People of the Tongass

• •

K. A. Soderberg
Jackie DuRette

People of the Tongass
Alaska Forestry Under Attack

• •

A Free Enterprise Battle Book

The Free Enterprise Press
BELLEVUE

FIRST EDITION
Published by The Free Enterprise Press

Typeset in Times Roman on Iconix computers by The Free Enterprise
Press, Bellevue, Washington.

The Free Enterprise Press is a division of the Center for the Defense of
Free Enterprise, 12500 N.E. Tenth Place, Bellevue, Washington, 98005.

This book is distributed by Merril Press, P.O. Box 1682, Bellevue,
Washington, 98009. Additional copies may be ordered from Merril
Press at $14.95 each.

LIBRARY OF CONGRESS CATALOGING-IN-PUBLICATION DATA
Soderberg, K. A.
    People of the Tongass.

    "A Free Enterprise battle book."
    Bibliography: p.
    Includes index.
    1. Tongass National Forest (Alaska) 2. Forest policy--Alaska--Tongass
National Forest. 3. Wilderness areas--Alaska--Tongass National Forest. 4.
Logging--Alaska--Tongass National Forest. 5. Mines and mineral resources--
Alaska--Tongass National Forest. I. DuRette, Jackie. II. Title.
SD428.T6S63   1988   333.75'09798   88-31097
ISBN 0-939571-04-8

PRINTED IN THE UNITED STATES OF AMERICA

CONTENTS

Table of Contents   *v*

Introductions: the Congressional Delegation of the State of Alaska

        Senator Ted Stevens   *viii*

        Senator Frank Murkowski   *ix*

        Representative Don Young   *xi*

Authors' Preface   *xiii*

Maps   *xvi*

PART ONE: THE PEOPLE OUTRAGED

Prologue: Mountains in the Sea   3

Chapter One: Liars   19

PART TWO: THE COLONY

Chapter Two: Homeland   53

Chapter Three: Stepchild of America   91

Chapter Four: The Forest Service   129

PART THREE: THE WORKING FOREST

Chapter Five: Loggers   155

Chapter Six: Pulp Mills   213

Chapter Seven: Sawmills   247

PART FOUR: THE PEOPLE ASPIRING

Chapter Eight: Proving Ground for Lawyers   261

Chapter Nine: Voices   281

Chapter Ten: Agenda for Renewal   313

Sources   337

Index   351

DEDICATION

TO THE PEOPLE OF THE TONGASS

The people of the Tongass are themselves a valuable resource that should not be dismissed lightly. Their life on the land, their natural wisdom and their productivity all give depth and shape to the meaning of America. Far from being a threat to the forest as extremists portray them, these diligent and dedicated people are good stewards who increase the natural gift of productivity on our timberlands through wise use and sound silvicultural practice.

Socially, the people of the Tongass are a priceless asset teaching our affluent society the forgotten value of basic economic commodity production, industriousness, foresight and endurance in the face of overwhelming obstacles, both natural and manmade.

Charles S. Cushman
Former Member
National Parks System Advisory Board

● ●

SENATOR TED STEVENS

● ●

Ever since the Alaska lands battle of the 1970s, extreme environmentalists have been trying to shut down Southeast Alaska's timber industry. Alaska's Tongass National Forest has been the prime target.

Non-Alaskans and organizations based thousands of miles from Alaska have promoted -- so far unsuccessfully -- legislation that could devastate the economy and the lives of the people of Alaska's Southeast.

Those extreme environmentalists want to close even more of the Tongass to timber harvesting than the 5.4 million acres contained in the 1980 Alaska Lands Act. One third of the timber base is already off limits, managed as wilderness or roadless areas.

It's obvious that reducing the timber base would affect the timber supply. In turn the logger, the equipment supplier, the grocery store owner, the school teacher and every other resident of the Tongass would be adversely affected.

The authors, both Southeast Alaskans, understand what that could mean, from the economic and human standpoints. They present the commodity users' side clearly. They also explain why there is no sound environmental reason to reduce the Tongass timber harvest.

The Alaska Lands Act provides for the multiple use of a portion of the Tongass National Forest. In the best interest of our nation, as well as Southeast Alaska, this is the way it should remain.

Ted Stevens
U.S. Senator, Alaska
October, 1988

• •

SENATOR FRANK H. MURKOWSKI

• •

How do you put a price tag on a forest? It's a vexing decision that over the years Congress has been forced to make when determining the costs and benefits of setting aside portions of the National Forests as Wilderness.

On the one hand there are human costs to be considered -- the loggers, their families and their communities that depend upon the forests for their livelihood. On the other, there's the inherent value of preserving pristine timber lands, for future generations to enjoy.

With these two most basic interests at stake, it is no wonder that whenever Congress has attached a dollar figure to the designation of Wilderness, the price has been high.

In 1980, Congress reached such a compromise on the Tongass National Forest in Southeast Alaska. It set aside a significant portion of the forest as Wilderness, and at the same time committed federal dollars to make sure people could continue working the region's timber industry.

Today, there is an effort to renege on that compromise. In the late '70s, during the debate on the Alaska Lands Bill, Congress faced the challenge of balancing costs and benefits of land designations. The dilemma was classic. On one hand, timber production from the Tongass Forest provided the economic base for more than a half-dozen Southeast Alaska communities. On the other hand, because of the forest's unquestionable beauty and abundant wildlife, many people wanted as much of it as possible put off limits to any kind of development.

·   When Congress crafted its Tongass compromise in 1980, millions of acres were designated as Wilderness. Nearly one-half of the commercial forest land, previously available to support the timber industry, was put off-limits to logging. With the loss of 1.4 million acres, the timber industry was forced to log in areas considered only marginally commercial, due to difficult access or logging conditions. This meant significantly higher costs to the industry. To compensate, Congress established the Tongass Timber Supply Fund.

The price tag for the Federal government for making Tongass a Wilderness is high. But it's only a fraction of what the government has paid elsewhere.

Congress now cannot walk away from one-half of the Tongass compromise that took years to craft. With the 1980 decision on the Tongass, Congress reaffirmed its commitment to the people of Southeast Alaska, and recognized the responsibilities that go along with federal ownership and the costs associated with the value of Wilderness. The compensation in the Tongass permits the people of Southeast Alaska to maintain an industry to which the federal government and Alaskans have been committed for thirty years.

Senator Frank H. Murkowski
Washington, D.C.
October, 1988

• •

REPRESENTATIVE DON YOUNG

• •

America's system of national forests is one of this nation's greatest contributions to the world's wise use of natural resources. From the smaller units such as Vermont's Green Mountain National Forest, to the largest, the Tongass -- the subject of this book -- the national forest system provides enlightened management of our timber, wildlife, watersheds, mining, wilderness, recreation, and many other uses.

The U.S. Forest Service has been charged by Congress with the responsibility for administering our national forests. Its mandate is based upon the principle of "multiple use," the principle of providing "the greatest good for the greatest number over the long run." However, as our nation has grown, the Forest Service and its "lands of many uses" have become the center of increasing controversy.

How much land should we devote to each of the competing multiple uses? How much land should we devote to wilderness? How much to timber harvest? How much to motorized recreation? How much to mineral development? How much to each use?

These questions have been debated in one form or another for nearly a century, since the Forest Reserve Act of 1891 authorized the vast preserves that evolved into today's national forest system. This book, *People of the Tongass*, brings a fresh voice to the debate. We have long heard advocates for timber harvest and mining speak from the corporate board room or through lobbyists in Washington, D.C.

But here we have the voice of the people, grassroots voices from all walks of life, speaking on behalf of the wise use of the resources of Tongass National Forest. A corps of citizen supporters has finally come to the fore to speak in the public interest for industry's sake.

PEOPLE OF THE TONGASS

The two authors of *People of the Tongass* are remarkable Alaskans. Not only do they bring deep personal experience and conviction to the subject, but they also possess the wisdom to put others in the limelight. They have filled this book with the authentic voices of the people of the Tongass, letting them recount their own stories through extensive and probing interviews. The lively result is a colorful array of viewpoints knit together in a compelling narrative that will at once entertain and educate the reader.

People of the Tongass will be a revelation to most Americans. Its path of discovery will outrage some and inspire others. Even though I may not agree with the authors on every point, I can vouch for their honesty and I admire their daring. This is a book long overdue. These are voices long overlooked. I commend them to you.

Representative Don Young
Washington, D.C.
October, 1988

● ●

WHY WE DID IT

● ●

An ounce of truth to cure a ton of lies.

That's what this book is and why we wrote it.

We have done our best to provide here a necessary antidote to the massive dose of media poison presently being penned against the resource users of the Tongass National Forest. This book is the outraged response of two Alaskans to an unscrupulous campaign of environmentalist slander being waged by media ranging from the respected *Life*, *Reader's Digest*, *The New Republic* and *Sports Illustrated*, to tourist periodicals including Conde Nast's *Traveler*, *Alaska* magazine, and *Trailer Life*, to publications clearly having a special-interest axe to grind such as *Sierra*, *Audubon*, and *Backpacker*.

Yet we hope you discover here more than just a response, more than a mere knee-jerk reaction.

For, as *People of the Tongass* developed, we found it turning into a celebration of the very aspect of Alaska that our current crop of detractors deplores: the working world of the forest products industry -- and the miners and the fishermen and all the others who make the rain forest of the Tongass a fascinating place to live. We realized that we had opened a vista totally unknown to the average American.

We had etched a provocative word portrait of an American place and an American people previously unchronicled -- a place drenched in rain and sweat, a people radiant with joy and struggle and hope and all those things that make ordinary humanity transcendent. Best of all, the boldest strokes on our paper canvas had been laid down in that most lasting of literary pigments, the affirmative hue of the people themselves -- the grassroots people of the Tongass.

So what we have produced is the true story of a remarkable forest. It is a tale of people, land, and trees. The trees, Sitka spruce and Western hemlock for the most part, thickly mantle all but the highest peaks as they island-hop a rain-soaked arc of North America's broken western coastline known as the Alexander Archipelago, an international caucus of place names such as Chichagof, Revillagigedo, Malmesbury, Kosciusko, and Hoonah.

The land is America's largest national forest, the Tongass of Southeast Alaska, five hundred channeled and sea-battered miles long and a hundred steep and mountainous miles wide. At 16.78 million acres (or 26,221 square miles) the Tongass is bigger than West Virginia and vastly rich in natural resources, all administered by the Forest Service of the U.S. Department of Agriculture.

The people are loggers and car dealers, miners and newspaper editors, fishermen and high school coaches, bush pilots and legislators, barge operators and boutique owners and bureaucrats and bums -- just-folks and movers-and-shakers: America in miniature, but with a special frontier-to-front-page Alaskan tang.

The Tongass National Forest and its people have for decades been the center of a great national debate. As the current plague of environmentalist propaganda demonstrates, the debate is profoundly emotional, clothed in rhetoric as difficult to penetrate as a Tongass mist, shifting, obscuring the view, tantalizing now and then with a suggestive glimpse of something you can't quite define. Behind the fog lies a single basic question: How shall Alaska develop its resources and who shall make that decision? *People of the Tongass* is our argument for the wise use of Alaska's resources.

We owe this book to many people. We first want to thank the dozens of people who got together and formed The Tongass Book Fund, without whom we wouldn't have had the budget to do the extensive research and interviewing we faced, much less the writing and photography. Next we owe a debt of gratitude to Ron Arnold, editor in chief of The Free Enterprise Press for his long hours of advice and encouragement when the going got rough. Our thanks also to Alan M. Gottlieb, president of the Center for the Defense of Free Enterprise for accepting this project for publication. Center staff researcher Andrea Arnold and National Inholders Association researcher Ramona Hage spent many hours digging out facts in university libraries, state and federal records repositories and the National Archives and helped make important discoveries.

At the National Archives in Washington, D.C., natural resource archivist Mary Frances Morrow was instrumental in locating records that led to the identification of William Steele Holman as the true founder of the 1891 forest reserves that evolved into today's national forests. Senate Historian Richard Baker provided valuable insights into the origin of the

PREFACE

forest reserves. Indiana State Manuscripts Librarian Marybelle Burch provided essential letters and biographical information on Holman. Indiana Historical Society Manuscripts Cataloger Sally Childs-Helton provided useful Holman letters.

Lawrence Rakestraw, Ph.D., provided invaluable service as historical consultant, and also granted permission to quote extensively from his many books and scholarly articles. He kept us from many errors of fact. Harold K. Steen, Ph.D., executive director of the Forest History Society kindly granted permission to use materials from *The Journal of Forest History*.

Rollo Pool turned in an outstanding photographic assignment on logging in the Tongass. Ketchikan Pulp Company and Alaska Pulp Corporation provided helicopter transportation to remote sites so editor Ron Arnold could verify facts and take many of the photographs in this book.

So many people in the U.S. Forest Service helped that it would take another book just to list their names. Our special thanks to Michael Barton, regional forester, Alaska Region; Kenneth Roberts, special assistant to the regional forester for timber; Wayne Nicolls, director of public affairs; Jim Wolfe, director, engineering and aviation management; John Standerwick, group leader, inventory, plans and silviculture; Gary Peterson, group leader, timber valuation group; Carl Holguin, group leader, legislative affairs and public involvement; Wanita Williamson, public affairs specialist. All of these people are located at Alaska Region headquarters of the Forest Service in Juneau. Don Lyon, team leader, Tongass National Forest Plan Interdisciplinary Team - Juneau Ranger District, provided valuable insights into the forest plan revision process.

We owe the most to all those hundreds of people who agreed to be interviewed for this book. We hope you will all accept your printed interview as our acknowledgement, and for those whose materials we couldn't get into the finished product, our apologies and many thanks for your assistance.

Responsibility for this book's flaws, including any errors of fact or judgment, rests solely with the authors. And if this book may have merit, it comes from where you'd expect: From the people of the Tongass.

K. A. Soderberg
Jackie DuRette
The Tongass, Alaska

• •

MAPS

• •

The Tongass is a mapmaker's nightmare: It is too large for a single map to show reasonable detail. Government maps showing its complex topography and administration are nearly impossible to read. Thus we have prepared four maps especially for this book. They provide minimal detail and maximal readability. They show only selected major features discussed in the text and eliminate all else; rivers, for example, are not shown. These maps are not intended as travel guides, but rather as reader guides. Consult more detailed maps for features not shown.

Map Key

Feature	Location
Admiralty Island	Map 2
Alaska Pulp Corporation mill	near Sitka, map 2
Angoon	Admiralty Island, map 2
Annette Island	Map 3
Baranof Island	Map 2
Chatham Area	Map 2
Chichagof Island	Map 2
Clarence Strait	Map 4
Coffman Cove	Prince of Wales Island, map 4
Craig	Prince of Wales Island, map 4
Craig Ranger District	Map 3
Dall Island	Map 4
Frederick Sound	Map 2, Map 3
Freshwater Bay	Chichagof Island, map 2
Haines	Mainland, map 2
Hawk Inlet	Admiralty Island, map 2
Heceta Island	Map 4
Hollis	Prince of Wales Island, map 4
Hoonah	Chichagof Island, map 2
Hoonah Ranger District	Map 2

MAPS

Map Key (continued)

Feature	Location
Hydaburg	Prince of Wales Island, map 4
Juneau	Mainland, map 2
Juneau Ranger District	Map 2
Kake	Map 2
Ketchikan	Revillagigedo Island, map 3
Ketchikan Area	Map 3
Ketchikan Pulp Company mill	near Ketchikan, map 3
Ketchikan Ranger District	Map 3
Klawock	Map 4
Kosciusko Island	Map 4
Kuiu Island	Map 2
Kupreanof Island	Map 2
Lisianski Inlet	Chichagof Island, map 2
Metlakatla	Annette Island, map 3
Misty Fiords	Map 3
Naukati	Map 4
Pelican	Chichagof Island, map 2
Petersburg	Kupreanof Island, map 3
Petersburg Ranger District	Map 3
Point Baker	Map 4
Prince of Wales Island	Map 4
Revillagigedo Island	Map 3
Skagway	Mainland, map 2
Stikine Area	Map 3
Thorne Bay	Prince of Wales Island, map 4
Tongass Island	Map 3
Tongass National Forest	Map 1
Tuxekan Island	Map 4
Ward Cove	near Ketchikan, map 3
Wrangell	Wrangell Island, map 3
Wrangell Ranger District	Map 3
Yakutat	Map 1, map 2
Zarembo Island	Map 2

Note: Features identified as "near" another feature are not shown, but noted only for general location. North on all maps, as conventional, is toward the top of the page. but no direction arrows are shown.

Map 1: Tongass National Forest, Alaska (shaded area)

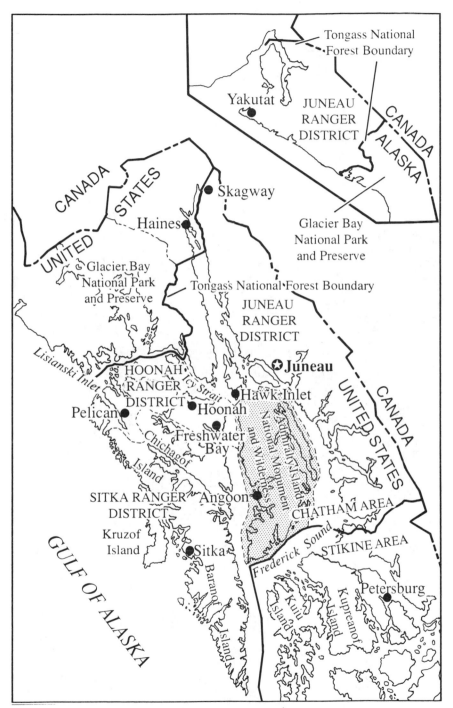

Map 2: Chatham Area, northern Tongass National Forest

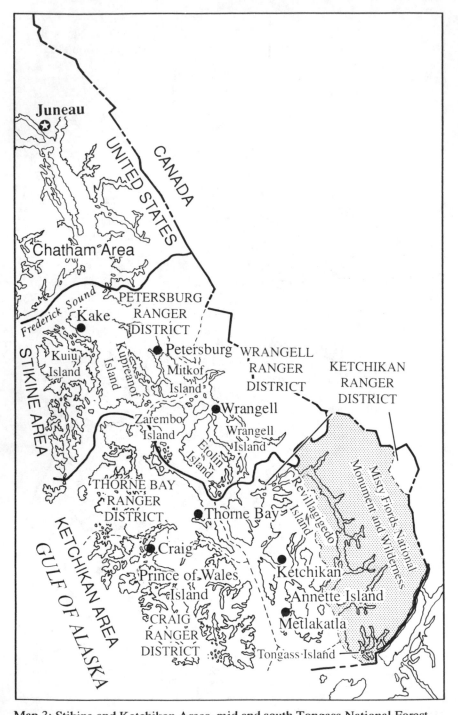

Map 3: Stikine and Ketchikan Areas, mid and south Tongass National Forest

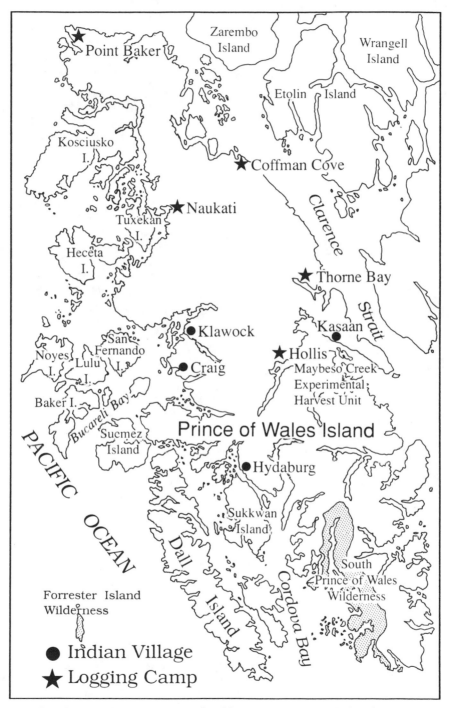

Map 4: Prince of Wales Island, pride of foresters, Tongass National Forest

Part One

THE PEOPLE OUTRAGED

MOUNTAINS IN THE SEA

• •

This book is a gamble. It's risky for two first-time authors to invite their readers into the controversial world of Alaska's natural resources. It's chancy for us to defend working foresters and mining engineers and all the other resource users in the Tongass. And it's downright hazardous to speak out against the sacrosanct environmental movement. We know we're stepping into the minefields of a propaganda battleground where belief does not come easy. Yet we're ready to take the gamble. By the time you've finished the last page, we expect you to believe us.

Why? Because of who we are: grassroots Alaskans whose vital individual interests are tied to the fate of Alaska's natural resources. We know what we're talking about because we live Alaska's "ecology wars" every day. Both of us are working wives in family-owned construction and logging companies. We're honest enough to tell you exactly where we're coming from: we defend the wise use of resources in the Tongass. And we're advocate enough to insist that there *is* such a thing as the wise *use* of resources.

So consider this prologue as an authors' self-introduction, an inspection tour for the wary, if you will. This is who we are. Here our voices speak as separate and distinct personalities, two people of the Tongass, unlike the amalgam we've tried to form in the rest of the book. Take a few pages to get to know us.

K. A. Soderberg

Welcome to my Alaska! Or at least to that part of it I can put into a book. It's a place where the average person can respect and admire logging and loggers, mining and miners, development and developers -- as passionately and compassionately as you admire the trees, the mountains, and the wildlife. If you think admiring a logger or a miner is a tall order, you're due for exactly the kind of self-examination this book offers.

3

Author K. A. Soderberg   Ron Arnold photo

One of the things you'll learn about me in these pages is that my views on the environment may be hard to understand at first. You might conclude that because I say sharp things against environmental groups I care nothing for nature, but you'd be wrong. My profound love of nature will show itself plainly enough. You will find that it differs from the standard environmentalist philosophy in that I regard humanity as an integral part of nature -- and that the wise use of natural and human resources is a sound philosophy in itself.

You'll hear me indict the organized environmental movement on many counts, dishonesty among the foremost. I'll point out that in our national quest for environmental purity we've saved "the last wilderness" at least a hundred times in a hundred different places. I'll document that we've locked so many virgin forests in anti-industry chastity belts for so long that billions of virgin trees have now aged into wizened old maid forests, rife with heart-shatter and butt rot. Which is my way of mixing a metaphor asserting that the environmental establishment is both deceitful in its rhetoric and inattentive to actual natural processes.

Who am I that asserts this? I'm the K.A. Soderberg who remembers stepping out of my front door one September day when I was seven, feeling the chill north wind through my favorite sweater, and suddenly becoming aware of my surroundings beyond the wide encircling porch. I looked across my front lawn, across the street, across the parade grounds, across the little town of Haines, past the broad saltwash of Lynn Canal to the forested slopes of the mountains in the sea.

I thought: This is my world, this village at the southern foot of the Takshanuk Mountains with the lofty glacier-clad Chilkat Range for an everyday sunset backdrop and thousands upon thousands of bald eagles up and down the Chilkat River for winter companions.

I'm the K.A. Soderberg who remembers as a child standing there, suddenly aware: Alaska! This is My Alaska! My home! These are my mountains, these are my trees, my water, they're all part of this town, part of the house that I live in up on this hill, part of *me*. This is what people mean when they say 'beauty.' And I am a part -- I insist that I am a part -- of that beauty, part of it all.

Ron Arnold photo

K. A. on the front porch of her childhood home in Haines

I kept that secret feeling as I grew up. I see it in people all around me. No matter where we may live in the Tongass, every one of us feels the same way. We feel the beauty. We are part of the beauty. The people of the Tongass are not despoilers of their own homes, despite what the Wilderness Society may tell you. If I have any single message to submit in this book, that's it. We people of the Tongass love our land. We do not destroy it.

To my friends I'm simply K.A. I was born Kathie Anne Gregg in the Tongass in 1954, but everyone calls me K.A. My mother started calling me by my initials because of the Territorial Delegate's daughter: Doris Ann Bartlett lived in Haines when I was very small, and she went by her initials -- D.A. My mother picked up the idea I've been K.A. ever since.

Don't let that give you the false impression that Mimi Gregg -- my mother -- is casual about things. She was clerk of the court and deputy magistrate of Haines for twelve years. Before that she owned and operated a small business called The Craft Shop for twenty-five years. She's been a teacher and once ran for the Alaska legislature. And she's been a driving force in practically every civic improvement campaign Haines has seen for forty years. She's simply unique, like my Dad, Ted Gregg.

Dad is a sculptor, a furniture maker, a carver of Indian artifacts and a retired longshoreman. He started the Haines tradition of the Strawberry Festival, a Fourth of July civic extravaganza, and managed it for a good twenty years, developing the event into a key summer attraction for our town.

Dad says our address has been the informal Haines Hilton since he and Mom arrived in 1947. A great many Alaska notables have passed through our portals. Mom always had room for one or two more at the dinner table.

My parents had a lot of government friends because they lived in Washington, D.C. before moving here, so coming into contact with Territorial Delegate to Congress E.L. Bartlett and his daughter would be nothing unusual. And our home itself is an attraction in its own right: it's a turn-of-the-century military outpost.

Tell them about how you got here, Dad.

"Just after World War II Mimi and I belonged to a group of veterans who wanted to leave the East Coast and carve a new life for ourselves in the hinterlands of Alaska. The bunch of us bought this whole place, the sprawling 1902-vintage Fort William H. Seward -- a complete town with its own water supply. The Fort was up for sale by the U.S. Department of the Interior as surplus after World War II, and our group won the bid. It was in pretty sad shape as far as appearance goes, but the construction was basically sound. Each of us fixed up one of the old officers' quarters and this one's where we've lived ever since.

"Fort Seward had been renamed "Chilkoot Barracks" back in 1922 to avoid confusion with the growing town of Seward, Alaska. It was Chilkoot Barracks when we bought it, a name that didn't appeal to some of us veterans. The Fort actually lies up the hill and around a zig and a zag in the road from Haines proper. It's called 'Port Chilkoot' on maps today, even though the two towns merged many years ago."

I weighed into this world in Juneau because it had a hospital. And that hospital lies only forty-five minutes south of Haines. That's forty-five minutes by small plane. The sheer size and natural obstacles of our great land have naturally led Alaskans to think of distances in terms of time by small plane -- "as the crow flies."

"Well, daughter, in those days if you had a baby you flew to Juneau or you were out of luck, you might have it on the kitchen table.

"But I had an easy time with you in Juneau. And Ted came down to see me the day after you were born. You came May twenty-seventh, right over our anniversary time, which was May thirtieth. He brought a little bouquet of flowers, took me out to dinner right from the hospital."

Well, because I was born in Alaska that makes me a native but not a Native. Capitalized, Native means a member of a local Southeast Indian tribe. With a small "n" it means someone who was born in Alaska. And until I was a year old I was officially a cheechako -- someone who has yet to put in his or her first year in Alaska. But time caught up with me and now I'm a Pioneer -- someone who's been in Alaska so long they can't remember being a cheechako. Official membership in Alaska Pioneer Igloo chapters requires 30 years residence.

Doris Ward photo

Mimi and Ted Gregg at home

Back to the 'fifties. I was the youngest of four children. This K. A. toddled, started kindergarten, finished high school and in between did her growing up in Haines/Port Chilkoot, the picturebook Alaska town etched above the gravel banks of Portage Cove. It was a fascinating little community, half local Tlingit Indians (Tlingit is pronounced "KLINK-it"), half U.S. immigrant old-timers and newcomers from Norway, Italy, Sweden, the Philippines -- what a writer once called "a distinctly Ellis Island sort of place."

Mom says I was "the baby-doll of the family," i.e., the youngest of the four children. Somehow the Greggs of Port Chilkoot put us all through college. Today my oldest brother Tresham is an artist,

Allan is an electronics engineer, and my sister Annette works for Wings of Alaska, an airline that serves Haines.

Strangers wonder about the isolation. I can recall as a kid being asked by visitors young and old, ''What is there to do here?'' ''Plenty,'' was always my answer. Haines was a community with camaraderie: we staged shows to entertain each other, school life involved everyone, we took Girl Scouts and Boy Scouts seriously, we cooked up myriads of home-grown events and special occasions that left us few dull moments.

It's truc that isolation is part of being Alaskan, but it doesn't mean you don't see the world. It's true that you can't drive to the state capitol at Juneau because there are no roads from ''outside.'' But you can book passage from Haines to anywhere, and Haines and Skagway up Taiya Inlet are the only towns in the Tongass connected to the rest of the United States by road.

When I was young we took little trips to Whitehorse, the nearest town you could drive to -- 250 miles away in Canada. We went to see my older brother Tresham graduate from Stanford, I got to stay with my sister at Scripps College in Santa Barbara and the whole family visited my younger brother Allan at the Air Force Academy in Colorado. I toured Mexico during my high school years, took my junior year of college in Spain and later visited Europe with my parents.

I think many Alaskans feel they have to prove they can make it in the ''big world'' out there. I saw the big world, was duly astonished and went back to Alaska. When I returned from Colorado Women's College, degree in hand (majors in anthropology and Spanish, if it matters), I decided to make the Tongass my permanent home, and have never since dwelt anywhere but in ''Southeast'' -- Alaskan for ''the Panhandle region,'' the site of Tongass National Forest, the place of Mountains in the Sea.

My husband Virgil is an adoptive Alaskan, born in Washington State in the Lower 48. He grew up in Alaska logging camps, undoubtedly the most remote and isolated communities in America. It didn't seem to do him any harm: He's a logging camp kid who got an advanced degree from the Harvard Graduate School of Business Administration.

Virgil and I met during the early 1980s while I was working clear down at the other end of the Tongass, 300 miles south of Haines in Ketchikan. After college I had found a job there as Public Information Officer for Alaska Loggers Association. I stayed for three years working on matters of public interest. I developed the association's information programs, coordinated press tours, produced slide shows and even created the ''Levi Logger Color Book Tour.''

During an Association convention in Juneau, legendary logger Pat Soderberg and his wife Hazel introduced one busy K. A. Gregg to their son Virgil. I didn't pay much attention to him at the time, immersed as I was in the crush of convention business. But there were soon a lot of long phone calls and cards with witty remarks.

As time went on I found myself at odds with the Loggers Association. I felt my hands were unnecessarily being tied with red tape and saw important industry projects languishing for lack of funds. Frustration! Then one day a job offer came in from Soderberg Logging and Construction Company, in the tiny Indian village of Kake on the west side of Kupreanof Island. It meant I'd be working side by side with Virgil, and by then we'd gotten pretty involved. I decided to make the break.

So I moved and took on the challenging task of dispatching and running supplies for major contract logging operations at Kake and around the corner at Portage Bay. Seeing at first hand the painstaking care

Ron Arnold photo

Virgil Soderberg reads a construction map aboard Wavos Rancheros

modern loggers use to protect ecological values while obtaining material values for human use impressed me tremendously. Virgil's father Pat had once experimented extensively with balloon logging -- a simple but costly way to lift logs clear of the ground to avoid dragging them across streams or damaging standing timber. He often found himself referred to by friends as the Commanding General of the Alaska Logging Air Force.

When I first got to the new job, Virgil wanted to get married right away, but I was hesitant. Everything was so new and frenetic. And there was so much going on, so many problems to handle. That was the last time he asked!

There wasn't much time for asking. I found I had joined Virgil's operation during a time of indescribable crisis. Since the late 1970s one restrictive land designation after another had come to the Tongass, hemming in vast stretches of productive timber and reducing the annual allowable harvest. Less timber, less work. Like a line of dominoes the economic impacts fell first upon the giant pulp firms, then down the supply line to equipment dealers, transportation companies, teachers, doctors and grocery stores -- and contract loggers. Our industry was crumbling around us and all we could do was put band-aids on its skull fractures. For you Ayn Rand fans, I sometimes felt like we were Dagny and Hank looking for John.

We were so involved with surviving in the politicized world of Alaska logging that it was five years later when we caught our breath one day and I said to Virgil, "Weren't we going to get married once?"

I became K. A. Soderberg in 1985 in a five-day wedding celebration that will be long remembered in Haines.

During the economic chaos of the mid-1980s, the proud name of Soderberg no longer flew over a logging operation. But we survived: We won a major road-building contract for the Greens Creek Mining Corporation on Admiralty Island. As I write this on our company's word processor, I look through the office windowpane dripping rain to see the dock and headquarters where our roadway winds around the mountains to the mine site. Greens Creek is the largest silver mine in the country. The ore also contains significant concentrations of gold, lead and zinc.

Our office is one of half a dozen structures floating on log booms in the lashed-together gypsy fleet that is our work camp. The float camp, including our house, was hauled to its present site on Hawk Inlet by our reworked military landing craft, the *Beacher*. Float camps are an old tradition in the Tongass. Southeast is littered with mountains in the sea, prodigious peaks, formidable barricades that force our coast-hugging culture to travel by sea or air. Our homes travel by sea.

Our floating company headquarters consists of a storage float, a generator float that supplies our electricity, our camp guard's house, our superintendent's quarters, the office float, and at the end of the line, our house, occupied by me and Virgil and a new kitten named Missystuff.

D.C., my 23-year-old calico cat, died while I was writing this book. (Even my old cat went by her initials. D.C. originally stood for "Damn Cat" when my family took her in as a young stray, but it changed to "Duchess of Chilkoot" as age and dignity caught up with her.) On this job we have no cook shack or bunkhouse float: Our crew here lives ashore in Greens Creek Company facilities. But now we also run a logging operation on Heceta Island where our crew lives on a barge complete with cookhouse and bunkhouse facilities.

Our floating conglomeration of dwellings is technically a marine vessel named Wavos Rancheros. (If that sounds suspiciously like the Mexican egg-and-tortilla dish *huevos rancheros*, we'll admit there's some word play there. We came by the name quite logically, however. You see, Portage Bay, where our logging camp was located, is in the banana-belt of the Tongass -- less than 100 inches of rain per year -- so Virgil chose three palm trees as the company logo, even though the only palm trees you're likely to see there come in through the satellite TV dish. Our camp became known as Rancho De Las Palmas. Perfectly reasonable. When we

moved the Rancho onto floats, it only seemed logical to name it Wavos... Hmm, maybe it isn't all that logical.)

At home we can tell that the phone's ringing when the Alaska Marine Radio Network operator says in his staticky voice, "Calling WTU two-two-four-niner, Wavos Rancheros, Wavos Rancheros. Over." Your phone call will be relayed to us by radio. Don't call if you have a secret. You'd have more privacy in Juneau's

Red Dog Saloon on a sailor's Saturday night. Everybody from Eagle River to Taku Harbor listens in to the radio.

Life on the float camp isn't as rosy and romantic as it may sound. Yes, we have a magnificent panoramic water view of Hawk Inlet. We also have incessant creaking and swaying on stormy days, layers of glare ice to chip from the walkways after winter storms -- not to mention the snowdrifts we have to shovel off in order to keep the camp from sinking -- and container gardens that require hauling every pound of dirt by hand (only to have the superintendent's cat use them for a sandbox).

Now all this is more than the chit-chat it seems. I'm making the point that life in the Tongass is emphatically not life in Boston or New Orleans or San Francisco. It is uniquely precious, a ruggedly beautiful thing of its own. Yet decisions made by Americans in those faraway cities count for more in shaping our destiny here than our own voices do. People who know nothing of the care we take in harvesting timber join campaigns that condemn us to bankruptcy and despair because they mistake the temporary raw appearance of a clearcut for its enduring biological viability. People who have never seen a modern mining operation denounce us because some high-paid environmental group executive such as the National Wildlife Federation's Jay Hair ($150,000 a year) tells them they should. The laws Congress passes with the support of such people are strangling the people of the Tongass, depriving us of our land, our state, our livelihood, our homes, our way of life. It is a gross injustice. It has gone far enough.

JACKIE DuRETTE

I'm the other side of the Tongass coin from my co-author K.A. She represents the native-born Alaskan while I'm the picture of the immigrant. I was born in Canada on Prince Edward Island at Prince County Hospital in the town of Summerside in 1951. My parents, Stanley and Mary Howatt, operated a lobster cannery in the farming and fishing community

Author Jackie DuRette   Ron Arnold photo

of Victoria, and lived about twenty miles away in Carleton Siding, a staid little town of some two or three hundred souls making what they could of life on Canada's austere North Atlantic Coast. My family has traditionally lived by harvesting natural resources. We lived in Canada until I was sixteen. It was a good solid life.

In 1968 my father semi-retired. Translated, that means he went into another business. He had owned some property on the coast of Oregon in Manzanita, and decided to build a motel on it. I came west the summer I turned seventeen. It was a different country and a new world, but I adjusted rapidly and thoroughly enjoyed the Pacific Northwest. I spent my senior year at Neah-Ka-Nie High School in Rockaway, a nearby coastal Oregon town.

After high school I took a job in a local medical clinic where I met a young man named Robert Ralph DuRette -- "Butch" to everyone. At the time he was a student at Northwestern College of Business in Portland. He came in with a minor injury while working summers as a logger. He asked me out and I said yes. His family, I discovered, had lived as loggers in the Willamette Valley for several generations.

Ron Arnold photo

Butch DuRette at a loggers meeting

Fate decreed that we were cut out for each other and about a year later, in August of 1970, we were married in Nehalem, Oregon. Butch had graduated from college and received a computer job offer from AT&T in Chicago. We immediately moved just outside the Windy City. It was a terrible transition for me. After about six weeks I was beginning to wonder how I could ever tolerate suburbia when one day Butch walked in and said,

"It'll take me about two hours to pack. How about you?"

"Me too. Did you quit your job?" I asked.

"Not formally. I'll call them from the West Coast. Let's go home."

Butch had always been a questing, restless soul but firmly realized in Chicago that his destiny lay along the logger's path. We returned to McMinnville.

There Butch joined Von Logging, the firm owned by his uncle and brother. We settled in at McMinnville, a modest-sized countrified town not far up the Valley from Portland. During the next two years I regularly drove the distance to Chemeketa College in Salem, taking business courses.

Logging suited Butch just fine. We began to sink our roots in McMinnville. There our two sons Corey and Rob, Jr. were born. As possible, I worked off and on as a ward clerk at McMinnville Community Hospital while the boys were small. Things went well. Occasionally I'd see that questing spirit sparkle in Butch's eyes, urging him to pick us all up and move on, but nothing happened until 1977.

Then Alaska happened. The Mountains in the Sea happened. The Tongass happened. It happened first to Butch.

"One summer I came up to visit my Dad for a couple of weeks -- he was working on a road construction job. When I came back I told Jackie if I had an opportunity I'd move to Alaska. I love the country: the beauty's here, the industry's here, and I like to fish and hunt. I got the chance because of a log trucker named Jerry Larrabee I met working for Von. He'd left Oregon to come up here and contract log with Alaska Lumber and Pulp in Sitka and I'd just about forgotten about him. Then that winter we got a call from Larrabee asking if I wanted to be a siderod for his logging operation. [Logger lingo: siderod -- a job boss with authority over workers and equipment assigned to a specific logging location, the combination of place, workers and equipment being called a "side."]

"'Course it didn't take me five minutes to decide. But I sat down and really talked to Jackie about it. It took us about a day and a half before I called back and said yes to the job in Freshwater Bay, about 60 miles south from Juneau."

Butch talked me into it. He went first and the family soon moved up with him to a tiny camp at Kennel Creek on Freshwater Bay. In actuality Freshwater Bay is a saltwater spur of Chatham Strait flowing into one of the many mountain-and-valley crenelations of Chichagof Island. There were a few dozen portable float houses, a little camp store and a school. Everybody knew everybody else because there were not a hundred of us there. The nearest village on the island was Tenakee Springs, about 9 miles away with -- emphatically -- *no* connecting road. Not that the Tenakee folk are unfriendly, they just seem to enjoy bringing lawsuits to stop logging roads. So we were absolutely isolated. The locale and circumstances may sound spartan and uninviting, and it weeds out the weak in a hurry, but for those it fits, it is a pure and rugged and altogether satisfying life.

It was like logger's heaven, the Tongass. It's the northernmost stretch of the familiar humid forest that extends from southern Oregon to Kodiak Island. The Douglas fir component had dropped out in the march northward to the Tongass, leaving Sitka spruce and western hemlock dominant in a dense rain forest choked with groundcovers of huckleberry and devilsclub, a wicked thorny shrub named by somebody who knew it well. Scattered stands of Alaska yellow cedar and western redcedar ensconced along favored bottomlands.

We lived in the rain forest with the rhythms of nature, the turnings of sun and moon, the season of eagles nesting, this year's crop of salmonberries giving way to next year's, the longer cycles of deer lifetimes and bear histories, and the overarching periodicity of timber harvest in a forest that had been cutover back at the turn of the century and was now bountiful again. The things we didn't have we didn't miss. The perennial rains from the vast Gulf of Alaska rinsed the night sky so we could see all the stars at once. We would ooo! at the fairy glow of the Northern Lights. We lived on Freshwater Bay for seven years while Butch served as logging and road superintendent of Larrabee Logging.

Our second year there we began to hear rumbles from Congress that the environmentalists wanted to take 5 million acres of land from the timber base of the Tongass National Forest for Wilderness set-asides. It soon became clear that we faced a legislative battle royal, something that would emerge as the Alaska National Interest Lands Conservation Act of 1980. I felt I had to do something -- but what?

The question answered itself in the form of Sandra Nutting, who visited the Tongass as president of a group called California Women In Timber. Despite its quaint-sounding name with overtones of the old-fashioned ladies' auxiliary and raffle society, CWIT was in fact a grass-roots activist lobbying group that had cut its eyeteeth on the Redwood National Park Expansion campaign, fighting to preserve the private lands of three large timber firms that provided a sizeable fraction of California's North Coast employment. They lost that one. Congress condemned 58,000 acres of private redwood timberland -- already logged and re-planted timberland, at that -- to expand a national park at a cost of over a billion taxpayer dollars in ''just compensation'' and a cost of 1,754 actual jobs, for which there can be no justice.

Carol told her story and inspired a few of us, K.A. Soderberg, Jewell Larrabee, Nancy Eliason, Linda Larson, LaVern Sullivan -- and others you'll hear more of later -- to join the fight and form the second WIT organization. Some time later I was on the activist road myself.

AWIT members made several trips in 1980 to Washington, D.C. lobbying for the logger on the ANILCA bill. When Congress passed the act, we had lost 5.3 million acres of the Tongass to Wilderness, which pushed us into more and more marginal lands. But we received a sort of just compensation, a congressional fund for the Forest Service to use for the extra work required in planning timber sales on the rougher, less accessible lands remaining. We had a deal. Or at least we thought we had a deal.

I became increasingly involved with Alaska Women In Timber. In 1982 I was elected as a member of the board of directors, and in 1984 as board member and vice-president. During my first term I was in charge of membership and also served on the education committee. We developed a classroom learning tool for fifth and sixth grade teachers called ''Alaska's Great Green Forest,'' to teach the wise use of timberland and the benefits of forest products.

In 1984 Jerry Larrabee's operation was reduced substantially. We were working on a project called the Kadashan Drainage Timber Sale over at Corner Bay, close to Freshwater Bay, just across Tenakee Inlet. A preservationist group brought a lawsuit against the Forest Service, claiming that the provisions of the National Environmental Policy Act of 1969 had not been followed. The Environmental Impact Statement (EIS) was ruled inadequate and logging had to stop while the planners went back to the drawing board. Preservationists who had never worked in the woods and knew nothing of its sturdy ways had prevailed.

After being pushed by environmentalists from good timber to marginal jobs to break-even projects to impossible situations, we found the market going against us as well. The timber industry entered a slump as bad as the Great Depression of the 1930s. Jerry was literally out of logging work. Butch was out of a logging job.

We made a hard decision then. The kids were still in the logging camp's grade school, the oldest boy only an eighth-grader. Our idyllic lives at Freshwater had been shaken by ambitious environmentalist lawyers and then shattered by an economic collapse; there was nothing there for us any more. But we were determined not to let either the misbegotten or the bear market get us down. We made the decision to move into Juneau and establish some sort of roots, at least to get the kids in school.

So one sad day we left Freshwater Bay on a landing craft that held all our belongings, everything that we owned. My sister in Oregon tried to cheer me up: ''You know,'' she said, ''most people move in an Allied Van. Think how romantic your way is.'' We moved not knowing really what we were going to do. We just left. I couldn't bear to look back.

Three weeks later, after we'd found a house in Juneau and tried to think of unemployment as a vacation, Butch got a call. His reputation as a top-notch logger saved us.   Steve Seley, owner of Wrangell Forests Products and one of Alaska's fabulous entrepreneurial success stories, was contracting a Forest Service road construction job out of Petersburg. The job had a deadline and Steve was looking for a good man to meet it.

So Butch relocated to Petersburg by himself and I stayed in Juneau with the kids. Our boys were old enough now to deal with a working mother, so I went to work as an assistant credit manager for the credit department of NC Machinery Company, the Caterpillar equipment dealer in Ketchikan and Juneau.

Butch finished Steve's job on schedule eight months later. Then he hired on as project manager with Leo Gellings of Phoenix Logging and did some logging and road building for another eight months. Needless to say, we were getting tired of bouncing around in short-term jobs and being separated all the time.

We made the final leap to independence in January of 1986 when we founded DuRette Construction Company, building timber access roads for Ketchikan Pulp Company on their 50-year Forest Service contract lands. I said goodbye to my job at NC and took over the bookkeeping, parts chasing, equipment financing, business negotiation, inventory control and a little of everything else for DuRette Construction. It's not that different from the role of a farmer's wife. Now the bear market has turned around and we're busy making a living and providing jobs for our own employees. Butch runs the crew and gets the production in from the woods and I do all the headwork here in Juneau and over at the camp at Thorne Bay on Prince of Wales Island.

And now that we've struggled to our feet once more, a man from New York and his preservationist cronies want to knock us out for good. Congressman Robert Mrazek has introduced legislation that would take more land from the Tongass timber base for Wilderness and cancel the fund established by ANILCA. It's a cheap environmental vote. It will destroy us, but hurt none of his constituents.

So, in the Spring of 1988 I found myself on a lobbying trip to Washington, D.C. with Alaska Women In Timber, fighting again for the logger and his right to exist. I was anxious to speak with Congressman Mrazek, to tell him of the care we take in the forest, of the strict environmental protection measures we observe, of the forest's resilience and fantastic productivity. I didn't get to speak with him, but others of his opinion that I did speak to replied with the functional equivalent of "My mind's made up. Don't confuse me with facts."

In the capitol building, late one afternoon after walking all day through five congressional office buildings, I stopped in the vast rotunda under the high dome, leaning against the wall to rest my aching feet. I idly watched the sauntering tourists and the professional lobbyists swirling in the wake of some aloof striding congressman. What an alien landscape. How different from the Tongass. Power and policy in place of water and trees. How did I get here? What am I doing here? I'm an immigrant to these United States, to me the greatest country in the world. Why is it up to me to save it from foolishly destroying its own industry, from stupidly putting its own people in the unemployment lines?

Knowing the obvious answer, this woman resting her feet in the capitol building got up and walked on to the next appointment.

The answer is a perennial truth: Somebody has to do it. If I don't do it, nobody will.

I knew that the members of the Alaska Women In Timber delegation were feeling the same way as they covered the offices of the 535 Members of Congress.

Their hurt has made them strong women. I know that sometimes they don't want to be strong. I know they'd like to rest once in a while. I know they ask themselves, "Just this once, can't somebody else do it?" And I know the answer they all tell themselves: No, not in a nation where the top ten environmental groups have a combined annual income in excess of a hundred million dollars and employ the most savvy lobbyists on The Hill. They will push us into oblivion if we don't push back.

I'm tired of being chased out of one job after another by ruthlessly aggressive, self-righteous and ignorant preservationists. I'm tired of having to defend an industry that does more good for the world than it will ever get credit for. I'm tired of taking the blame for evils that exist only in public relations inventions of the Sierra Club and the Wilderness Society.

It is not only the loss of our jobs and our money and our way of life caused by environmental groups that hurt us Alaskans so much, although such losses are indeed sufficient to daunt anyone. The deepest root of our pain lies in humiliation, the knowledge that these fellow citizens who call themselves "environmentalists" have lobbied away Alaskan lives and in their victory only smile at our misery. I've cried enough about it to salt Freshwater Bay. But the time for tears over environmentalists is gone by. It's time to take them down a notch or two.

Now we're ready to tell you the reasons for the anger of the Tongass. To mix my own metaphor of fair warning, if "environmentalism" is a sacred cow to you. prepare to have your ox gored.

LIARS

•••

Alaska. A magic word. Some dictionaries say it came to us through Russian (*Alashka*) from an ancient Aleut word *alakshak*, meaning "a peninsula." But we prefer the derivation most Alaskans use, the Aleut word *alyeska*, The Great Land. That's much more satisfying. It's also much more to the point in describing the home of the people of the Tongass.

But The Great Land does not mean the well-known land. Ask Helen Finney, one of the Alaska Women In Timber of Ketchikan. "Every summer," says Helen, "I go on board the Inside Passage cruise ships that stop in Ketchikan Harbor. I give little lectures to hundreds of passengers telling them about our section of the Tongass. But I learn more than I teach. Visitors ask things I'd never dream of. The three questions I hear most often are:

1) Do you take American money here?

2) How high above sea-level are we this far north? and

3) Where's all the devastation?"

Well, we're sure Alaskans seem a little silly to New Yorkers when we ask dumb questions in midtown Manhattan. So, in order to avoid embarrassing anyone, we'll sneak you the answers to Helen Finney's Terrible Trio:

1) Yes, as fast as you're willing to spend it. The tourist season lasts only four months a year. But we assure you that Alaska is one of the United States of America, the forty-ninth, admitted to the Union in 1959. It's only *treated* like a foreign country.

2) On the C Deck of your cruise ship you're about 35 feet above sea level. Sea level doesn't rise or fall the farther north you go. Or south or east or west. It varies with the irregular shape of the Earth and local gravitational anomalies.

3) The devastation is in the propaganda of irresponsible environmentalist writers. Not in the Tongass.

Our Problem: Creative Symbolization

Richard M. Griffin -- we all call him "Grif" -- is director of Islands College of the University of Alaska, Southeast. He says in his Sitka office, "Emotionalism about the Tongass is so effective it's become what I call The Official Version. If you're like most Americans, you were introduced to The Official Version in the lavish pages of the *National Geographic* or in the electronic flickers of the Public Broadcasting System. The Official Version is a myth that there are no trees left in the Tongass, that there is no wildlife left, that we've depleted our fishery stocks, that the bear, the deer, the wolves are all gone. And it's all totally false."

Grif is a professional educator with a background in physics. As a scientist he holds a strong commitment to the truth about the Tongass. And, like Helen Finney, he enjoys sharing his knowledge with visitors on tourist ships.

"On Sunday mornings I take visitors out on Sitka Sound to St. Lazaria Island, which is a National Wildlife Refuge, a bird sanctuary. I'm an avid bird watcher. The visitors I take along are generally people from the Midwest or the East Coast who've read or seen on television that there are no such things as bird sanctuaries in Alaska, there are no vast wild spaces for animals in the Tongass, that we've chopped all the forests down.

"I'm amazed by the misconceptions people have about what's going on up here. And our visitors are amazed by what they find that's *not* going on up here. I guess the reason I have trouble with emotionalism about the Tongass is that it preys on the innocence of good people. Ignorance is our greatest enemy."

Richard M. Griffin at the college.   Ron Arnold photo

Because of this simple innocent ignorance, our fellow Americans readily believe the distortions and flat lies about the Tongass now flying fast and furious in some of the nation's most respected print media. Telling lies in print may seem harmless enough, a time-honored media sport -- it's a free country, isn't it? We have freedom of the press, don't we? But the current crop of "Trash the Tongass" articles -- from late 1986 to late 1988 -- is not harmless. They form a well-orchestrated smear campaign in support of a deadly serious legislative program in Congress, a program intended to destroy the entire resource economy of Southeast Alaska -- for no good environmental reason.

Trashing The Truth

One of the most dishonest "Tongass Trashers" we've ever seen was published in the March 14, 1988, edition of *Sports Illustrated*. It ran ten text-and-photo pages, from page 77 to 88, bearing the title, "The Forest Service Follies." Author John Skow, a New London, New Hampshire, contract writer and self-styled wood-splitter, knows exactly what he's doing: making you hate the Tongass forest industry.

Skow presses into service every cunning device you'd expect to find in the professional propagandist's pouch of ploys: name-calling, glittering generalities, plain folks, band wagon, and appeal to prejudice.

He easily puts on the "plain folks" chatty locker-room style familiar to *Sports Illustrated* readers, devoting a whole paragraph early in his article to the special point that he works simultaneously on his stories and his winter woodpile. Skow proudly claims to switch off his computer "whenever a paragraph seizes up, like the transmission of his old logging truck," so he can whack on his woodpile for half an hour or so until he feels that "the fashioning of English prose seems much the easier chore."

It's Skow's macho-simpatico way of proving he knows that you have to cut down trees to get forest products -- his sole qualification for writing this article, as far as we can see.

Either one of us has forgotten more about logging than Mr. Hotshot ever knew, don't you imagine, Jackie?

You can't tell he ever knew anything about it, K.A.

Anyway, the implied similarity between Skow's hatchet-job approach to the woodpile and his writing style is a bit of unintentional self-parody -- the only thing funny about "The Forest Service Follies."

Although *Sports Illustrated* is not what you'd call a respected journal of natural resource management, as a heavily promoted property of Time-Life, Inc., it does occupy more waiting room space than anything including

National Geographic. Circulation director Michael Loeb, speaking from his Rockefeller Center office in New York City, says *Sports Illustrated* has a net paid circulation of 3,355,000, verified by the Audit Bureau of Circulation. Yes, that's much less than *Geographic's* 10 million-plus membership. But total readership of the March 14, 1988, edition, counting pass-along to non-subscribers, was an enormous 19,029,000 people, verified by Simmons Market Research Bureau. Think of it: Nearly eight percent of the total U.S. population is likely to have seen Skow's splitting-maul technique applied to the people of the Tongass.

If some crafty environmental group had been searching for the right place to plant a hand-tailored propaganda piece, they'd have a hard time doing better.

"The Forest Service Follies" -- catchy title -- is a compendium of inaccuracy, bias and rancor so unethical that both of Alaska's Senators, Ted Stevens and Frank Murkowski, characterized it in a letter to the *Sports Illustrated* editor as an "attack." It's worth examining in detail for what it reveals about the attacker -- and what it hides about the attacked.

Devil's Door into the Tongass

This is a heck of a way to become acquainted with the Tongass, but you might as well get used to the perennial controversy -- we locals have to.

So, here goes. Skow's story opens on page 77. The first thing you see is a stark photo of a clearcut. Over the logging photo a bold-face headline reads: "In Alaska, as in the Lower 48, the U.S. Forest Service is turning the timberlands it is supposed to preserve and protect into mismanaged tree factories."

Now, that's a sentence you could fairly call a "glittering generality." And it's a marvel of rhetoric. Look how it establishes the rules of debate to be employed in the article's body copy: It levels serious charges against a large federal agency, setting up the David-and-Goliath syndrome so you'll identify with author Skow as the underdog; it asserts that the big bad guy is supposed to "preserve" America's timberlands, even though "timber" by definition is "forests" designated for *use* rather than *preservation*; and it misdirects your attention with the name-calling expression "mismanaged tree factories" so effectively that you'd never think to ask if there could be such a thing as a "well-managed tree factory" or "a forest properly managed for wood production."

Behind the headline, the photo of the logged area is designed to hammer your aesthetic sensibilities so painfully you'd never wonder whether the clearcut technique might have living *biological* merit in promoting forest regeneration that one photo frozen in time could never reveal. It hides the prodigious regeneration typical of Tongass clearcuts.

Think what's just happened. Every idea that could possibly favor the Forest Service or the forest industry in the Tongass has been banished from your universe of discourse by a single headline over a single photo. A masterpiece of manipulation. Balance? Fairness? Forget it. Just hate them loggers, buddy.

You've already been brainwashed and the article hasn't even started yet.

Now that you're angry, console operator Jack Skow -- he goes by "Jack" -- can begin to push your buttons. Punch. Jack brings you into the Tongass on a melodramatic note: "Great claw marks, the half-healed scars left by ancient glaciers, run from northwest to southeast across Chichagof Island, which is part of the forested archipelago that sprawls below Glacier Bay and Juneau along the Alaska Panhandle."

So far so good. Claw marks and all, Skow's at least got our state's basic geography down according to the maps. As most folks know, the huge entirety of Alaska pokes out on the northwestern verge of the North American continent, skirted by the Arctic Ocean on the north and the Pacific on the south. Dipping southeast along the coast from the Gulf of Alaska, our narrow Panhandle virtually coincides with the Tongass National Forest. This Panhandle, or just plain "Southeast," as we locals call it, consists of two parts: The narrow continental coast, which cuts into British Columbia's mainland mountain mass; and a fantastic jigsaw puzzle maze of emerald-and-gray offshore islands -- the Mountains in the Sea -- called the Alexander Archipelago.

But we do need to warn you about a couple of little details as you enter the Tongass, because Jack Skow isn't going to tell you about the first one until he's punched your buttons for five pages: This national forest is bigger than West Virginia. At 16.78 million acres, it's three times the size of any of the other 155 U.S. national forests. And Jack won't tell you at all that only ten percent of it is scheduled to be logged during the next hundred years. Just keep those points in mind for a little perspective.

Skow follows the glacier's claw marks for 25 miles over northwest Chichagof until he comes up Lisianski Inlet to "a narrow, heavily wooded upland valley." He explains correctly that this valley of the Lisianski

Southeast Alaska fishing industry thrives   Alaska Department of Fish and Game photo

River is part of the huge Tongass National Forest. The Tongass, he writes eloquently, is "the last largely untouched rain forest in either of the world's temperate zones."

Punch. You didn't notice that this feelgood "largely untouched rain forest" is the feelbad "mismanaged tree factory" of the headline, did you? Hmm... He doesn't explain that only ten percent of the Tongass is scheduled for harvest in the next century. But ask yourself, if the last rain forest is largely untouched, why spend ten pages blasting decent people about logging the small touched parts? Well, you can weasel-word your way out of that little inconsistency, so it's no big deal, eh? Just hate them loggers, man!

Anyway. In the Lisianski River valley, Jack sets you up but good. He draws an idyllic glacier-shaped landscape, "a lovely, roadless place, a Wilderness in all but official designation." It hosts stands of 400-year-old Sitka spruce six to eight feet in diameter at the base and topping out at 175 feet, and it produces "stupendous numbers of pink salmon" for Southeast Alaska's $75 million annual salmon catch. Ah! Paradise rumbled by grizzlies, guarded by bald eagles and abundantly larded with Sitka black-tail deer steaks for the hungry folk in the nearby fishing village of Pelican (pop. 276). That's the setup.

Now the punch line: "If you want to see this rare, small valley, don't lollygag. The odds are that the best of it soon will be scraped bare again." Punch. The evil Forest Service is to be the clawing glacier this time, operating out of the Death Star in Juneau -- that's what environmentalists actually call the Forest Service Regional Headquarters building, after the *Star Wars* movie planet-killing space station. If you tune in to Skow's oratory, Forest Service Darth Vaders are going to stomp up the Lisianski River and smash every last tree to smithereens with bulldozers for the sheer meanness of it.

But worse, Skow asserts, the Forest Service won't pay attention to some of the folks who live in Pelican who would rather not have any logging up in that valley. "Agency men," says Skow, "hear but rarely heed, public critics." Punch. Skow insinuates that even if all 19 million *Sports Illustrated* readers objected to cutting timber in the Lisianski, the Forest Service would still rape it, scrape it, murder every living creature down to the last amoeba, and harrow salt into the wreckage. After the first couple of pages, things are looking bad for the Forest Service.

You can almost hear the *Sports Illustrated* cheerleaders chanting with glee, "Hit 'em, Jack! Hit 'em, Jack! Whack! Whack! Whack! Yaaaay JACK!"

Then, in a mere three column inches on page 78, Jack Skow accuses the Forest Service of 1) chronic malfeasance, 2) of selling timber below cost, 3) of entering a pair of ''50-year bargain-basement pulpwood contracts'' with the two pulp mills in the Tongass -- Louisiana-Pacific's Ketchikan Pulp Company and Japanese-owned Alaska Pulp Corporation in Sitka -- 4) of making sweetheart deals with the Japanese, 5) of selling giant 400-year-old trees for $2 each, 6) of not serving the forests, 7) of not serving even the forest industry, and 8) of being an obstinate bureaucracy.

Punch, punch, punch, punch, punch. Whew! What a slugger! Jack Skow, the best virtuoso voice of venom, vituperation and viciousness we've ever heard. You have to admit that when he gets through, there's not much left.

Then Jack dusts his hands off and turns toward you as he leaves the crumpled form of the Forest Service dead on the floor, great claw marks on its back. Skow explains earnestly why he has focused so intently on this particular site: ''The Forest Service's proposed trashing of the Lisianski Inlet is worth a hard look because it is representative of what is happening in the rest of the country.''

A hard look at the Lisianski Inlet? All right, let's take one. First, our U.S. Geological Survey map of the Sitka, Alaska Quadrangle, scale 1:250,000, indicates the narrow Inlet trends southwest from its mouth about thirty miles to where the Lisianski River empties into its headwaters. The village of Pelican is on the north shore not quite two-thirds of the way up the inlet. It's twelve and a half miles from Pelican's town boundary to the nearest proposed logging site. It's two miles from Lisianski Inlet saltwater to the nearest proposed logging site. The Environmental Impact Statement's logging proposal, Alternative J, reveals that the proposed harvest site is a series of ten clearcut openings averaging 78 acres each, 780 acres total, widely scattered in a valley about two miles wide and four miles long in a vast forest encompassing 26,221 square miles. Tree growth tables show that the forest's ability to regenerate itself in this valley is unsurpassed in North America.

Jack didn't bother to mention any of that. If you flew over such small clearcuts during their first years of regrowth you'd have a hard time distinguishing them from natural muskeg openings -- and we frequently see folks looking out Alaska Airlines windows at natural muskeg, complaining ''look what those condemned loggers did!'' Skow's ''trashing of the Lisianski Inlet'' parlance makes Alternative J's clearcuts sound like gaping thirty-mile-long scars you could see from the Moon. And it makes the scars sound permanent. Been at the woodpile again, Jack?

Now, what about this trashy logging proposal? Let's go into the dreaded Death Star in Juneau and examine the active Forest Service logging plan file for the Lisianski. After an hour's fruitless search for what Jack's talking about, let's go up to the fifth floor and talk to Wanita Williamson, a veteran Forest Service public information officer. She's a pleasant woman who doesn't look the least like one of George Lucas's *Star Wars* storm troopers. She smiles at our questions about Jack Skow and the Lisianski Inlet.

"Mr. Skow came in one day during August of 1987 and talked to our public affairs director Jim Caplan and Mike Barton, the regional forester. I didn't meet him personally," Wanita tells us. "We flew him to so many places he may just be a little confused. But the fact is that in December of 1986 we deferred timber harvesting in that Lisianski area for the present 5-year harvest period."

What? Jackie, did you hear that?

I heard it, K.A. The Lisianski logging plan was deferred months before Skow came visiting.

Wanita Williamson at work. Ron Arnold photo

"Yes, it was," says Wanita. "I just don't understand why *Sports Illustrated* fact checkers never contacted us about it. The deferral was in the public record for more than a year before they went to press -- and on such a vital point for Mr. Skow's argument, too. But why don't you talk to our legislative affairs officer Carl Holguin?"

So we do. Carl reads us the public statement he prepared on the Lisianski Inlet logging issue: "Our public participation meetings clearly showed that the residents of Pelican did not want logging in the Lisianski River drainage. In deference to their requests, and the fact that we could meet our contract obligations by logging in other areas, timber sales in the Lisianski

River units will not be offered for the present 5-year harvest period.''

Oops! There's no doubt about it. The official deferral of that timber sale has been on the public record since December of 1986.

Now, wait a minute. Let's figure this out. If Jack is right, and the Lisianski case *is* representative of what the Forest Service is doing in the rest of the country, then there's only one possible conclusion. The Forest Service is listening so compassionately to every single objector that there won't be a stick of federal timber cut anywhere in the United States for five years. No punch. Swing and miss.

The *Sports Illustrated* cheerleaders return glumly to the bench, pom-poms drooping.

Carl Holguin verifies Lisianski timber sale deferral.   Ron Arnold photo

Jack! How could you? Just when we were really getting into your ''Hate the Forest Service'' claw mark routine. Your whole sensational setup turns out to be nothing but hot air. Utterly without meaning. A non-issue.

How do you judge something like that? Is it a careless mistake by a hired contract writer? Is it a cunning lie? How are we to decide? But the Lisianski Inlet setup is certainly representative of what Jack Skow is doing in the rest of his *Sports Illustrated* article. Punching your buttons. About problems that either don't exist or aren't as he represents them. Without a peep in defense of the forest industry.

But that's environmentalist justice: a hanging preceded by no trial at all.

Fatal Errors

By now we've undoubtedly made you want to rush out and buy a back copy of the March 14 1988 issue of *Sports Illustrated*. That may sound feebleminded on our part, but it's not. We have nothing against *Sports Illustrated*. We have nothing against John Skow. We only have something against lies. It's immoral to tell lies. It hurts people when you tell lies about them. We simply found more concentrated falsehood in Skow's *Sports Illustrated* article than in any other single Tongass Trasher.

Now, we certainly don't propose to drag you line by line through Jack Skow's whole pungent garbage scow. Oh, we'll deal with all his bogus accusations, to be sure, and we'll handle the hostile hogwash printed in a dozen other magazines over the past couple of years. But we'll do it our way, spending a whole chapter letting lots of locals tell you about each of the important issues on the Tongass. We'll set the rules of debate here, more factually, we hope. And we're ethical enough to let you know up front that we're writing by our own rules. We've also provided a whole section of source notes in the back of the book so you can verify everything we say, if you're that interested.

But, since Jack handed us that helpful three-column-inch menu of malevolence on *Sports Illustrated's* page 78, we might as well rub his nose in it a little more. We never thought we'd see the day that we should defend the Forest Service. We loggers and road builders fight with them on a day-to-day basis ourselves. But when a cheechako carpetbagger like Skow comes jet-hopping into our home for ten days, smilingly claims he's going to write "a balanced article," goes away an "expert," and then spouts malignant rubbish about the people of the Tongass to an audience of 19 million of our fellow Americans, we'll defend the Forest Service even if it sticks in our craw.

In the first place, logging is not harming the environment on the Tongass. *Period*. Not even with the Forest Service managing things. Logging produces employment, useful products and no permanent damage. The best evidence is the wildlife count. Pardon us if we sound like number crunchers. Sitka blacktail deer harvest in southeast Alaska has increased from 4,800 in 1980 to 18,791 in 1987, and in places the bag limit has even been increased from four deer per hunter to six. That's deer harvested legally by licensed hunters and represents a genuine increase in deer population as counted by the Alaska Department of Fish and Game, not just more hunters or better reporting.

There is genuine controversy about the effect of logging on deer habitat despite the increase in numbers. David Anderson, Regional Supervisor of the Division of Game in the Alaska state fish and game department -- and no friend of loggers, in our view -- says, "The high-volume old growth forest provides wintering habitat for large numbers of deer because the high canopy of the forest intercepts snow and protects the abundant understory vegetation. When an area is logged, there is a relatively short period of time, say twenty-five years, when vegetation comes up in great abundance in the clearcuts. Deer use clearcuts extensively in the summer months and they're also usable in the winter months -- absent snow.

"But that's the one difference between the Tongass and more southerly Northwest forests where logged areas provide adequate deer habitat: the winters here are generally much more severe and you get snow accumulation in clearcuts that makes them unusable. Then too, the second growth, after about twenty five years, grows up so that the canopy closes and shades out the understory vegetation. The area then becomes impoverished. It takes between 200 and 300 years for the forest to thin itself out to where the understory vegetation regenerates and once more becomes favorable deer habitat."

Most biologists agree with that assessment. We don't dispute it. But to turn it into an argument to stop logging is absurd, for a very good reason: Skow's assertion that we're turning the *whole* forest into a "tree factory" is false. Again, the numbers tell the story. Of the 16.78 million acres of the Tongass, more than 9 million are covered by forests. Of that 9 million forested acres, about 5.7 million acres are commercial forests. Wilderness already covers nearly 4 million acres of that land, leaving commercial timber harvest scheduled for 1.7 million acres, a tenth of the Tongass (or about a fifth of the forested area), over the next century, or about 17,000 acres (a thousandth of the Tongass, or one-five-hundredth of the forested area) each year. About ten percent of the Tongass is all that will *ever* be logged under current plans. Yet environmentalists begrudge us even that. And they have more than twice as much Wilderness as we have logging land in the Tongass.

In terms of deer habitat, the fact that only a fifth of the forested area will ever be logged, and only one-five-hundredth in any given year, means that the overall Tongass deer population will be only slightly affected during any given year. Add to that the fact that foresters thin the growing forest, which improves its habitat characteristics, and you have minimal overall impact on the deer.

Some anti-logging advocates claim that the deer population has increased only because of an unusual string of very mild winters, and that the Sitka blacktails will all be wiped out as soon as the next hard snow comes. That doomsday warning doesn't explain why the deer population has in fact been growing so long and so steadily, even through several normally cold winters since 1975, particularly in the very places in the Tongass where the most logging has been done such as Prince of Wales Island, which Skow did not write about.

The salmon harvest is at an all-time high. Bald eagles are so abundant they're being transplanted to other states which need to increase eagle populations. High numbers of brown and black bear are reported every year. The wolf population is healthy. What more could you ask? All the complaints are couched in evasive language such as "Logging proposals *could* have a bad effect," or "*Experts say* logging has a bad effect."

The facts themselves tell you we have not harmed the spawning streams of salmon, the habitat of the Sitka black-tailed deer, the nesting sites of the bald eagle, the life-style of the bear or the

Forest Service photo

Logging has not harmed the Tongass.

ways of the wolf. All major wildlife species are doing well on the Tongass after decades of logging on the "touched" ten percent.

And on that other 90 percent of the Tongass, the casual observer doesn't realize that the Forest Service has management prescriptions for non-logging lands that are vastly different from its timber harvest lands. The Forest Service manages appropriately and differently for watersheds, Wilderness, archaeological sites, high value fish streams, wildlife areas and other sensitive areas. Listening to Skow you'd think every forest ranger is a logging engineer. Believe us, logging engineers are vastly outnumbered by just about everybody else in the Tongass National Forest.

Now, another point. Jack makes out that timber is "a dying industry," so it's unimportant. Let us assure you, our industry won't die before Jack stops living in wood houses and stops writing stories printed on paper. We're sure he'd like to give us that final nudge into oblivion, and we *have* just emerged from the worst slump in a generation, but we're a hardy bunch. There were about 2,700 direct in-the-woods workers employed in the Tongass area in 1987. Including induced jobs the number goes up to 3,093 for total wages of $80.1 million. Alaska Loggers Association claims there were 3,100 workers as of May 1988. ALA has 110 member firms working every day in Alaska's forest industry, not just the "corporate giants" that own the two pulp mills in the Tongass -- Ketchikan Pulp Company (a division of Louisiana-Pacific Corporation) and Alaska Pulp Corporation. ALA's "associate member" list, consisting of firms that supply equipment and services to the logging outfits, numbers over 200. Counting those related industries, we forest folk employ about 4,500 people.

In 1986, the Tongass supported some 10,500 direct and induced jobs in fishing, tourism and timber, generating more than $231 million in earnings. Those 4,500 timber-related jobs comprise nearly half of the Tongass area's natural resource economy, and nine percent of the *total* Tongass area's economy -- even counting those thousands of government jobs in Juneau. And that was in a depressed year for timber. The Tongass couldn't do without us.

And Skow writes in one snotty sentence, "Most of these are five-month-a-year jobs, right?" Wrong, Jack. Are you deliberately misleading us? Mill jobs are year around and logging in the woods is ten to eleven months a year. It's the tourism and fishing jobs that are highly seasonal and turn into unemployment for seven or eight months a year. The tourist season is barely four months long, five in rare years, three in bad years. And tourism job pay rates are little more than half of forest industry wages.

So we think the Forest Service is serving the forests and the forest industry just fine -- of course, the landlord could always treat the forest industry a little better, especially us small business types, right Jackie?

Right, K.A.
But that's "family" squabbles.

Mystery of the Missing Facts

What about that "pair of 50-year bargain-basement pulpwood contracts?" What the heck is Jack talking about? He doesn't bother to
explain, because that might let in an alien hint of fairness. But back in
1947 Congress passed a law called the Tongass Timber Act, which was
designed to attract capital investment to a place we'd call a Third World
country today. Things were pretty rough in the Territory of Alaska back
then. The Tongass was all federal land, with no place for private enterprise. Alaska as a whole is still 59.2 percent federal, 28.4 percent state
land, 11.9 percent Native-owned and 0.5 percent non-Native private.

Back in Territorial days the Forest Service had a regional forester in
Alaska named B. Frank Heintzleman. A remarkable guy. Since 1937 he'd
been trying to attract pulp mill operations to the Tongass. Why? The
place had no economy to speak of. The trees were here. Pulp trees. More
than half of the trees in the virgin Tongass were Western hemlock, many
of them over 200 years old, dying or dead, their gray skeleton top-branches
showing like tombstones all over the mountainsides. The forest industry
can use such trees for pulp, but not much else. They're too rotten for
lumber, generally. So pulp mills were the ideal investment. However,
with no private pulpwood land in the Tongass, and federal land notori-
ously subject to non-market political pressures, financiers weren't interested.

Then, too, about that time the Native Americans in the Tongass were
pressing so many land claims that if they won them all in court, the Forest
Service would shrink right out of Alaska. Congress wanted to be fair to
the Natives, but also wanted to maintain federal control over as much of
the Tongass as they could in order to promote the settlement and development of an American territory. The Tongass Timber Act of 1947 was the
solution. It authorized the secretary of agriculture (the boss of the Forest
Service) to make contracts for timber sales, but the receipts had to be kept
in a special fund until the Native land claims could all be settled. So it was
Congress itself, not the Forest Service, that set up the contract framework
for Skow's disparaging "pair of 50-year bargain-basement pulpwood
contracts." It was national policy in the public interest.

Heintzleman used that congressional authority to bring pulp companies to the Tongass. Even so, he practically had to beg firms to come buy
Tongass timber. Finally he convinced American Viscose Corporation and

Puget Sound Pulp and Timber to form the Ketchikan Pulp Company. He offered them a 50 year contract to buy Tongass hemlock pulpwood at a market price to be renegotiated every five years and adjusted annually. The "bargain-basement" price accusation Skow makes is pure poppycock. The price of Tongass wood is determined by the market. It is *not* set by arbitrary Forest Service "sweetheart deals." We'll show you the actual process step-by-step in a later chapter.

Now why 50 years? Isn't that excessive? Put yourself in the investor's place; think about a pulp mill coming out of your own pocketbook. Then ask yourself, why invest in the Tongass? On political lands, you're not going to risk the immense capital required to construct a pulp mill -- it was about $70 million in the 1950s, but it's $200 to $400 million in 1988 dollars, and that's a chunk of cash, friend -- without some guarantee of raw material supply.

Weathering the well-known boom and bust cycles of the pulp market is hard enough with a reliable pulpwood supply on private land. If you're going to recoup your investment on political land you need a raw material supply guarantee long enough and secure enough to deflect the fickle fingers of political football players. Fifty years is the magic number and a legal contract is the magic instrument. If the people of the Tongass were to have a business base, the Feds had to act in a businesslike manner. Since the Forest Service had been authorized by Congress to do so, they did, and the Ketchikan Pulp 50-year contract was signed on July 26, 1951, marking off a segment the size of one-fifth of the Tongass for their exclusive bids.

Okay, now what's this garbage about sweetheart deals with the Japanese, Skow? Another bum rap. And an appeal to prejudice to boot. The same year that Ketchikan Pulp signed its all-American contract, 1951, a Japanese consortium approached the Forest Service asking to buy Alaska timber. Why? It seems that President Franklin D. Roosevelt had made a secret deal at Yalta with Joseph Stalin to give Japan's main pre-World War II source of timber, Sakhalin Island, to the Soviet Union. The military government the U.S. had set up in post-war Japan developed a system of forestry, but its timber supply was insufficient. So Japan came to its conqueror for relief.

At first the Forest Service refused, saying it wanted Tongass timber to stick around for local use. Public sentiment in Alaska, however, favored another pulp mill, Japanese or not. After much haggling, a system was agreed upon by which a Japanese company would incorporate in the United States, using its own money and a loan from the Export-Import

Bank of Japan to construct a pulp mill and a sawmill at Sitka. But all the jobs -- in the mills and in the woods -- were to go to Americans forever. The second 50-year contract was signed in September 1953 with what is today known as Alaska Pulp Corporation.

Some sweetheart deal! You pay your conqueror for wood to replace what he gave away to the Soviets, you pay corporate taxes to your

Tongass National Forest Long-term Timber Sales

Timber contract sale name	Contract date	Expiration date	Timber volume (MMBF)	Volume remaining FY 1987 (MMBF)
Louisiana-Pacific Ketchikan	7/26/51	6/30/2004	8,250.0	3,600
Alaska Pulp Company Sitka	1/25/56	6/30/2011	4,974.7	2,500

Forest Service chart

conqueror, and your conqueror gets all the jobs in the mills that you have to amortize with your own money. Kiss, kiss, kiss.

Perhaps Jack didn't tell us about this because he didn't know about it. His English prose chore might benefit from working less on his woodpile and more in the national archives and university libraries. What's that, Jack? Archives? Libraries? Come on, you remember: Where they keep the facts.

The archives, Jack, reveal that there were originally going to be *five* pulp mills and *five* 50-year contracts in the Tongass. *Five*, Jack, not the *zero* you'd like to see. Five because there is more than enough of the low-grade hemlock pulpwood to supply them, and it would bring Southeast Alaska's economic base up to a level comparable with, say, Northern Idaho or Western Montana. Or a ten-block area of lower Manhattan. Two of the potential mill companies couldn't get the financing together. But an environmental group, the Sierra Club, blocked the other mill through a war of attrition in the courts. The most bitter irony here is that once the environmentalists got us down, they kicked us with charges that having only two existing mills constituted "no competition" in the Tongass. More on that later.

As things stand today, the contracts work this way: together the companies are guaranteed access to about 300 million board feet of wood per year averaged over a five-year period. A board foot is a unit of measurement of wood 1 foot by 1 foot by 1 inch -- yes that last measurement is an *inch*. If it was 1 foot by 1 foot by 1 foot it would be a *cubic foot* of wood, a measure that is commonly used in calculating pulpwood volume, while board feet is the common measurement used for sawlogs that end up as lumber.

You should also realize that an additional 150 million board feet per year are available on the Tongass to *any bidder*, not just to the two big companies, Ketchikan Pulp and Alaska Pulp. Of that 150 million board feet, about 80 million per year are reserved for small loggers through a 1977 agreement with the Small Business Administration. We have more than 100 logging, road building, log towing and log processing companies on the Tongass in addition to the two big pulp mill companies. It's a little more complex and involved than Jack would have you think.

Let us stress again: Of the Tongass's total 16.78 million acres, about 1.7 million, a tenth of the Tongass, is scheduled for harvest in rotation over the next century, or about 17,000 acres per year, a thousandth of the Tongass. *Only ten percent* of the Tongass will ever be "turned into tree factories," as Jack the Razor Tongue so contemptuously says of our workplace. We could call his computer a "lie factory" with much more justification. So that's that.

Subsidizing Wilderness

While you still have the 50-year contract "sweetheart deal" fresh in mind, we're going to jump to something Skow says on page 80 before we go back to his charges from page 78. You'll see why.

Apropos of the 50-year contracts, Skow wrote, "In 1980 a poorly drafted federal bill, the Alaska National Interest Lands Conservation Act (ANILCA), made the deal even cozier. ANILCA directed the Forest Service to give the two pulp companies a total of $40 million a year in aid 'or whatever sums are necessary' to achieve the timber supply goal."

That's pure invention.

Good grief, Jack, you're foaming at the computer.

Witness: ANILCA was so "poorly drafted" that the environmentalists in 1980 hailed it as the most comprehensive and far-reaching environmental legislation ever enacted by Congress. It created more acres of national parks, wildlife refuges, and national monuments than any single piece of legislation before or since. Among other things, it created 56 million acres of Wilderness in Alaska, equal to the combined size of New

York State and Ohio.

Witness: The two pulp companies don't receive a penny of this $40 million fund as Skow claims they do. The Forest Service gets it all. In fact, $25 million of it is the regular Forest Service budget for the Tongass! Only $15 million of it is devoted to special Forest Service tasks that guarantee an adequate timber supply to make up for losses due to the massive Wilderness designations. This must be one of those paragraphs that seized up on Jack like his old logging truck's transmission -- but never recovered. It's totally false. Lies, lies, lies.

Then what did happen in ANILCA? For one thing, Congress designated 5.4 million acres of the Tongass as Wilderness. That erased a lot of high quality timber from the existing logging maps because you can't log in a designated Wilderness. ANILCA's new Wilderness Areas pushed timber harvesting out of the fine stands into worse timber areas: rougher terrain (skyrocketing road building costs) and marginal timber quality (more cost to log because you get less usable wood for the same amount of work in rotten stands).

To their credit, Congress recognized that Wilderness comes at a price. Part of that price, Congress decided, was to make good on the 50-year contract. Congress decided to guarantee the forest industry 520 million board feet per year for timber harvest, but the environmentalists thought that was too much, so the industry compromised for 4.5 billion board feet per decade, or 450 million board feet per year as an annual average.

You already know the breakdown: 300 million to the two pulp mills; 150 million to all other bidders, with 80 million of it allocated for small loggers. Now remember, that guarantee only means the Forest Service has to *offer it for sale*, not that it's *mandatory to cut it*, although a number of opponents call it "The Mandatory Cut."

The other part of the price of Wilderness was to create a $40 million per year fund for the Forest Service's increased expenses to plan, administer, and prepare for sale an average offer of 450 million board feet per year over ten years in the rougher, more marginal land left to log on. But one thing has to be made especially clear about that $40 million, as we've already tried to do: $25 million of that $40 million is the Forest Service's everyday budget, the normal running expense of putting up regular timber sales. Only $15 million of the $40 million is allocated to the Tongass Timber Supply Fund to build roads into submarginal areas, do some logging technology research for coping with submarginal areas, and perform thinning to promote more rapid timber growth.

That $40 million-a-year fund is not a subsidy to the timber industry, it's a subsidy to pay for the Tongass Wilderness that took away easy-to-plan, easy-to-access timber areas. That 450 million board foot per year guarantee is a subsidy for the Tongass Wilderness that took away prime logging lands and left the industry with less accessible, more expensive-to-operate submarginal timberlands.

But now the environmental movement wants to change the deal. With Skow as their apparent catspaw, they're out to renege on the 1980 ANILCA provisions. They want to eliminate the $40 million fund and cancel the 450 million board foot a year timber supply guarantee because they want all logging stopped permanently in the Tongass. Yes, the total destruction of forestry and the timber industry in the Tongass.

In one of the most shocking discoveries we made while researching this book, numerous sources described a 1986 meeting held in the Juneau regional office conference room between Wilderness Society chief lobbyist Gaylord Nelson (his official title is "Counsellor") and Forest Service officials in which Nelson said bluntly,

"Alaska is The Last Frontier. Philosophically, we want to keep it that way. Practically, the Wilderness Society will work to make the Tongass completely wild. We see no acceptable place for the timber and mining industries."

Industry's death should come little by little, of course. The environmentalists don't want to look *too* ruthless. More on this later.

Now back to the lumpy laundry list from Skow's page 78. What about his charge that the Forest Service sells timber below cost? Skow's no better a timber appraiser than he is a legislative analyst on ANILCA. To put it tersely, the "below cost timber sale" flap is all a matter of bookkeeping. It comes out looking great or awful depending on what you count and which column you put it in.

The "below cost" brawl began about 1979 when the forest products industry nationwide hit its worst slump since the Great Depression of the 1930s. And the fracas has meaning only in the context of the Forest Service's appraisal process. You can't get "below-cost" sales on private land. The definition reads like this: "For a timber sale to be defined as below cost, the net public benefits of a forest following timber harvest (recognizing all anticipated benefits and all costs, monetary and otherwise) must be less than if the timber was not harvested." Since it's technical and boring, Skow didn't bother his *Sports Illustrated* readers with it. Environmentalists use "below cost" as a value-laden code word, without paying any attention to what it means. What the heck, the facts don't matter when simple hate seems to be your objective.

In the Tongass National Forest, they use what's called the residual value appraisal to determine timber sale costs. The residual value appraisal takes the estimated end product value and subtracts from it the cost of producing that product, working step by step back to the stump, which could get down to a certain minimum acceptable bid, below which the government will not sell timber. Not too hard to grasp, is it, Jack?

The end product value is estimated by looking to see what end products -- such as a bundle of dissolving pulp or a boxcar of lumber -- have been selling for on the market. It's all there right on the invoice. The market dictates the price, not the Forest Service.

And from that end product value you subtract the logging costs, the road building and maintenance costs, the log hauling costs, the lumber or pulp manufacturing cost, environmental regulation costs, payments to the state in lieu of taxes, a return on investment allowance based on comparable profits -- and what remains after that is the return to the U.S.

Sitka blacktail deer: population healthy and thriving   Forest Service photo

Treasury, or the "stumpage" price, as it's called, but that price is not allowed to sink below a minimum base rate. Jack? Did we lose you there someplace?

It's not too hard to see that when markets are depressed and the end product value is pennies, you're going to spend more preparing and operating a Forest Service timber sale than you can sell it for. Then you have a "below cost timber sale" in which the government receives less money for the timber removed from its lands than the cost of preparing and operating the sale. But remember, the Forest Service always sells the timber for at least a base rate -- a minimum established rate below which the government cannot sell timber.

Here's the irony. If you subtract the environmental regulation costs from this arithmetic problem, you have a profitable sale, *above* cost.

We're not talking environmental *protection* costs that actually do something good on the ground, such as redesigning a logging layout so you can avoid a wildlife area or installing culverts to prevent rainwater from eroding your roadbeds.

We're talking environmental *regulation*, the cost of *red tape*: Twenty-pound Environmental Impact Statements that merely describe what will happen when you log an area, and other regulations that do nothing but jump through legalistic hoops, paper that will never have the slightest effect on the ground.

We're talking the millions of dollars worth of Forest Service planning that has nothing to do with logging, but only with following the elaborate details of environmental laws. The cost to plan a properly engineered *and environmentally sound* timber sale is minimal. Add to it the incredible maze of laws that the environmental movement has lobbied into existence these past 20 years and you have non-logging costs making up more than three-quarters of the so-called "timber sale budget." Most timber sale planning today has *nothing to do with logging*, yet the logger gets blamed for its high cost.

We're also talking the hundred-pound lawsuit documents generated by environmental groups that fight every timber sale on the Tongass through administrative appeals, federal court lawsuits and appeals court proceedings. Fighting over environmental regulations can add a million dollars to the cost of a timber sale without helping the environment an iota. Just remove the environmentalist lawyers' fees from the cost of a timber sale, Jack, and you make a profit nearly every time.

And do give a thought to the overhead costs for Forest Service salaries and benefits, which are a not inconsiderable part of the cost of running the national forests.

Now stop and think a moment. Have you ever wondered why there are no "below cost timber sales" on Native corporation timberlands in the Tongass, Jack? Probably not, but try. It's because the Indians own their own land, private land they won in the Alaska Native Claims Settlement Act of 1971. These private Native corporation lands are scattered among Forest Service timberlands -- no different forests. The Native corporations log their forests without an army of environmental group lawyers obstructing them with federal lawsuits at every turn -- because it's not federal land. And, just as important, because it's not federal land, Native corporations don't have to obey federal environmental laws and regulations.

For example, Native loggers don't have to prepare costly Environmental Impact Statements under the National Environmental Policy Act of 1969. Native loggers don't have to adhere to the costly restrictions of the Forest and Range Renewable Resources Planning Act of 1974. And they can export round logs at top dollar to world markets, while loggers on Forest Service land must process the wood in the United States. Native loggers don't have to follow the incredibly costly rules of the National Forest Management Act of 1976 -- they don't have to limit the size of their clearcuts or pay for a mountain of paperwork that talks about non-logging uses of the forest. Native loggers don't have to pay the salaries and benefits of battalions of Forest Service bureaucrats. Getting the picture? Low overhead.

But the Native corporations do have to log their forests under Alaska state environmental laws, which are much more rational than federal environmental laws. And under these less rigid laws, Native loggers do such a good job of logging they've even won environmental awards. Obviously, you can log *and* protect the Tongass environment without *any* of the federal laws that every logger and timber firm must follow on Forest Service lands. And if you don't have all that ridiculously expensive non-logging federal and environmentalist overhead, you *never* have a "below cost timber sale."

And have you ever wondered why there is no outcry about "below cost Wilderness use," Jack? Again, probably not, but try. It costs tons of money just to build hiking trails into Wilderness areas, much less carry on the unending studies of Wilderness carrying capacity, wildlife management, salmon enhancement, and so forth, but there are no user fees for Wilderness. Nowhere. Never have been. You pay to get in at a lot of national parks. But not Wilderness areas. Not a thin dime has ever come back to the United States Treasury from any Wilderness area entry fee. If you hold Wilderness to the same standard as the timber industry and demand a payback, Jack, Wilderness comes up boondoggle. Timber pays. And pays and pays. Wilderness areas *always* lose taxpayer money, Jack, not just during severe depressions. Always. Wilderness only costs, it never pays.

Why doesn't that make you sore, Jack? Could it be, as you admit on page 82 of your article, that "whacking the Forest Service for fiscal wastefulness is so satisfying?" That you don't really give a hoot about the U.S. Treasury, but merely want to get your jollies doing a claw-mark number on the Forest Service? That's pretty kinky, Jack. You wouldn't do anything that irresponsible, would you? Jack? Is that the sound of cordwood splitting?

Advocacy Against Ethics

Anyway. We can't argue much about the Forest Service being an obstinate bureaucracy -- all bureaucracies are obstinate in fulfilling their mandate, including the *Sports Illustrated* bureaucracy in Rockefeller Center. Secretary of Agriculture Richard Lyng -- who is the Cabinet officer responsible for the Forest Service -- was so upset by the falsehoods contained in Jack Skow's article that he wrote a letter to the editor of *Sports Illustrated* presenting the story's more patent errors along with the correct data. The obstinate bureaucrats of *Sports Illustrated* replied with the functional equivalent of, "We don't believe you." They wouldn't even look at the errors, much less print the secretary's letter. So much for obstinate bureaucracies -- and journalistic ethics: failing to check your facts sounds like reckless disregard of the truth to us. And *refusing* to check your facts sounds like malice, doesn't it?

Sports Illustrated also obstinately refuses to print any Forest Service response to Jack Skow's charges of chronic malfeasance.

If they won't, we will. Here's what Juneau Forest Service public affairs director Wayne Nicolls wrote that *Sports Illustrated* won't print:

The Forest Service is the agency:

- that leads the world in forestry and forest products research, to benefit forest lands and the forest products industry, thereby the people.

- that annually suppresses or otherwise manages thousands of acres of potentially unimaginably devastating wildland fires.

- that manages the land and facilities which accommodate the largest number of recreation visits of any public land system in the United States.

● that administratively started the National Wilderness Preservation System 40 years before the 1964 Wilderness Act.

● that conducts research and management to significantly increase salmon production through habitat protection and improvement for the benefit of commercial, sport, and subsistence fishing in Alaska.

● that through effective management provided base acreage for numerous additions as recently as the 1980s to the National Park System.

● whose founder, Gifford Pinchot, also maligned in Mr. Skow's article, along with Bob Marshall, after whom a National Forest Wilderness is named, were charter and founding members of the Wilderness Society.

If examples of malfeasance in the Forest Service are known, Mr. Skow should come forward with names, places, and facts. It will be stopped and appropriately prosecuted.

Skow scuds dangerously close to the shoals of libel in accusing the Forest Service of criminal behavior -- chronic malfeasance is a felony offense. Skow's comments about forest supervisor Ken Roberts come even closer. Turn to page 88 of Skow's article. Jack is still harping on the Lisianski non-issue on this tenth and last page, making his non-case that the Forest Service doesn't pay attention to Tongass residents who don't like logging nearby.

In leading us up to Ken Roberts, Skow describes how one day in August of 1987 the residents of Pelican wait for Forest Service floatplanes to bring in several strongly environmentalist members of the House Committee on Interior and Insular Affairs on a congressional investigation. Several Pelican residents, asserts Skow, complain about the proposed logging of the Lisianski to Robert Mrazek of New York and Mo Udall of Arizona, both Democrats. Skow pointedly notes that Alaska's Representative Don Young, a Republican, is not included on this junket. (And think about that: Alaska has only *one* congressman.) Interestingly, Skow does not mention that influential California Rep. George Miller *was* at Pelican, about which more later.

Next, Skow bubbles about several Pelicaners who "have bumper stickers that read I'm proud of my congressman Bob Mrazek." A publicity shot on page 82 (provided by Mrazek's office) bears the caption, "Some Alaskans think of Mrazek (D.,N.Y.) as their congressman."

That's laying the partisan politics on a little thick, and it vastly overstates the case, but now we come to a paragraph that Jack probably regrets. Ken Roberts, Skow claims, announced a few days after the meeting at Pelican that the Lisianski sites would be offered as timber sales, which is flatly untrue. Then Skow writes, "Roberts is a sharp advocate and a patient, polite listener. He seems typical of the service's field-level managers. Giving the public its say, and then patiently and politely ignoring objections, is something they do very well." We think that's tantamount to an accusation of felony malfeasance.

We talked to Ken Roberts in Sitka. "I've seen too many 'Trash the Tongass' articles to let unbalanced reporting get me down," he smiles with resignation. Ken, incidentally, is one of numerous Native Americans who have made the Forest Service their career. "And federal officials must be able to take heat from journalists. Maybe Jack's accusation is a little jolting because our deferral of the Lisianski timber sale was on the public record for eight months before he got here. I didn't see Jack in Pelican when we brought the congressional delegation there, so I don't know how he got his information for that part of his article.

"But a few days later I spent some time with Jack over near Hoonah and got to know him a little better. As forest supervisor, I drove him through the woods for three or four hours, showed him all our operations. He's a pleasant fellow, really. Good company. He took that picture of me on page 80 himself, you know, the one with the caption, 'Agency men like Roberts hear, but rarely heed, public critics.'"

Ken laughs as he recalls the event. "What I was really doing in that picture was counting the rings on a big stump where loggers had recently felled this tree. Jack had been talking a lot about 800-year-old trees, and I'd been telling him that there may be a small percentage of trees that old."

Not likely. George B. Sudworth's standard textbook *Forest Trees of the Pacific Slope* says of Sitka spruce that "Large trees attain from 400 to 750 years." Interestingly, Skow talked to Roberts about 800-year-old trees but only wrote about "400-year-old trees."

"But," continues Roberts, "I told Jack that we never had any 800-year-old stands in the Tongass. Trees that old usually show up as isolated individuals or in small pockets scattered here and there. Well, about then we drove by this great big fresh stump and I said, 'Let's see how old this one is.' I backed up and we got out. Jack took my picture while I counted tree rings, one for each year of the tree's life. I used a common forester's method: I counted a six inch segment of growth rings and extrapolated the tree's age from its radius: 140 years, give or take. The tree was about 140 years old, 150 years tops.''

Forest Service photo

Ken Roberts and biased magazine: Misrepresentations galore.

So there's no question that Skow knew he was stretching the truth when he whacks home ''400-year-old trees'' page after page as if every tree in the Tongass is a venerable patriarch. To paraphrase his own accusation, we could write rudely but truthfully, ''Advocacy men like Skow hear, but rarely heed, the objective facts.'' If some environmental group were setting him up to write the article, he couldn't have been less objective.

We already knew that *Sports Illustrated* fact checkers never called anyone in the Juneau office to verify their writer's assertions. We asked Ken Roberts if anyone had contacted his Sitka office. ''No one from *Sports Illustrated* ever called me, or anyone in my office. Neither did Jack. We put him on a Forest Service airplane and that was the last I heard of him. Until his article in *Sports Illustrated* came out.''

On a Forest Service airplane? Jack got free rides at taxpayer expense? Oho! Forest Service records verify that after Skow visited Sitka, he was flown in an airplane under contract to the Forest Service to Hoonah at the northern end of Chichagof Island on Monday, August 17, 1987. Tuesday,

August 18, Skow was driven by Forest Service personnel to the logging
float camp where Jackie and her family lived for seven years at Kennel
Creek on Freshwater Bay. After Ken Roberts showed him the neighbor-
hood in a Forest Service vehicle, Skow was flown by Forest Service plane
to Lake Hasselborg on Admiralty Island where he stayed the night in a
Forest Service cabin. On August 19 the Forest Service flew him to
Juneau, where records show he had arrived ten days earlier. All at
government expense. From Juneau Skow presumably departed for his
New London, New Hampshire woodpile. After *ten whole days* in the
Tongass. Yippee-Skipee!

On occasion, the Forest Service transports journalists to remote sites
on public lands at government expense. The public has a right to know
and the responsible agencies sometimes provide access to qualified journalists in the public interest. We don't object to that at all, even though we
didn't avail ourselves of the service for this book. We paid our own way,
as logging folk are accustomed to doing. What's curious is that the exalted
Jack Skow, consecrated champion of fiscal austerity, sanctimonious slayer
of subsidies and stainless defender of the U.S. Treasury, never volunteered
to reimburse the government for the taxpayer dollars that subsidized his
article. Neither did *Sports Illustrated*.

Cahoots

Aside from exposing Skow's hypocrisy in decrying "subsidies" to
the forest industry while accepting free rides himself, Forest Service
records of Jack's visit reveal a most embarrassing linkage:

Jack Skow visited Juneau in the company of Steve Richardson, general counsel of the Wilderness Society. We examined the business cards
Richardson left behind to verify the connection. Forest Service personnel
report that Richardson did most of the talking during Juneau meetings and
Skow remained mostly silent. Who was in charge?

Skow's entire itinerary in the Tongass was guided by the Wilderness
Society. Forest Service public information officer Jim Caplan offered to
have District Ranger Pete Johnston host Skow on Prince of Wales Island,
where he could talk to loggers at Thorne Bay and see abundant examples
of excellent forest regrowth. Wilderness Society lawyer Richardson was
heard to veto the idea, even when a staff member of the Mrazek-Udall congressional delegation recommended it. Skow's whole trip, his whole
article appears to be a setup by the Wilderness Society.

Skow appears to have been picked for this assignment because of his
allegiances, not his knowledgeability. He was not well informed about

national forest matters when he visited Juneau and Sitka in August 1987. For example, Skow argumentatively asserted while interviewing an official that Regional Supervisor Mike Barton did not have jurisdiction over the Chugach National Forest in South Central Alaska, a sophomoric error.

Skow, according to records we obtained, visited only the northern "A-B-C Islands," Admiralty, Baranof and Chichagof, and a cannery on Noyes Island, covering less than one-quarter of the Tongass.

Skow is not listed as a qualified writer in the Outdoor Writers Association of America 1988-89 directory. OWAA's Creed requires that "I will present my audience only that which I can present ethically. My financial returns will not influence my judgment, nor will I evade my personal responsibility to search for facts. I believe in honest representation and conscientious performance...."

The views Skow expressed in *Sports Illustrated* hew strictly to the Wilderness Society party line.

The Wilderness Society's leadership has vowed to push the timber and mining industries out of the Tongass.

Did *Sports Illustrated* publish a paid political propaganda piece for the Wilderness Society designed to destroy the Tongass timber industry under the guise of legitimate freelance journalism?

This much is clear:

● A high ranking officer of the Wilderness Society traveled in the Tongass with Skow.

● Skow saw only what the Wilderness Society wanted him to see.

● Skow wrote only what the Wilderness Society wanted to see in print.

● Skow wrote nothing that would indicate the slightest independence from Wilderness Society designs.

Which leads us to ask further: Did the Wilderness Society provide part or all of the material for Skow's article? Did the Wilderness Society subsidize any part of Skow's article?

Was *Sports Illustrated* aware of the Wilderness Society's influential role in shaping their writer's itinerary and material?

Why didn't *Sports Illustrated* do any fact checking to verify their writer's quotes with the Forest Service?

The answers would be illuminating. But our discovery of the Wilderness Society's direct power over this article casts its own light.

Political Fallout

You may ask: Even if all this is true -- which you're still skeptical of -- so what? Who does it hurt? Consider: Two weeks after Skow's *Sports Illustrated* article appeared, on March 30, 1988, Rep. George Miller, who was in the Pelican delegation but not mentioned by Skow, sent out a "Dear Friend" letter to his biggest environmentalist campaign contributors. It began:

> If you heard that a government was destroying a rain forest by selling 400-year-old trees for less than $2 each, you would probably assume that it was a Third World country run amuck.
>
> Incredibly, the government running this scandal is the United States. The threat is to the Tongass National Forest in Alaska -- the largest, most pristine and most beautiful old-growth forest in the nation.

Who wrote that? Jack, are you back there in the woodpile somewhere?

This letter from Rep. Miller is a persuasion piece written specifically for the environmental lobby in Washington, D.C. to help a House bill through the Senate. Rep. Miller continues:

> The U.S. Forest Service spent over $275 million in the last five years on a timber subsidy program that has returned only $32 million in revenue to you, the taxpayers who own the Tongass timber. Because of a fiscally, and environmentally, unsound deal made years ago, two large timber corporations are profiting from tens of millions of your tax dollars each year, while at the same time destroying priceless salmon streams and wildlife habitat.
>
> Fortunately, we have taken a decisive step to stop the rip-off. The House Interior Committee has passed legislation which I authored to make fundamental reform on the Tongass. Under my plan, the mandatory timber cut and special timber fund which are the major culprits in the current scandal will be repealed. The Forest Service will be forced to renegotiate outrageous sweetheart contracts held by the two giant lumber companies. My bill also places 1.7 million acres of the

most valuable fish and wildlife lands into protected
status.

I will keep you informed on the progress of my
legislation to restore fiscal and environmental integrity to the management of the Tongass Forest.

Sincerely,

GEORGE MILLER

Member of Congress, 7th District

Lies.

More lies.

And damn lies.

(A Harry Trumanism.)

But hauntingly familiar, eh?

Isn't it a little coincidental that *Sports Illustrated* published an article
by a flaming anti-industry writer-for-hire just when a key piece of flaming
anti-industry legislation needed a boost to pass the Senate? And a dozen
other magazines such as *Life* and *Readers Digest* and *The New Republic*
and Conde Nast's *Traveler* have been peddling the same falsehoods and
misrepresentations as Jack Skow during the anti-industry Tongass legislative campaign of the past two years.

Why should Congress and the public not believe all these lies?
There's been no champion of the forest industry allowed into the pages of
Life or *Reader's Digest* or *Sports Illustrated* to say them nay. Does
anyone know what's actually going on in the Tongass? Does anyone
know that we're doing an outstanding job of logging our small part of the
Tongass and protecting our resources at the same time?

Do you take American money here?

If we hadn't filled you in on a few details, you'd assume that Congressman Miller was saying, like hired-writer Jack and his Wilderness
Society puppet-masters, that the government has given $275 million in the
last five years directly to Ketchikan Pulp Company in Ketchikan and
Alaska Pulp Corporation in Sitka, which is false.

How high above sea level are we this far north?

You'd never know that Rep. Miller's 1.7 million acres of "the most
valuable fish and wildlife lands" is the very 1.7 million acres we're
allowed to log on now. That 1.7 million acres is all we have left in the

Tongass. Take it away and you will leave us nothing. Nothing! How long do you think we can survive working on nothing?

Where's all the devastation?

Rep. Miller has softened his stand somewhat since he wrote his letter. He appears to be reasonable, but not Robert Mrazek and the Wilderness Society: they don't want us to survive. If all the anti-industry legislation now on the table passes, that will be the end of the Tongass timber industry. It will be the end of our personal businesses. It will be the end of our way of life. And it will be the end of Alaskan independence.

Where's all the devastation?
In our hearts.
In our minds.
In our lives.

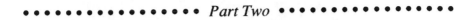

Part Two

THE COLONY

HOMELAND

• •

We've seen what the Tongass is *not*. That's devastated. Now let a couple of locals take you around to see what it *is*. That's equal parts of two things: great land, great people.

If you come to see us from the south, what the Tongass *is* is *isolated*. You get here by water or by air. But not by road. Another little gift from the environmentalists. All the natural access corridors that could have brought roads, power lines, railways and pipelines from Canada and the Lower 48 to the Tongass were blocked by environmentalists drawing Wilderness Area lines on maps in strategic locations that Congress approved. If it's Wilderness, you can't build a road through it. So there goes another permanent chunk of our economic potential. Nice.

Anyway. Come with us on an imaginary but entirely plausible trip through the Tongass. Let's make our approach by water. We'll start from Prince Rupert, British Columbia's northernmost coastal port (which *is* connected to the Lower 48 by road, rail, etc.). And by all means let's take a Blue Canoe -- Tongass slang for the nine blue ferries trimmed with white and yellow belonging to the Alaska Marine Highway system. The system in 1988 celebrated their twenty-fifth year of operation. We could take the Columbia, the large thousand-passenger 180-car ferry, or the 750-passenger 120-car Malaspina or Matanuska, or the 500-passenger 105-car Taku, but they don't serve some of the little places we're going.

We'll be taking the Aurora, a 300-passenger 44-car vessel, one of the five "village boats" that serve as lifelines to little logging and fishing communities and carry mostly locals. The Blue Canoes aren't as posh and the ride isn't as smooth as the Sundancer or other summer cruise ships that ply the Inside Passage. But on the four big vessels you can get a nice stateroom with a bed, and if you're *really* tired, you can even sleep in it. On the Aurora, bring your sleeping bag, a sack of groceries and a deck of cards.

Good Morning, Alaska

A passage to Ketchikan. The Aurora's full of cars and the purser's collected the fares. Deckhands, heave in that hawser! First mate, blast that horn! Let's run this bucket of bolts out of the slip!

The heavy screws churn up a thundering turquoise ferment in the still gray harbor and we're away. Goodbye, Prince Rupert, we'll see you again. We turn into Venn Pass, glide past the buoy light, put Tugwell Island astern and head into open water. Now we travel the whale's road at 14 knots. Watch the sea otters splash in the kelp. Yes, that's our Alaska, Tongass rock-and-ice poking up over the horizon, dead ahead thirty nautical miles.

We diesel up Chatham Sound against a beam sea coming in off the Dixon Entrance to port. Let the sun and the ancient tang of brine spume and long rolling ocean swells roust your senses. It's a good day to be alive. We slice through a light chop past Melville Island, then the Moffats, then Dundas Island. Then...

We're across the International Boundary and into American waters. See the red, white and blue ensign go up. This is Revillagigedo Channel, named for Don Juan Vicente de Guemes Pacheco de Padilla y Hocasitas, Count of Revillagigedo, a Viceroy of New Spain in the late 18th century. You really wanted to know that, didn't you?

The maps may greet you with our Spanish heritage, but the land meets you with breathtaking splendor: Off the starboard bow, the Misty Fiords National Monument and Wilderness. Cloud-piercing peaks plunge a thousand feet straight down to chiseled straits rivaling Norway's famed fjords. And guarding the southern entrance in Nakat Bay are the low hills of smallish Tongass Island, once the home of the people for whom the Tongass National Forest is named.

The Meaning of Tongass

Aside: Tracking down the origin of the word *Tongass* became quite a chore. We first asked a number of Forest Service officials in Juneau and in Ketchikan what the name of their national forest meant, but not one of them knew offhand. "It's probably a Tlingit word," they all said. But what does it mean? "Damfino."

The *Dictionary of Alaska Place Names* published by the U.S. Geological Survey wasn't much help. Its entry reads:

> Tongass: *locality*, on E coast of Tongass I., Coast Mts;
> 54°6'30" N, 130°14'30" W; *Var.* Fort Tomgas, Fort Tongas,

TAn-ga'sh, Tongas, Tont-a-quans, Tungass, Tungass-kon, Tun-grass.

Former Tlingit Indian village or camp named for the island. In June 1868 a military post, called "Fort Tongass" was established, and maintained here until September 1870. Population recorded as 273 in 1880 and 255 in 1890.

K.A., you have a degree in anthropology. And you grew up with the Tlingit. What does Tongass really mean?

I wish it was that easy, Jackie. A degree doesn't tell you everything. And my Tlingit schoolmates and friends never talked much about what Tlingit words mean. We'll just have to snoop out the meaning of "Tongass" ourselves. But I do know something about the people.

You have to understand that long before European settlers arrived in the Tongass, fourteen tribes of the Tlingit group lived in all this land, from the Yakutats and Chilkats up north to the Shee-Atikas and Hoonahs and Stikines in the middle, to the Sanyakwan and Tantakwan down south. They were the first users of the Tongass forest. The Indians of the southeastern Alaska coast and islands -- the Tlingit first, then the northward migrating Haida and Tsimshians -- were a people of prosperity who lived on the abundance of the sea.

Although the Alaska coast Indians dined from the sea they expressed their advanced, stratified and highly complex culture in wood -- hemlock, spruce and cedar. They used the forest for both utilitarian and artistic purposes. And the great Tongass forest favored the development of woodworking crafts then as it does today.

Houses were large rectangular gable-roofed dwellings built of logs and split boards, the front often decorated with strong designs of surpassing beauty. There's a reasonably authentic replica right across the square from my parents' house in Haines, and a number of others throughout the Tongass. The Indians developed techniques using steam and fire to augment their advanced wood-carving and splitting tools.

Water travel -- and we all know what a necessity that is in the coastal region -- was carried on in wood vessels shaped by fire and adze. Tlingit craft ranged from ten-foot paddle canoes for river passages to expeditionary war canoes sixty feet long with stepped masts and sails of cedar bark. And can you imagine, Jackie, the Tlingit commonly ranged for hundreds of miles and reportedly sailed as far south as Baja California!

To get out of the rain, K.A.?

No doubt. Archaeologists have been studying sites in the Tongass dating back more than 8,000 years. Recent evidence indicates early inhabitants fished from boats, a technology they are believed to have brought in migration from Asia.

Their weapons -- spears, bows, arrows, lances, pikes, war clubs -- were made of wood. Their household furnishings -- bowls and utensils and exquisite bentwood boxes -- were made of wood. Their ceremonial and artistic life made elaborate and sophisticated use of wood -- the most striking examples are their masterfully carved masks, rattles, totem and mortuary poles. Their everyday baskets were woven from spruce roots and their rain clothes and hats they shaped from cedar bark. Their rich and complex ceremonial rituals were heavily influenced by wood as a material and by the forest as an environment. You can see it brought to life in the performances of the Chilkat Dancers in Haines and similar groups all over the Tongass.

What kind of environment was the Tongass for its original inhabitants, K.A.?

Let's ask somebody who knows: A professional historian, Dr. Lawrence Rakestraw. You'll find his name on several distinguished histories of the Alaska forests as well as on numerous articles in scholarly journals. Dr. Rakestraw?

"Well, the Tlingit's world for the most part was the beaches and low benches just above the tide zone. That's where their homes were built and their daily functions and rituals played out. They were equally at home on water and in the woods, gathering food, hunting, fishing, raiding for slaves, a practice which they kept until the 1860s. But the forest overshadowed everything, literally and figuratively.

"The forests of southeastern Alaska are the northernmost stretch of a humid West Coast forest that extends from the southern Oregon coast to Kodiak Island. It is composed of Sitka spruce (*Picea sitchensis* to the biologist) and Western hemlock (*Tsuga heterophylla*) in the southern Panhandle, with Alaska cedar (*Chamæcyparis nootkatensis*) and Western redcedar (*Thuja plicata*) in some areas. It does not contain the Douglas fir so common farther south. It is a dense rain forest, with a thick ground cover of devils-club, huckleberry, and other woody shrubs, and an abundance of naturally fallen trees.

"Because of the heavy rainfall, this coastal forest has been little modified by the action of fire. Big conflagrations happen occasionally, but they are the exception. The coastal Indians had very little influence on the original forests, unlike some of the Indians of the Alaska interior who caused innumerable fires that had profound ecological effects.

Forest Service photo

Forest of the Tongass region, aboriginal home of the Tlingit.

"The forest comprises a relatively narrow strip along the coast and islands, reaching up to an elevation of about 2,000 feet in the south and 1,000 to 1,500 feet in the north. The country is mountainous, and, except along inlets and river bottoms, the forest is largely located within three miles of the coast."

Can you help us find the meaning of Tongass, Dr. Rakestraw?

"My specialty is history. Unfortunately, that is a problem in linguistics. But I can give you a clue."

It's a Tlingit word?

"Exactly."

That's what we thought, Dr. Rakestraw. All right, Jackie. We'll do it ourselves. Let's take two paths: the library and the living source. First let's ask our friend Walt Begalka of Ketchikan Pulp Company to find the oldest living Tlingit for us -- Walt knows quite a few Southeastern Alaska Indians. Surely the oldest living Tlingit would know what *Tongass* meant.

Walt found her for us and, sure enough, she knows.

Emma Williams dwells in Ketchikan, at 90 the oldest living Tlingit, at least of the Tantakwan tribe. And a distinguished person, at that. She and her late husband Frank, who was chief of the Tantakwan, once provided linguist Jeffry Leer with Tlingit-language stories that he edited and transcribed into English. They were published as *Tongass Texts* by the Alaska Native Language Center at the University of Alaska, Fairbanks, in 1978.

Emma Williams, born in 1898, told us that the word *Tongass* was originally *Tantakwan*, from *Tan* or *Taan*, the Native name for what is now called Prince of Wales Island, plus the additive element *ta,* plus *-kwan*, meaning People. Tantakwan was the name of her tribe -- you could render it in English as "people of the island." Emma Williams does not know who first altered Tantakwan to Tongass. She's been trying to find out herself, without luck. Our research shows that the general area was already called "the Tongass" when President Theodore Roosevelt proclaimed it a national forest September 10, 1907. Mrs. Williams' best guess is that "Tongass" was transmogrified from "Tantakwan" because the European settlers couldn't pronounce the Indian sounds properly.

Emma Williams' account checks closely with the scholarly version from the library. Come on, put up with the linguistics class a little longer. It's important. You'll see. In 1922, anthropologist Thomas J. Waterman, working for the Smithsonian Institution of Washington, D.C., published "Tlingit Place Names for Extreme Southeast Alaska." He had interviewed a Tantakwan named Pete Williams, who turns out to be no relation to Emma Williams, although she remembers stories about him. Waterman, who developed his own style of recording Tlingit language, rendered it in English characters as *Tantakwans*. English spelling just isn't well adapted to dealing with the Tlingit language, which is not primitive at all but is highly developed in phonology and grammar. Pete Williams told Waterman that *Tantakwans* came from Taan, "the sea lion island," a slightly more elaborate name for Prince of Wales Island, plus *-kwans*, people. Tantakwans was the name of his tribe -- you could render it in English as "people of the sea lion island."

These are the roots of the word Tongass. People of the island. People of the sea lion island. Either way, the very name *Tongass* resonates with the human presence. That's the lesson to be drawn from the original meaning of *Tongass*. It's a lesson that The Official Version refuses to transmit. The Tongass is People. People of the Island. People of the Sea Lion Island. There's something symbolic here, and more than symbolic. The Tongass is not uninhabited wilderness. It *should* not be uninhabited Wilderness. It has been the home of people, humans, men and women and children, since the last ice age, and probably long before. People. Islands. Wildlife. We all belong.

Neighbors

You can see the old Tongass Island campsite flats out the deck window -- oh, oh, it must have started raining while we were gabbing. Well, you could see Tongass Island a minute ago. They don't call it Misty Fjords for nothing, you know.

You won't be able to see the beautiful scenery of the Tongass for the rest of the trip -- typical except in July and August -- The captain is navigating with his weather radar.

We're approaching our first stop, Annette Island, a fistful of stone knuckles boxing the raindrops, hiding milky glacial lakes between its rocky fingers. You can just make out the shapes of Chenango Mountain and Purple Mountain in the drizzle as we dock. This is Alaska's only federal Indian reservation -- other Native peoples hold their lands through Native Corporations, a completely different arrangement.

Annette Island's town, Metlakatla, comprises Alaska's sole Tsimshian community. From a different language group than the Tlingit, their ancestors came to the island from British Columbia in 1887, following a lay religious leader named William Duncan. Duncan had persuaded them to speak English, dress in European style and abandon their communal houses for single family dwellings. In Canada, religious issues and a dispute about the U.S.-Canadian boundary encouraged them to leave. Duncan talked Congress into giving Annette Island to his followers. He arrived on Annette Island with 800 Tsimshians who named their new town Metlakatla after their old home near Prince Rupert.

Let's disembark while the ferry unloads. We can mosey down to City Hall and talk a few minutes to Metlakatla Mayor Harris Atkinson and Annette Hemlock's Ken Gazzaway and a few other people.

Ken Gazzaway is general superintendent of the island's two sawmills. "I'm not Native, but I married a member of the island community. I've lived here with my wife and three children for nine years."

Some people express surprise that the Indians log their tribal lands, Ken. We consider that a racist carryover from the literary romanticism of the nineteenth century and the ethnic-chic idealization of the 1960s.

"I think you're right. Real live Native Americans need to eat and pay their bills like everybody else, and they need jobs to do it."

Mayor Atkinson, a businesslike but friendly and personable man, agrees. He explains his tribe's economy. "We have two main sources of income on the reservation, fishing, which is highly seasonal, and the timber operation, which is our big year-round employer. Actually, we have two separate timber operations, one logging, the other milling. We contract with large firms to do both. Currently, ITT Rayonier is our logging contractor and Annette Hemlock does the milling -- Annette Hemlock is a division of Ketchikan Pulp Company, which is owned by Louisiana-Pacific Corporation. But the two operations are completely unrelated. Gordon can fill us in.''

Gordon Thompson is Director the Annette Natural Resource Center. He tells us, ''Our logging operations provide jobs at peak times for about 40 workers, half of them island residents. ITT Rayonier just won the bid on two timber sales we put up, the Tent Lake and Triangle Lake sales. It's on a standard Bureau of Indian Affairs contract under the trust doctrine.''

Tribal forester John Bruns continues: ''We fell the trees, yard them to the truck landings and haul them to saltwater. All the timber harvested on Annette Island can be exported as round logs right on our docks at Port Chester. There'll be dockside employment there through Southeast Stevedoring which gives hiring preference to our island residents.

''The logs will go directly to foreign markets, primarily Japan. None of them go through the Annette Hemlock sawmill. Unprocessed round logs usually bring top dollar in the world market, and our responsibility is to get the best possible return for our tribal timber.

''And from what we see in the places where we logged from 1972 to 1982, the second growth forests will be much more productive than the old growth we're harvesting now -- they're coming back so strongly we'll get half again as much wood from the same acre of ground.

''In fact, we're doing what we call pre-commercial thinning to make sure the new forest is highly productive. It will also produce good deer habitat. Some of our island residents have formed small companies to go in with chainsaws and reduce the thick natural growth of 2,000 stems to the acre down to the ideal of 800 well-spaced stems, which will then naturally thin themselves as the forest matures. We select for the best trees to improve the forest's gene pool.''

Ken Gazzaway explains how Annette Hemlock gets its logs. ''Our logging is done by the Timber Division of Ketchikan Pulp Company over at Thorne Bay on Prince of Wales Island. Like Mayor Atkinson says, L-P owns the KPC operations.

''The log rafts are towed here by tug. Every stick of timber that goes into the Annette Island mills came from Forest Service timber sales. We have a Small Mill Operation that cuts only two sides of the log and leaves the other two round. It produces two sizes of rough cants and employs 14 people. Our Large Mill Operation cuts 3 and 4 sides of the log to make four sizes of rough cants, which are exported to world markets. The large mill employs about 85 people in two shifts.

"The law forbids Annette Hemlock to export any Forest Service hemlock or spruce as unprocessed round logs, although it does allow us to export, under permit from the regional forester, round logs of Alaska cedar and Western redcedar, which we log in small quantities.

"We have 114 people in all, hourly and salaried. About 60 percent are Tsimshian tribal members. It's strictly Native preference for employment in the reservation. The non-members now working for Annette Hemlock had to obtain work permits through TERO, the island's Transportation, Employment, Rights and Operations department, and can only be employed if they hold a technical skill that can't be filled here on the island. Even Natives from different tribes have to get a work permit like any other outsider."

That brings up something "Trash the Tongass" articles don't usually mention: *Forest Service* timber sales provide employment to a significant number of Native workers.

Mayor Atkinson concludes, "We've got 1,500 people on this island. If Congress passes any law reducing the amount of timber Louisiana-Pacific can cut on Forest Service lands in the Tongass, it'll probably mean the elimination of 114 jobs in my community. Our economy would take a super nosedive."

There's the ferry whistle. The Aurora's ready to go. Don't miss the boat -- the seagoing taxi comes to Metlakatla only once today. This next leg of the trip will be short: It's only fifteen miles to Ketchikan.

A Tongass Town

The ferries don't go into downtown Ketchikan like the cruise ships do. You have to get off out by the airport. Which is across Tongass Narrows on Gravina Island. No bridge over there. Only American airport we know of that has its own ferry system, one vessel named the MV Ken Eichner, another the MV Dick Borch, and a third the MV Bob Ellis, all local notables. Look at the sign on that little eatery as we drive off the ferry dock toward town. It reflects a certain typically Alaskan irreverence: Mexican Food and All-American Junk Food.

Ketchikan is a strip city hugging Revillagigedo Island's tidewater below the sheer flanks of Minerva Mountain and Deer Mountain. There are two driving routes: north to the end of the road (not quite 20 miles) and south to the end of the road (a little more than 10 miles). Oh yes, and the road up to Lake Harriet Hunt -- a beautiful setting with campsites and great fishing. City Dock downtown is the tourist hub of Ketchikan. Our most photographed feature here is a ten-foot-tall "Liquid Sunshine Gauge." It brings up once more the main subject of conversation in the Tongass. Rain.

If you want to know about the Tongass, you have to know about rain. In Juneau it rains 223 days a year. Over most of Southeast, about thirteen feet of it annually. Just as the Eskimos of Alaska's North Slope are reputed to have developed at least 16 different words for snow, so the people of the Tongass have numerous expressions dealing with rain, some even fit to print.

Here's a little **Lexicon of Tongass Precipitation**.

Tongass weather: a term defined by Darrell Pruett, meteorologist for the U.S. Weather Service station on Annette Island (they make the Ketchikan area forecasts), as drizzle, occasional showers, chance of showers with periods of rain, cloudbursts, storm warnings. After several weeks of rain in a row, you develop more colorful personal definitions.

Horizontal rain: Bill Moran, banker and former Mayor of Ketchikan, defines it as the endless resource of the Tongass, the flat form of round droplets once they've hit the ground. It's good for making puddles, generating hydroelectric power, filling home water cisterns, keeping the forest green and giving the salmon something to spawn in.

Tongass tennis shoes: Also known as Sitka sneakers and Southeast sandals. Usually red, brown or black calf- or knee-high rubber boots worn to Tongass occasions from picnics to formal weddings. Essential for hiking muskeg (*see* muskeg).

Tongass pickup truck: tugboat.

Tongass tan: rust.

Outside: Any place it doesn't rain all the time. (*See* Paradise).

Sun-shock: acute agitation of the central nervous system when the sun shines. Symptoms are walking around with your hand shading your eyes or with baseball cap pulled low over your face.

Paradise: Hawaii, Mexico or any place the suns shines in winter.

Muskeg: Horizontal rain disguised as solid ground.

The Original Tongass Yarn: "The fog was so think we shingled the barn and six feet out on the fog."

Down South: Where you go to get out of the rain. We're not talking about the land of cotton. Anything south of Tongass Island is "Down South" to us.

Webfoots: People who live where it rains less than in the Tongass. We don't develop webbed feet, we get fins.

Igloo: Temporary hunting shelter built from blocks of ice. Melts rapidly in the Tongass. Try the North Slope.

You learn to tolerate bad rain jokes in the Tongass.

Listen as we walk by the grocery store. Grant Smith's SeaMart is getting a radio call.

"SeaMart. SeaMart. This is Polk Inlet. Over."

"This is SeaMart. Go ahead, Polk Inlet."

"Hi! We've got our grocery list ready for you. Here goes -- one ten pound bag of flour, five pound bag of sugar, two large cans of coffee, large bottle of ketchup, four dozen eggs, four fresh chickens, and two heads of lettuce. That's it for this order."

"We'll have the order on the Postal Service plane tomorrow morning. Thanks for the business, Colleen. SeaMart Out."

"Polk Inlet. We're clear."

With logger wives like Colleen Gildersleeve ordering groceries all over the remote Tongass country, Grant can keep the product flow running at two standard shipping containers per week from the Lower 48.

"The more product flow running through the community," says Smith, "the fresher and higher quality the products you get. Take away the loggers and I'd be down to one big shipping container per week. That means the town folks here in Ketchikan would find their food quality going down."

The population of all of Southeast is 58,464 people. People. The human econosystem is interconnected by webs and chains just as nature's ecosystem. Uproot a huckleberry sprout and you find it hitched to everything else in the universe. Uproot a logger's wife and you find the same thing.

Come into the office of the *Ketchikan Daily News* in the big frame building on Dock Street. Meet our friend Lew Williams, 64, veteran newspaper publisher and Alaska pundit. He was born into a newspaper family -- his mother was a reporter on the *Tacoma News Tribune* and his father was an editor at the *Tacoma Ledger* when they met. Lew has run the *Alaska Sunday Press* in Juneau, the *Wrangell Sentinel* and the *Petersburg*

Press, and he's turned out the *Ketchikan Daily News* since 1966. He's won a wall full of journalism awards and has irons in all sorts of civic fires. He's a member of the state's Citizens Advisory Commission on Federal Areas. He understands the Tongass intimately.

Tell us about the current environmental battle, Lew.

"Well, the current controversy is pretty typical of past ones. The environmental community wants to reduce timber cutting in the Tongass National Forest. And they want to eliminate the $40 million annual Tongass Timber Fund, which they call a subsidy for the timber industry. We call it a subsidy for putting 5.4 million acres of the Tongass into wilderness classification. But what Alaskans think is beside the point."

What do you mean by that?

"I was talking to Governor Cowper about it just yesterday. I asked him about the possibility of reaching a compromise with the environmentalists on repealing the parts of ANILCA they don't like. The governor said, 'Well, I hear that the environmental community isn't too eager to get a compromise because they use these kinds of issues to raise money.' And I know they do. I get mailers from them all the time. You know, 'the last vanishing rain forest is threatened so please send us your contribution.' That's how they make their living. I think that's pretty unethical."

Do the environmentalists have so much clout they don't have to compromise? Can't the timber industry stop them?

"The timber industry used to be a power, a real political power. Today they're definitely the underdog. They simply can't match the huge multi-million dollar environmental lobby. They haven't won a fight against the environmentalists for almost twenty years.

Have you seen the *Sports Illustrated* article?

"Oh, yes. The national environmental community has found they can get access to the big circulation media. You can see why they do it. If you can misrepresent the Tongass on the east coast, you're hitting quite a

Lew Williams   Ron Arnold photo

few million people. There's no way the Alaska Loggers Association here can respond. Nowadays it's just stylish to rant about industry-caused environmental damage, whether it's true or not. So it's easy to cream industry, but it's hard for industry to cream back."

What does that do to public opinion?

"It distorts it. The national media pander to the mass market. The masses don't stop to ask whether *Sports Illustrated* is right. They see a distorted article about the Tongass and then write their congressman -- and he doesn't know anything about it either. We had one senator here out fishing with an Alaska logger and the senator said, 'Gee, I'm really looking forward to getting into that Tongass National Forest tomorrow.' He'd been in the Tongass for two days. The logger explained to him, 'That's the Tongass all around you, this water, those mountains, farther than you can see. It's three times the size of Massachusetts.' The senator literally didn't know a single fact about the Tongass, not even that he was in it.

"And that's where you run into the problem of the environmental community's power -- they can say anything they want. Anything. There's no countervailing force. They've been able to expand their voice into the mass media. Alaska's industry hasn't. The facts never even get into the public debate."

Prop Wash

The single-engine floatplane is the lifeblood of Alaska. It is taxi, grocery boy, ambulance, school bus, letter carrier, retail outlet and "flight-seeing" escape valve. From the way bush pilots talk to their airplanes, we'd guess the pontoon single-prop job is also father confessor, psychologist and whipping boy.

The Alaska bush pilot's reputation has become wreathed in mythology, most of it true. Among the typical pilot-brags we hear: "Alaska flying is a mixture of exhilaration and sheer terror." And "The Alaska wind turns you every which way but loose -- and then it turns loose just to confuse you." And "I backed into Elfin Cove the other day -- my airspeed was 90 knots but the headwind was 100."

Come bounce with us through Alaska's rowdy skies as Ken Eichner takes us with a load of freight over to Thorne Bay on Prince of Wales Island. Ken's quite a guy. He's a founder and the long-time president of Temsco Airlines, one of the busiest aviation companies in Southeast Alaska. They named one of the airport ferries for him because of his long community service, in particular because he was the founder of the Ketchikan Volunteer Rescue Squad.

Even though Ken's got more than 100 employees, including 35 helicopter pilots and 28 airplane pilots, he likes to do the flying himself every now and then.   His red-with-yellow-stripe floatplanes look like shiny new toys lined up along the Ketchikan waterfront.

Ken is tall and agile and folds into the driver's seat like he been doing it for more than forty years, which he has. He's got a photo tucked into one of the instrument panel gauges showing him holding a mean looking cudgel labeled: "A Sierra Club."

Ken gives us the seat belt lecture, yells "Clear!" out the window, cranks her over, and slowly sails us out into the takeoff pattern next to the downtown harbor. Over townside, half a dozen bald eagles sit on the fleet docks, waiting for fishing crews to throw them a little dinner.   The overcast has lifted a little, so we may be able to see some of the sights.

Ken's voice penetrates the prop noise. "Temsco's pretty big for a private locally-owned aviation company. It gives a kind of home-town control to it, makes a difference in the service we give. We do a lot of government contract work since the environmentalists locked up the mining lands. We fly Fish & Game and Forest Service and Wildlife Department folks into remote sites."

Flaps into takeoff position, throttle up, off we go. You're going to like this.

"We've had to get a little creative at Temsco, too. In the summer we helicopter tourists onto Mendenhall Glacier near Juneau. They get to walk on a glacier while we give them a nature talk. That's a real popular flight. And we floatplane them over Misty Fjords. Makes them realize most of it is inaccessible with anything but a helicopter. There are a few mountain lakes stretched along the fringes of Misty Fjords, and people go fishing and camping and hunting there, all within very few miles of the coast. But farther inside Misty Fjords, there's just no way you can get there on foot."

We look down on an Alaska Airlines 727 jetliner on its final approach to the Ketchikan airport. That's the Ketchikan Pulp mill over to the right in Ward Cove.

"People don't realize the immense size of Wilderness we have around us and how inaccessible it is. We have 5.4 million acres of Wilderness, more than twice the amount of logging lands. When you think of a forest, you usually think of a place with a nice carpeted floor where you can stroll underneath the trees. The Tongass isn't that way. This is a new country geologically. It's mostly muskeg and rock, with trees growing on thin

Ken Eichner's "Sierra Club."   Ron Arnold photo

soils and in little cracks in the rock, places you'd think were impossible."

We're out over the open water of Clarence Strait now. Whack! Don't mind the bumpy air. Our Alaska's just teasing you.

"Muskeg is incredible to anyone who's never seen it. When the glaciers retreated, they left scoops in the rocks all over the Tongass. Of course, the hollows filled up right away with horizontal rain, and the only thing that would grow in the water is sphagnum moss. The moss grew and grew until it filled these depressions completely. You look at a muskeg, it looks solid as anything. It even has a few little scrub trees growing in it here and there, mostly shore pine. A lot of people mistake it for a logged area. You step in it, though, and you might find yourself in anything from a pair of wet britches to a very serious fight for survival.

"You have to learn the color and texture of muskeg to know where to step. I didn't know that when I had my first experience with it -- and we're talking ancient history here. It was after I had shot a deer up in the high country. I was carrying it out, and walking around the edge of this muskeg, and I stepped in the wrong place. I just vanished. Had a terrible time getting out from under the deer and then trying to get my head above the sphagnum, trying to survive the muskeg.

"The muskeg is just a sponge made of decaying vegetable matter. You can take a stick and shove it down into most muskegs, take out your cigarette lighter and light the hole, and it will burn sometimes for hours and hours on end from the methane gas.

"But you learn to walk around the edges of it, you learn where the tree growth is, where you're safe. Generally if the vegetation is real fine grained and green, don't walk on it. You'll end up over your Tongass tennis shoes."

As we approach the shores of Kasaan Peninsula on Prince of Wales Island, Ken smiles and points silently to a black bear prowling the beach below. She's a big one.

"But there's always somebody thinks he can beat the Tongass. Misty Fjords has several fairly good whitewater rivers -- the Chickamin, the Marten, and the Unuk. Once some oldtimers built a crude thirty mile trail from the Chickamin through to the little town of Hyder, working in the gold prospect rivers around Banded Mountain and Texas Lake. It was a month's job just to *hike* their trail.

"I remember three boys from the Ketchikan Fire Department here a couple of years ago decided that they were real he-men and could tackle that kind of country. A pilot dumped them off at Portage Bay on the back side of Revillagigedo Island, which is in Misty Fiords Wilderness. They were going to hike without any special equipment all the way to Ketchikan over thirty miles or so of really fearsome terrain. Well, three days later we picked 'em up not too many miles from where they started.

"Then not long ago two boys wanted to shoot the rapids of the Chickamin in a rubber boat, so I took them up there, left them off at the headwaters. Four days later I rescued them 3 miles down the river. There's always somebody in trouble.

"It takes more than just a desire to use the Tongass wilderness. Experienced outdoors enthusiasts know how to travel it. But your average hiker can't deal with it."

Ken circles us in over the city of Thorne Bay, permanent population 475, and sets us down without so much as a splash. We glide silently to the town dock. Gloria the local Temsco agent awaits us on the plank walkway and grabs one of the hanging lanyards flapping from the plane's left wing. With expert body-English she tweaks the floatplane to a stop and lashes it to the dock.

"Hi, K.A. Welcome home, Jackie," she grins. "Hey, Ken, good to see the boss doing some real work flying. Did you bring the bouquet of roses for Mrs. Sullivan's birthday? And the pizzas for the Nicholas family? And the medical supplies for the clinic?

"It's all right back there by the mail. And the pizza's still warm."

Island Rivulets

Welcome to P.O.W. No, around here it doesn't stand for Prisoner of War, it stands for Prince of Wales. As Emma Williams reminds us, the word Tongass originally meant "people of the island," and Prince of Wales was the island. And Thorne Bay is P.O.W.'s biggest town.

Thorne Bay may have been incorporated under Alaska State Law as a Second Class City on August 9, 1982, but it's been a first class logging base since the first float camp moved in twenty years earlier. During the 1960s it was the world's largest logging camp, producing over 100 million board feet annually for several years. Even today, just coming out of the worst depression the timber industry has seen in 50 years, Ketchikan Pulp Company's log sort yard runs about 60 million board feet in a year's time.

Logging camps are normally temporary. Thorne Bay is a logging camp that wouldn't die. There's a lot of business here nowadays. The initial five miles of 1962 logging road has grown into an island-wide network of 1,500 miles that all lead to Thorne Bay. Bill and Colleen MacCannell publish *The Island News* here. This is the home of DuRette Construction, where Jackie and the two boys join Butch during the summer school vacation. You can buy your groceries at ClearCut Market, a genuine old-fashioned general store, or you can purchase a cooked meal at Ken and Jeri Gallagher's Galley, where they make sourdough pancakes from a starter twenty years old.

If you happen in to Gallagher's Galley on the right evening, you'll encounter Thorne Bay's gift to American culture, the International Order of Illiterate Pigs, founded by Swede Ecklund and presided over by Frank McKinney.

K.A., don't tell them about that. IOIP's not exactly mainstream Thorne Bay!

It's local color, Jackie.

Good grief. Oh, well, go ahead.

IOIP wears the crown of scorn heaped by environmentalists on Tongass working folk as a badge of honor. Their motto, "Generosity and knowledge is the flip side of greed and ignorance" perfectly reflects the mask and face of Alaska's detractors. IOIP is dedicated to preserving Alaska's way of life by creating a positive piggy attitude. They'll gladly sell you an I'm An Illiterate Pig T-shirt for ten bucks and let you start a local chapter of IOIP in your hometown. Smile and the Illiterate Pigs will "root" for you.

Nick Gefre and Tom Beck run Island Fuels, Inc. in Thorne Bay. The Boyer Alaska barge Callapooya fuels their tank farm direct from Mobil's Ferndale, Washington refinery. Nick says, "We sell Mobil fuel and lube products -- number one and number two diesel, regular and unleaded gasoline, greases and oils and hydraulic fluids and transmission fluids -- to eleven towns and logging communities on P.O.W.''

Tom says, ''Don't forget we also deliver fuel up to Hobart Bay and there's some outer camps over at Coon Cove and Salmonberry Point for Klukwan Forest Products. And the City of Thorne Bay generates its electricity with our fuel.''

Nick, you've gone back to Washington, D.C. to testify as an expert witness before Congress.

''Yes, I testified before the Subcommittee on Energy and Environment of the House Interior and Insular Affairs. It was a hearing on the environmentalists' latest attack on the Tongass.

''I told the subcommittee that those contracts were entered into over thirty years ago to provide year round jobs so we could build a self-sufficient economy in Southeast. I pointed out that the poor markets during this last economic downswing resulted in major financial losses to both KPC and ALP. But they both kept up their end of the contracts and kept people working.

''I also told them that all during that time the Native corporations were making profits on their own private lands because they're permitted to sell top dollar round logs to the Orient. There isn't any private timberland for us non-Natives. It's all Forest Service. Political lands.

''I just flat said that our Thorne Bay economy will collapse unless the jobs for timber remain. Over 80 percent of our city's economic activity is generated by timber harvest.''

Tom Beck, who is the former Mayor of Thorne Bay, adds, ''Now, the two big companies will collect damages from the United States for breach of contract if H.R. 1516 passes. But the small logger and the dependent communities won't -- we'll be devastated, destroyed by the stroke of a pen. So if the environmentalists are trying to hurt big business, they're going about it the wrong way. KPC and APC will each walk away with billions of taxpayer dollars from court settlements. It's us little folks that will get squashed. That's not fair and it's not right.''

Nick nods agreement and continues: ''If Congress is afraid of what logging does to the environment, P.O.W. has been logged more heavily than any other island in the Tongass and it hasn't hurt the environment. I listened to the Wilderness Society's deer expert testify that logging had harmed our deer population. I challenge him to actually demonstrate that his claims are true -- I know he can't. While I was driving the other day between Labouchere Bay and Thorne Bay -- an 80-mile stretch -- I counted 34 deer *on* the road, and I didn't even look in the brush *beside* the road.

''We have the highest concentration of wolves per square mile anywhere in the Tongass. Each wolf eats approximately 52 deer per year. Even at that rate we're seeing a deer population increase. When one of the congressmen questioned the environmentalist's deer expert about the amount of wolf kill, he answered, 'I'm a deer expert, not a wolf expert.' He was just evading the question. He didn't want anybody to even *think* that something besides logging might harm deer.

"Then too, we hear a lot of environmentalist anguish about 'roads to nowhere.' That's their comment on the fact that during the downswing some timber sales went begging after the logging roads to them had been built. We have about 1,500 miles of logging road on P.O.W. They're open to the public and they connect eight of the island's major towns. The reason we have any tourist industry at all is that logging road system. P.O.W. is the only island in the Tongass with a well-developed road system. The Forest Service has set up campgrounds and other facilities along these logging roads for fishing, hiking to the high country, beach-combing, and just enjoying the scenery. That 'roads to nowhere' remark is a disgusting insult: Those roads lead to our future."

Muscle And Blood

Let's talk a little about Tongass wildlife. David Anderson of the Alaska State Department of Fish and Game is regional supervisor of the Division of Game and an expert. "The Tongass is in some ways typical of the Northwest Coast and in other ways unique. Five species of salmon dominate our many streams: king, or Chinook; coho, or silver; red, or sockeye; pink, or humpback, sometimes called "humpies"; and chum, or dog salmon There is both a sport and a commercial halibut fishery. And there are shellfish such as shrimp and Alaska king crab. Our streams play host to Dolly Varden trout and our lakes are home to cutthroat trout.

"Of the forest mammals, the most important economically as a food source is the Sitka blacktail deer. It's a smaller version of the Columbia blacktail found in Washington and Oregon. There are no caribou in the Tongass, and seven efforts to introduce elk have failed. However, moose have come into the Tongass across the mountains from the Yukon down the major river systems. The only places moose are found is in the major river valleys, the Yakutat forelands, the Chilkat near Haines and Skagway, the Stikine in the Wrangell area, and south to the Unuk. Mountain goats are native to the mainland. We've also transplanted them successfully to Revillagigedo and Baranof Islands.

"We have two species of bear, the black and the brown or grizzly bear. Black bears are abundant throughout the Tongass with the exception of what we call the ''A-B-C Islands'' -- Admiralty, Baranof and Chichagof -- where there are only brown bears, and in the highest density anywhere in the world. North Admiralty Island, only eight miles from Juneau, has about one brown bear per square mile. The Tongass is broken into two sections when it comes to bears. On the islands south of Frederick Sound

Forest Service photo

Brown bear.

-- Prince of Wales, Kupreanof, Kuiu, Revillagigedo -- there are mostly black bears and hardly any browns.

"Wolves range throughout the Tongass, again, except for the A-B-C Islands. The excellent brown bear habitat there, the rich salmon streams, have probably led to the brown bear becoming such an efficient predator it has left no room for other predators.

"The mainland has some wolverines in typically low numbers, but they are present. Beavers occur essentially everywhere, the mainland and the islands of the archipelago. Raccoons are not native here, but there are some in the Tongass, probably escapees from boats where they were kept as mascots. Skunks are absent while porcupines are common all through the Tongass. Up in the rocks in the mainland high country there are hoary marmots and pikas.

"Among the fur-bearers we have the marten, which probably produces more revenue in commercial trapping than any other species. They're most abundant on Admiralty Island and Prince of Wales. There are some minks, no fishers. We have two species of weasel, the short-tailed or ermine, and the long-tailed. We have both sea otters and land otters throughout the Tongass.

"Birds include the largest concentration of bald eagles in the world, which, along with our abundant ravens played an important part in Indian clan groupings -- the Tlingit divided themselves into the Eagle and Raven moieties. There are also hawks and crows in large numbers. The Tongass is home to seabird species by the dozen, gulls, petrels, terns -- as well as temporary quarters for the Pacific flyway's migratory waterfowl and songbird species.

"We don't have polar bears or other arctic creatures, but we do have an unusual natural predator species that has lived for thousands of years with the Indians -- domestic dogs."

Rain Winds Blow Doors Open

Sitka is situated on the west side of Baranof Island. It's another floatplane trip from Thorne Bay. In 1799 Russian sea otter pelt traders established the post of New Archangel here with permission of the Kiksadi, the local Tlingit. The Kiksadi changed their minds in 1802 and their warriors destroyed the settlement. Alexander Baranof, manager of the Russian American Company, came back in 1804 with troops and a gunship to explain why the company should be allowed to rebuild its settlement.

Sitka blossomed into a commercial and cultural center. As the blurb on today's official Sitka City Map says, "When San Francisco was a collection of huts, Sitka had a cathedral, a large library and fine residences appointed with crystal and lace." After U.S. Secretary of State William Henry Seward bought his folly from the Russians in 1867, Sitka served as the capital of Alaska for the next 45 years.

Then nothing much happened until World War II when Sitka became a military staging center, and later in 1959 when the $70 million Japanese-owned pulp mill came to Silver Creek, down the road about three miles south and east.

Today, at the other end of town, Trish White runs a drug store with her husband Dirk. Both are pharmacists. Dirk came from the Midwest, Trish has lived her whole life in Sitka, yet she was born in Boston, Massachusetts.

"The only reason I was born in Boston instead of Sitka is my mother married a Coast Guard officer from there and they went back for a while. I've been here since I was 5 months old. Mom was a native Alaskan, born in Cordova, and my grandmother came in the gold rush on Chichagof, so we're Alaskans from way back.

"I took my five-year pharmacy degree at Oregon State University in Corvallis, so I've seen some of the world outside the Tongass. I travelled a lot during school, went to Europe. But there's no place like home. Sitka is a beautiful place to live.

"A lot of people from the big cities come here and can't handle it, they feel very isolated. It doesn't give

Ron Arnold photo

Trish White in her family pharmacy.

me that feeling. Sure, in wintertime we definitely get cabin fever. We're dark fifteen hours of the day or more and we get a lot of rain. This is rain forest country. But I'm used to it. I'm one of those finned people. It doesn't bother me.

"But the conflict over natural resources on the Tongass does bother me. It's made me aware of how fragile everything is, which I didn't realize while I was growing up here. You get the feeling that the forest is always going to be here and that our timber jobs are always going to be here. But now I realize that both can be taken away from us by outsiders and we have no say in it. The forests can be locked up. The timber people can be kicked out.

"It's the helplessness of the people who live here that disturbs me so. Jackie, you've gone to Washington, D.C. to lobby our issues. You've said that it's the congressional aides, the administrative assistants on staff that actually make many of the decisions about the Tongass. Is it true?"

Yes, Trish, those aides are running a lot of the government. It's scary because nobody elected them. They have a lot of prejudices and lot of misunderstanding of what's actually going on in the Tongass. They spread it to their elected officials.

As a result, Congress has become hostile to Tongass industry. Their hostility is completely groundless. They have no idea of the size of this country. And they haven't been here to see what a logged area looks like after a few years. They don't see the before and the after a few years down the line, they have no perspective on the power of the land to regenerate the forest. You've seen it, Trish.

"I know, Jackie. They don't understand that Alaskans are true conservationists anyway. We believe in the wise use of resources. I think the appreciation of the outdoors, the appreciation of the wildlife, the appreciation of the resources we have here is so ingrained in you that you can't help but have respect for it all.

"The Tongass is our livelihood, it's our recreation, it's our future. We hope that others respect that. I want it to be here for my children and my children's children. And I want to be able to use it. Wise use will keep it here forever."

Thad Paulson, publisher of the *Sitka Sentinel*, points out that there was no controversy 30 years ago when the Japanese came looking for wood in the Tongass. Environmentalist criticism of the forest industry is fairly recent history. The Tongass struggle is a veritable case study of how economics and social values have changed in America in three decades.

"Millions of board feet of timber was going to waste," Paulson says. The government "dragged the lumber corporations up here and begged: 'Please buy this timber.'"

In contrast to Paulson's defense of the forest industry, the *Seattle Times* printed a 1988 feature story on Sitka's pulp mill, quoting a sour-eyed critic as saying, "The pulp mills will stick around until they've taken all the old-growth timber, then they'll move on." Not even a whisper that Tongass logged areas are growing back at nearly two times the volume of the old growth forest. The *Times* wrote its story using nothing but the viewpoint, definitions and assumptions of the environmentalists. Fair comment on the Tongass forest industry is hard to find.

Michael Kaelke, Ed.D., is more than able to provide fair comment: He's a respected scholar and educator, president of Sitka's Sheldon Jackson College, Alaska's oldest existing educational institution, established by the Presbyterian Church in 1878. Dr. Kaelke speaks with the measured deliberation of the academician.

"I can say this about the use of the Tongass National Forest: Sheldon Jackson College recognizes that the planned, organized use of our natural resources is very critical. So, some five years ago our faculty, with subsequent approval of our Board of Trustees, initiated a four year degree program in natural resource management and development. It was one of the first programs in Alaska that really began to address the integrated use of our natural resources.

"So our students, while receiving a sound background in political science and the setting of government policy and regulations governing the use of our resources, get a basic understanding and working knowledge of our natural resources, both in the forest and beyond the forest, whether it be fisheries or aquaculture.

"I like to believe that in Alaska we are capitalizing on and helping to prevent the mistakes we've seen in other areas. I'm quite proud of what we've done with the forest. I'm quite proud of what we've done with our other industries in Alaska, for example in Prudhoe Bay in the petroleum industry. We realize that we can't expend resources unwisely as we've done in other parts of the world, yet we also realize that natural resources are here for the betterment of the quality of life. And that with the right kind of management the people on this good earth are going to have the benefit of these resources for centuries to come."

Dr. Kaelke, we understand that Sheldon Jackson College played an important role in the realization of James Michener's recent bestseller, *Alaska*.

"Quite true. Mr. Michener came to our campus and resided here for the better part of two years as he wrote his historic novel on Alaska. He had travelled widely in Alaska prior to taking residency with us, but while he was with us he travelled to many other places in Alaska and so became quite familiar with the issues of our state.

"He was already a scholar of the history of our state, and of course I'm biased, because I'm the one who invited him to come here, but he in his book not only presents the historical basis for where we are today, but also recognizes the pivotal place that Alaska plays in the proper management of our abundant natural resources.

"Although I can't speak for Mr. Michener, I've heard him say that he's proud of what we've done in the management of Alaska's natural resources. And he's a person who thinks as we all do that prudent and wise use -- and nothing to excess -- is the most appropriate approach."

Nothing to excess -- what do you think of the recent *National Geographic* television special that characterized the timber industry as devastating the "pristine Tongass wilderness?" Isn't such falsification and bias an excess?

"I see a lot of things broadcast on the Public Broadcasting System or on the Arts and Entertainment network that lead people who come to Alaska to look for only what the producer wants them to see. I think that in the main, the media and the public information that has been disseminated about the Tongass National Forest is very biased.

"For example, it's ludicrous for people to broadcast in the Lower 48 that we're destroying the forest in Southeast. One can take people out in the forest, if they want to take the time to spend five or six days, and show them second and third generation growth that is fantastic.

"That suggests one of the most exciting things about our Michener project. I think it will encourage many people to come to Alaska as visitors and as students of our great state. After reading *Alaska* they will come with a historical basis which they may not have had before. It will prepare them to see what is actually here. That's a very exciting spinoff of the book."

A Woman

Like all state capitols, Juneau is a town of lobbyists and pressure groups. The environmental movement sends a number of lobbyists here. The forest industry sends lobbyists here. And the Resource Development Council of Alaska shows up to represent all extractive resource developers. Becky Gay is RDC's executive director. She's an extraordinary woman. She speaks to us as a personal friend.

"I moved to Alaska in 1969 after growing up in Indonesia, in real rain forest, and I've seen a lot of timber harvest. I'll tell you in Alaska we may not do it perfectly but we do it a lot better than anywhere else.

"I'm an Alaskan by choice. I'm very outdoors oriented -- I'm a wind surfer and cross country skier, I'm a snow machiner. With a friend I built a log cabin south of Mt. McKinley and it's 12 miles from a road so you have to ski to get there. I've lived out at the cabin, I've lived at the Naval Arctic Research Laboratory in Barrow as a science research staff member and I was all over the North Slope in that capacity working with everything from marine biologists to freshwater biologists to terrestrial mammal biologists. It was there that I began to realize how much influence from outside was affecting Alaskans and that we didn't have the wherewithal to get to the politicians who were making Alaska's decisions for us.

"So I went back to school, became the Truman scholar for Alaska, got my degree in economics at the University of Wisconsin at Madison, came back to Alaska, paid off my student loans, and went to work for Resource Development Council. I was a volunteer at first, then went on staff, and through a long series of fortunate circumstances, I now serve as executive director.

"For about the last five years we've been working issues involving the Tongass. And our worst problem is that the issues are so complex. For one thing, the Tongass is considered to be an old-growth forest and that's an emotional red flag, for another there's controversy over the condition of its wildlife, for another it has the two fifty-year contracts, for another there's total ignorance about what the forest industry actually does -- and that's only the beginning of the list.

"As you know, K.A. and Jackie, 59.2 percent of Alaska is owned by the federal government, 28.4 percent is owned by the state, and the 11.9 percent that remains is owned by the Natives and is their private property. You might wonder where the non-Native private property is. Well, it's the rounding error in all those other numbers. We have *half a percent* in non-Native private property. So if we citizens want any say at all, we have to be able to affect the bureaucracy and the Congress that rules our lands.

"I feel like we're getting a really raw deal on the Tongass. That's exactly how I feel about Congress. I travelled with Congress last August when the House Interior and Insular Affairs Committee came on its investigative tour. That's the same tour that Jack Skow of *Sports Illustrated* followed around. The congressmen were flown in on Air Force One to Juneau and then Governor Cowper took them on a special ferry trip from Juneau to Sitka.

"I was fortunate enough to be invited, but found resource users vastly outnumbered by environmental group leaders from the East Coast. I made a special effort to make myself known to the Congressmen, to really get close to them, particularly the ones who were affecting us most with hostile legislation, George Miller and Robert Mrazek and Mo Udall. And I was so insulted -- not by the congressmen so much, but by their staff members who made derogatory comments about 'Alaskans and their lack of regard for their own country.' In most cases, these staffers make the actual legislative decisions for their congressmen.

"It was such an indignity to travel with these people. It was an affront to every American to see the ignorance and the imperiousness with which they judged the Tongass issues. It was absolutely galling to think that they should be the ones who decide the fate of the Tongass National Forest.

"My real feeling is that if we've got the largest national forest in the country in Alaska, we darn well ought to be able to harvest some timber out of it. We've given plenty to the wilderness movement in Alaska. We have 55 million acres of Wilderness in Alaska, a tenth of it in the Tongass. Over half of the whole nation's wilderness is in Alaska and they're coming back for more. And we just can't survive any more designations.

"That's something that Americans have to realize. That Alaska has a living, breathing economy that supports real live people. We don't have that many people, fewer than half a million, but the people that we've got here are good, salt-of-the-earth people and they depend on the earth and its resources to bring us a decent standard of living, even though it's below most of the United States.

"We are not a colony. We are a state. We contribute quite a bit to the national security, both in strategic military location and in energy supplies. There is absolutely no reason for the rest of our fellow Americans to believe the rhetoric that they hear about Alaskans raping and ruining our home. We live here, we recreate here, we want to raise our children here and remain here. And Americans have got to believe that Alaska residents know best. You tell them, K.A., Jackie."

We will, Becky. We will.

Workers of the Moist Woods

Meet Bob Loescher, who lives in Juneau and was even born here.

"It's true. I was born and raised in Juneau, went to school here. I'm a Tlingit Indian, and my family heritage comes from Hoonah and from Sitka. During my early working years I was a fisherman and a construction worker. I graduated from Fort Lewis College in Durango, Colorado, and came back to Alaska in 1969 to work in a law office for a couple of years. After that I was asked to work as a planner for the Tlingit-Haida Central Council, which was a tribal governing body of the Tlingit and Haida Indians recognized by the federal government. And then I was assigned to the Tlingit-Haida Regional Housing Authority, and the Tlingit-Haida Regional Electrical Authority. I was responsible for the construction of a number of houses and the electrification of a number of Native rural communities of Southeast.

"One day back in the 1970s I was on my way to Washington D.C. to be a special assistant to the U.S. Secretary of Housing and Urban Development. But a new Native organization named Sealaska Corporation was in the process of nominating its lands and seeking conveyance of title about then, and they needed somebody who knew how to deal with the government and somebody who knew Southeast Alaska, so they asked me to work for them.

"I should explain how Sealaska Corporation came to be. It's a little involved. The basic fact is that Tlingit Indians originally owned all of the Tongass forest and our heritage goes back to prehistory. Within the past few centuries many people started coming to the Tongass forest, the British from Canada, the Spanish from down the coast, the Russians, then the Americans.

"In the late 1800s, three chiefs from Southeastern Alaska went to the Congress of the United States and explained that they were concerned about the encroachment, the use of resources, the fish and timber. The Tongass was ours. But that assertion was in dispute. There was a question whether we had access to the courts to settle the dispute.

"It wasn't until the 1930s that we actually filed suit before the U.S. Court of Claims and then it took about thirty years to hear our cases. One of the claims we brought was that we owned the forest. And we also owned the fisheries and other aspects of the Tongass. We had six claims in all.

"In 1965, the court and the Congress established that we had certain rights in the Tongass and they awarded us a judgement of seven-and-a-half million dollars. But they only settled two claims out of six, and they didn't address our land claims. So we joined with the other Alaska Natives across the state in seeking a legislative settlement for our land interests in Southeast and thence came the Alaska Native Claims Settlement Act of 1971, or just ANCSA, as most people call it.

"Sealaska Corporation was incorporated in 1972 as a regional for-profit Native corporation pursuant to the provisions of ANCSA. So Congress authorized Sealaska. Now, what it means to be a 'regional' Native corporation is a little complicated. Within Sealaska's region there are twelve independent village and urban corporations that own shares in both their corporations and in Sealaska. For the first five years after 1972 Sealaska had a fiduciary relationship to them, but that's long gone.

"Under the provisions of ANCSA Sealaska has received or expects to receive conveyance of approximately 330,000 acres of land in the Tongass National Forest, including both the surface and subsurface estates. Sealaska has to date received 245,000 acres, which is private land. In addition it is anticipated that the village and urban corporations in Sealaska's region will receive conveyance to 289,000 acres within the Tongass National Forest, on which Sealaska will own the subsurface estate and the urban and village corporations will own the surface estate. Of that total, 259,000 acres have been actually conveyed, all private land.

"We had the opportunity to nominate the exact lands to be conveyed

Ron Arnold photo

Bob Loescher.

to us from selection areas established by Congress. It wasn't a very perfect process. The non-Natives aren't the only ones dissatisfied with how the federal government has treated them. Our region of Southeastern Alaska received much less land than other regional corporations across the state.

"I've been with Sealaska Corporation now for over ten years, first in the capacity of land selections and then gradually developing inventories of timber and minerals and other land resources. As time went on, I helped form the timber division and Sealaska Timber Corporation, which is a marketing and sales company. I now work as senior vice president, not only with forest products, but also with mineral and real estate development.

"Sealaska has begun to use the land we received. One of the first things we have undertaken on our private land is timber harvest, round log export of old growth spruce and hemlock and some red and yellow cedar.

"The logging rules for private Native lands and federal Forest Service lands are quite different. The Forest Service sells timber under the 'Primary Manufacture' rule, which means that any timber cut on a federal forest has to be either chipped for pulp or sawn into lumber or cants here in the United States -- what is called primary manufacturing. Our loggers on private Native lands are not required to perform primary manufacturing. We have benefitted greatly in the marketplace because we can export -- in the round -- quality old growth spruce and hemlock logs. It's a top dollar product that is highly valued in the Orient, primarily in Japan and South Korea.

"There's a large profit difference in selling high priced round logs and selling lower priced manufactured products from federal forests. There is a certain envy on the part of non-Natives in the Tongass. They have no

Forest Service photo

Roundlogs being loaded into cargo ship for export

private land and must log in the federal forest. They say, 'We'd sure like to export round logs from federal lands because the return on the products we manufacture is very low.'

"Theoretically, we would not object to export of federal timber in the form of round logs -- but only if everything was equal. If the two pulp mills had no long term contracts, no exclusive bidding areas, if we, if everybody could go in and bid on every available acre of the Tongass National Forest, we would support federal round log exports. But I don't think that's going to happen, so we oppose it.

"We operate our private timberlands by contracting with existing logging companies for timber harvest and road building, and we use existing towing companies. But we've been handling our own marketing and sales. Our volumes just for Sealaska corporation have been some-where between 45 million and 150 million board feet a year, and the overall Native timber industry output has been from 100 to 250 million board feet export a year. We've also been selling some domestic pulp logs to the pulp mills in Ketchikan and Sitka.

"We're part of the forest. We're Alaska Natives, we're Tlingits and Haidas and Tsimshians, we've been here since time immemorial, we owned the land in the beginning. We live here, we live in the rural communities. We have to eat and build houses and shelter our children and clothe them just like any other people and we deserve to have a part of the Tongass, a living part of the Tongass just like anybody else who comes here."

By Emerald Shores

Haines, K.A.'s home town, is about as far north in the Tongass as you'll find timber operations. Although there's some harvesting up at Yakutat beyond Glacier Bay, the last sawmill in the Tongass is just east of downtown Haines.

We're here to visit Bob and Margaret Andrews, old friends of Jackie and Butch, close friends. They're school teachers just up the road in the Native community of Klukwan. But not so long ago they lived a great Tongass adventure: They taught at the remote logging camp at Kennel Creek on Freshwater Bay.

Join us in a conversation in their Haines living room. Jackie's husband Butch has come with us.

Yes, we know it reads like the script of a play, but put up with it.

K. A.: "Margaret, I don't know you two as well as the DuRettes do. How did you and Bob meet?"

Margaret: "You know, it's ironic. Bob and I met as VISTA volunteers. He was from Minnesota and I was from Oregon and we met in Kentucky."

Bob: "We came to Alaska because I'd taught in Sitka before going into VISTA and couldn't get Alaska out of my mind after getting out. We got married in 1970. We taught in Ketchikan at first."

Margaret: "Then we went to a couple of other sites to teach. We taught one year in Hydaburg. And then we taught in Metlakatla. We quite literally got the Kennel Creek job because of a paper airplane flying through a teacher's lounge."

Bob (laughs): "We intercepted it and it turned out to be a job announcement. It talked about Freshwater Bay. We both said, 'Where's that?!' We looked it up on a map and it sounded GREAT!"

Margaret: "But Bob was already in the process of taking a position at a different school. Luckily, the superintendent said, 'You don't want to go there. You want to stop by Freshwater Bay. You'll kick yourself if you never go there and check it out. That's where you guys want to be.' So Bob dropped in by floatplane on Freshwater Bay.''

Bob: ''I was familiar with the area from looking at maps and charts. But I wasn't prepared for a logging camp. It was a great little bay and up at the head of the bay was this little white camp nestled along the side of the dark green mountain. It was very small. It was just picturesque, like something you'd see in an Alaska book.

''I kind of expected all of this hustle and bustle but there was nobody around. Just a few people. Everybody was up in the woods working. The school teacher Don Brown took me around and introduced me to Jerry Larrabee, the contractor who ran the logging operation.

''The fact that it was out by itself was what was important to me. There were no roads to any town, only logging roads. At that time there were very few and they didn't go very far. There was basically nothing. If you didn't have a boat you were stuck.

''It was love at first sight. I said to myself, 'This is where I want to be.' The superintendent really read me right.''

Margaret: ''We signed on for only one year. Our two boys were getting to be of school age and we weren't sure about teaching our own children for more than a year.''

Bob: ''But we stayed for five. It turned out to be the best thing we

Ron Arnold photo

Author Jackie DuRette (center) interviews Bob and Margaret Andrews.

ever did. We'd still be there if they hadn't shut the camp down.''

Margaret: ''We moved to Freshwater in 1978. The kids and I came first on The Goose [Tongass slang for a reliable workhorse type of floatplane], and Bob came up later by boat. I'll never forget the way we landed. The kids woke up, Jeremy was four and Joshua was six, and they said 'we're crashing.' We didn't glide up to any dock, the pilot just trundled The Goose right up the beach. I'd done a lot of floatplane flying, but I'd never come out on the beach before. They've got a regular floatplane dock now.

''Jackie, you were really good to us, me and the kids, the way you welcomed us that very first day. But I can still see the look on your face a couple of days later when you saw Bob coming up Chatham Strait in the boat.''

Jackie: ''Oh, yes, tell that one for sure!''

Margaret: ''I had forgotten something, a can opener or something, and was over at your place. And you looked out there and said, 'There's a Volkswagen bus coming down the channel.'

''And I said, 'I think that's my husband.' I could tell you were really wondering what you were getting as teachers.''

Jackie: ''Well, you have to admit that you don't usually see a Volkswagen bus on floats in the channel.''

Bob: ''It was a large Boston Whaler type hull with our VeeDub bus mounted on the deck. The VeeDub had a camper roof. It was my house. I spent a lot of my time in the summer out fishing, and I wanted my house to be high enough so I could stand up. I'll admit it looked... well, it was unique.''

Margaret: ''The Natives came up and walked around it and looked at it and said, 'It's too high.' And it had a canoe on top of it, so you got this whaler, and this VeeDub bus, and this camper roof and a canoe on top.''

Bob: ''Butch, you and Jackie really took us under your wing when we moved in.''

Butch: ''Just being neighborly.''

Bob: ''When we moved in we had tons of stuff and Butch told me that we needed to build a wanigan onto the trailer so we'd have a place to store things. I wasn't sure what a wanigan was, but it sounded good.''

Margaret: ''It was the night before school started and we'd been there for just a short while, and Butch's father showed up at the back of the trailer.''

Bob: ''Noise was coming from back there and I wondered what all the pounding was and it was Butch's Dad. He said, 'Well, are you goin' to build this thing or aren't cha?' He was out there with his saw and we worked until the wee hours, got the deck all laid and the next day the walls were up and we had a wanigan, just like that.''

Butch: ''That's my Dad.''

Margaret: ''Some people had lawns and flowers. It was a homey place. I always figured it was home. The school district superintendent didn't like our trailer when we first moved in. But I didn't want a fancy one, I'd rather keep with our old one and just add wanigans.

K.A.: ''What was it like teaching in a logging camp?''

Bob: ''It wasn't similar to anyplace I've ever taught before or since. We walked into this school that was basically unsupplied. It had nothing.''

Margaret: ''Nineteen-forties encyclopedias -- two truckloads of stuff that we pretty well let go, it was just junk.''

Bob: ''And between Margaret and I, we had all the grades from K through 12. So we taught all subjects and all grades. And, of course, some things you're good at and some things you're not so good at. So we traded off a lot. She'd take my high school kids and do something with them, and I'd take her grade school kids and do science and stuff like that. It was fun.''

Margaret: ''It's a good thing the state had a lot of oil money in those days, because our district was very good about supplying us with things, and we told them we needed everything.

Bob: ''There was plenty of money so they said 'okay.' It was just a matter of taking the time to do the paperwork and we had everything we needed.''

Margaret: ''I think one of the rudest awakenings coming to a logging camp was a film I showed the first week. I showed a wildlife film on eagles. And I got about ten minutes into the film and it was an anti-logging film. And I had Jerry Larrabee's daughter in there, and I had all these logging camp kids in there. I didn't know what to do. I could turn it off. I could reverse it. But that wouldn't be very graceful. I thought, 'Oh Lordy, I've really stepped in it. This is horrible. My first week and here I am giving them an anti-logging film.'''

Jackie: ''You did right. You just showed it and then asked the camp people to review it.''

Bob: ''It was a typical propaganda piece. It showed log dumps in the water and said how you don't see fish out there and you don't see whales out there. Which is bullshit. Some of the best fishing we ever had was right off the log dumps. And the whales would go out there all the time and play with the logs. It was misrepresented to say the least.''

Margaret: ''I remember the first time the whales came. We went out at lunchtime one day and lined the kids up on the beach because a pod of killer whales had come into the bay. We went out in the skiff with a few kids at a time and -- when did we get back, about three o'clock? We were out there all afternoon playing with the whales next to our logging camp. A lot of kids had come up from Down South and had never seen whales. So we all went out to see them. It turned out that it was nothing unusual because we soon found that the killer whales came into Freshwater all the time.''

Bob: ''And another thing, I don't think we've ever taught in a place where there was that much community support. We had parental support, we had the campowner's support. The kids were great to be with. They were well mannered and polite. It was a teachers' dream. We had big money raisers and we raised big money to take trips and things like that, more in that isolated logging camp than we ever did in a city school. You start figuring it out per capita and it's amazing.''

Margaret: ''We always took the kids out of camp at the end of the year to show them things they'd never seen. It's real hard to explain stoplights and trains to a logging camp kid.''

Bob: ''The kids raised the majority of their trip money. Like the high school kids did taxidermy. They'd auction off critters or the camp would hire them during the month of winter shutdown to shovel five feet of snow off all the roofs. The whole setup sounds primitive, I know, but you can't imagine how good the life was.''

Margaret: ''We had a good library for all levels. We had a complete darkroom. The kids put out their own yearbook, it was a combination school/camp annual, which increased our market. We had an engine repair shop that the camp mechanics helped us with.''

Bob: ''One year the older kids would go trapping in the daytime when they had light, and start school at 5 o'clock in the evening and go from 5 to 11.''

Margaret: ''I'd bring popcorn over about nine o'clock. I felt sorry for them.''

Bob: ''It was all older kids, seventeen through nineteen, and they were nightowls anyway. They didn't really start to function until about 5:30 p.m. All the kids in the school ran trap lines and made good money selling pelts. It worked out.''

Margaret: ''We could go on and on. More people came and the camp grew. More trailers were lined up. The fourth year the school district put up a TV satellite dish.''

Bob: ''That didn't impress me much. While my kids grew up, before they went to bed at night they'd read. I think that was a lot more worth while than watching the tube. The isolation of camp gives you an inner strength that's pure and clean. Butch and I fished halibut, the kids would work with us, make good money, get good experience.''

Jackie: ''Then the environmentalists won that lawsuit over in the Kadashan drainage. That was the beginning of the end.''

Bob: ''Yes, it was. I don't think we realized it. We went to Freshwater knowing full well that this was a logging camp. We knew that logging is a temporary kind of thing. But that feeling didn't last long. We just identified with Freshwater and it became home. All we thought was, 'We live in Freshwater Bay, Alaska, and that's my home.' 'You live there?' 'Yes, I live there.' I was proud of it and I loved it. Leaving it was one of the hardest things I've ever done.''

Butch: ''If the environmentalists hadn't got us the market downturn would have.''

Jackie: ''I keep thinking that with just a little more to work on we could have weathered it. If the environmentalists just hadn't shoved us out...''

Butch: ''You could never prove it.''

Margaret: ''But everybody left. Last one out, turn off the lights.''

Bob: ''Yes, everybody left. That was four years ago and I'd go back there tomorrow. We just got finished moving into this new place in Haines. It's a nice house. I'm heating up the hot tub right now for us later. I'd move out tomorrow if I could go back to Freshwater and stay.''

Jackie: ''Bob, you and Margaret taught our boys how to think for themselves, how to study, how to look out at the world and how to see what they're looking at. We owe you so much.''

Bob: ''You don't owe us. We were doing what we loved to do.''

Margaret: ''I remember the very end. There were no barges coming in. As long as there had been logging supplies to bring in and out, barges came. But then one day there were no barges.''

Bob: ''We had to hire a landing craft from Juneau, which Butch and Jackie knew all about, because they had just moved out on a landing craft. We knew exactly how to do it.''

Margaret: ''We had more junk than they did. We moved all the school equipment with us because we knew we were moving up here to Klukwan, which is part of the same school district, so we just brought all the equipment.''

K.A.: "Ever feel homesick for Freshwater?"

Bob: "Daily."

Margaret: "We've had to go by Freshwater on the ferry every now and then. It's so hard. There's such good memories there. It's hard to keep from..."

Awkward silence.

Margaret (finishes): "We know we can never go back. What was there when we were there is gone. We know. But there at Freshwater, there are our memories, and our kids' memories. And..."

Bob: "Our kids are growing up now and they're into girls and cars and things, but they say every now and then that if they had the chance they'd go back to Freshwater tomorrow."

Great land, great people. Raw and refined. Tough and tender. Compliant and defiant. Glad and sad and mad. The great land feels what we feel. Glad we are its children, sad that we're sad, mad that we're mad. We can feel the bond, just as the Indians have always felt it. The resilient land provides and we tend it every day. It does not begrudge us what we take. We do not begrudge it the care we give back.

But now the people of the Tongass are under attack by a powerful lobby centered thousands of miles away. We know we haven't much chance. But we won't give up without a fight. It's like Hemingway wrote in *The Old Man and the Sea*: We can be destroyed. But not defeated. The environmentalists have everything their way now. They can destroy us, we realize. They're ready to dump us in the hottest water they can arrange.

But time changes everything, you know. There's something in the wind. And there's something about us. Something indefinable. Perhaps it's this: The people of the Tongass, we're like tea bags -- we don't know our own strength until we get into hot water.

STEPCHILD OF AMERICA

• •

There are 867 watersheds in the Tongass National Forest.

Purling streams splash everywhere, ten thousand of them feeding and glutting those 867 watersheds with liquid magic, sky sap dripping from damp clouds to dank soils, nourishing the hungry trees that eat the filtered sunlight, trees with enchanted emerald cells that convert energy from the nearest star, photosynthesizing a sugar called cellulose, generating a binding glue called lignin, storing star power in the form of wood waiting in the forest for us to unlock in later years. And the trees all the while, in a vast cycle of elements, exhale freshets of oxygen to kindle the metabolic fires in the beasts of the forest.

Live in the Tongass long enough and you'll feel these thoughts whether you can say them or not.

The Tongass has great psychological power. That power lies engraved on the souls of those who have dwelt all seasons with it, those who have recruited personal character from its amiable toughness and its indomitable self-renewal, who know its sundry moods and uncanny spells, who've trembled when the Tongass is brooding and stormy and murderous, who've watched it cooing in springtime over its people like tender cradled babies, who've ventured its waters by night and found it immense and mystical, who've watched its magic aurora, outshining the Milky Way's galactic fires, reach out with a filament to tap the shoulder of Orion in winter.

The psychological power of the Tongass finds expression in a cartographer's litany of lyrical place names: Cape Decision, Mount Fairweather, Peril Strait, The Glory Hole, West Crawfish Inlet, Eagle Reef, Dangerous River, The Basin, Suicide Falls, Green Monster Mountain, Deadman Beach, Fat Lady Creek, Whale Cove, Ford's Terror, Point Retreat.

And for some of us, that psychological power makes the Tongass home, the only possible home. It's a home you cry for when you're away. It's a home that owns you. It's a home that intimidates loquacious poets

91

into silence and prompts taciturn loggers into spontaneously blurting "Damn, what a place!" How we love you, Tongass! We love you like a son, like a daughter. We love you fiercely, compulsively, jealously.

Yet the Tongass we love is a colony, America's Third World Settlement. It's been that way since the Czars occupied Sitka. But now it is time to examine the changing Tongass times seriously, to consult those who know them and understand them. We cannot understand the present unless we know the past.

Probably nobody knows the story of the Tongass better than Lawrence Rakestraw, who we met briefly in the last chapter. As we noted there, he is the author of several distinguished histories of conservation dealing with Alaska as well as of numerous articles on the subject in scholarly journals.

Forest Service photo

The Tongass: a timber ship threads the mountains in the sea

Early in his career he worked for the Forest Service and, even though his doctoral degree is in history, he later became a professor of forestry at Michigan Technological University. Dr. Rakestraw has spent nineteen months of intensive on-site research in Alaska plus uncounted thousands of hours sifting through federal and private archives and interviewing many veteran Alaska hands, digging out the story of what really happened in the Tongass. His research on the subject is universally respected.

Be our muse, Dr. Rakestraw. Tell us of the Tongass.

"I don't know about being a muse, but perhaps you'll settle for a historian. However, there is indeed a certain epic scale and classic spirit to the story of the Tongass, and that I will try to convey."

The Outland

"We have already discussed the first users of the forest, the original dwellers in this place: the Tlingit and the Haida and the Tsimshian. But others came and the forest changed. During the Russian occupation beginning in 1799, the forests of the Tongass received use characteristic of a frontier: as the economic base of extractive industry. The Russian-American Company utilized the forests largely as building material for the purposes of the settlers while ruling the fur trade in the Alexander Archipelago and the rest of Alaska.

"Houses, official buildings and churches were made of wood, ranging from the massive stockades and government buildings at New Archangel, present site of Sitka, to individual wooden dwellings made of logs and held together with wooden pegs. Some shipbuilding was carried on at New Archangel. Wooden dams and fish traps were constructed. The Russians established a few sawmills, three of them near New Archangel. They were small-capacity, waterpowered mills for the most part, though one was run by steam. But much of the lumber was laboriously whip-sawed by hand.

"The Russian occupation left few marks on the forest. Contemporary photographs and paintings show the Russian settlements, like most frontier towns, as clearings in the forest. Their greatest impact was to deplete the supply of Alaska yellow cedar around Sitka. Russian scientists collected and classified plants in the Tongass. Interestingly, they also made a major attempt at forestry in 1805. In that year a plantation of Sitka spruce was made on the Aleutian Islands at Unalaska, a thousand miles from the Tongass and far beyond the conifer belt. Surprisingly, some of the trees have survived to the present day.

In 1833 Baron Ferdinand Petrovich von Wrangel, governor of the

Russian colonies in Alaska (later director of the Russian-American Company), sent Lt. Dionysius Zarembo from New Archangel to build an outpost near the mouth of the great Stikine River. Its purpose was to prevent encroachment by the Hudson's Bay Company fur traders. Zarembo's crew completed Redoubt St. Dionysius on the north end of Wrangell Island (named after the baron, despite today's different spelling) in August of 1834, logging nearby forests for materials. The Russians built a number of similar outposts throughout the archipelago using logs from the Tongass forest. But in all, the effect of the Russian era on the Tongass forest was inconsiderable.''

What about the American era? After 1867 when Seward bought Alaska from the Russians? When the Tongass became an American colony.

"Well, the subject of economic colonialism -- the twin themes of neglect or suppression of an area by the federal government and exploitation by absentee landlords and carpetbag politicians -- is an old one in American history. The more developed sections of the United States have always been wary of frontier areas as potential economic competitors, and have always wanted to keep them subservient.

"Many historians have used economic colonialism to explain events, particularly in Alaska. I still recall the wrathful titles that Ernest Gruening selected for three sections of his 1968 book The State of Alaska: 'The Era of Total Neglect,' 'The Era of Flagrant Neglect,' and 'The Unconcern.' Gruening, of course, was not complaining of the absence of federal programs to help Alaska, he was asking for the self-determination that would enable Alaskans to develop their country according to their own vision.

"Alaska still feels the sting of economic colonialism because it was the last major area acquired by the United States to be considered part of the 'public domain,' land to which the federal land laws have applied. It still cannot develop its land according to its own vision, but remains largely under the control of a bureaucracy based 3,000 miles away in Washington, D.C.

"Anti-development or anti-economic forces have always been an important component of economic colonialism. The current dominance of the anti-development environmental lobby, which, if you'll notice, is funded by numerous large Eastern corporations, is merely the latest phase. The idea is strictly old hat. The Alaskan novelist Rex Beach complained in a 1936 letter to Anthony J. Dimond, Alaska's territorial delegate to Congress:

> Bureaucratic control of Alaskan affairs, misapplied theories of conservation, Congressional experimentation with new fangled nostrums forcibly fed through the noses of Alaskans have combined to just about put that country on her back. Her coal and iron are permanently locked up, her timber and pulp wood is rotting faster than it can be cut, capital is discouraged, and private enterprise in many lines is hog-tied.

"You could find similar complaints with different specifics from frontier settlers a century ago in South Dakota or Nevada or Oregon. So you see that public domain lands are historically the primary site of economic colonialism."

We can also see that folk singer Utah Phillips was right: There's nothing as revolutionary as a long memory.

Genesis of the Public Domain

But before you go on, Dr. Rakestraw, how did this public domain get started in America? We thought the original thirteen states had no federal land in them -- didn't it all belong to the states and private citizens?

"An astute question, and your observation is quite true. The original thirteen states did not contain any federal lands -- any 'public lands.' However, from colonial times, seven of the thirteen states had claimed a vast patchwork of 'Western lands' located generally between their borders and the Mississippi river, an enormous area. Those Western lands became quite a bone of contention when the Constitution came up for ratification. The six non-claiming states wanted the other seven to give up their Western lands. The seven land-claiming states wanted to keep their claims with the wealth and political power they could bring.

"The dispute was bitter and even threatened to derail Constitutional ratification. But in 1780 the Continental Congress reached a compromise, pledging that all Western lands ceded by the original states to the U.S. 'shall be disposed of for the common benefit of the United States, and be settled and formed into distinct republican States, which shall become members of the Federal Union, and have the same rights of sovereignty, freedom, and independence, as the other States.'"

And that settled the argument?

"Not entirely. It was only after the greatest legacy of the Continental Congress, the Northwest Ordinance of 1787, that orderly westward expansion could come about. The Ordinance specified that the Northwest Territory, a large area stretching from present-day Ohio as far west as

today's Minnesota, and which had been ceded by Virginia and Connecti-
cut, would evolve from being a colony with a governor appointed by
Congress, to self-government with an elected assembly, to statehood 'on
an equal footing with the original states.'

"When the Constitution was finally ratified, it validated the process
and gave Congress the power to admit new states and regulate territories.
After much wrangling and foot dragging that stretched from 1781 to 1802,
the holdout states -- Georgia being the last -- ceded their Western lands to
the federal government. The first public domain lands were thus acquired
by the federal government from land claims of the original states. And
that's where the public domain started."

We hadn't known that. But we all know the textbook story of how
the nation expanded its public domain through the 1803 Louisiana Purchase, the purchase of Florida in 1819, the addition of the Oregon Territory in 1846, the admission of California in 1850, and the Gadsden
Purchase in Arizona and New Mexico Territories in 1853. We know that
Hawaii's annexation in 1898 was the last to result in statehood (in 1959,
the same year as Alaska's admission to the Union). Congress may have
made good on its promise to dispose of all lands ceded to it by the original
states, but today *one-third of the entire nation* is still owned by the United
States government. It was never disposed of into private hands. Explain
to us how the public lands developed into such a gigantic bureaucratic
boondoggle.

Stages of Transformation

"Land economists and historians have an interesting answer. They
have identified five major phases of federal land ownership in the American past. The initial one was that of acquisition, during the nineteenth
century when the United States acquired territory by treaty, purchase,
political maneuvering, or as the fruits of war to obtain satisfactory national
boundaries and to extend these boundaries in the interest of security,
national pride, or economic welfare.

"Next came the era of disposal, in which the public lands were used as
a substitute for capital in helping to develop and settle the country; they
were sold, leased, or given away to individuals, states, and corporations. It
was during this second phase, incidentally, that the term 'public lands'
became commonplace. It originally meant 'land intended for disposal to
the public.' It is somewhat ironic that the same term today has come to

mean the exact opposite: the one-third of America's lands that will never be disposed of to the public. Our current notions of 'public' land as being somehow owned by 'all Americans' -- who cannot exercise any of the powers of ownership over them whatever -- would have seemed ridiculous or even subversive to our settler ancestors.

"The third stage was that of reservation, in which individuals and interest groups became concerned over the consequences of unrestricted land disposal for a variety of reasons, ranging from the aesthetic to the moral, political and scientific, and during which lands were 'reserved' -- that is, kept in federal hands and withdrawn from the disposal process -- to protect areas of unique scenic beauty, protect watersheds, prevent land speculation, or retain a regulated timber supply.

"Of most consequence to the Tongass, and all America, was the law that led to the formation of our national forests. In 1891, Congress passed an act allowing the president to proclaim forest reserves on the public lands. It was tacked on as a 68-word rider to a voluminous general land law revision bill. The law was imperfect because it did not allocate appropriations or provide for administration of the reserves. Presidents Benjamin Harrison and Grover Cleveland proclaimed a total of 17.6 million acres in the West as forest reserves -- and then left them sitting there with nobody able to do *anything* with them, to manage them for either preservation or use. Not even the Department of the Interior, which was charged with administering all the public domain, could manage them. The first proclamations resulting from this law simply stated, "Warning is hereby expressly given to all persons not to enter or make settlement upon the tract of land reserved by this proclamation." The early forest reserves were literally 'No Man's Land.'

"Of course, settlers and timber cutters, as usual, cheerfully ignored the law's absolute lock-up. President Cleveland grumped that it was pointless to proclaim any more reserves until there was some way to manage them or protect them, so he suspended the practice in 1893."

Why didn't the government do something about the illegal timber cutters?

"Usually there was no federal officer within several days' ride. And the outcry against the locked-up reserves from Western land users was so great that in 1897 Congress finally passed an act providing for the management of these forest reserves, allowing controlled timber harvest and livestock grazing.

"This 1897 law was also tacked on as a rider to another bill, in this case the Sundry Civil Appropriations Bill of that year. This law gave the

General Land Office in the Department of the Interior the appropriation money needed to manage the reserves. But here we find another imperfection: The Division of Forestry, which employed foresters with the requisite expertise to manage the forest reserves, had been situated in another agency, the Department of Agriculture, since 1881. Long encumbered by cronyism and incompetence, Interior's General Land Office proved ineffectual at running the forest reserves. Although the two agencies attempted cooperative forest reserve management programs, the situation degenerated into inter-agency rivalry.''

This forest reserve era sounds like total confusion.

"It was. Finally in 1905 Congress transferred the forest reserves to the newly created Forest Service, a reorganized version of the Division of Forestry in the Department of Agriculture. The first chief of the Forest Service, Gifford Pinchot, who had served as head of the old Division of Forestry since 1898, coined the term 'conservation' to mean 'the wise use of resources' and set up wise use as the main purpose of the reserves, which were renamed 'national forests' in 1907.

"The creation of the Forest Service heralded the opening of the fourth period of American public land ownership, *extensive* management, in which the government gave to the reserved areas management that was compatible with the state of scientific and technical knowledge of the time. Gifford Pinchot's theories of efficient use of resources became the guiding policy of the Forest Service. The concepts of American forestry as we know it today were largely shaped by Pinchot, although he had a number of important predecessors in the field such as Franklin B. Hough, Nathaniel Egleston, and Bernhard E. Fernow that we'll talk about later.

"We are today moving into the final era of *intensive* management; the body of technical and scientific knowledge is now sufficient to bring resource management to a state of maximum productivity.

The Great Rooms of Time

"The Tongass is unusual in that disposal was slow, and there were fewer private inholdings than was characteristic of the Lower 48. Disposal on a large scale came only with statehood in 1959, and with the disposal to Native Alaskans in 1980. In territorial days not very much land was disposed to settlers in Alaska even though it was purchased by the United States in 1867, during the heyday of the disposal movement in the frontier West. The Homestead Act was virtually unused in the Tongass, but thousands of settlers before the turn of the century took up land through squatters' rights granted by several Preemption Acts, intermarriage with

Natives, fox farming under special lease -- strange as that may sound -- and mineral claims. A number of small sawmills and fish canneries sprang up, but the area they occupied was minimal.

"Ironically, the period of actual disposal in the Tongass came out of sequence, in the 1970s when the government gave substantial federal lands to the Indians in the Alaska Native Claims Settlement Act of 1971. However, almost no land outside town-limits belongs to non-Native private parties today.

"By 1892 the period of reservation began: the first forest reserve came to Alaska, on Afognak Island across the Gulf of Alaska from the Tongass. A presidential proclamation permitted the U.S. Fish Commission to establish fish culture stations on Afognak and Kodiak Islands. But that wasn't all.

"You can understand why all Alaskans were furious and frightened over this Afognak reservation by reading the final clause of President Benjamin Harrison's proclamation:

> Warning is hereby given to all persons not to enter upon, or to occupy, the tract or tracts of land or waters reserved by this proclamation, or to fish in, or use any of the waters herein described or mentioned, and that all persons or corporations now occupying said island, or any of said premises...shall depart therefrom.

"Not exactly the kind of treatment settlers, fishermen and sawmill owners expected from their government. You can imagine their outcry. Protests against similar forest reserves reverberated in the halls of Congress for years from all over the West. The Department of the Interior, which administered all the public lands through the General Land Office, became a favorite whipping boy of Western politicians.

"When conservationist Theodore Roosevelt succeeded to the presidency in 1901, he wanted to know about the possibility of creating forest reserves in the Tongass region. Yet he had no intention of locking out commerce or arousing the settlers to anger. He was methodical about it and sent a well-known authority on Alaska, Lieutenant George Thornton Emmons, to survey the area for the department of the interior and make recommendations.

"Emmons reported to the president:

> In setting aside of Government timber reservations, I understand that it is the department's desire to interfere as little

as possible with the settlement and development of the country, and where conditions are equally favorable to select islands -- the limits of which are clearly defined by nature -- which are the more sparsely inhabited, and to this end I would suggest the following list of localities fulfilling these conditions:

(1) The Prince of Wales Island and associate islands to seaward

(2) Zarembo Island

(3) Kuiu Island

(4) Kupreanof Island

(5) Chichagof Island and associate island to seaward.

"Emmons found that the islands had a total of about 1,400 Native inhabitants and no white settlements of any size. There were small sawmills at Howkan, Shakan, Kasaan Bay and Hetta Inlet, and a few canneries. There was a mission on Chichagof Island at Hoonah and a small settlement in Tenakee Inlet. Roosevelt cautioned Interior Secretary Ethan Allen Hitchcock to use softer language in the Tongass proclamation:

> Ought not the proclamation to be made to conform a little more fully to the real objective of the case? I have been told that at present they have rather the effect of scaring, and of conveying the idea that we are trying to drive all the people out.

"On August 20, 1902, President Theodore Roosevelt established by proclamation the Alexander Archipelago Forest Reserve, the first in the Tongass. The missionaries objected loudest, because the Indians they served were 'loggers by occupation,' and with timber cutting regulated, would have to 'revert to primitive conditions or else starve.' The secretary of the interior sent out reassuring letters, logging went on, and the protests were short-lived.

"A second reserve was created September 10, 1907, 2 million acres of mainland between the Canadian border on the south and the Unuk River on the north: it was called the Tongass National Forest -- forest reserves were renamed 'national forests' that year. On July 1, 1908, the Alexander Archipelago and the Tongass were consolidated into a single national forest, the Tongass, with a total area of 6.7 million acres. Ten million more acres would be added before the Tongass National Forest was complete and the era of reservation drew to a close."

So that's how the Tongass National Forest began.

"Indeed it is. The subsequent long period of extensive management is essentially the story of the Department of Agriculture's Forest Service in the Tongass. Among the arguments for bringing the Forest Service into the Tongass by way of proclaiming reserves and creating new national forests was the problem posed by timber sales. Unreserved public domain lands, as opposed to forest reserves, remained under the jurisdiction of the General Land Office of the Interior Department. Although the secretary of the interior was authorized to sell timber to mill operators in Alaska under the Trade and Manufacturing Act of 1898, no timber was ever sold under it. Instead, the logger went where he pleased and cut whatever he wanted without getting permission from anybody or notifying any government official. Once a year a special agent of the General Land Office visited each mill in the Tongass to inquire how much timber had been cut. Settlement was made on the basis of innocent trespass, at twenty cents per thousand board feet for sawtimber, one-half cent per linear foot for piling, and twenty-fire cents per cord for firewood."

That's a bit informal.

"Many thought so. Such casual procedures outraged the professional foresters in the Department of Agriculture and spurred the creation of forest reserves in the Tongass. Another spur was a peculiar feature of federal law: export of lumber from the unreserved public lands of Alaska was forbidden, but, on the other hand, lumber cut on national forests *could* be exported. Obviously, large sawmill owners in Ketchikan, Wrangell, Juneau and Douglas wanted more reserves created in order to tap the potential export market.

Notes From The Fog Mountain

"The Forest Service, or rather its predecessor, the Division of Forestry, had been in the Tongass since 1903 in the person of William Alexander Langille, a mountaineer, adventurer and forest expert. He was a large man of magnificent physique and keen intellect. However, he spent much of his time in a canoe visiting sawmills and investigating timber theft by Canadians, and was not able to bring any sort of real management to the vast region until 1905. Even then he worked alone most of the time arranging timber sales and settling cases of timber trespass.

"Langille was forester, business manager, law enforcement officer and bureaucrat. Like all bureaucrats, he found himself increasingly tied up in red tape. When grazing fees were authorized in the national forests,

Mrs. Ivan Langley Collection

William A. Langille in 1902 in Washington for a
report to Pinchot and Roosevelt

Langille was responsible for submitting an annual report on his collec-
tions. Now, farming and livestock grazing were out of the question in the
Tongass. A forest ranger assigned to work with Langille said it all in this
1906 report on livestock grazing fees collected in the Alexander Archipelago Forest Reserve, which reads in its entirety:

> Foxes are the only live stock on the reserve, and they
> graze on salmon at the rate of 4 cents an acre.
>
> There is a trespassing mule somewhere in the Klawak
> region but he cannot be located.
>
> Attempts at grazing cattle have absolutely failed on
> account of the ruggedness of the country and the prohibi-
> tive cost of winter feeding. The same holds true for
> sheep.

"Forest Service veterans will tell the rest of the story of extensive
management in the Tongass in a later chapter. The transition to intensive
management has occurred with dramatic suddenness since the pulp mills
came in the 1950s, masses of complex environmental laws came in the
1960s and the old style forest ranger such as Langille -- ruler of the district,
jack-of-all-trades, and respected by the community -- gave way to hordes
of resource-management teams who study problems with a multi-discipli-

nary approach. The ranger's disappearance was inevitable as part of the shift from custodial management to intensive management, but with his disappearance an element of the romance and poetry and comedy of natural resource history has vanished.''

Lures and Promises

But Dr. Rakestraw, merely dividing up American land ownership into five phases doesn't explain *why* it happened.

"Aren't you the sharp ones? Very true. Dividing a phenomenon into parts, indeed, gives you only a set of still photographs, so to speak. It sorts things out and makes them a little more understandable, but it doesn't explain the *dynamics*, what makes it happen. Here's what I make of the *why*. It will require that we backtrack in time.

"It's plain enough to everyone that the earliest stage of land acquisition after the American Revolution came from powerful motivations for national security. Remember, when Jefferson sent Lewis and Clark to see what he had got from Napoleon for his 15 million dollars, the Oregon Country was claimed by Great Britain, Russia, Spain and the United States. We were involved in a dispute with Spain over ownership of Texas and the stretch of Gulf Coast from New Orleans to Mobile Bay. Then the British burned Washington during the War of 1812 and our northern boundary with British North America became an armed border.

"But behind the need for security lay a feeling that America had a natural right to expand, a feeling that journalist John Louis O'Sullivan summed up in his coinage of 1850: 'Our manifest destiny is to overspread the continent allotted by Providence for the free development of our yearly multiplying millions.' The lure of land and the promise of freedom were the pioneer spirit of Manifest Destiny. That slogan combined the elements of security, national pride and economic development. It drove us to the Pacific. It was the spirit that led Seward to purchase Alaska and prompted later officials to annex overseas territories such as Hawaii and Puerto Rico. It was the guiding principle behind the disposal of public lands to the public: Getting settlers on the ground was the best way to assert the national claim to ownership 'from sea to shining sea.'

"The Civil War disrupted the vision of Manifest Destiny only briefly, but things were never the same afterward. The decade of the 1860s saw the beginning of two contradictory tendencies that profoundly altered the course of history. On the one hand, settlers exploited the forests and grazing lands of the advancing frontier with increasing fervor. On the other, growing nature-appreciation and the professionalization of resource management led strong personalities to demand government control of the forests and grazing lands. And both of these conflicting tendencies developed long before Alaska came into the picture.

"Many forces caused the increasing exploitation of our forests. The

Forest Service photo

Logging operation at Whitewater Bay circa 1909

Homestead Act of 1862 encouraged settlers to push the frontier ahead with promises of cheap land. The General Land Office became one of the busiest agencies in government. 'Doing a Land Office business,' is a phrase that still lingers in our speech as the epitome of hustle and bustle.

"The Homestead Act offered small plots of 160 acres, just enough for one family to farm in average soil, to anyone who would take up residence for five years and make certain minimal improvements.

"In the timber industry, technological developments and engineering refinements sped up the rate of production, both in the woods and in the mills. The lumber industry moved from the Lake States to the vast West Coast forests as the frontier moved. The federal government was reluctant to punish timber trespass -- illegal timber cutting by settlers and corporations -- fearing that too harsh a treatment of violators would discourage settlement and economic development. Business organization shifted from individual owners or partnerships to corporations. National demand for wood and wood products boomed. A close alliance between business and politics developed.

"Then too, Congress passed two laws that liberalized the Homestead Act: The Timber Culture Act of 1873 which expanded on the Homestead Act by allowing the settler to substitute planting trees for part of the residence requirements, and the Timber and Stone Act of 1878, which authorized the sale of nontillable public timberland for private use. Neither law was designed with conservation in mind: Both were intended to liberalize the timber supply to meet Western needs. But you can't operate a commercial sawmill with the timber on only 160 acres.

"Lumber companies throughout the West solved the problem by hiring farmers, sailors -- any available person -- to file under the Timber and Stone Act. Dr. Harold K. Steen put it succinctly in his book *The U.S. Forest Service: A History*, 'These benign conspirators would then sell their claims to the lumber company for a small sum and go about their business.' One General Land Office agent found that the going rate for dummy entrymen ranged from $50 to $125; you could buy a witness for $25. He estimated that three quarters of the claims filed with him were fraudulent. As historian John Ise put it, fraud was a frontier way of life.

High Wind In The West

"For each of these forces there developed a counterforce. Such men as pioneer landscape architect Frederick Law Olmsted, the designer of New York City's Central Park, argued that aesthetic appreciation of forests near cities as well as in remote places such as California's Yosemite must be encouraged to prevent the "nervous exhaustion" of constant city living from undermining the human spirit. This meant retaining in government ownership areas of unique scenic, historic or recreational value. It was this feeling that helped bring about the establishment of the world's first national park at Yellowstone in 1872, which, incidentally, was lobbied into existence by the Northern Pacific Railway Company and a group of distinguished citizens of Montana, so the national park movement certainly had a tinge of economic opportunism about it as well.

"A second and stronger counterforce was the growth and professionalization of science and the desire to bring the expertise of science to the management of natural resources. We can see this force in the creation shortly after the Civil War of federal scientific agencies such as the Bureau of Fisheries, the Geological Survey and the Division of Forestry, which supplemented the scientific work carried on earlier by the Topographic Engineers and the Smithsonian Institution. The scientific managers felt that retaining natural resources in government ownership offered a better opportunity for 'orderly and permanent development' than what they saw as 'hasty and ill-considered occupation' by the private landowners who settled the West.

"A third force was the desire by reformers such as Interior Secretary Carl Schurz, Theodore Roosevelt and Senator George Edmunds of Vermont, to bring morality into public life and to check an often corrupt alliance between business and politics. The reformers abhorred the illegal entrymen who helped Western corporations accumulate large land holdings from the public domain against the intent of homestead laws designed to help only 'actual settlers.' They abhorred timber trespass. They abhorred the lobbyists who convinced Congress and government agents to look the other way -- sometimes by outright bribery. Several administrative officials such as Schurz and Land Commissioner Edward Bowers recovered lands stolen or defrauded from the public domain and made efforts to establish better land laws -- but adamantly refused to increase the 160 acre maximum homestead allowance in the arid West, which only invited further flaunting of the law. The reformers uniformly urged Congress to retain at least part of the public domain in government ownership.

"A fourth counterforce was sectionalism, in particular the desire of politicians and financiers of the Eastern Seaboard to restrict the growth of the West and thus reduce both the labor force drain resulting from outward migration and the threat of economic competition. Sectionalists not infrequently hid their true motives behind the rhetoric of the reformer, the nature lover and the scientific resource manager. For sectionalists, keeping the public domain under government control kept it under political control. The West may have had the natural resources of land and timber and minerals and later petroleum, but the East had the money and the votes.

"These two contradictory tendencies fed upon each other. From the 1860s, reports of Western homestead scandals or timber trespass by settlers and corporations provoked intensifying outrage and political reaction in the East among the naturalists, resource professionals, reformers and sectionalists. In turn, every complaint from the East hardened the settlers and corporations in asserting their right to use the West's natural resources, intensifying their outrage and political reaction to outside interference. In large part, their debate was a matter of talking through each other, because neither could understand the other's viewpoint. It was this conflict between Western land users and Eastern objectors that led to

the creation of the forest reserves that became today's national forests --
including the Tongass.''

   That's remarkable. We were unaware of this background. In telling
us about something that happened over a hundred years ago, Dr. Rakestraw,
you've described exactly what's going on today in the Tongass. American
fighting American over natural resources. We're still making the same
mistake.
   "All too true. It was a Greek general and historian named Thucydides

Lawrence W. Rakestraw, Ph.D., our historical consultant
receiving accolade at his *alma mater*, Clark College

who warned us twenty-five-hundred years ago that history repeats itself,
and the modern philosopher George Santayana who added that those who
are ignorant of history are doomed to repeat it.
   "Today the debate over the Tongass is carried on in mass market
magazines such as *Sports Illustrated* and *Reader's Digest* by people who

are totally unaware of how the national forests evolved and what their actual purpose is. Many do not know the difference between a national park and a national forest. Their audiences, likewise unaware of history, react emotionally and without information. The result can be disastrous for all concerned: The forest industry in the Tongass can be needlessly crippled or even obliterated, the Forest Service can be shackled with overly rigid new laws by a Congress reacting to noisy militants, and the nation as a whole can be saddled with onerous breach-of-contract settlement payments -- while absolutely nothing results which will improve the biological state of the Tongass forests.

"The only unconditional winners in such a conflict will be environmentalist pressure groups, whose political agendas will be forwarded and their coffers filled with misguided contributions. The key to a sound solution in the Tongass is an understanding of how the national forests developed and what they're actually for."

The Hounding of History

And for that we turn to our editor Ron Arnold, who has uncovered previously unknown facts about the origin of the national forests.

"It's unorthodox for an editor to intrude like this."

You made the discovery. You tell the story.

"Very well, then. We began this research on another book, but while checking the facts in K.A. and Jackie's manuscript, my research staff gathered everything that was known about the forest reserves and how they evolved into our great system of national forests. As we sorted the documents, we began to realize that this was no routine research task. The origin of these forest reserves, we found, was shrouded in mystery. They had been authorized by an 1891 law no one understood -- even at the time it was enacted. Today it is generally called "The Creative Act of 1891" or "The Forest Reserve Act of 1891," although in fact it was a general revision of the land laws and repealed several obsolete homestead laws, including the Timber Culture Act of 1873.

"Interestingly enough, Sections 11 through 14 of this law opened Alaska lands to trade and manufacture occupancy (sawmilling, for instance), and Section 15 is the provision that made Annette Island a reservation for the Tsimshian Indians. However, it was the notorious Section 24 of that Act which gave the President power to unilaterally withdraw from disposal portions of the public domain as forest reserves so that settlers could not enter.

"Section 24, we discovered, had been added as a last-minute rider to

'An act to repeal timber culture laws, and for other purposes.' This is the law that Gifford Pinchot in his autobiography called 'the most important legislation in the history of Forestry in America...[and] the beginning and basis of our whole National Forest system.'''

Isn't it strange that a law with such enormous consequences would be added as a rider to another bill?

"It's not unheard-of. And nobody could foresee the consequences. Then we established that the momentous rider had been tacked on in a House-Senate conference committee -- but was not referred back to the originating Public Lands Committee of either the House or the Senate, a completely illegal procedure. It went straight to a floor vote and nearly every commentator says that Congress passed this most important law without being aware of its content. Now, that *is* virtually unheard-of.''

Who added Section 24? What interest group of the time -- preservationists, professional foresters, anti-monopolists, sectionalists or what-not -- pressured for its addition, and who yielded to the pressure?

"Government documents contained no information.''

Why was Section 24 added? What was the 'congressional intent' behind these epoch-making forest reserves? Aesthetic preservation? Arrest of timber thieves? Preventing damage to watersheds? Assurance of future timber supplies? Thwarting speculators? Suppression of Western development to guarantee Eastern economic dominance? Anything that could shed light on the proper modern interpretation of our national forests?

"Again, no information. Yet the bill passed both chambers without difficulty and became law March 3, 1891.''

Quite fascinating.

"And perfectly baffling. The language of the law presents problems of its own. Here's what it says verbatim:

> Sec. 24. That the President of the United States may, from time to time, set apart and reserve, in any State or Territory having public land bearing forests, in any part of the public lands wholly or in part covered with timber or undergrowth, whether of commercial value or not, as public reservations; and the President shall, by public proclamation, declare the establishment of such reservations and the limits thereof.

That's it?

"Yes, that's the puzzling 68-word clause that generated our vast national forest system, in all its oracular splendor. As Dr. Rakestraw noted, it gave the president power only to *proclaim* forest reserves. It did not confer the power to *administer* the reserves thus created nor did it provide *appropriations* for management of any kind. Even more baffling, the first forest reserve created under Section 24 was not even related to forestry, but added a huge section to Yellowstone National Park by presidential proclamation after Congress had just rejected a bill proposing the identical enlargement! Section 24 has bewildered historians for almost a century.

"Dr. Harold K. Steen, executive director of the Forest History Society, pointed out to me that the clause is so poorly drafted it doesn't even make sense grammatically: The first sentence lacks a necessary noun, it doesn't say *what* the President may 'set apart and reserve' 'as public reservations.' However, the gist is clear: The President may reserve any public land he damn well pleases for any purpose that tickles his fancy.

"Dr. Steen wrote in his book *The U.S. Forest Service: A History*, 'Much of the original documentation has been lost for what is now called the Forest Reserve Act of 1891. It is unfortunate that one of the most important legislative actions in the history of conservation is so obscure.'"

It seems to us more than unfortunate: The arguments we're hearing over the true purpose of the national forests could ruin the Tongass timber industry.

"I agree. Preservationists do argue forcefully that the national forests are for preservation and not for use. Casting light upon the origins of the national forests could resolve some of those disputes, so it seemed to me both vital and urgent. I resolved to find that lost original documentation."

But how?

"The first step was to find out what historians have said about Section 24. I quickly found they've said conflicting things. At least half a dozen improbable people have taken credit for attaching the rider. At least half a dozen improbable explanations for its intent have been offered. The controversy over Section 24 is as murky as the clause itself. This was not going to be easy. But you have to start somewhere, and I decided to begin with the most generally accepted account.

"It tells a story something like this: The idea of creating forest reserves goes back to the 1870s, so it was nothing new when Section 24 was passed in 1891. Numerous newspaper stories had been written advocating reserves. More than 200 forestry bills had been introduced in Congress during the twenty years from 1871 to 1891 and they all failed. Most were intended to protect watersheds and -- don't laugh -- attract rain."

You can't be serious.

"I am. It was then generally believed that forests influenced the climate, bringing rain. Numerous rainmaker schemes proposed to stipple the Great Plains with trees for the farmer's sake. Cutting timber was seen as an invitation to drought. It's possible that Section 24 was some sort of legislative rain dance.

"But the reservation clause is thought by professional historians to have originated in 1889 with the law committee of the American Forestry Association, a professional organization founded in 1875. AFA's law committee consisted of three distinguished professionals: Bernhard Eduard Fernow, a German forester who had immigrated to the U.S. and in 1889 was the chief of the Division of Forestry in the U.S. Department of Agriculture; Nathaniel Egleston, the immediate past chief of the Division; and Edward A. Bowers, commissioner of the General Land Office in the U.S. Department of the Interior.

No Better Witnesses

"This law committee met with President Benjamin Harrison in April 1889, presenting a petition advocating an efficient forest policy. The president was cordial but took no action. The following year the American Forestry Association memorialized Congress to create forest reserves and to provide a commission to administer them. Congress likewise took no action.

"The law committee tried again, this time with Secretary of the Interior John W. Noble. Fernow, Bowers and Egleston were joined by others, including John Wesley Powell, head of the U.S. Geological Survey, who earlier in his career had led the first daring expedition down the Colorado through the Grand Canyon. Fernow impressed upon Secretary Noble his responsibility to protect the public domain.

"As Dr. Steen wrote of the meeting, 'Accounts vary as to who said what, but it is generally accepted that as a result of the meeting, Noble personally intervened with the congressional conference committee at the eleventh hour to get Section 24 added.' If this story is true, the intent of the forest reserves was clearly forestry, i.e., the professional management of reserves for both protection and use. Historian Samuel Hayes calls this 'the gospel of efficiency' and sees it as a technocratic rather than ecological viewpoint."

Do you think it's true?

"We'll get to that. But one problem with this account is that, as I've already noted, the first forest reserve created under Section 24 was an addition to Yellowstone National Park. National parks have no connection to forestry or the efficient use of resources: they are managed by the dual legislative mandate of 'public use and enjoyment' and the 'preservation of lands and features in their natural condition.'

"However, John Ise, the historian who in 1920 wrote the first comprehensive history of U.S. forest policy, seems to have confirmed that Noble added the rider. In *The United States Forest Policy* he wrote: 'Noble, who had been influenced by Fernow and Bowers, and perhaps by other members of the American Forestry Association, asked the committee to insert a rider authorizing the president to establish reserves.'"

How did Ise know that?

"He based his assertion on a letter from Fernow, who replied to Ise's correspondence, 'My memory is, that at the time the story was current, Mr. Noble declared at midnight of March 3, in the Conference Committee, that he would not let the President sign the bill...unless the Reservation clause was inserted. Since these things happen behind closed doors, only someone present can tell what happened, Secretary Noble or one of the conferees. All we, that is, Bowers and myself, can claim is that we educated Noble up to the point.'"

Now we're getting somewhere.

"True. Noble's secretarial papers would tell the tale of what Section 24 actually intended. But, as Dr. Steen pointed out in a footnote, those papers have yet to be located.

"It didn't take long to find the institution to which they were bequeathed. Noble was from St. Louis, Missouri, and a few phone calls to the area located Peter Michel, Director of Library and Archives, Missouri Historical Society. He remembered something about Noble's papers. Michel examined the register of the Society's archives and found a notation that Leona B. Halstead, sister-in-law to John W. Noble, gave the secretary's papers to the Historical Society shortly after his death on March 21, 1912. Aha! We found them! Then the next notation, from February 19, 1928, shows a Mr. Tibbott, who was writing a book on President Benjamin Harrison, asking to look at Noble's papers. A thorough search came up with nothing. Somewhere between 1912 and 1928 Noble's papers had disappeared. Oh, hell! We didn't find them!"

Back to the drawing board?

"Right. I went to Washington, D.C. and talked to Senate Historian Richard Baker. Maybe there was some clue dangling somewhere about Noble and what had happened in that House-Senate conference committee meeting. Baker could find nothing about it. He did have a helpful observation: there is little likelihood that any executive-branch officer could violate the separation of powers doctrine so blatantly as to thrust himself into a closed-door legislative session making imperious Cabinet demands and threatening a Presidential veto. Baker suggested that the Noble story was probably fabricated.

The History Student

" I could find nothing that a professional historian had written suggesting the same thing -- except a footnote in Dr. Steen's book:

> see Herbert D. Kirkland, "The American Forests, 1864-1898: A Trend Toward Conservation," Ph.D. dissertation, University of Florida, 1971, pp. 171-75. Kirkland casts doubt upon Noble's specific role and whether Fernow was even aware that the amendment was under consideration.

"So I saw Herbert D. Kirkland, pages 171-75. I could hardly believe *what* I saw.

"Kirkland, a young doctoral candidate at the time, had dug up massive amounts of documentation that professional historians have missed. Primarily through letters that have been gathering dust in the National Archives for nearly a century, Kirkland showed decisively that neither Forestry Division chief Fernow nor Interior Secretary Noble even *knew* that Section 24 had been added, much less had anything to do with putting it there."

That's remarkable.

"Quite. Kirkland writes, 'nothing at all appears on the Forest Reserve Act in the Division of Forestry papers until March 16, 1891, almost two weeks after it became law. These papers indicate that it was quite likely that Fernow was not even aware of this legislation until after it had passed.' Yet, as a result of Fernow's statements and their interpretation by Ise and others, nearly everyone gives Noble credit for initiating the Forest Reserve Act.

"Kirkland lists an inventory of historians who fell for the Noble story: Thomas Manning in *Government in Science*; Richard Lilliard in *The Great Forest*; Stewart Udall in *The Quiet Crisis*; Robert Sterling Yard, *Our Federal Lands*; E. Louis Peffer, *The Closing of the Public Lands*; Samuel Trask Dana, *Forest and Range Policy*; Treadwell Cleveland, *Forest Law*;

and W. N. Sparhawk, *History of Forestry in America.* It is appalling that such a register of distinguished personages should parrot secondary sources without checking the facts first.

Mythogenesis

"All evidence indicates that Noble found out about Section 24 on Monday, March 16, 1891, when Arnold Hague, a preservationist and Interior Department employee in the U.S. Geological Survey assigned to Yellowstone, took the news to Noble in a private meeting."

This is getting to be quite a cast of characters.

"We're not finished yet. Our research assistant Ramona Hage followed Kirkland's lead and copied a series of Hague's letters in the National Archives. They show that he and a Washington lawyer and Yellowstone advocate named W. Hallett Phillips discovered the enactment of Section 24 late the previous week. Hague realized the implications of Section 24 in rectifying the recent crushing defeat of a bill asking Congress to expand Yellowstone National Park southward. Hague took Section 24 to Noble, who asked him and Phillips to draft an appropriate proclamation establishing a Yellowstone Forest Reserve with the exact boundaries of the failed proposal to Congress. Hague delivered it to Noble on March 25. Noble forwarded it immediately to President Harrison, who signed it March 30, not two weeks after Noble found out about Section 24.

This Hague was no dummy.

"Oh, he was shrewd. The very day he told Noble about Section 24, he discreetly spread the word to fellow preservationists. In a March 16 letter to park enthusiast John Nicholas Brown of Rhode Island, Hague wrote:

> The matter of setting aside the land adjoining the Yellow-stone Park, which it was proposed to add to the Park by the bill, had already received some attention from me at the time of the receipt of your letter. I had seen the Secretary of the Interior upon the matter and he seemed much interested and asked Mr. Phillips and myself to prepare the necessary papers which we propose doing. I will keep you advised from time to time if we accomplish anything of what form the matter takes. In the meantime I would suggest that you say nothing about it as it might defeat our object if it in any way came to the ears of those who are interested in the lands out there or feared that it would in some way interfere with their pecuniary schemes. We hope to get the land set aside without any newspaper discussion until the thing is accomplished.

Not much different from the tactics of environmentalists in the Tongass.

"Not much.   But this reduces Fernow's importance as a reliable source on Section 24.   In fact, many years later Fernow responded to a request for information from *Forest and Stream* magazine publisher George Bird Grinnell April 10, 1910, admitting

> I do not know who drafted the exact clause, but I know it would never have been inserted, if we ... had not educated the Secretary of the Interior to the propriety of this move.

A Little Taffy

Okay, why did Noble ever get the credit in the first place?

"Again, Arnold Hague's letters reveal the answer.   You have to realize first, however, that this *Forest and Stream* magazine publisher George Bird Grinnell is considered by at least one qualified historian to be the true "inventor" of the wilderness preservation idea, rather than Aldo Leopold, or Arthur Carhart, or Frederick V. Coville, who are variously claimed to hold that distinction.   But, in an April 4, 1891 letter to Grinnell (who, as noted above, was years later to ask Fernow who wrote Section 24), Hague provided "such data as you may need in order to make up an editorial for your paper."   After citing Section 24 verbatim, Hague guessed:

> It was put in, I suppose, as a "sop" to those who believe in timber preservation.

So Hague didn't know who put it in or why, either?
"No, he didn't. But he cautioned Grinnell

> In your editorial you had better give the Secretary of the Interior a little taffy for his seeing the necessity for this thing. You can also congratulate F. and S. [Grinnell's *Forest and Stream*, a vocal park expansion advocate] in the fact that the country has been set aside, and if you see fit to congratulate the undersigned, I would make no objections.

"And that's how the Noble myth entered American literature.   A nature magazine gave a little taffy to a political appointee who had been prompted by an ambitious self-serving preservationist bureaucrat to misuse a law based upon no facts whatever."

Why does that sound so familiar here in the Tongass?

"Stay with me. We're still wondering: If Noble didn't add Section 24, who did? And why?

"Doctoral candidate Kirkland, who so brilliantly uncovered Hague's key role in throwing credit to Noble, could not penetrate further. 'This writer,' he concluded, 'has been unable to determine who specifically drafted the forest reserve clause and attached it to the 'Act to Repeal Timber-Culture Laws.' It appears, however, that it came from someone within the conference committee rather than from Noble, Bowers, Fernow, Hague, Phillips, or the variety of other people sometimes given credit for publicizing the idea of reserving forest land.'"

The conference committee?

"Yes. The House-Senate conference committee that met to resolve differences between their two versions of the land law revision act that ended up containing the illicit rider. It was my court of last resort. My daughter Andrea, one of my research assistants during her senior year at Stanford, searched the *Congressional Record* for the names of those assigned to go to conference on the bill. They were not hard to find:

Senate	House
Preston B. Plumb,	Lewis Edwin Payson,
Republican, Kansas,	Republican, Illinois
Chairman, Senate Public	Chairman, House Public
Lands Committee	Lands Committee
Richard E. Pettigrew,	John Alfred Pickler,
Republican, South Dakota	Republican, South Dakota
Edward Carey Walthall,	William Steele Holman,
Democrat, Mississippi	Democrat, Indiana

"Six men. None of them stellar names in the firmament of American history. Certainly none of them recognizable champions of forestry, or preservation, or any of the things for which today's national forests are noted. One of them -- at least one of them -- is the actual father of the national forests. But which one? Andrea located the papers of each of these men and we wasted a week failing to set one conferee apart as a forest reserve advocate."

Sounds like a dead end.

"Not quite. There was one thing left: to go over the *Congressional*

Record with a fine tooth comb. The conference report containing the
Section 24 rider was debated on February 28 1891 in both the House and
the Senate. Andrea researched the details.

What did she find?

"First the Senate. Senator Preston B. Plumb, Chairman of the Public
Lands Committee, submitted the conference report to the Senate and
recommended that it pass (with the new Section 24). The Secretary of the
Senate proceeded to read the conference report. Immediately, Senator
Wilkinson Call of Florida interrupted the reading, saying he felt the
conference version 'should be printed so that we might all understand it
before acting upon it.' Plumb blandly asserted, 'there is nothing in the
report on any subject whatever that has not already undergone the scrutiny
of this body, and been passed by this body.'

"Now, that was true of everything in the bill -- except Section 24. The
Senate had never seen it before."

Why would Plumb lie? Had he added Section 24, not for forestry
reasons, but perhaps as a closet sectionalist out to suppress Western
growth?

"Unlikely -- he was from Kansas, still regarded in those days itself as
'The West.' Upon completion of the reading of the report, which ended
with Section 24, Senator Call pounced on the amending rider and said, 'I
shall not willingly vote or consent ... to any proposition which prevents a
single acre of the public domain from being set apart and reserved for
homes for the people of the United States who shall live upon and cultivate
them.'

"Senator Plumb then told a real whopper: 'no bill has passed this
body or any other legislative body that more thoroughly consecrates the
public domain to actual settlers and home-owners than does the bill in the
report just read.' The Senate immediately voted its approval of the bill.
As we've seen, President Harrison used Section 24 of that bill to conse-
crate the Yellowstone Forest Reserve to keeping actual settlers and home-
owners the hell out forever."

Shades of the Tongass.

"So the Senate was perfectly aware of what Section 24 contained
when they voted. They had just heard it read to them. Senator Call of
Florida clearly pointed out its flaws. The charges that Section 24 was
passed in ignorance are false.

"In the House, a similar drama played itself out. Representative
Payson, Chairman of the Public Lands Committee, presented the conference report to the House, where the Clerk began to read it. The chief

objector here was Mark Dunnell, who back in 1873 had originally introduced into the House the Timber Culture Act -- which this bill repealed.''
    Sour grapes?
    ''Probably. Representative Payson patiently answered Dunnell with-
out lying about the bill's contents. The Clerk then read the whole bill,
including Section 24. Dunnell regarded himself as a champion of forestry,
but he vociferously opposed Section 24, feeling it important enough to
merit its own fully detailed law. A number of Representatives asked
questions, mostly about details that might affect their constituencies.
Payson and conference committee member William Steele Holman answered them.

Shadows In The Misty Past

    ''Then something strange happened. Andrea came to me and said, 'I
have a hunch about Holman.' She showed me the debate. We read it
together. In the middle of a page, we found a fascinating exchange.
Thomas Chipman McRae of Arkansas arose and said

> I do believe, Mr. Speaker, that the power granted to the
> President by section 24 is an extraordinary and dangerous
> power to grant over the public domain, and, if I could, I would
> move to amend by striking out that section. I would cordially
> vote to strike it out, and am sorry that it is in the bill.
>   Mr. HOLMAN. What section?
>   Mr. MCRAE. Section 24. I do not believe, Mr. Speaker, in
> giving to any officer, either the head of a Department or the
> President, power to withdraw from settlement at will any part
> of the public lands that are fit for agricultural purposes and not
> required for military purposes. There is no limitation upon this
> extraordinary power if the land be covered with timber.

    ''McRae continued for two more paragraphs, deeply worried about the
power granted by Section 24. Then

> Mr. HOLMAN. My friend will remember that the bill in
> regard to the withdrawal of forest land is exactly the same as
> the bill passed last session, after very careful consideration.

    ''What bill? Had Section 24 been passed by the House last session?
Andrea said with utter certainty, 'It was Holman.'''
    Omigod.

"Exactly. The clue we'd been looking for, the clue dozens of historians had looked for. Staring us all in the face in the pages of the Congressional Record for nearly a hundred years.

"We tore open the *Congressional Record* for the 50th Congress, 1888, turned to the index, and found H.R. 7901, 'A bill to secure to actual settlers the public lands adapted to agriculture, to protect the forests on the public domain, and for other purposes.'

"We turned to the text. The bill was introduced February 29, 1888, by William Steele Holman, Democrat from Indiana, *Chairman of the Public Lands Committee*! The Democrats ruled the House in 1888 and a Democrat therefore chaired every committee, unlike the Republican-dominated 51st Congress which relegated Holman to ranking minority member of the House Public Lands Committee in 1891, and therefore to lowest man on the totem pole of the famous conference committee.

"Almost shaking, I ran my fingers down the pages. Section 8. There it was.

> Sec. 8. That the President of the United States may from time to time set apart and reserve, in any State or Territory having public lands bearing forests, any part of the public lands designated in this act as timber lands, or any lands wholly or in part covered with timber or undergrowth, whether of commercial value or not, as public reservations, on which the trees and undergrowth shall be protected from waste or injury, under the charge of the Secretary of the Interior; and the President shall, by public proclamation, declare the establishment of such reservations and the limits thereof, and may employ such portion of the military forces as may be necessary or practicable in protecting such or any other reservations, or any other public timber land from waste or injury; and all the provisions of this act, or of any law touching the public domain which relates to timber lands, shall be subordinate to the provisions of this section.

"This is the original model for Section 24, but here it stands in its entirety. There is no question about it. There were plenty of forest reserve bills introduced in both the 50th and 51st Congresses, but none contained language even close to that of Section 24. Its similarity to Section 8 is too precise to be coincidence. And Section 8's grammar is correct.

Light The Lights

"Section 8 immediately answers several questions, the most obvious being why Section 24 is grammatically incorrect. Someone in the 1891 conference committee cloned Section 24 word for word from the template of Section 8 -- but purged the clause which referred to 'designated timberlands' because the 1891 act made no such designation. A splicing phrase had to be added, which was evidently done under pressure of time, because no one seems to have noticed that the splice added the innocent-sounding word 'in' at just the wrong place. Here is the 1888 prototype with the extracted words of the 1891 paraphrase shown in boldface type and the added splicing phrase shown in italics within brackets, i.e., the boldface and italics are Section 24.

> Sec. 8. **That the President of the United States may from time to time set apart and reserve, in any State or Territory having public lands bearing forests**, [*in*] **any part of the public lands** designated in this act as timber lands, or any lands **wholly or in part covered with timber or undergrowth, whether of commercial value or not, as public reservations**, on which the trees and undergrowth shall be protected from waste or injury, under the charge of the Secretary of the Interior; **and the President shall, by public proclamation, declare the establishment of such reservations and the limits thereof** [.], and may employ such portion of the military forces as may be necessary... [et cetera]

"At least now we know the paradigm for Section 24. And we're sure that the conference committee knew it too. We see that they deliberately eliminated the power to administer the forest reserves, not wishing to entrust them to the Secretary of the Interior for some reason, and also deliberately eliminated the power to allocate military appropriations to protect the reserves with troops."

It's puzzling that the model for Section 24 contained administrative and appropriations provisions yet Section 24 itself did not.

"We'll soon see why. The last portion of Section 8 was omitted from Section 24 because it was clearly inappropriate to the 1891 bill. Astoundingly enough, Holman's 1888 bill was accompanied by a full report from the Committee on Public Lands explaining exactly why Section 8 said what it said. Here are significant excerpts:

> It is generally understood that the timber lands are being rapidly exhausted. The sale of those lands on the Pacific coast

at $2.50 per acre, in Alabama...and elsewhere, at $1.25 per acre...indicates clearly enough how rapidly these lands will go into private hands and perhaps, in spite of public vigilance [sic], into large holdings. Public attention has been aroused on this subject. It is, in the opinion of your committee, time that a stop should be put to the destruction of our forests. The influence of these forests on the mountain slopes and at the heads of our great rivers in regulating the regular flow of the waters and preventing devastating floods, as well as their influence on climates, temperature, and the public health, are well known. The experience of older nations than ours and the result of our own experience in recent years surely suggest the commanding importance of this subject....

One of the most radical changes proposed in the existing laws is in regard to timber lands. The bill provides "that lands chiefly valuable for timber of commercial value, as sawed or hewed timber, shall be classified as timber land;" that the land shall not be sold, but the timber on the land in legal subdivisions of 40 acres shall be appraised and sold on sealed proposals to the highest bidder, and shall be removed from the land within five years from the date of sale....

Your committee are satisfied by their investigations that high public interest will be subserved by only allowing the sale of timber on lands when the timber is of commercial value. This bill does not specially provide that the land after the timber is removed, if valuable for agriculture, shall be subject to homestead entry, for the reason that it is not clear what should be the policy of the Government in that respect, while the land may be subject to be embraced in a public reservation of timber land. If not so embraced, in the opinion of some members of the committee it should be subject to homestead entry....

As examination of the reports of the successive Secretaries of the Interior and Commissioners of the General Land office for years past confirm the fact that our public lands, instead of being carefully husbanded for the high purpose of securing homes for our landless people and enlarging the number of our freeholders, are being steadily and rapidly absorbed under the present laws into great private possessions, to be held for speculation or permanent landed estates, thus defeating the spirit and purpose of the homestead law; and your committee submit that the history of our land system fully establishes the fact that (together with the excessive grants of public lands made by Congress) the pre-emption law, timber-culture law,

the desert land law, and the unfortunate commutation clause of
the homestead law are chargeable with this fraudulent misap-
propriation of this public wealth....

It seems proper here to remark that in the preparation of
this bill the purpose of making the public lands a source of
revenue to the national Treasury has been wholly ignored as to
lands that are available or can be made available *in securing
homes for our people, so that only mineral lands, timber lands,
town sites, and reserved lands made especially valuable by the
improvements of surrounding lands and forest reserves are to
be exempt from the homestead principle.* [Italics in the origi-
nal] ... The increase therefore of the number of homesteads in
the disposal of the public lands is the leading object of this bill.
The committee submit that the bill, in its purpose, general
scope, and in its details, is essentially a homestead measure,
and carefully guards against any form of monopoly of this the
most valuable of the public wealth....

"That is the legislative intent of Section 24. The documentation
wasn't lost. We were simply looking for it in the wrong place. But there
is a good reason it appeared to be lost: Holman's 1888 bill passed the
House but died in the Senate. Bills that die tend to vanish from history.

"And that's exactly what happened. When the 50th Congress ad-
journed, H.R. 7901 expired on a Senate Public Lands Committee table. So
all the extensive documentation for the reasons behind Section 8, later to
become Section 24, fell into obscurity, unused. But now we can see that
Noble and Fernow and the American Forestry Association had little if
anything to do with either Section 8 or Section 24. Fernow drafted a
comprehensive forestry bill himself in 1888, but he dealt with the Senate
where Senator Eugene Hale of Maine introduced it, and its forest reserve
language and provisions are significantly different from the Holman
committee's: Fernow's bill authorized military protection, but also proposed a new bureau of forestry in the interior department, which was not
part of the Holman committee proposal. Numerous notables supported
Fernow's bill, and the American Forestry Association memorialized Congress on its behalf, but it was tabled in committee in the Senate. It went to
the House, but Holman's committee used it as a reference at most, because
there is no evidence it was used at all in constructing the committee's
overall land reform bill. Fernow's friend Bowers may have been more
influential because the House of Representatives in 1888 requested a
report he had written for the interior department the year before, "Plan for
the Management and Disposition of Public Timber Lands." However, the

Bowers plan, like Fernow's bill, called for a new bureau of forestry in the department of the interior, which the Holman committee rejected in favor of military control. Secretaries of the Interior before Noble, Carl Schurz for example, and General Land Office reports of land fraud, had more obvious influence in shaping the Holman bill overall, but the language of its Section 8 and the later Section 24 can only be traced to Holman.

"Even at that, the House Public Lands Committee acted in 1888 because of so many influences that no single one can be accurately characterized as *the* major influence: committee members received homesteader complaints about too-small plots in arid lands, cattlemens' complaints about homesteaders, moralists' complaints about dummy entrymen and monopolies, letters from preservationists, memorials from the American Forestry Association and pressure from other personalities on the committee."

But the *purpose*, we can see the purpose now.

"Yes we can. The forest reserves had no original *primary* purpose, but a mixed one not too different from today's 'multiple use' principle. Forest reserves were intended to specifically preserve watersheds and attract rain -- as silly as that sounds -- to provide for controlled timber cutting within reserves, to prevent fraud, monopoly, speculation and the buildup of private landed estates, and to generally intersperse settled areas with non-settled timberlands where nothing but commercial quality trees could be cut under government control. The original forest reserves were intended for both preservation and use.

"Had we know that fact, had we known the legislative intent of the original forest reserves, had we known that Gifford Pinchot's 1905 policy that 'Forest reserves are for the purpose of preserving a perpetual supply of timber for home industries, preventing destruction of the forest cover which regulates the flow of streams, and protecting local residents from unfair competition in the use of forest and range' was virtually identical to the original legislative intent, modern court cases such as the 1973 Monongahela lawsuit *Izaak Walton League v. Butz* would likely have had an outcome more favorable to timber harvest. We would have known that the Forest Service's long traditional practice was right on target with the actual intent behind the forest reserves.

"The report bears the signature of William Steele Holman, Chairman, Public Lands Committee, House of Representatives, United States Congress. So does H.R. 7901.

"Although we cannot say for certain that Holman *wrote* the language of Section 8 and Section 24 (he probably did, as we shall see), we can

certify that he is *legally responsible* for that language as committee
chairman and signator. That makes him the father of the forest reserves.
And the grandfather of the national forests. Andrea was right.

"Ironically, there's probably not a forester alive today who ever heard
of William Steele Holman. The Forest Service has raised no monument in
memory of him because they have no memory of him. Sadly, Holman
died in 1897 without realizing what he had set in motion. Not surprisingly, the preservationists ran away with his law ignorant of whence it
came or what it was for and used it for their own narrow park expansion
purposes."

Is that too different from what is happening today in the Tongass?

Grandfather of the National Forests

"Who was William Steele Holman? He was a pioneer lawyer born
on a farm near Aurora, Indiana, September 6, 1822, who lived to serve
more terms in Congress than anyone else had at the time. He became a
classic Jeffersonian Democrat of unquestioned integrity, embodying the
ideals of a nation of frugal yeoman farmers and mistrusting every kind of
intemperance or concentration of power, political or economic. His entire
life was without scandal of any sort and he remained ever a stickler for the
proprieties. He was self-effacing and personally modest. Were it not for a
dedicated and capable biographer's scholarship in the 1940s we would
know almost nothing of him today.

"Early in his career as Democratic Representative from Indiana Holman stood one day on the House floor listening to a measure he found
unacceptable and uttered the cryptic but lawyerly response, 'Mr. Speaker,
I object.' It became his trademark. Whatever Holman didn't like met with
'Mr. Speaker, I object.' Newspaper reporters tagged him 'The Great
Objector' and efficient *Congressional Record* printers paid him the unin-
tended compliment of stereotyping the line:

Mr. HOLMAN. Mr. Speaker, I object.

"As a member of the Appropriations Committee he slashed funding
for every imaginable project, characterizing government spending as a
'carnival of luxury and extravagance.' His zeal for thrift became legendary and he gained the title 'Watch-dog of the Treasury.' Committee
chairman and future president James A. Garfield had to deal with Holman
regularly, good-naturedly explaining the merits of an appropriation or
cajoling him to remove an objection. Frequently to avoid delay, Garfield

accepted Holman's suggestions on small points.

"In 1885 Holman was appointed chairman of a congressional committee to investigate the expenditure of appropriations for Indian Schools and for Yellowstone National Park. The inquiry would take three and a half months, out to the Pacific coast by the northern route and return through Arizona by way of the southern. The investigators included Joseph G. Cannon of Illinois and other high ranking members of Congress.

"Holman exasperated the committee by forcing them to practice a rigid economy on the entire trip. He would honor requisitions for Pullman berths only at night, making the members ride coach by day or pay their own Pullman fares. Holman refused to use a sleeper at all, sitting up all night while his colleagues rode in comfort. He lectured committeemen that he and his wife had traveled in an ordinary coach all the way from Indiana to California and back. At hotels he demanded rooms without bath, but the committee rebelled and made him approve rooms with baths. The Watch-dog of the Treasury barked at every requisition."

He was what might be termed today a 'cheap S.O.B.'

"Irreverent, but true. He saw Yellowstone first hand, visited many homestead settlers and traversed public lands that would one day encompass more than fifty national forests. He was well aware of the many measures that had been introduced to Congress proposing forest reserves and felt personal sympathy for such protection. His biographer, Israel George Blake, described Holman as 'a botanist of no mean ability.' He also noted that, 'Holman saw to it that his farm contained many beautiful flower gardens filled with unusual plants. He transplanted trees from various historic spots which formed a sort of arboreal avenue of history. It is said that when one or another of these old friends of the forest was marked for the axe he would be heard to say in as startling tones as he ever addressed to the Speaker of the House, "I object." ' "

"When three years after his investigative trip West Holman led his Public Lands Committee in writing H.R. 7901, it is obvious that if he was not sole author of the Section 8 forest reserve clause he concurred with it completely."

Why do you say that?

"As chairman of the committee he would have had the power to force its alteration or removal.

"Holman the Jeffersonian Democrat was fanatically against land monopoly of any kind. A speech he gave on the floor of the House in 1870 denouncing railroad grants and other 'land monopolies' and sympathizing with 'the landless and laboring people' was reprinted in booklet form and widely circulated. He believed that the whole tendency of the government since the Civil War had been to foster the growth of gigantic businesses and 'overgrown estates,' and that these corporations now considered themselves responsible to no one, not even to Congress itself. Holman could not tolerate that idea and did everything he could to prevent public land monopoly and help the actual settler.

"Knowing this about the man who is legally responsible for the language of Section 24, we can speculate more intelligently on how it actually came to be added to the 1891 bill to repeal the timber-culture act.

Holman Alone

"First, there is no reason to believe that anyone but Holman inserted the rider. No one on the Senate side of the conference committee had any vested interest in the language of H.R. 7901, certainly not enough to copy it almost verbatim: Remember, after H.R. 7901 passed the House in the 50th Congress it died in the Senate Public Lands Committee. The Senate conferees of the 51st Congress probably knew Section 8's forest reserve language, but clearly held it in no special regard. The other House conferees were Republicans who had no particular interest in forest reserves.

"Second, Holman came to the conference committee as the sole House Democrat and a dethroned one at that. Republican Lewis Edwin Payson of Illinois had replaced Holman as House Public Lands Committee chairman and John Alfred Pickler of South Dakota was second ranking majority member. These party relationships are important. The Republicans in the 51st Congress held only a slender majority of seven votes in the House. They knew their control was precarious, and that a powerful Democratic minority could easily block any Republican legislation. So Speaker Thomas B. Reed promulgated new rules that allowed the chair to entertain no motions whose purpose would be to block legislation. Holman, 'Watch-dog of the Treasury,' seethed with resentment, censuring the Republicans as a 'petty oligarchy.' He entered the conference committee meeting in no fine mood.

"Third, Holman saw that the land law revisions contained in the 1891 bill were markedly inferior to the bill he had introduced during the previous session of Congress. He undoubtedly felt the need to improve it.

"Fourth, the 1891 session of the 51st Congress was a short one, scheduled to adjourn March 3. If the Republicans wanted their land law revision enacted, they had to move fast. Holman was the only real roadblock. Senate Democrat Walthall of Mississippi was not detectably concerned over the Western lands, as his voluminous correspondence shows.

"Fifth, once the major disagreements were cleared up on the main body of the bill -- those first 23 sections nobody remembers today -- Holman must have insisted on having some say in shaping the new law. He probably seized upon the forest reserve clause of his beloved H.R. 7901 because it thwarted the Republican tendency to favor corporate capitalists -- and it was sufficiently technical and obscure that the other conferees would scarcely risk the whole bill just to keep Holman from adding a pet provision, especially one that had already passed the House in an earlier version.

"So Holman, during the closing moments of the conference committee meeting, pulled out his battered copy of H.R. 7901, opened it to Section 8, eliminated the *administration* and *appropriations* provisions -- Watch-dog of the Treasury or cheap S.O.B., take your pick -- and also removed the inapplicable reference to designated timberlands, hurriedly patching up the language as best he could. Nobody in the conference cared a whit about Section 24 anyway, so nobody checked the grammar. Just as James A. Garfield had done earlier, the conference committee gave in to Holman on a small point to avoid delay.

"Holman the stickler for protocol knew his amendment was illegal -- there was clearly no time during this short session for the bill to go back to the originating committees. He probably obtained assurances that his amendment would be read aloud at the floor vote so both chambers would know its content, stressing Section 24's earlier passage in the House.

Editor Ron Arnold

"So Plumb had the amended bill read to the Senate and said it contained nothing they hadn't passed before -- he probably confused the *House* passage of Section 8 in 1888 with the new 1891 Section 24. He was suffering terrible headaches and had been diagnosed with aphasia. He died of a stroke before the year was out.

"Payson had the amended bill read to the House and Holman said it contained nothing they hadn't passed before, which was true.

"Both houses passed the bill, President Harrison signed it into law, Hague read about it in a newspaper and told Noble, Yellowstone National Park was expanded, *Forest and Stream* magazine spread the Noble taffy tale, Fernow repeated it to historian John Ise, every historian since has repeated the myth to the next generation of historians, the forest reserves perplexed everyone so badly that administrators and legislators made up the rules as they went, Congress finally passed an administration and appropriation measure for the forest reserves in 1897, the forest reserves went to the Forest Service in 1905, their name was changed to national forests in 1907 and the rest, as they say, is history."

But it pays to check out what *really* happened in history.

THE FOREST SERVICE

• •

An old miner who spoke in epigrams once told us that Time Changes Everything. A particular newsreel from the 1930s concluded each weekly episode in stentorian voice: Time Marches On! A graffito documented in a Seattle tavern restroom informs us: Time is Mother Nature's way of keeping everything from happening at once. And we all know the French motto: The more things change, the more they stay the same. Time has played all these tricks on the Forest Service.

We don't present this chapter out of boundless affection for the Forest Service. We have to talk about it because the Forest Service is the air that the people of the Tongass breathe. It is landlord over all, except for a few towns and except for Native corporation timberlands. And the Forest Service is people, too, remember -- people of the Tongass.

The bureaucracy that began in William Steele Holman's truncated forest reserve rider of 1891 -- the bureaucracy that hobbled along with the weak powers of the 1897 Forest Reserve Administration Act (The "Organic Act") until the Forest Service was created in 1905 -- that bureaucracy still struggles today with the tensions bequeathed to it by Holman's rediscovered House Public Lands Committee Report of 1888: Its lands are meant for both preservation and use.

Although the doctrine of blending preservation and use that we now call "multiple use" was not enacted into law until 1960, the first Chief of the Forest Service, Gifford Pinchot, discussed the idea in 1906 -- and he was certainly unaware that the embryonic concept had been embedded in the legislative intent behind the first forest reserves. Pinchot realized that his fledgling Forest Service had been born with a permanent case of schizophrenia: He wrote both protection and use measures into the first Forest Service "Use Book" of regulations for his foresters to enforce.

Every subsequent Chief has realized the schizophrenic position of the agency in one way or another. Outside the Forest Service, informed observers for more than eighty years have seen the need to keep some forest lands in their natural state and to use others for the commodity needs of civilization. Somewhere along the trail to the present the dialectic struggle between preservation and use became institutionalized and grew into a Forest Service way of life. But not until our generation did a social force emerge with the intent to eliminate use and dictate nothing but preservation: the environmental movement.

A man who has seen most of this change in the Forest Service in Alaska is John Sandor. He served as regional forester in Juneau from 1976 to his retirement in 1984. His experience is doubly significant for us because his early Forest Service career brought him to Alaska from 1953 to 1962. He earned his undergraduate degree in forestry from Washington State University and his master's degree in public administration on a conservation fellowship at Harvard. He helped form the Alaska chapter of the Society of American Foresters and served on the national council of the Society. He was the charter chair of the natural resources and environmental administration section of the American Society for Public Administration. He's a walking compendium of comparative forest administration.

A Veteran's Ruminations

Come with us to John Sandor's home on Douglas Island, overlooking Gastineau Channel and downtown Juneau across the water. He'll fix you a cup of coffee or tea if you like.

John, when you returned to Alaska in 1976, what changes did you see from the 1950s?

"Well, you recall that during the 1950s the Forest Service developed the long term sale agreement first with Ketchikan Pulp Company and later with the Alaska Lumber and Pulp Company at Sitka, which is now called Alaska Pulp Corporation. We had very strong Territory of Alaska and local community support. Prior to these fifty-year timber sale contracts, timber harvesting on the Tongass was very limited. The investments and associated economic benefits of the new pulp mills were widely hailed as being beneficial to the communities and people of Southeast Alaska. By 1976, organized interest groups had formed in opposition to timber harvesting generally, and in opposition to the long-term timber sales specifically.

"Another interesting contrast was the reaction to a 1954 Forest Service proposal to designate Tracy Arm - Ford's Terror as a Wilderness Area -- ten years before the Wilderness Act was passed. The opposition and lack of enthusiasm for this proposal was so great it precluded any Wilderness classification. The secretary of agriculture nonetheless went ahead on

Ron Arnold photo

Former regional forester John Sandor interviewed at his Juneau home by authors Jackie DuRette (left) and K.A. Soderberg

the Forest Service's recommendation and established a 283,000 acre Tracy Arm - Ford's Terror Scenic Area.

"However, in 1976 Congress passed the National Forest Management Act, or NFMA, and mandated that every national forest must develop an integrated Land Management Plan for all resources under the guidance of an interdisciplinary team, or IDT. When the Tongass Land Management Plan, or TLMP, was developed from 1976 to '79, our IDT recommended the designation of 3.48 million Tongass acres as Wilderness.

"When Congress enacted the Alaska National Interest Lands Conservation Act of 1980, or ANILCA, they designated 5.4 million acres of the Tongass as Wilderness. ANILCA also reduced the timber harvest on the Tongass, which had previously averaged 520 million board feet per year, down to an average of 450 million board feet annually.

"Thus the strong support of a pulp industry and opposition to Wilderness designations in the 1950s stood in sharp contrast to interest group and political opposition to the pulp industry and support for Wilderness in the late 1970s."

That's a fascinating change, and we'd like to hear more about it. But let us butt in here with a note on speaking in abbreviations: The National Forest Management Act's nickname, NFMA, is pronounced "NAFMA" by some and simply the letters "N.F.M.A." by others. Loggers call TLMP "Tee-Lump," but that offends some Forest Service officials. ANILCA is pronounced "Uh-NIL-kuh" by almost everybody. Better get used to federal alphabet soup -- TLMP and NFMA and IDTs and ANILCA are only the beginning. Wait'll we get to NEPA with its EAs and EISs and the RPA and.... Excuse us, we're getting carried away. Go on, John. Were you surprised by these political changes?

"Not by the increasing support for Wilderness designations. I'd seen it in other parts of the nation. But I was surprised at the strong opposition to timber harvesting on the Tongass based on the false perception that most of the Tongass was planned for timber harvest and that such harvests were destructive of other forest values."

Explain that.

"Well, although these perceptions were false, a highly organized campaign of misinformation was leading people to believe they were true. This campaign has been so effective that many people are surprised to learn that only 10 percent of the Tongass National Forest is planned for timber harvest over the 100 year rotation period; that clearcut areas average less than 100 acres in size; and that special measures protect wildlife, fisheries, recreation and other values."

And what about the political fallout of these false perceptions?

"The current proposals to enact legislation in Congress cancelling the Tongass Timber Supply Fund and abrogating the long term contracts are a mistake. They would preempt the public's and the communities' role in revising the Tongass Land Management Plan, a revision process required by the NFMA and now well under way. A draft revised TLMP is scheduled for release by December of 1989. Local meetings in Southeast Alaska communities have already been held to identify issues. It's important to preserve the integrity of the TLMP revision process. It would be an especially serious mistake to enact current legislative proposals without public hearings in the affected local communities of Southeast Alaska."

And we notice there are no such local hearings scheduled. John, we appreciate your candor. But you've discussed a lot of things about the Forest Service that invite further unfolding. And our main interest, of course, is to get as quickly as we can to showing how the forest industry actually works. Actually, we don't do anything in the woods before the Forest Service figures out what we can do legally. We don't send out the logging trucks. We don't send out the chainsaw crews. We don't send out the road construction crews. We don't sign a logging or road-building contract. We don't even bid on a job. Not until the Forest Service has spent millions of dollars and thousands of hours drawing up plans that comply with more than a dozen ultra-complex environmental laws. We want you to know about both the Forest Service and the forest industry. Perhaps we can do both by tracking the path of a timber sale through the Tongass bureaucracy.

Getting Ready to Get Ready

Let's go across the Douglas Island bridge to the Juneau Ranger District office out by the airport and talk to Don Lyon. He's a man we love to grouse about. He's the Forest Service's Interdisciplinary Team Leader who's responsible for the Tongass Land Management Plan revision -- the creation of TLMP II.

TLMP I was the Master plan with a capital M, and TLPM II will be the same. It tells us industry folk everything we can and can't do on the Tongass. It tells us where we can log and where we can't. It tells us how we can log and how we can't. It tells us how to take care of fish streams and wildlife habitat and recreation areas and a dozen other things. You don't know complicated until you've seen a Forest Plan like TLMP.

Don, tell us a little about TLMP.

"Well, the Forest Service has done planning of one kind or another since it was created by Congress in 1905, but modern highly detailed integrated Forest Plans like TMLP were mandated, as John noted, by the National Forest Management Act of 1976 or NFMA.

"The Tongass was the first of all the 156 national forests to complete its forest plan, TLMP, in 1979. Each forest's plan must be revised at least every fifteen years according to NFMA, but the Forest Service is targeting for every ten so we can respond to changing public attitudes. We're scheduled to release our draft revision, TMLP II, in December of 1989. Since the Tongass turned out the nation's first forest plan, it will also turn out the nation's first revised forest plan."

Don, that's what we in the forest and mining industry want to see before Congress goes off half-cocked with these Wilderness Society bills introduced by Rep. Mrazek and others. We want to see the revision draft first so Congress can act on information and not on misleading emotionalism from the environmentalists.

"Information is what you're going to get. The planning team I've led here for the past couple of years is made up of many specialists working together. This Interdisciplinary Team approach is a key feature of today's Forest Service planning. It avoids emphasizing one resource over others. The Tongass IDT has about seventeen members: a team leader -- that's me; a planning analyst, an economist, a social scientist/public affairs specialist, a recreation planner, a landscape architect, an archaeologist, a wildlife biologist, a fish biologist, a timber resource planner, a soils and water specialist, a minerals specialist, a lands specialist, a transportation planner, a fire/insect/disease specialist, a database manager, a writer-editor, an administrative assistant -- and don't forget the clerical support.''

Have you ever done this kind of thing before, Don?

''Yes, I was team leader on another national forest plan, the Wenatchee, down in Washington State. One of the things I learned there is that as one forest's plan is developed it becomes the guideline for the next forest's plan. The public criticism each plan gets causes the next plan to be a little bit better. So the TLMP revision will not only be the first forest plan revision, it should also benefit from all we have learned from previous plans -- and may set a standard for improving future plans.''

Tell us about the public criticism.

''We're required by NFMA to actively solicit public involvement in the planning process. The Tongass has a few unique problems in getting that public involvement: What other national forest has so many small fishing and logging communities living right in the forest? And when we go there to get comments or hold hearings, we don't get in the car and drive. We've got to get in an airplane or on a boat. So just to get out and visit with our clientele is a little tougher job.

Ron Arnold photo

Don Lyon, TLMP Revision Interdisciplinary team leader

"But we did it, just as John Sandor said. We did the public scoping for the TLMP revision during November 1987 through February of 1988. We went to every community in Southeast Alaska. There's very few people in the Tongass that can honestly claim they don't know what we're doing. We put some 30,000 copies of our public response newsletter, the 'Tongass Review,' in most newspapers in Southeast Alaska.

"We've got three distinct publics we're talking to. First we've got the people in these little comunities that live right in the national forest -- not adjacent to, but actually *in*, so anything we do influences their life. We've got the more urban people in southeast Alaska that are strongly concerned about what we're doing. And then we've got the rest of Alaska and the Lower United States."

You have to solicit comment from Down South for the Tongass?

"Yes. You're aware of the national interest in Alaska. That's why we're talking. National magazines and east coast papers routinely carry stories on what's happening in the Tongass. There's an organization in Washington D.C. called the Friends of the Tongass, organized by the American Forestry Association. We provide them information and they distribute it to all the interest groups back in the D.C. area. How many national forests have a special organization interested in them 3,000 miles away? The people of all the United States care what happens here on the Tongass."

We know. Sometimes we feel like we're living our whole lives under a microscope. But go on with the TLMP.

"The revision has to be performed through a series of ten steps. First we identify public issues, management concerns and resource opportunities. The revised plan is supposed to be a set of management actions which help solve present or anticipated problems on the Tongass. Public comment gives us the issues, and there's quite a list of them: Visual issues, recreation issues, wilderness issues, unique areas issues, fish and wildlife issues, subsistence issues, human and community development issues, timber issues, mineral/energy resource issues, land use/ownership issues, transportation/utility corridor issues and others. But management concerns and opportunities are identified by Forest Service and other agency people."

What kind of comments did you get?

"Well, take visual issues. Deirdre Buschman, our landscape architect at the Supervisor's Office in Petersburg, reviewed all the comments about visuals on the Tongass. She found three general positions: 1) Maintain all forest lands in a pristine visual condition; 2) Timber industry needs should be a priority over the visual resources and should not be a concern; and 3) Minimize visual impact while allowing some timber harvest to occur."

What about Wilderness?

"Chuck McConnell, recreation planner on the Interdisciplinary Team in Juneau, reviewed the Wilderness comments. He found two basic positions: Some people feel additional areas should receive Wilderness classification primarily to protect them from timber harvest. Many, on the other hand, believe there is enough Wilderness but that a better balance between the various resources should be achieved."

Was this anti-timber, pro-timber polarization typical in all the issues?

"Yes, on nearly every issue."

Not surprising. What do you do after getting this public comment?

"Second, we develop planning criteria -- set the ground rules, so to speak. We develop criteria from a lot of sources: existing laws, Executive orders, regulations, agency policy, the Alaska Regional Guide, plans from state and local governments and Native corporations, among others.

"Third, we collect resource information. The Interdisciplinary Team does most of that, working with every unit on the Tongass, many people. We've been working on information collection for more than two years. We gather information on all forest resources -- vegetation, soil and water, fish and wildlife, recreation, and timber."

We notice timber is last on that list.

"The order is not significant. We also gather cultural and social information. We look for how forest resources respond to management and interact with each other. We collect data on the cost of doing business and the value of forest outputs to individuals and the surrounding economy.

Electrons In The Mist

"All this information will be incorporated into a Geographic Information System or GIS. GIS is our high-tech automated resource database and mapping system. It's state of the art. In fact, we're developing the state of the art. It gives us extremely fine detail and that gives us the best ability to determine what our forest's capabilities are. Look here at this map."

I recognize that map. It's Craig, on Prince of Wales Island. DuRette Construction has built roads in this area.

"Right, Jackie. GIS uses standard U.S. Geological Survey quadrangle maps, 2 inches to the mile. It takes more than 220 maps this size to cover the Tongass."

What are all these little shapes?

"This is the soils map. This is the basic soils data based on a recent inventory. You can see that every little enclosed shape, or polygon, as we call them, is labelled with a soil-type number. There's three or four hundred different kinds of soils on the Tongass. Each polygon represents some feature of the geology and soils and landforms of this quadrangle."

Good grief. Such incredible detail. You've done this with the whole Tongass? How did you do it?

"These maps are based on aerial photography, on-the-ground surveys, even remote sensing -- satellite photos. After the information was verified, they were drawn first on paper, and then digitized, electronically put into the computer by a scanner and a mouse. And this is only the basic layer, essentially soils. All right, what's the next resource?

In the Tongass? The trees.

"Right, the vegetation. This next sheet is in green ink, again the same Craig quad, and this is the vegetation, whether it's spruce or hemlock or alder or muskeg, or meadows or whatever. It's not only the species, but when you get into the timber, it'll tell you the volume class, what size stands, whether it's a fresh clearcut, or a seedling/sapling stand or thrifty second growth stand or an old-growth stand."

That's fantastic.

"That's computers for you. Here's the next sheet. You'll be particularly interested in this one. What you see here in green is suitable timberlands -- these are the lands that could, from a biological standpoint, produce wood crops for ever and ever. The suitablity criteria were developed using input from all interest groups, including environmental organizations. The red shows where we've already harvested the timber. We now can identify in map format what lands are suitable and what are unsuitable for timber harvest."

There's so much suitable land. More than we thought.

"You noticed. Which brings us to the real issues we have on the Tongass. To me, and this is my perspective only, this is not the official stance of the Tongass National Forest, you really have only one big issue: Do you develop or don't you develop? And where? And when I talk about development, I'm talking about timber harvest, road building, mining. Those are the big developers. And that's the question before us. And we have to answer it.

"That one real issue establishes where the battleground is. We talk about how large the Tongass is -- 16.78 million acres. It *is* a big forest.

But the Tongass battleground is a much smaller piece of ground than the whole Tongass.

"Now in TLMP I, we have 1.75 million acres scheduled for harvest. TLMP II may schedule a different number. Or it may schedule that same number.

"But the battleground is not the 1.75 million acres now scheduled for harvest in TLMP I. It's the plus-or-minus 3 million acres of what we call 'tentatively suitable lands.' The tentatively suitable lands are the lands that are biologically capable of producing timber in perpetuity, physically, biologically capable of producing forest products for ever and ever. I say 'plus-or-minus 3 million' because we're in the process of determining that right now. We're building the computer maps, but we haven't made the final run to know exactly what that figure is. That's where the battle's going to take place, the battle of development versus non-development.

"Where does that tentatively suitable timber show up? Predominatly along the shorelines. But what else takes place there? That's where the prime wildlife habitat is. That's where the scenic visuals are. The battleground isn't 16.78 million acres. And it isn't 1.7 million acres. The battleground is roughly 3 million acres."

That's almost twice the land in our current harvest schedule. And it's capable of producing timber forever?

"Yes. Forever. But let's get back to our GIS maps. One more step. Again the same quad. And this is the composite map that will go into FORPLAN, as our forest planning computer model is called."

This map has little code numbers in each -- what was it, polygon?

"Yes. On this composite planning map each polygon represents what we call an Analysis Area. Each number is an Analysis Area identifier. Each Analysis Area represents a homogenous unique piece of land out there on the ground. An Analysis Area is typically very small, ranging from 500 to 1,200 acres each. There are 3,300 of them on this one little quad map in the Craig area. And any given Analysis Area will react to management the same way every time."

Look at all these different kinds of maps! Soils, timber, streams, wildlife habitat....

"And every acre on the Tongass will be covered by each one of these different kinds of maps. With a few simple commands we can ask the computer to go into any level of detail or any level of information. Here, for example, from this map we can judge timber operability, how the land can be harvested, whether by tractor or standard cable or long span cable, whether the access is limited or if it's an isolated patch. Another level we can ask the computer for is what its access is, whether there are existing roads, is the terrain suitable for additional roads, and so on. And whether it's above or below 800 feet. Here on this map level is the coniferous vegetation and whether you have high, medium or low productivity. On this level is non-forest lands, water, rock-and-ice, unsuitable lands.

"Another level is critical fish spawning streams, another is wildlife habitat. Another is whether it's in a long term contract or out of a contract. Whether it's up in the Yakutat area or down on Revillagigedo Island. Whether it's in a Wilderness. Just ask the computer for whatever level of information you want to know and it will tell you, based on firm on-the-ground and/or aerial mapping information. The value of the computer is when you have to lay one resource over another or over several others, you get the same answer every time. You can calculate new combinations of resource use overnight as opposed to taking months by earlier methods."

Think of the work that must have gone into this!

"Two years so far. Probably as much as 85 to 95 percent of the information we're using to build TLMP II is new. Our timber yield tables, our economic tables will be new, our mapping for *all* resources will be new. Nothing like this has ever existed before on the Tongass."

A forest in a computer.

"Those have existed for many years. But not at this level of detail and not covering so many different resources. And this is just a tool. Computers can't make decisions. So our Step 4 is analyzing the management situation based on all this information. We use the computerized information to determine the Tongass National Forest's ability to supply goods and services.

"And then the fifth step is formulating alternatives. We'll consider a number of things that could be done with the Tongass. As a minimum, we'll outline the environmental, economic, and social consequences resulting from long-term implementation of each alternative.

"The next step is estimating the effects of each alternative. This will provide the decision maker with a sound basis for comparing alternatives.

"Then we'll evaluate the alternatives, comparing them to determine how well it satisfies the issues identified by the public in the first step. This will provide the three Tongass Forest Supervisors a basis for recommending a preferred alternative to the Regional Forester. The preferred alternative identified in the Draft Environmental Impact Statement will have been selected and approved by the Regional Forester.

"In Step 8 we'll comply with the National Environmental Policy Act of 1969, or NEPA. We'll distribute a draft environmental impact statement (EIS) and the draft revised Tongass Forest Plan for public review and comment.

"In Step 9, public comments will be incorporated and a final EIS and final Forest Plan will be approved by the Regional Forester.

"In Step 10 we'll monitor and evaluate to see how well the revised plan is working, and determine if changes are needed."

Culture Of Duty

Uh, you'd better explain about your regional forester and the three forest supervisors, Don. I don't think many of our readers understand your bureaucracy.

"It's time for you to go talk to Mike."

Down at the Death Star?

"Are they still calling the Federal Building that?"

Mike is Michael A. Barton, Regional Forester. Mike is a genial man and welcomes us to his corner office on the fifth floor of the Federal Building. Okay, Mike, you know the question.

"Let's start with the basics: Who does what in the Forest Service? You have to understand that the Forest Service is part of the federal bureaucracy. That means we have many levels of authority. I'm what's called the Regional Forester of the Alaska Region. The 156 national forests in the system are grouped into nine geographic regions, each with a regional forester. All nine of us report to Chief Forester Dale Robertson, who is the highest official in the Forest Service. He in turn reports to the Secretary of Agriculture who reports to the President of the United States.

"A regional forester like me usually has authority over ten or more national forests. Here I have

Ron Arnold photo

Michael A. Barton, regional forester

responsibility only for Alaska's two, the Chugach and the Tongass, but combined they're the size equivalent of a dozen or more average national forests. Each national forest is managed by a forest supervisor and divided into ranger districts run by a district ranger, who is our basic on-the-ground administrator.

"The Tongass is so large, however, that it's divided into three administrative areas, each with its own forest supervisor and staff, just as if it were three separate national forests: the Chatham Area with a supervisor's office in Sitka, the Stikine Area with its supervisor in Petersburg, and the Ketchikan Area with its supervisor in Ketchikan. Each area has a normal national forest office staff and is broken up into ranger districts just as other national forests around the country."

Thanks, Mike.

Getting Ready

The actual planning of a single timber sale is just as complicated as the overall forest planning process -- and it too is a committee job. *Interdisciplinary* is more than a buzzword with the Forest Service.

There are actually three kinds of timber sales on the Tongass National Forest: First, the 50-year long term contracts belonging to Ketchikan Pulp Company and Alaska Pulp Corporation. Ownership of that timber was vested in the respective pulp companies at the beginning of the contracts back in the 1950s. Therefore, the harvest units planned for any given year are not technically called "sales" since the pulp companies already own the cutting rights. But the pulp companies did not pay in advance for the whole 50 year supply -- they pay stumpage fees for each individual harvest area as they enter it. But they're not exempt from any environmental law. Each harvest unit on the long term contracts must jump through the same legal hoops as every other Forest Service timber sale. The long term contracts are subject to the same planning process as any other timber sale.

Then there's the 150 million board feet per year in the short term sale program. It's divided up into 80 million board feet of annual Small Business Set-Asides (obviously for small loggers only) and 70 million board feet that anybody can bid on -- faithful reader, you could bid on it yourself if you wanted to. So those are the three types of timber sales on the Tongass National Forest. They're all planned much the same.

Now let's go down to Ketchikan and find out how a timber sale is actually prepared. Joe Thompson is a Supervisory Forester in the Ketchikan Area Supervisor's Office. Tell us how you do it, Joe.

"We're going to be talking primarily about the independent timber

sales -- those 150 million board feet per year for small businesses and open
bidding. Every timber sale actually starts back at the Forest Plan level that
Don Lyon told you about. Two things happen there: The Forest Plan indicates roughly the amount of timber that's to be harvested; and it also
makes the land allocations that tell you where there's timber available for
harvest.

"The Forest Plan, even though it's highly detailed, is a policy plan,
not an action plan: It tells us what we can and can't do and what we should
be doing, but it doesn't tell us where and when we ought to harvest a
particular stand of timber. For that we have what we call the Ten Year
Action Plan, which is updated annually. Every timber sale that's actually
completed has to first get on that Ten Year Action Plan. And to get on that
Ten Year Action Plan, a timber sale has to go through an elaborate
screening procedure.

Through Many Doors Together

"To keep timber sales orderly, we have a process called the Gate
System. It's a sequence of six crucial steps or 'gates' we go through to get
from start to finish on a timber sale.

"Gate 1 is the Position Statement -- we informally call it the 'Feasibility Report' -- which results from initial reconnaissance and examination of
an area to see if there's a feasible timber sale proposal that could be
developed in a given area, like a certain watershed of a part of an island.
The Position Statement outlines our preliminary position on whether a
timber sale area ought to be added to the Ten Year Action Plan or not. We
do a great number of those Position Statements. Every year when we
update the Ten Year Plan we do Position Statements for all the new timber
sale proposals.

"Position Statements are not usually done in Juneau at the regional
level, but at the Forest level in Sitka or Petersburg or Ketchikan, and
frequently at the Ranger District level in all three areas. It's a decentral-
ized process. How the reports are actually done is relatively straightforward. Our planning team will take a quick look at a given area to see how
much timber might be available in total, what kind of other resource values
exist in the area and how long it would take to do the planning necessary to
get a timber sale at that location on line. We'll do an area logging/
transportation analysis, too.

"Then we decide which areas ought to be proposed for inclusion in the
Ten Year Action Plan -- we decide which proposed units to harvest in what
sequence and how much timber we want to harvest out of each area, the

budget and scheduling. The staff sits down and says 'No, we don't like this one,' or 'Yes, we like this one,' or 'Something else needs to be done with that one.' After an extensive weeding process the best timber sale proposal Position Statements are added to the Ten Year Action Plan.

"Once a timber sale is listed on the Ten Year Action Plan that really kicks everything off through Gate 2. From this point on you'll get better answers from our logging engineer Tom Bobbe here at the Supervisor's Office in Ketchikan. Come on over here, Tom. Tell 'em about the rest of the gates."

"From Gate 2? Okay, that's the Sale Area Design stage, but its proper name is simply 'Decision.' That's where we do the public involvement and the environmental analysis, and then develop different alternatives, come up with logging plans, and end up with a signed NEPA document, usually an 'EA' or Environmental Assessment, which is simpler, less voluminous, and less expensive than a full EIS, or Environmental Impact Statement."

We know about the expense of a full EIS, Tom. It can easily cost over a million dollars if it goes to court and has to be redone.

"Getting through Gate 2 is fairly complicated. We first put together an interdisciplinary team to do the public involvement and actual design of the sale. Normally our timber sale ID teams include a timber forester, a fisheries biologist, and a wildlife biologist, as a minimum. Then, depending on specifically what you found in the Position Statement, anywhere from three to five other specialists could be added to the team: A landscape

Forest Service photo

Sitka, location of Chatham Area headquarters, Tongass National Forest architect, a soils scientist, a recreation and visual specialist, and a transportation planner who performs an engineering function for road and bridge design. It's not a cut-and-dried number. ID teams are usually made up of those people required to address whatever resources are in the area.

"Once the ID team is assembled, they go out and involve the public to find what issues people are concerned about in the timber sale area. Then they sit down and look at how they can address the issues identified by the public and blend those with Forest Service objectives, such as harvesting a certain amount of timber out of the area.

"Next, they go on the ground with aerial photographs and topographic maps to determine how the different units and roads look on the ground. The interdiscipinary team develops different alternatives for each timber sale. Each alternative is developed to respond to the issues identified in the planning process. The ID team determines where logging roads need to be built, they establish the locations of each logging unit, looking out for soils that may slump after logging, writing down the considerations that went into each desicion, telling what they want to see on the ground as far as logging unit layout.

"They identify streams that need protecting and how to protect them. We have different management prescriptions for different classes of stream: for water quality streams, for resident fish habitat, for anadromous fisheries habitat, whether it's spawning or rearing tributaries. The prescriptions range from leaving uncut buffer zones along the streams, to selective cutting, to clearcutting up to the stream banks where it's biologically appropriate. And where logging will occur over a stream, we have various cable suspension requirements to prevent dragging logs through the stream channel.

"The ID team determines what logging techniques must be used to best protect the environment, which include the cable yarding methods known as highlead, running skyline and slackline, which are methods of pulling log from where they were felled up to the truck landing for loading and transport. And so on -- everything but the detailed layout which will come in the next gate.

"The ID team documents the logging and environmental standards, addresses the public issues and concerns, and when they get through they'll have produced a draft NEPA document, either an EIS or an EA. These display the impact of various action alternatives and are made available for public comment. The final step incorporates the public comment and Gate 2 then yields two products: A signed NEPA document from the Forest Supervisor and a Sale Implementation Plan or SIP.

"Gate 3 is called the Timber Sale Preparation Report and our activities consist of sale plan implementation. The Sale Implementation Plan is given to the next crew, the people on the ground who will physically lay out the timber sale. The plan contains all the documentation the ID team created. It identifies our resource coordination needs: You have to make sure that the people who are going to lay out the roads understand what is envisioned or required for that chunk of ground out there, whether it has soils concerns or water quality or fisheries concerns. If the plan has originated on a Ranger District, the same people who did the SIP may do the actual sale layout.

"But the bulk of our Sale Implementation Plans originate at the Forest Supervisor's Office level and get passed on to a Ranger District crew for actual layout. On the long term sales we have a core team in each Forest Supervisor's Office that do a lot of Gate 2 work. But whichever way it works out, the Gate 2 team is responsible for getting all the maps, aerial photos, and documents to the Gate 3 team in the form of the Sale Implementation Plan.

"I work mostly with the Gate 3 and later teams. We'll actually lay out the technical details of the sale on the ground and perform the timber cruise to measure how much timber the sale contains.

Those Who Go Forth Before Daylight

"Ranger District foresters and engineers work in the field and locate all the specified roads -- mainline roads or arterial roads -- and spurs to

Forest Service photo

Petersburg, location of Stikine Area headquarters, Tongass National Forest

logging units. They actually 'hang the flags,' tie the brightly colored ribbons on stakes and tree branches showing where the roads will go. They paint certain trees with an X, marking the boundaries of the cutting unit. Foresters work with the engineers on road locations, making sure they're going in the right place as far as timber is concerned.

"But roads are located for other uses as well as timber harvest: recreational and fish and wildlife management. In fact, the Ranger District's recreation, fisheries and wildlife specialist has input into the location of roads. But typically for timber sales the forester has a lot of say about where we put spurs and landings for yarding and truck-loading machinery. A landing is really just a place in the road wide enough to accommodate one standard sized yarding tower and a log loader, which are huge pieces of equipment.

"The forester and engineer do all this by walking the ground, and in the rain forest that can be strenuous indeed. 'Pounding-the-ground' people, layout people, whether they're foresters or engineers or wildlife biologists, must possess highly developed skills at reading aerial photos and maps and walking the ground and recognizing where they are on the ground in relation to the map. They have to be able to take a grease pencil out and mark on a soggy map in a dripping wet plastic case, 'OK, I'm here and I want to put a landing there' with absolute precision. They must be able to look out from this landing where the cable tower will one day stand, down across the slope below and up the far side of the valley to correctly identify "tailhold" trees over there -- trees strong enough to anchor 40 feet up the trunk the end of a thick logging cable strung from the tower, a cable that will carry formidable loads of logs up and out of the valley. The only way to tell is to walk over and make sure that adequate trees are there.

"You do a lot of bush-whacking and fern-hopping in this job and those who don't like running up steep slopes in the rain need not apply.

"Say I'm planning a cable logging job, a long span of 1,500 feet across a valley, and I know I can't rely on scrubby marginal timber to anchor the far end of my logging cable. I know I have to have tailhold trees over there at just the right elevation to get adequate deflection, or sag, in the logging cable. The more sag, the greater the load the yarder can pull to the landing. I have to make sure I've got big enough trees, rooted strongly enough, and in the right place to give me enough deflection. You can't guess about these things, so it's down the slope and up the other side to make sure. You've got to make sure you can do what the Gate 2 team wants.

"Now we don't pick the exact tailhold trees at this stage -- the logging contractor will do that during actual logging -- but we do make sure that along the backline, along the rear boundary of the sale, that there's a selection of trees that can be rigged with a cable, rigged more than 40 feet up the trunk.

"Sometimes if you can't find adequate trees you can do some artificial anchoring, attaching the cable to a dozer, but that costs money. Sometimes it's the only choice, and you have to build that expense into the timber sale appraisal.

Ron Arnold photo

Author Soderberg radios planning team.

"We run profiles of the terrain using surveying techniques so we can do computer analysis to make sure that with a given configuration of landings and tailholds that the contractor can get a payload that's adequate, that we can actually log the trees that are out there on the slope.

"If we can't get adequate deflection by some means, if we can't design the unit so that the logger can rig his equipment to follow the Sale Implementation Plan successfully, then we have to modify the layout or maybe cancel the unit even though it's already approved.

"It's our job to lay out a sale that can be logged as originally envisioned by the ID team, and done safely and in an environmentally sound manner.

Counting The Trees

"Let's get John Standerwick on the horn. He's our group leader for inventory, plans and silviculture at the regional office in Juneau."

Tom reaches Standerwick and puts him on the line.

"How do I explain what we do? Let's start here: If you're going to manage the resources on a national forest you have to determine what's there first. The best way of determining what's there for timber purposes is to make a statistical analysis, to compile an inventory of the standing timber. Now, that doesn't tell you what you're going to do with it at all. It only tells you what you've got to start with.

"The inventory is a systematic sampling of the timber volume on the forest. We use a combination of aerial photo interpretation and ground plots. Basically what the whole process amounts to is counting trees, measuring them, assessing them. We compile all this data so we have a statistically acceptable measure of the timber volume on the forest. We do this for the whole forest once every ten years on the Tongass and that information is used in the forest planning process.

"We compile our inventory with a separate statistical analysis for each of the three areas of the Tongass, then lump them all together to obtain the total picture. That's the basic procedure for determining the forest's total timber volume, but the annual allowable sale quantity is based upon *only* that volume which you are committed to schedule for harvest. In the case of the Tongass approximately ten-percent of the national forest's land base has been scheduled for harvest under forest plan.

"We have people at the Ranger District level who actually go out on the ground and do all this. Tom's one of them. He can fill you in on the actual process."

Back to Tom.

"Concurrently with the unit layout," Tom says, "foresters will take the unit's cruise information -- the actual measurement of the timber -- or forest mensuration, as it's also called. There are a lot of cruise designs, but we use the Variable Plot technique, one of the most common cruising methods. It begins with the laying of a grid on the timber sale map and generating random-number sequences which are matched to points on the grid. That gives us a randomly selected set of cruise plots. We don't measure every single tree -- yet. Then we go out on the ground and find those points and measure the trees in a plot surrounding each point, writing on data cards the volume, the species and the grade estimate, which tells us how much defect or rot there is to subtract from the gross volume. That data is extrapolated for the whole sale to come up with a total estimate, which is essential for the appraisal.

"Our end product for Gate 3 is the Timber Sale Preparation Report.

"Gate 4. It's called Advertisement or Notice. This is where we prepare the Timber Sale Package. It involves making the cost appraisal, preparing the timber sale maps and instruction documents, writing the contract and prospectus, and making the sale offering.

"We take the Timber Sale Report from Gate 3 to an appraisal specialist who'll take all the cruise information, all the acreages on all the cutting
units in the sale, and come up with the market value for the amount of
timber in that sale based on the grade and volume and species composition. Here, let's call another Juneau guy, Gary Peterson. He's group
leader for timber valuation at the regional office."

Tom dials a number in Juneau and we're soon connected to Peterson.

"At the regional level we're responsible for the collection of cost and
sales information from the timber industry and providing our people with
direction, training and appraisal data to do timber valuation," says Peterson.

Gary Peterson, timber valuation group leader in Juneau   Ron Arnold photo

"What I basically have responsiblilty for is providing our appraisers
with data which they need to appraise timber, -- we do it through a
handbook, a regional handbook which we update annually -- it's actually a
continual process, though.

"The appraisal process we're using in this region is called the residual
value appraisal, in which we will take the estimated end product value and
subtract from that the cost of producing that product, working our way
back to the stump. So what that means stated as a formula would be: The
selling value minus the manufacturing cost (milling costs to produce
lumber or cants or pulp -- whatever each log is best suited for), the cost to
haul the timber along the road system to the mill, the cost to build the
roads and bridges, the cost to maintain the roads, the costs of yarding the

timber from the units and putting it on the log truck, the costs of felling and bucking the trees into logs, and some consideration of a profit or return on the investment of the timber purchaser.

"In the Tongass we have another consideration to factor into the appraisal, the payment of twenty-five percent of forest receipts in lieu of taxes to the State of Alaska. In the Lower 48 these in-lieu payments usually go to the counties adjacent to Forest Service land. The intent is to make up for the taxes that counties lose because of federal land, which is not on their tax rolls. In Alaska we don't have a county system, so the payments go to the state -- twenty-five percent of everything the Tongass National Forest receives from all users, timber sales, cabin use fees, whatever. The in-lieu money is then managed by the state just as if it were tax receipts for the usual things that taxes pay for: schools, improvements, cost of government, whatever the state decides upon. That twenty-five percent is factored into our appraisal process. What remains after that then would be the return to the government, or the "stumpage" as we call it.

"All this cost information comes from surveys our people make, on-site, of actual mill sales invoices, log trucking receipts, yarding and loading ledgers, and so forth: strictly from the market place. Even though our numbers are averaged, there's nothing predetermined about them at all. The Forest Service itself does not arbitrarily set any cost or price whatsoever, but derives them only from market data.

"The appraisal accounts for all the costs along the way from the stump out the end of the mill as a finished product and tells us the fair market price or minimum bid we'll accept for the sale: there is a price floor below which the government may not sell timber. We have people out on the Ranger Districts do all this. Let me give you back to Tom."

"Thanks, Gary."

Tom goes on with his gates.

"Then we put together a Timber Sale Package with the maps, documents and the contract. The contract contains all the specifications on what's required to complete the timber sale. It describes where the roads are to be built, what kind of culverts the road contractor must supply, the quantities of rock required to build the specified road. Contract requirements are spelled out for log suspension over parts of the units for soil protection. There's a very detailed map showing all the streams that have to be protected and specifying what kind of protection. It shows the cutting units and exact boundaries. And then you have all the legal language that goes along with the contract. Now the sale is ready to offer.

"The end product of Gate 4 is an advertisement in the newspapers of the Tongass area after which we wait a specific amount of time for responses. Then we hope somebody puts in a bid.

"In normal times we have no lack of bids. And Gate 5 is Bid Opening Date. This gate is not very complicated. We open and review the bids and see who the highest bidder is.

The last step, Gate 6, is awarding the contract. We inform the high bidder of winning the contract. We complete the technical paperwork and work can begin, although some of these sales will not be completely harvested for anywhere from three to five years. The buyer is gambling that the market will be there for the logs at a future price that will leave him a profit. And that's the gate system.

"Now you should notice that each one of these gates is a quality control step. We don't proceed to the next gate until we have the work in the previous gate done. For example, it's not appropriate to lay out a timber sale before you have a completed NEPA document. And of course you wouldn't advertise a sale that's not laid out. The Gate System is a logical sequence of events and a quality control process to make sure you do the job right."

Stewards' Thoughts

But wait, there's more, right?

"Of course. We monitor the timber sale work, just to make sure the contractor complies with all the specifications of the contract."

We always comply.

"We always make sure. Then too, in the NEPA document we may have identified some monitoring needs to follow up on even after timber harvest is complete and the contractor has gone on to another job. For example, we may have some reforestation needs -- we may have to hand plant seedlings to make sure we get adequate stocking of new growth within a specific time period. But the Tongass is generally so productive that nature needs no help. We have only one seedling nursery in the Tongass, near Petersburg. Seeds are brought in from each seed area, germinated in containers, and the seedlings are planted back in their area of origin. But we don't need a lot of artificial regeneration here. This is a very vigorous forest.

"We also monitor soils we consider to be sensitive. If any hillside slumps or if we find bare soil areas, then we seed them or do what's necessary to get the area to heal again. Our seeding is done by hand with a mixture of grass seeds and fertilizer.

"Once we're satisfied that we have adequate restocking, we go back into all harvest units after five or ten years to see if they need thinning. We'll monitor each stand for many, many years. We do precommercial thinning for wildlife purposes and, to open up the thick regrowth and create suitable habitat for Sitka blacktail deer. We also do precommercial thinning for silvicultural purposes, to encourage more rapid tree growth. We'll go in with chainsaw crews and thin out the natural 3,000-stems-per-acre regrowth down to about 300 stems an acre. 'Precommercial' means that we expect no monetary return from the trees cut because they're too small yet for commercial use. We precommercial thin for the sake of the future forest's better growth and to provide improved deer habitat. We simply leave the cut saplings on the forest floor to recycle their nutrients. We're doing a lot of research right now to see what kind of thinning regimes will get the best results on the ground for timber and deer both.

"A commercial thinning schedule is something we're also looking at now. We can go back into stands in the age class of 60 to 70 years and thin out commercial size trees while opening the forest further for the benefit of the Sitka blacktail deer. This program should pay for itself. We already have one demonstration project of commercial thinning, over on Heceta Island, a sale where the operator commercially thinned a stand that was about 80 years old."

Well, Tom and Joe and Mike and and Gary and Don and John. You've told us what happens before the logger gets into the Tongass timber and after.

Time has certainly changed how that works. It's a far cry from the logger of the 1890s going where he pleased and cutting whatever he wanted without getting permission from anybody or notifying any government official, isn't it, K.A.?

Maybe it's a bit far to the other extreme, Jackie.

But one thing it is for sure: Nothing like what the environmentalists say.

Part Three

THE WORKING FOREST

LOGGERS

• •

Wake up. It's five a.m. Time to rise and shine. We've got places to go, people to see, work to do. It's logging day!

You're on board Wavos Rancheros in Hawk Inlet. We're going to show you road building here on Admiralty Island at the Greens Creek mining operation. Then we're going to take you over to Whitestone Logging Company, based out of Hoonah. There you'll see actual timber operations. We'll end up tonight in Coffman Cove, down on Prince of Wales Island at the Alaska Women In Timber picnic. Between now and then we're going to cover a lot of Tongass territory.

Get on your logger's uniform: Longjohns, hickory shirt, stagged jeans with suspenders -- jeans are "stagged" by tearing the hem off of each pantsleg so there's no cuff for sticks and limbs to hang up on in the woods. Same reason you don't wear a belt. You'll need a tin hat and a pair of caulks (pronounced "corks") -- boots with spiked studs in the soles so you can walk the downed timber in the brush without falling all over yourself. Bring along your work gloves; you don't want to get jaggers in your hand from old choker cable. Jaggers are nice sharp steel strands that stick out of worn wire rope. And be sure to bring your Tongass tennis shoes and your rain gear. It's going to drizzle all morning.

Virgil's on the deck talking to our siderod Everett Turner, planning out the day's work. Come with us over to the cook house on shore and stoke up. Virgil will be right up. Don't slip on the wet planks. Did you know that a busy logger needs about 4,000 calories a day?

Well, the ambience here in the cookhouse isn't Uptown Yuppie, but the food's as good as you'll find anywhere. Oh, and be sure to compliment the camp cook: He won't take a meat cleaver to you if he thinks you don't appreciate his cuisine like he might have a century ago, but it's tradition -- and common courtesy.

Here, have a seat beside us. The coffee's steaming and this is as good a place as any to get to know us better. You notice that everybody in our crew says good morning, or at least scowls in recognition, depending on

155

their mood today. When you work in this business, you discover what closeness really means on a social scale. Our crew and their families at Soderberg Logging and Construction are our extended family.

It's that way at DuRette Construction, too, K.A. It's that way at every logging operation. It's the nature of the timber industry in the Tongass. We practically live in each others' hip pockets. You can't avoid the feeling of family. When you run a logging camp you're always doing something, ordering cough syrup for kids with a cold, just being there when

Fish dinner at Rodman Bay   Rollo Pool photo

somebody needs you -- while you're chasing dozer parts and making sure there's enough manpower on the crew and arguing with the Forest Service and getting the production in. You get to know everybody inside and out. You know everything about them whether you want to or not.''

Here's Virgil, K.A. Let's get breakfast.

Virgil, tell Jackie about how you got through school.

"You want to hear the logging camp kid story again?''

I never get tired of it. And Jackie's never heard it.

"Okay. Let's order breakfast and I'll spin that yarn for you.''

Were you born in Alaska, Virgil?

"No, Jackie. In Pe Ell, Washington.''

Where?

"I know, nobody ever heard of it, it was a little timber town Down South in Douglas fir country. Dad was a logger.''

Don't be shy, Virgil. Your dad isn't just "a logger.'' Pat Soderberg is about the best known logger in Alaska. Even though he's now retired.

"Of course, *I* think he's the best. Anyway, we followed the logging jobs around. I went to kindergarten in Forest Grove, Oregon. Then we moved to the redwoods, lived in Eureka, California, where I went to public school for the first grade. Then from the second to the fifth grade I was in Catholic school in Eureka.

"That was 1959, about the time Alaska Lumber & Pulp had their new modern pulp mill on line and needed loggers. Dad came up, took a look, decided it was good place to avoid the old problem of too many people chasing after too few jobs. He came up as a contract logger for ALP and started the logging camp at Rodman Bay."

So your dad was the one that built that camp?

"Sure was. When we came up my little sister and I enrolled in the one-room camp school. We had an experienced teacher that could take us through junior high. When my freshman year in high school came, I enrolled in a correspondence course from the University of Nebraska, which published the outpost curriculum that had been approved by the State of Alaska. It was a nice little program. We still had the grade school teacher to supervise the two or three of us, and she looked after our studies and gave us our tests."

What's it like going to a camp school?

"'Fun' is the best way to say it. A one-room school is actually a fun place to grow up. Of course, we kids didn't know any better. The quality

Virgil Soderberg (left) and crewman on Wavos Rancheros.   Ron Arnold photo

of education was good, but I think that more important was the quality of community. Everybody in Rodman Bay was close, it was very tightly knit. The school was always putting on little activities for the community, and the community always took good care of us school kids.

"And the life was unbeatable. Once we got our bookwork done we had the best playground you could ask for: Alaska. We'd play around camp, go fishing, whatever. I was always able to ride along in the log trucks, and that was really fun. And during shutdown months I spent a lot of time playing pool with the crew guys who spent the winter in camp.

"And Christmas in camp was always the most fun. I remember when the camp's first stereo buff put speakers on his porch and played Christmas carols. We could hear them all over the place, playing out in the snow, up in the hills around camp."

Virg, that reminds me of our last Christmas back at Portage Bay. Remember?

Virgil laughs between sips of coffee.

What, K.A.?

I make Christmas stuff every year, homemade goodies for the home guard. Virgil was anxious to leave camp, we were going away, camp was shutting down for the winter break. I had rushed and baked all day and I was dog-tired, but I had all the baskets fixed up. And I said, Virg, we've got to take these around tonight or we're not going to get them out.

So we went to the place next door and, of course, the couple there insisted that we have a little holiday cheer with them, which we did. Then we said we absolutely had to go to the next place and they said, hey, we'll come along too.

So the four of us went to the next neighbor.

"It was six, K.A. Don't forget their two kids."

That's right, Virg. So the *six* of us barge into the next place where the adults have some more Christmas cheer, and that couple thought they'd like to come along to the next place.

Every place we go through the whole camp we pick up more couples and more kids. Then finally here's a dozen or more of us at the last place: the cooks' house, Kathy and Jim, and they had the smallest place in the whole camp. It was kind of sparkly and wintery with the snow on the ground and the kids thought it was wonderful sneaking up to the cooks' trailer. Then we start singing Christmas carols outside their window, this mob of loggers. And we got the cooks out. And then somehow we all crammed into that little trailer with hardly any room to move around.

This, you have to realize, is a time full of emotion. You've got to say your goodbyes. We've lived with them for ten months. And we'll all be scattered to the four winds and won't see each other for a couple of months. With Kathy and Jim we were especially sad because this was their last season. This couple is one that won't be coming back to camp because they're going to settle Down South and we want to say a special goodbye. The whole camp just spontaneously got together.

Those were special times.

Oh, don't remind me of goodbyes, K.A. It's too early in the morning. Virgil, how did you finish school in camp?

"Well, I didn't. When I was a sophomore, and sis was getting into junior high, our parents felt they ought to get their kids out of camp before we got too weird. So they bought a house in Portland, Oregon, and we lived there for the school year, dad would come home for the month or two of winter shutdown, we'd come back for the summer, but we'd be split up during the fall and spring, mom and us in Portland, dad in Alaska."

Don't skip over that too lightly, Virgil. Hazel had to endure a lot of separation from Pat all those years. A lot of logging wives do.

"It was tough. But we didn't complain. I'd come up in summer and work in camp, get jobs running the fuel truck, changing tires in the shop. Eventually I worked my way up to dump truck driver. I gained some early first-hand experience in road construction. When college time came I went to the University of Santa Clara, a Jesuit school in California. I enrolled in the Army ROTC program and graduated with a commission as an infantry lieutenant.

"That last summer I worked up here a season before going into the Army in October 1971. I went through officer boot camp and then jump school at Fort Benning. Just when we came out, the Defense Department had started its Vietnamization program -- no more American infantry officers went to Vietnam. Instead I got to defend the Monterey peninsula for the rest of my hitch at Fort Ord.

"Then I came back and got a job logging with my dad. Dad retired in 1978 and that left a void in ALP's contractor pool. I had done some supervisory work for him over the years where I was visible to ALP. I'd kind of felt in the back of my mind that one day I'd like to go into the business. I worked out an arrangement with ALP and formed my own logging company. I also picked up some work from ITT Rayonier when they got cutting rights on the Kake Indian lands."

And you got an advanced degree from the Harvard Graduate School of Business Administration. You didn't mention that.

Sea-Drift

Well, did you get enough of breakfast, faithful reader? Don't forget to make a sack lunch for yourself. The fixin's are all laid out on the tables by the far wall. You can fill your steel Thermos with coffee over there in the corner.

Now come on out to the staging area and let's get on our way up the road. The siderod's just getting our crew on the crummies [logger lingo: buses that shuttle between camp and the work site.]. Pile into our pickup and let's go see how we build roads. From up here on the hillside you can see back down to Wavos Rancheros as we head out to the Greens Creek mine.

Virgil?

"Yes, Jackie?"

I'm curious about the Beacher, your landing craft tied up down there. How did you ever come by a landing craft?

"Well, I had just started up Soderberg Logging and Construction and we were in the process of moving our logging camp from Kake to Portage Bay -- Rancho de las Palmas -- which is on the same island that Kake is but it's on the other side and there aren't any roads connecting. We needed equipment on both sides during the transition, so we couldn't just move all the equipment on a barge at one time.

"I thought a landing craft would be just what we needed to bounce equipment back and forth as needed. So we looked for a landing craft and the only one with a good hull and good engines turned out to be in Okinawa."

Okinawa?

Virgil and the Beacher   Ron Arnold photo

"Okinawa. You take them where you find them. We bought it and had it shipped to Seattle, then Ketchikan, then Kake, and christened it The Beacher. The skiff's name is Son of a Beacher."

A little word play, Virgil?

"Very little. Anyway, we started our first haul with the Beacher, which was a dump truck load of culvert pipe. A big event -- the first official voyage of the Beacher. We all went down to the dock and waved it off. My dad was running the boat. It had very loud engines -- you could hear it even after it rounded the last headland. The sound of the engines got fainter and fainter and we went on about our business.

"The next thing we knew the engines started getting louder and louder again. Then here comes the Beacher back to the dock. We go down and my dad says, "'This isn't going to work. Number one, two of the four engines are starting to overheat and number two, I can't see where I'm going.'

"In the military version of the landing craft the captain's deck was just a little turret mounted on the back of the boat, designed to travel and take hostile fire at the same time. So when you're standing on the back of the boat and you're only five-foot-eight to start with, dad's problem became readily apparent as soon as he pointed it out.

"We beached the Beacher at high tide that fall and didn't put it back in service until the following June. We replaced the engines and replaced the little turret with a brand new wheelhouse that we had built in Seattle with radar and sleeping quarters and a galley and everything but a shower. Since we put it back in service we've just about worn the boat out we've used it so much. We've hauled airplanes and house trailers, heavy equipment, everything except our biggest logging towers.

"But the logging ended. In 1983 the market turndown was getting pretty bad. ALP revised its entire logging plan and decided not to log in Portage Bay. Our contract was terminated. Fortunately we found a fill-in Forest Service road job for a while. Meantime, we had heard about this Greens Creek job we're working on now. Mining and road building looked like a new field. The logging industry depression left too many people chasing too few jobs. We hadn't been able to get any introductions to the mining people, but our good reputation allowed us to at least submit a bid on the Greens Creek project, and we were the successful bidder."

Trail Blazing

We're coming to an area where road construction is in progress. But let us tell you about road building before we get there so you'll know what you're looking at.

A road crew is normally about eight or ten people. That would be four or five truck drivers, a front-end loader operator, a driller, a powder monkey, a cat skinner, a backhoe operator and a supervisor. High skill, high pay jobs. And you have support personnel like mechanics and fuelmen and grease monkeys backing them up.''

But what we'll start with is a ribbon-staked line the Forest Service layout crew has left in the woods. The Forest Service has jurisdiction over our roads here on Admiralty Island even though they're mining roads rather than logging roads. We'll put our right-of-way cutter in there and he'll go down that line clearing the right-of-way to the specified boundaries -- it's like a long narrow clearcut snaking up to the mine or the timber harvest unit. Here, we're turning off onto a spur road that's under construction now. It doesn't go directly to the mine, but rather to one of our rock quarries.

Most visitors ask what we do with the right-of-way timber that's cleared to make way for the road. It goes to the appropriate mill depending on whether it's a pulp log or good for dimension lumber. It's counted and paid for just like timber from a harvest unit. So even road building involves a good bit of logging.

Rollo Pool photo
Helicopter view of narrow right-of-way with felled timber on future roadway

Our right-of-way cutters are highly skilled, our best. It's one of the most difficult and dangerous falling and bucking jobs in the woods. It's difficult because you have to protect the adjacent trees and you're confined to the boundaries of the right-of-way, mostly for a fourteen-foot-wide roadbed, but sometimes wider depending on what has to travel them -- lowboys and big yarding towers get wider roads.

Virgil says, "We've got some big chemical tanks up at the mine site that had to be hauled on a wide right-of-way."

You have to fall right-of-way timber with great precision to stay within the narrow boundaries. It's dangerous because the falling trees always brush against standing timber on their way down -- you're never out in the open -- and that can leave branches from the fallen tree hanging loosely far up in the standing timber, ready to drop at any moment as the cutter below bucks the felled tree into log lengths. They're called widow makers.

The right-of-way faller also has to take into account that he has a backhoe equipped with a log grapple coming up behind him that has to handle that fell-and-bucked timber efficiently. A good right-of-way cutter can speed up the road building process considerably by falling his trees in neat rows right down the middle of the right-of-way, and a poor one can make a mess, like a pile of jackstraws, half in the right-of-way, half in the woods, that takes forever to unscramble.

We strip rock pits for the driller coming behind the cutter. The pits will run one to three acres. A driller is a highly expert person who drills holes in rock with compressors and power tools. The powder monkey then stuffs the holes full of powder and touches it off and gives you shot rock to build your road.

A good driller can normally drill six or seven hundred vertical feet a day. It takes about a week to drill one shot and we get about twelve to fifteen thousand cubic yards per shot, which is about the amount it takes us per mile on the road overlay.

We try to get the pits spaced along the road every mile and a half. But because of environmental pressures in the Tongass the Forest Service is trying to stretch them out to as much as three miles, which will increase rock haul costs.

Okay, we're coming up to the end of the road. You see that big machine beyond the dump trucks? The one mounted on tracks with the long boom and grapple? We call it the backhoe out of habit, although with the grapple mounted on its boom I guess it's really a log loader.

Everett Turner with front-end loader in rock pit   Ron Arnold photo

We turn around on the narrow rock road and Virgil tells us, "I've got to get down to Heceta Island today and check out the new road job, so I'm going to leave you with our superintendent Everett Turner now. You can go back to Wavos Rancheros in his rig. He'll show you the rest of our road building operations. You'll be off on your tour, K.A., so I'll see you in a couple of days."

We say our goodbyes to Virgil as he drives away leaving us in the silent forest and the drizzle. Then we walk with Everett Turner to watch the backhoe at the end of the road now being pioneered into a new rock quarry site.

The Technology Of Protection

Everett says, "You see the operator there taking the merchantable timber and stacking it to one side in a cold deck [logger lingo: a pile of logs that will be removed at a later time]. Now he's taking the non-merchantable material, turning the stumps upside down, walking the machine over the rootwad, picking up small brush, tops, limbs, whatever there is, breaking it up and making a debris mat, and he uses that to walk his machine on. Then the truck backs up to end dump a cover of shot rock over the debris mat, the dozer pushes it into the right places and the road is a few dozen feet longer.''

K.A., we ought to explain the care we take against erosion.

Go ahead, Jackie.

Okay, to prevent erosion, we install ditches and culverts while we're laying the rock. A culvert is a water path beneath the road -- it keeps runoff from gathering on the road and turning it into a creekbed of its own. Metal culverts vary from eighteen to as much as seventy-two inches in diameter. Some are flattened on the bottom, designed for a fish stream. Or it might be an arch pipe, doesn't have a floor in it. It's just a metal arch to leave the natural stream bed there for the fish. But it takes about an hour to install an eighteen-inch culvert and do it right.

Then the grader comes along and gets the road level and crowned properly for rain runoff. Once the road is shaped up you compact it so it won't fall apart, using either a heavy pull-type grid roller or a self-propelled vibrating roller.

Everett says, ''After the road has been compacted, you have to sell it to the Forest Service. They come along and inspect it. They measure every culvert, every road width, they look at the ditches, any bridges you might have put in. They are very, very meticulous. If they don't like it you have to redo it, and for no extra money. So the only place you'll find bad road builders is in bankruptcy court. And that's how you build roads.''

Forest Service photo

A properly built Tongass logging road: shot rock over a debris mat

Thanks for the guided tour, Everett. Don't forget to feed Missystuff while we're gone.

"I'll do it."

Back at Wavos Rancheros we call a floatplane to take us over to Hoonah on Chichagof Island, so we can visit Whitestone Logging.

The Employed

We get off the floatplane and meet Wes Tyler. He's the siderod for Whitestone. He's worked as a logger since 1967. He'll take us in the company pickup through Hoonah around the bay to Whitestone Logging. Hoonah? It's an Indian village on the northeastern shores of Chichagof Island. The Village Corporation, Huna-Totem, has its offices in Juneau, but some of its private timberlands are not far from here.

We enter camp by the Whitestone bunkhouse. The bunkhouse here is a row of mobile homes, each divided into separate apartments, not the one big open room with bunks around the wall like the old days. Come on out to the staging area and let's talk with Wes. Tell 'em what you do all day.

"It's my job to coordinate all of Whitestone's logging operations, the cutting, the yarding, the trucking. everything except roadbuilding. And I actually do a lot of road engineering too, making sure the roads and the landings are in the right places."

Let's visualize what Wes was doing here while we were coming out of the cook shack earlier this morning over on Hawk Inlet.

6:00 a.m. After breakfast, almost out of nowhere some sixty men materialize in the staging area. Wes walks among them, taking a man aside here and there for a few seconds. Let's listen in as he talks to a young Tlingit crewman.

"Louie, where's Patterson?"

"He's sick today."

"Still fishing with his dad more likely. Who's going to work second rigger for you?"

"I want Bradford."

"He just came up from Down South. Are you sure?"

"He's good with wet logs in the brush. Catty footwork. He logged in the redwoods."

"You tell him to stick to you like glue."

"He'll be fine, Wes."

"Beecher, got a full crew?"

"I took Mitchell and put him up on the landing in Hanson's spot. Hanson quit yesterday. We're okay."

For fifteen minutes before the crews leave, Tyler continues to readjust the lineup. Then the loggers are in the crummies and gone to the woods.

Tell us about your crew, Wes.

"As you well know, there's a fairly high turnover of manpower all the time in a logging camp," Wes explains, "so I'm always looking for a guy that can fill in for somebody who's quit or out sick or got hurt or whatever. Part of my job is to coordinate all of that, make sure there's enough men qualified for each crew."

This constant worker turnover may have been what Jack Skow was obliquely getting at in his *Sports Illustrated* remark that "Most of these are five-month-a-year jobs, right?" There are no "five-month-a-year jobs" in logging, but there is a wandering corps of loggers, mostly young unmarried "bunkhouse loggers" -- as opposed to the married men in family housing in another part of the camp -- that endlessly migrates from camp to camp and from Alaska to Down South and back. This corps includes every type you can think of: college students working a year, going to school a year; men running away from unhappy marriages; happy bachelors with itchy boots; alcohol problems perennially hoping the next camp will dry them out before the siderod fires them; men who fiercely love freedom and working outdoors. Each logger is a distinctive individual whose life would make a book itself. We wish we could tell you all the lives we've touched among these fascinating people.

Whitestone has about 80 loggers in the bunkhouse, some nomad, some long term, and 50 families in camp. But the nomads are becoming a minority: more and more loggers either stay put or get married, with their families living in camp. And the camps themselves work ten and eleven months a year -- in all but shutdown weather when most loggers take their year's wages Down South to Seattle or Eugene or Phoenix or Maui or Cancun or St. Croix. Even so, some loggers overwinter in camp for no other reason than that they love the Tongass.

We're in luck today because the owner of Whitestone Logging is going to take us out to the logging site. Meet our friend Bud Stewart.

"Come on, get in, K.A. and Jackie and your friend, don't just stand there getting wet. We can take my rig up to the Spasski Creek drainage where we're pioneering some new roads."

A burst of crew talk on the pickup's radio breaks the steady background chuckle of the eternal Tongass rain.

How long have you been logging out of Hoonah, Bud?

"Shirley and I moved here and began building road in the fall of 1981.

It's just a normal consequence of being a contract logger and roadbuilder for Alaska Pulp. When you finish one area they find another one for you. We'd been down near Wrangell for twelve years -- logged on Zarembo Island and at Cape Pole on Kosciusko Island and on Mitkof Island. Before that my family had logged Down South in the Willamette Valley of Oregon.''

Bud runs an impressive logging operation here. Bud's wife Shirley has run this whole huge outfit herself off and on when work took Bud up to Afognak Island on other operations. Shirley, like so many of the wives of contract loggers, has paid her dues as an active business partner, mother, wife, best friend, confidant, and endless wellspring of strength to be there for her husband, family and neighbors through the best of times and the worst of times.

This fact of the woman running a massive outfit, having to deal with everything, bad weather, running out of propane, making sure everybody is alive and well in camp, and getting the production in, this fact is something that the environmentalists don't understand, don't know about. Jackie has been there, I've been there, Shirley has been there.

Behind every logger we will meet there is a story of dedication and endurance and sacrifice that we can't do justice to, but never forget that the people of the Tongass you'll meet in this book are not cardboard-cutout stereotypes, they are all three-dimensional living human beings with hopes and dreams and sorrows like yours. Respect them.

We splash briskly through the camp puddles -- we don't have to watch for the kids on their way to school yet. We wave to the machine shop boss and rumble out onto the mainline road across Gartina Creek. A pair of bald eagles glowers down at us from atop a power pole next to camp.

Bud says, ''Right now we're logging about half Forest Service timber, half private Native corporation timber. If we could, I'd only work the Native timber because we can export round logs and make much more money. This is all Native land we're driving through now.

''Take a look around the hills here, as far as you can see in the downpour, anyway. At this end of Chichagof Island the forest is probably sixty-five percent hemlock, like most of the Tongass. Hemlock is a dominant species and it'll crowd the spruce out. But you'll see a lot of spruce today too. I've seen windthrown trees on the ground with dozens of spruce seedlings lined up on them. You'll see some of Mother Nature's timber harvest techniques, too -- windfall, insects, disease and rot, natural mortality, even some fire damage. We harvest the trees a little differently. Environmentalists think we do messy work, but you should see Mother

Nature's clearcuts after she's done with a hundred-mile-an-hour Tongass
tantrum.

"I hear that you talked to Joe and Tom down in the Ketchikan Area
yesterday. Hoonah's up in the Chatham Area of the Tongass, but you
know the Forest Service does things the same way here. You also know
they have aerial photos and detailed maps of the entire Tongass. They lay
these out and divide them up into Value Comparison Units."

Value Comparison Units? What's that? Nobody mentioned those to
us.

"It's just another bureaucratic designation the Forest Service uses to
define an area of the forest for allocations under TLMP. A VCU's
boundaries are based on natural watershed boundaries. There are several
hundred VCUs on the Tongass. A few have odd boundaries. There's one
up at Endicott River, half Wilderness, half timber, where a watershed was
split into two VCUs, but they're all heavily watershed-oriented.

"Within an unlogged Value Comparison Unit they'll identify what
they call a 'first entry harvest' and then put people on the ground to go in
and actually walk it, lay the roads out, paint the unit boundary trees. Then
we come along behind and build the roads and cut the timber."

Bud says into the radio microphone, "One empty."

The scratchy reply comes back, "One point five loaded."

One empty? One point five loaded?

Log trucks: empty leaving camp, loaded coming back   Rollo Pool photo

"See the pie plate nailed to that tree coming up, got a big black "1" painted on it? That's mile marker one, and there's a blind curve ahead. So you say 'One empty' over the radio if you're going out from camp and 'One loaded' if you're coming back. I just found out there's somebody coming this way half a mile ahead, so we should pull over into the next turnout. Unless you'd like to argue with a ten-foot-wide loaded log truck on a fourteen-foot-wide logging road."

No contest. We pull over and a vast behemoth appears around the bend, laden with logs and momentum. It flashes by and the ground shakes.

"This road is built over muskeg. You go out a hundred yards and the ground still shakes."

Why does this man, Bud Stewart, our old friend, common as an old shoe, evoke so strongly in our minds a powerful line from Walt Whitman in *Song of the Broad-Axe?* Whitman saw loggers as:

The friends and home-givers of the whole earth.

Maybe it's because Bud is not as common as an old shoe, but is instead that rarity, a man certain and proud of what he does. When his men cut a tree, like Walt Whitman he doesn't see himself as destroying a forest, but as building a clinic or a church or a home somewhere with its finished lumber, or as clothing multitudes with rayon fabrics and providing photo-graphic film for cameras everywhere from its dissolving pulp. He doesn't see himself as an enemy of nature but as an agent of nature, moving resources into the webs and chains of man's ecosystem before they fall to wind and rot. He sees himself perpetuating the stored sunlight energy and vigor of the spruce and hemlock a time longer, a friend and home-giver of the whole earth.

But no, that's crazy, right? Loggers are crass and insensitive, aren't they? Rapers and scrapers, nothing more. You can't overcome prejudice and stereotypes. Or can you? Let's go on.

We drive on, now in the clear, and continue up to the spur road where Whitestone Logging is finishing a road into the timber.

"Say, look at this," says Bud. "That's a Forest Service rig alongside our forester's. Let's see what's up."

We pile out and watch Whitestone forester Keith Walker vigorously tapping a particular spot on a map held by two Forest Service men.

"That's the Forest Service construction engineer and inspector," says

Bud.

Keith Walker says hi and tells us, "I'm arguing about who's going to pay for what for the closeout of this new road when we're done with it."

The engineer says, "Keith's raised a continuing policy question: Since this road is being built to a specific standard for future recreation use, should the contractor be required to absorb the cost of restoring the road to its original condition after the industrial use is finished?"

The inspector remarks, "I think somebody raises that question on the Tongass about every other day, especially on logging roads."

What's the problem, exactly?

Walker tells us, "This applies more to logging roads than to the mining road system you're working on, K.A. In your situation the mining company pays for the road and that's that. But here on a logging job, when Whitestone Logging is finished using a logging road system, we as the logger have to restore it to its original condition so it can be used by the general public for other purposes. Let's say a road was built to a certain standard and we used it, we hauled X million board feet of logs over it, and we're through. We have to give the Forest Service back the same type of road they bought. That involves a whole bunch of different perceptions: Is the crushed rock thick enough here; is the radius of that curve wide enough there; that kind of thing. They perceive it one way and we perceive it another. If they don't like the road, we rebuild it to their desires without payment for the extra work. So there's a lot of give and take: We give and they take."

The engineer grins: "Ouch! I think I'll send this one to the Supervisor's Office in Sitka."

Bud Stewart says, "That brings up a more fundamental problem from the logger's viewpoint. We don't have any problem with the temporary logging roads -- building to low standard into a one-time harvest area, putting the road to bed when we're done, water-barring it to prevent erosion, even removing the crushed rock on occasion, that sort of thing.

"But I think these permanent Forest Service roads for the general public are built primarily with money designated for logging. These roads will be here as long as there's a forest. Yet their entire cost is deducted from the first entry harvest instead of being amortized over the life of the road through second and third entries to timber stands that will be harvested in another ten or twenty years. That's political bookkeeping, not business bookkeeping. It's that all-at-once deduction that makes many timber sales appear to be "below cost" when in fact they're *low cost* investments that will last many lifetimes. The Forest Service should change its accounting system to be more businesslike.

"When will people realize that these roads have incalculable public value, for administrative purposes, for silvicultural work -- for reseeding, planting, thinning, salvage logging -- and for game management, stream improvement, tourism, recreation, transportation from point A to point B, you name it. I think the public will be using them long after we're gone. Hoonah is connected with the Alaska Marine Highway system and we're getting a heck of a lot of people recreating on these logging roads. Some days we can't move a twitch around here, especially during hunting season. Logging is the reason recreationists and the general public have these roads. We should be thanked, but we're vilified. Worse, the environmentalists want to eliminate the funds that pay for these roads."

The engineer replies, "Even though there is a recreational road fund, mostly for those associated with campgrounds, it's true that timber pays for most Tongass roads. Under the ANILCA legislation the bulk of the roadwork on the Tongass National Forest has been done either by the logging contractors themselves -- with costs deducted from the timber sale appraisal -- or with money from the Tongass Timber Supply Fund."

Which is now under attack as a subsidy to the timber industry.

The engineer says, "None of that money goes directly to any company. None of it. The two long term timber sale companies, Ketchikan Pulp and Alaska Pulp do not get any of it. Some of that money has gone to pay contractors to build government roads and facilities related to timber sales or to pay for constructing capital investment facilities that are going to be there beyond the sale. But none of that money has gone directly as a subsidy to any company."

Keith steps in: "K.A. and Jackie, these Forest Service folks can get some real experts on road design over the radio if you've got any technical questions."

Give 'em a call.

Road Wizards

The Forest Service engineer raises Ken Vaughan and Ollie Bacus and explains, "Ken is the regional transportation planning engineer and Ollie is the regional transportation development engineer, both in Juneau. Ask what you want."

Virgil mentioned earlier this morning that many Tongass logging roads are built on muskeg. Explain to our readers how that's possible.

Ollie says, "The road is floated on an organic mat through muskeg. It's a floating road. First we end-dump truckloads of stumps, broken limbs and any other organic debris from right-of-way logging. After the truck dumps the debris, a large machine called a backhoe spreads it into place. That creates a debris mat in the sphagnum moss of the muskeg. Then we end-dump shot rock -- rock blasted from road obstructions -- over the debris mat. Of course, you can't operate equipment out there until after you get a large layer of rock on it, but you just keep working that layer of rock down into the right-of-way right across the muskeg. We use this technique over most Tongass soils, not just on muskeg.''

Doesn't the debris mat rot?

''The debris is saturated, under water all the time here in the Tongass and it'll last 50 years. It doesn't alternately wet and dry like it would Down South, it stays continuously wet. It will not rot. We've dug some of these debris mats out that have been in the ground for more than 25 years without any rot. It saves us enormous quantities of rock, which is expensive. That makes roads cheaper to build.

''It's a technique common not only here but also in the Lake States where they build roads much the same way across peat bogs. It's very strong. Once the road is in and has had a year to set, it can carry tremendous loads.''

Ken, the Forest Service sends planners out on the ground. With so much information in the ID team's computerized database, why do you do that? Isn't it a waste of money?

''No, it's not. We use other methods than going on the ground where we can. They range all the way from personally flying over the site in helicopters to doing extensive aerial photography to in some cases using remote sensing techniques, satellite photography. If the soils are sensitive, and it could mean the difference between catching or not catching a critical break point on a hillside, there's no substitute for a pair of trained eyes attached to two legs walking a line on the ground locating a road. And walking through makes things fit. Sometimes it takes four or five trips to make it fit.''

What's a ''critical break point?''

''It's a term used to identify places in a slope where we're likely to have soil failures on a hillside or other points where road locations are limited by topography. The Tongass, as I'm sure you're aware, is a geological madhouse. Welcome to glacial carving. We have a very wet climate and when a hillside's geological bedding planes are in the wrong places you can say 'boo' and end up with mass failures. You can look on the hillsides around here just about anyplace and see the scars of where it's occurred, courtesy of Mother Nature. It just slumps, predominantly in debris avalanches or debris torrents and failures of that sort. We don't want that to happen under a logging tower because we put the road on the wrong side of a critical break point.''

Every now and then we've had road failures on our operations. How can you prevent it?

"You can't every time. But there is a specialty within engineering that's called geotechnical engineering. Geotechnical engineers are specialists in slope stability and in building successful structures on the more difficult and precarious sites. We have a geotechnical engineer in the Juneau office who provides leadership for the region.

"The lower elevation Tongass soils are alluvial for the most part, relatively stable from the standpoint of raw erosion. They're what comes out of the end of a glacier, glacial tills and compact glacial tills, with some marine clays intermixed with bedrock.''

The Forest Service engineer breaks in, "I don't mean to be abrupt, but we've got to be going. More sites to monitor.''

Ken signs off, "Hope it was informative.''

The two Forest Service road men jump into their pickup, and the engineer calls back, "Keith, we'll tell Sitka about your problem. But you'll need a strong case to get any money from the recreation road fund.''

The Clean Chainsaw

We pull over to the side of the road and let a pickup overtake us. Bud waves to the driver, who stops and we all get out. Here's Keith Walker again. Remember, he's the forester for Whitestone Logging. Keith, what does a forester do in a logging company?

"A forester for a logging company is a very practical person,'' says Keith as we stand among shadowy trees dripping water. The overcast seems to be thinning a little. "I do a lot of work with water quality in relation to the fishing industry. I make sure that when we go into a unit we take good care of the fish streams. This Spasski Creek drainage flows downstream through both public and private Native corporation lands, and I fish in it myself.

"So I make sure our cutters don't dump timber in the creeks or the tributaries. I make sure we follow any buffer strip prescriptions the Forest Service has made, or if I don't think it's enough protection or the right kind, I'll argue with them about it.''

Leaving buffer strips is controversial.

"That's true. In many cases we'll come back after the first bad windstorm and find our streamside buffer strip has blown down right into the water.''

Whether that's good or bad is itself becoming controversial. Some fisheries biologists are discovering that the pools formed behind fallen logs in streams provide just the quiet environment some species of fish fry need during crucial stages of growth. We can see the controversy coming full circle from 'don't put anything in the streams,' to 'fell at least six large trees into the creek per thousand running feet of stream.' We know the environmentalists won't like that. It's okay if it happens naturally, but for man to do the same thing is a sin.

Well, enough of that. How do you actually do the timber cutting?

Come on and I'll show you.

"It'll depend on the size of the unit, but most of our cuts run a little under a hundred acres. We'll have probably five or six cutters in a hundred-acre unit. They'll start by looking to see which direction the timber is set.''

What does that mean?

"This Tongass timber, because of prevailing winds, will tend to take a prevailing set, or direction of natural lean. Once the cutters have figured out what the lean is, they'll open by taking down a strip about three tree lengths wide.

"The actual process of falling a tree is very involved and demanding. You begin by clearing away any brush that would interfere with cutting, for safety reasons, to prevent chainsaw kickback and such. Then you plan two possible escape routes about twenty-degrees behind the planned direction of fall.

"Cutting begins with the undercut, which is also called the face. Making the undercut involves sawing out a pie-shaped piece of wood facing in the direction the tree is supposed to fall. The undercut is sawed back to about a third of the tree's diameter in two stages: first the horizontal cut and then the slanting cut. The resulting pie-shaped piece of wood, or snipe, is removed, leaving an empty space pointing in the direction of fall. An expert faller can drop the top of a tree within a few inches of where he's aimed it.

"Then the back cut is put in, usually one to three inches above the facecut. The backcut is sawed leaving only a narrow strip of wood between the backcut and the face. This narrow strip is called *holding wood* and acts as a hinge for the falling tree. If you cut through this hinge, you lose control of the tree.

"When the backcut is properly completed, you insert plastic wedges in it and hammer them in. They gently push the tree off balance and it falls

1. Faller begins horizontal undercut   2. Faller makes slanting undercut

3. Removing "snipe" from undercut   4. Backcut leaves "holding wood"

5. Wedging the tree over

6. Holding-wood hinge guides tree

7. Leap from stump, lands unbroken

8. Bucking tree into log lengths

slowly and precisely, breaking the hinge as the top of the undercut strikes the bottom slant cut. The tree, already nearly half-way down, then jumps away from the stump and hits the ground without damaging its wood. Falling timber correctly is an art requiring the steadiest hand and the greatest delicacy.''

Not many people think of logging as delicate.

''How would they know? And delicate doesn't mean fragile -- our fallers are all pretty tough specimens. You just walk around behind one for a while and you'll see what I mean. It's his expert touch falling a tree that's delicate and precise. The faller then walks the fallen tree with a tape measure and bucks it into exact log lengths calculated to yield the highest possible recovery of wood in the mill. He also cuts away the limbs and leaves a fully manufactured log ready to be yarded to the truck landing.

''As they progress through the cutting unit, cutters try to fall every tree parallel with the hillside. Sometimes when they get in a gully, they might fall it straight up and down the slope to minimize breakage.

''We're very safety conscious. If we get a really windy day, we just bring the crew back into camp: the trees can land just about anywhere in a good blow. Or if we find a really bad cutting unit with a lot of over-mature trees and bad widow makers, our cutter laws require us to have two people on the scene, one guy acting as spotter while the other guy cuts. The most dangerous tree to cut is a big rotten hemlock with about a four inch rind of bark. You can't guarantee where that tree is going. I've had 'em so rotten they broom out at the bottom and come straight down around the stump standing up, like a volcano erupting downwards. All you can do is run like heck.

''We spend a lot of time on safety meetings because we want our loggers to retire hale and hearty at the age they planned on. And industrial insurance is expensive: This company alone pays out about $1.3 million a year in premiums.''

And now we drive past this cutting unit, winding further up the spur. A loaded log truck in compound low gear inches down toward us. Keith pulls off the gravel shoulder and waves the driver to a halt.

Judge Us Not With Hard Hate

''This is Johnny Ruckel. Listen to him a minute.''

''Hi, Keith. What's up?'' asks the driver, looking down at us from the open door of his big off-highway ten-foot wide rig (highway log trailers may be a maximum of only eight feet wide).

''Tell 'em how you got here.''

Forest Service photo

Choker setting on a large old growth Sitka spruce. Such high quality wood has provided homes for hundreds of thousands across the world.

"Me? I'm an Okie. I just got tired of the rigamarole Down South and the kids were all raised so the wife and I just bought a trailer and decided to come up here and see what this country looked like. I heard about this job and been here for years now."

"It's a beautiful country but the timber we're logging is overripe. In a few more years a lot of this would blow down anyway. Look right here at all these dead tops and blowdown already. We might as well make some use out of it before it goes. They say logging hurts the fish and stuff, but there's just as much fish as there ever was, more deer now than there ever was, bear all over the place. I can't see where we're doing a lot of harm."

"Tell 'em about the environmentalists."

"I don't know that much about them. But I can't see where they should take over everything. And spread such hard feelings about us. It isn't quite fair to the people that live here or the people that want to make a living out here. Just ask them if they want to lose *their* job and *their* livelihood. That might make a difference."

"See you, Johnny."

You see, K.A.? Here's another life story we won't be able to dig out and tell people about. What has Johnny's wife endured? What have his children become? We can never tell all these spin-off stories. Johnny is another person of the Tongass who will only appear and disappear in these pages, but whose real life and meaning goes on, important to us, perhaps forgotten by the reader.

Cable of Our Destiny

We drive over a heavily wooded saddle, around a bend and out into an opening of about eighty acres at the end of the spur. Here stands the log loader and the giant yarding tower. Seven-eighths inch cable winds around enormous drums at the base of the portable steel tower, reaching up to a huge block where the cable turns through a wheel and stretches out over the valley to the far side where the cable loops around another block, this one lashed forty feet up in a tailhold tree. Beneath the cable lays the fell and bucked timber of this unit, carefully lined up in horizontal rows that make the hillsides look like a contour map -- in fact, this technique is called contour falling, or "quartering the slope." The cutters here must have been really good. We can't see a broken log anywhere, the stumps are low to the ground to retrieve the maximum wood from each tree, the logs are free and in the open so the yarding crew can set chokers around them easily.

Keith says, "I make sure we put the tower yarder in a position so that

Perry Beecher · Ron Arnold photo

we're yarding away from these tributary streams and not across them. As far as soil damage goes, we try to put our tower landings in layouts so that we get the best possible cable deflection and lift so we can tightline the logs clear off the ground. We want to keep the soil intact as much as possible. Here comes Perry Beecher's pickup. Perry's a siderod that works with Wes Tyler. He's got an interesting viewpoint on things too. Perry, meet K.A. and Jackie. How long you been in the Tongass, Perry?''

"Let's see, I came to Alaska in 1981. I heard it was the place to go for a single logger. It was the ideal place for a single guy: There was a bunkhouse life, good people, good work, you lived right on the job. But I'm married now and this is home."

Why did you stay?

"When I first came up I fell in love with Alaska. Three kids later and another one coming, it's definitely my home. But like I was talking to Keith the other day, I think these environmentalists are putting my whole life in jeopardy. When I went to work here I felt very comfortable that we had a fifty year contract with the federal government. We thought we had security. And relying on that security we started doing things, bought a home, put down roots. Now I find out that we can lose everything because of some politician rolling over for some special interest lobby.

"If the environmentalists win and they shut us all down, the pulp mills are going to be reimbursed for breach of contract, billions and billions of dollars. But what about us? Just ordinary people who have invested ourselves here in Alaska, are we going to be reimbursed too? We'll get nothing but the shaft. If the federal government is going to reimburse the mills for their losses, they ought to reimburse the loggers and the mill workers for what we'll lose too -- our jobs, our homes, our way of life. I really have some very strong feelings about it."

We feel it strongly, too. From this home-giver of the whole earth. From his wife. From his children.

"I got family, I got kids, they're real young. We don't want to move out of the Tongass. It's our home. We love it. I think the environmentalists are attacking my kids. I work so they can have a good life, maybe even go to college if they chose to. I take it very personally. But you don't want to hear me grousing.

"Anyway, we got the rigging rats coming up for lunch here." [logger lingo: rigging rats make up the crew that works in the fell and bucked timber attaching logs to the yarding cable by means of chokers. Chokers are special lengths of cable designed to grip tightly around logs, and are fitted with quick-release fasteners.]

Skyfall

Keith yells to the crew leader: "Hey, Louie, come over here." It's the young Tlingit man Wes talked to in the staging area this morning. "Louie White, this is K.A. Soderberg and Jackie DuRette. They're writing a book."

"What kind of book?" asks Louie.

About loggers. How did you get into logging?

"Me? I started logging in 1982, my last year in high school. I was born in Hoonah in 1964 and I was going to be a senior in '82, and I needed money to go to college. Logging happened to show up about that time.

"I signed up and about 2 weeks later, right out of school, I went to the woods here. Setting chokers. It was pretty tough at first, but you gotta start somewhere."

Setting chokers is the entry level job in most logging firms, and is one of the most physically demanding jobs in any industry.

Louie White   Ron Arnold photo

"I went from there to second rigger, climbing trees and helping the hook tender in the back end."

A second rigger works with a crew boss called a hook tender, a term left over from the old days when cable yarding actually used hooks to drag logs to the landing. The tree climbing is necessary to rig a tailhold tree with the block -- which is a wheeled device, not a square object like the name sounds -- that holds the far end of the yarding cable stretching from the tower yarder. The block has to be high enough in relation to the tower yarder to get adequate deflection (sag) in the cable so it can be pulled taut by the yarder engine, giving it the power to lift logs off the ground and haul them up to the landing. The "back end" of the site Louie refers to is where the tailhold trees are.

"I'm hook tender now," continues Louie. "Took me a while."

Keith says, "Tell them about your tumble, Louie."

"Oh, that. It was back in '87, one day about ten minutes to four. I had climbed this tailhold tree with my regular climbing rope, looped around the tree and fastened to my safety belt -- you throw it up a little, lean away from the rope and climb the bark a couple of steps, throw the loop up another distance, take another couple of steps, and so on up the tree. You wear these long spurs on the inside of your calf that dig into the bark and give you a foothold. While you're climbing you have to cut the limbs away so you can rig the tree properly, which means you take this little chainsaw up the tree with you.

"Got that? I was just cutting the last little limb so I could pull up my blocks up there. And I was about 75 feet up. I threw my climbing rope too high and sawed right through it. And down I came in a hurry."

Good heavens! You fell out of the tree?

"That's what happened. I planned for such an eventuality ever since I started climbing: I always take a quick look down every few steps to see what's softest to land on. I never realized it would happen, but it did. I had enough time to kick my spurs out and that was it.

"I turned over in the air, trying to get my feet down. I threw the saw over this way and I started turning over that way. It was instinctive, because if I fell with the saw running I could have been sliced up bad. I landed on my right leg, right on a root, broke it. It was soft ground, but I rolled. The doctor told me I can't believe you did that and lived. Because at the time I had all my climbing gear on, my little climbing saw, I even had a guy line hanging from me. I still have a steel rod in my leg from knee to heel that braces it. So it doesn't bother me. The doc said I could work, so I do."

You came back for more after that?

"I came back for more. I didn't really want to, it took me an awfully long time to think it out. I had nightmares at first, waking up in the hospital. They put a full-length cast on me at first, and I'd wake up jerking really hard and kept snapping my bone, so they had to pin it. Two operations right in a row. I kept having nightmares about it. But there's something about logging that really gets to be part of you. I didn't go back to climbing for a while. But I'm climbing again. I've overcome my fear. This time I'm a lot more careful."

What happened to college?

"Me and my wife are going back to school again. I'm having the steel bar in my leg removed soon so the final healing can take place. I'll have to admit that logging is wearing out for me slowly. I think I'd like to study basic education and physical education. I play ball a lot and I like working with kids. I'd like to be a teacher here in Hoonah. I grew up here, graduated here. Logging is good money, but it's awfully hard work and once you have an accident or two, it's time to get the message."

The Turning Wheel of Terror

After our sack lunch we watch the finished product of Louie's crew being loaded onto log trucks and hauled back to Hoonah for scaling and water rafting to the mill.

Keith drives us south to a place where we're to meet our friend Jan Harbour who will explain another style of logging. So long, Keith, and thanks for everything.

This is a place Jackie knows well: Kennel Creek on Freshwater Bay. She doesn't say much. The camp is there again today at the bottom of the hill, what with the market coming back, but it's a different time with different faces. You can't go home again. You can see it in Jackie's eyes. Tell us, Jackie. What are you feeling?

No, it's too horrible.

What, Jackie? Tell us. Tell us what you're feeling.

You won't like this. It was here at Freshwater. Louie White's story reminded me. It was a young man that Butch had hired, had worked for Butch three years, his wife and two children lived here in the camp.

What, Jackie? What happened?

I was working in the camp office with everybody one morning and a radio call came in. I heard Butch call in telling us there was an emergency up on the logging site, to contact a MedEvac immediately, and that he was about to start CPR.

Logger releasing chokers dangling from butt-rigging   Forest Service photo

The atmosphere in the office turned to ice. Somebody had been seriously hurt. Butch didn't say who. I got on the radio and asked who is it, Butch? He only repeated get a MedEvac immediately and that he was going to start CPR.

A couple of guys ran out of the office, jumped into their rigs and tore up to the site, about twelve miles out. We called the MedEvac.

Then about five minutes later Butch came back on the radio and said cancel the MedEvac. He said get a plane here right away. He said call the state troopers and the safety people and the coroner. There's been a fatality.

Dear God. A fatality.

We were on the industrial frequency. Every other logger in Southeast Alaska was listening. Everybody stopped what they were doing. The bull cook in the kitchen fixing lunch in a camp three-hundred miles away, the Andrews couple teaching in the school next door. Tension covered the Tongass instantly. We knew we had lost one of our own.

I asked Butch to identify the victim. He told us it was our young friend with the two young children. He said the crew is coming in. He

said to let him know when the troopers and the coroner arrived, that he'd
stay up there until everything was taken care of.

The whole camp was absolutely still. The crew all came down off the
hill. Nobody said a word. It was utter shock. The only one up in the
woods out of the 120 men at Freshwater was Butch -- and the man who had
been killed.

About thirty minutes later the authorities arrived in a float plane and
some of the crew took them up to where Butch was watching over the body
of our young friend.

The authorities got to the work site, the coroner pronounced the man
dead, the state troopers did all their paperwork and took all their pictures,
the Department of Labor did their incident documentation.

Butch picked up our lifeless friend and put him gently, like a son, on a
stretcher, put the stretcher in the back of a crummy and drove the crummy
down the hill and stopped on the side of the road just up from the camp
while everybody else drove on by. I looked up and I could see the red nose
of the crummy sticking out by the trees. I couldn't figure out why he was
just sitting there.

He got out of the rig and flagged one of the guys to go get the dead
man's wife. She came up, and Butch told her I have him here, but I won't
take him down to the plane until you tell me you're ready to let him go.

She insisted on seeing him. Butch said I've known you for a long
time. Trust me on this. You don't want to look.

She said I have to. Butch said if you trust me you won't look. Finally
she went away without looking and another woman from camp walked her
back down.

So Butch drove the crummy down to the dock and put the body on the
plane and all the authorities were gone before he reentered camp. It all
took about four hours.

So Butch came back to camp. I kept out of his way. Our two boys
were in the house and kept quiet. There wasn't a kid out playing
anywhere. Butch had just been grilled by three layers of government,
talked to a bereaved wife and put the body of a friend on a plane to cold
storage in Juneau. He needed some breathing space.

He walked in the back door of our wanigan, stripped off his rigging
clothes and stepped into the bathroom. I heard the shower start. I saw the
pile of dirty clothes out in the wanigan and I turned on the washing
machine and put the soap in it. I figured I'd clean up his clothes and fix
some lunch and give him a chance to come back from the edge.

I was just bending down to pick up his hickory shirt and shake it off when Butch came out of the bathroom in his sweat pants -- he hadn't got into the shower yet -- and reached over me. He grabbed the shirt away from me so hard I almost went flying. He said keep your goddam hands off that shirt. I don't want you or anybody ever touching these clothes.

He grabbed everything off the floor, stormed outside to the burning barrel, threw the clothes in the burning barrel and set them all afire. I couldn't figure it out. I asked myself what in the name of heaven is he doing?

He came back in the house, took his shower, came out of the bathroom, sat down and stared at the wall for a couple of hours. I just left him alone.

Late that afternoon he started talking to me. When we'd talked a while I said, tell me, Butch, tell me: why did you burn your clothes?

He looked at me and his eyes filled with tears.

He said I did it because his brains were all over that shirt. I couldn't stand for anybody to ever see that.

This is not a story of Butch DuRette. It's a story of every logging contractor in the Tongass. More than a hundred of us. Virgil has been through it. Bud Stewart has been through it. We all have. You stay at this business long enough and someone will make a fatal move. This young man had stood in the wrong place at the wrong time and a buttrigging on the cable yarder got him. He knew better. We'll never know if he was distracted by worry over an early season shutdown caused by some lawsuit or if he was coming down with the flu or what. He was gone. That's all.

The next day the camp kids went gathering wildflowers in the rainforest of the Tongass and when they came back we held a memorial service in the school. It drew us closer. The death joined us in full tight bind. How few we are. How precious we are. How everything militates against us. How everything strikes us down.

You never get used to it. But you learn to survive it.

We learn this: Those who die in us live in us. Their memories build us an inner determination and an inner force. Then when the Jack Skows and the Steve Richardsons and the Robert Mrazeks of the world come to destroy us we don't hate them. We despise them for what they are, insects of the spirit, worms of the soul. Skows and Richardson and Mrazeks, how dare you make us suffer more who have suffered so much! You could not endure the thousand dangers we live with nor the thousand horrors we die with. Your hearts could not bear that hideous strength which dwells within us.

Keep your shameful lying selves elsewhere. You will never defeat us. We'll never give up. With your millions and your power you may destroy us, but you'll never defeat us. And if you come again and again and ask for roaring war, we will bring it to your doorstep. We will not go gentle into that good night. We are the people of the Tongass.

Something too much of this. I didn't mean to get so wound up in my feelings, K.A.

No, Jackie, the world needs to know. To see what we have seen. To feel what we feel.

The Sea In The Forest

Here, let's go down into the cookshack where Jan Harbour's waiting for us. Have a cup of coffee. Let the heavy mood dissipate.

Jan! Thanks for meeting us here.

"No problem. We're up here looking for work for our crew anyway. Jackie, you look terrible."

I just told them about the shirt.

"Oh. I haven't thought about that for ages. Are you sure you want me to do this now, to talk about A-frame logging for your book?"

Come on, Jan, you know us better than that. Business as usual. Isn't that the motto our critics denounce us for? Our ability to take the worst and keep going? Tell us about your operation. How has your company survived since Alaska Timber filed Chapter 11?

"Okay, Jackie, I'll tell you. Business as usual it is, then. Our operation? Well, Don and I got stuck with a million feet of logs in the water and no income. We had to close our camp, but Ed Head at Klawock sent us enough money to cover the payroll when the Native corporation went bankrupt. It could have been worse. I think we'll make it, but I don't know how well we'll make it. There is timber around.

"But there hasn't been much A-frame logging available, which has really hurt us. That's what we're set up to do. The Forest Service guys we deal with are willing to put up the A-frame sales, but orders from up high say no. It's a touchy thing with the environmentalists. They don't like the looks of it.

Tell us how A-frame logging works.

"I really don't know how to explain it without pictures. It's a form of shore logging. You start with a float camp, so there's no land disruption

A-frame logging: cable yarder A-frame on float, line straight into woods

for living quarters and your operating base. On a float there's the big A-frame boom made of two poles braced in the shape of the letter A. A cable from the A-frame pulls logs in from the woods directly to the water.

"Normally we leave a fringe of trees along the water to hide the oh-so-terrible logging we do back in the woods. We make very small breakout points in the fringe from the woods where the skidroad comes down. And you don't build a road system to A-frame log. There's no large-scale soil disruption. In road logging you have permanent log dumps and sort yards and leave permanent scars. When we move out there's nothing left to show where we've been -- only the actual logged area is touched, there's no land taken for our operating base because we're in the saltwater. My personal feeling is that A-framing is much easier on the ecology than putting roads in. And every A-frame logging operation that's been offered has been approved by every department you can think of in the government.

"Environmentalists don't like it because they say it causes water pollution from the loose bark that gets knocked off when the A-frame dumps the logs into the water. I think it's just because we're visible from the water and might attract favorable interest from cruise ships. The tannic acid that leaches out of the bark supposedly causes a low degree of pollution and the bark sometimes collects in unsightly floating clumps. Natural stream water where no logging has ever occurred is normally tea-colored in the Tongass. Bark from natural windfalls has leached into our streams for thousands of years. And A-frame logging is not done near streams, only in salt water.

"I've heard some fishermen whine about fish being damaged by A-framing, but we always catch a lot of fish under the floats. When we were in 'Chomley' Sound (properly spelled Cholmondeley) the king salmon moved right in and lived under our camp. They moved out when we did, too. They like having the floats to live under. We used to go back to that spot and fish after we pulled our camp out of there and there were no fish. They left too.

Like many of us, Jan, you seem to have been pushed out of one job after another by the environmentalists and then clobbered by the economic downturn. How has it all affected you?

"It takes a lot out of you. We've been tied up for years. For one thing I bought a house just before the bottom fell out on us, which I bitterly regret. It's been for sale for two years I can't seem to find a buyer for it. Just making the payments is real tough. It's frustrating."

Did you cry a lot at first?

"I skipped the crying part. I was just mad. You just can't let yourself fall apart. You probably could if you thought about it. I just got angry that so many people lie about us. They have no idea the hurt they've given us,

Rollo Pool photo

Tower yarding operation brings logs up in fan-shaped straight line pattern

and for no good reason.

"My son has worked for us, he spent probably two years with us working for less than fifty percent of what he could have gotten anywhere else, simply to help us. It frustrated Don and me, and it frustrated our son. The money is so short. I can't afford insurance on the company airplane, and in the Tongass, that's your lifeline. We haven't been able to keep our crew together. We've only kept three men working. And then these ignorant critics come and tell us we don't have any consideration for our own forests. Then they try to shut us down forever. They're evil, plain evil."

You said the environmentalists have hurt us for no good reason. Why "for no good reason?"

"It's harm to the wildlife that's always their emotional plea. That's nonsense. We don't harm the wildlife. We live with the wildlife, they come to live with us. We had a family of otters that hung around camp for several years. They'd come up underneath my float house and get on the under-decking beneath the top deck, and start squeaking and screaming just to annoy our dog. And the dog would go nuts trying to dig through these 2 inch thick top deck boards. The otters would be under there cracking up. Sometimes they'd bring up a fish to eat on the deck and leave fish guts all over the place. They're messy little eaters, but they're entertaining. The kids built a snow fort on the deck one winter day and an otter came up and used it for a slide. I noticed because I saw our cat on the porch crouched down like she was sneaking up on something. I wondered what she was after so I walked over to look and there was that otter playing on the fort. The cat made a big dash at him. He pretended he didn't even notice her, and waited until the last second and then just flipped over into the water and laughed. We entertain the otters, they entertain us.

"At Kah Sheets Bay on Kupreanof Island we were logging some blowdown timber from a bad storm. We had eagles everywhere, bears everywhere. It's an incredible wildlife area. Here's all this blowdown timber and this one big tree sticking up right out of it and our road ran right next to it about four feet away. Eagles came and built a nest in that tree after we'd been logging all around. Those eagles raised their babies in that same nesting tree every year we were there. They didn't care that we were logging under it. They seemed to enjoy just sitting and frowning at us. It was wonderful. People who say we're bad for the wildlife don't live with the wildlife every day like we do."

Thanks, Jan. The truth will get out. It has to.

Flyer

A helicopter waits for us on the landing pad. We say goodbye to Jan Harbour and hello to Arnie Johnson. He's going to fly us to Ketchikan. Get in.

"Strap yourselves in, don't smoke anything, and no dancing in the aisles."

Arnie breaks the last of our heavy mood. This is going to be one of those trips. Tell us something about yourself, Arnie.

"I came up to Alaska in May 1973 to fly helicopter for Alaska Lumber and Pulp, Alaska Pulp Corporation they call it now. Been doing it ever since, although I didn't start my own company until 1977 when I bought my first helicopter.

"I got seven people working for me. Three fixed wing pilots, a mechanic, two helicopter pilots, and one other helicopter on a contract for Sitka Gold. I do anything from hauling sightseers to campers, but the majority of the work is with industry people -- miners, loggers, fishing industry people.

"I fly in to their camps, their hatcheries, flying parts and stuff out to the boats, doing fish surveys. And politicians -- I don't know how many sightseeing trips I've given to show-me politicians. I've landed several politicians in 40-50 year-old second growth, and they didn't even look at it. You could tell they had their minds made up before they stepped foot out of the helicopter.

"All this agitation by environmentalists, it's political, it's not jobs oriented and not even reality-oriented. They've already got more than twice as much Wilderness in the Tongass as there is logging land. The environmental lobby is just a special interest group that has a lot of power with the politicians. Those people don't really care about Alaska, they just want to make a

Arnie Johnson

Ron Arnold photo

name for themselves, the Mrazek bunch, the Millers. They don't care if we lose our jobs or if they run us out of business, as long as a few of their campaign contributors can have their private little piece of the Tongass at our expense.

"The politicians don't seem to want to honor the long term contracts with our two pulp mills. They make it more and more difficult to operate all the time, tighten things up with a law here and a law there. Kill you by inches. And you watch, the politicians, through special interest groups like the Sierra Club and the Wilderness Society, once they get one industry shut down, they'll start attacking another industry. When they get logging shut down, next thing will be the mining, next thing will be the fishing.

"I think we're losing the battle, the industry people. I think that industry and preservationists can live together, but the preservationists have to learn how much is enough. We don't harm the deer or the bear or the eagle. I can't see locking the whole Tongass up just for a few individuals, and that's basically what they're after.

"I think logging the old growth is essential for the new growth to come in. We'll get better forest yields fifty years down the line. Second growth is going to give us more timber a hundred years from now on fewer acres, and its better growth."

Our route takes us over Thorne Bay, where DuRette Construction is based. On this side of the town, that flat area there on the water, is the Ketchikan Pulp Company log sort yard. That's where the logs go from cutting units on Prince of Wales Island. Down there the logs are unloaded from the log trucks, rolled out onto scaling decks, scaled by the Puget Sound Scaling Bureau to determine volume, species, defect and destination of each log. Then the logs are taken to a sorting area where large log loading machines sort them by species and size. Then they're bundled, put in the water, and rafted to Ward Cove about seven miles north of Ketchikan on the Tongass Highway where the Ketchikan Pulp Company mill receives them.

Purveyors to the Home-Givers

Our destination is right across Tongass Highway from the mill: Coastal Machinery, Inc., owned by Bob Elliot, a major logging equipment dealer in Southeast Alaska. We set down at KPC's helipad just down the road and meet Kirsten Held, public information officer of the Alaska Loggers Association, who will drive us to Coastal. She'll be with us for the rest of the day.

It's goodbye Arnie, and thanks for the ride. Hi, Kirsten.

Bob Elliot   Ron Arnold photo

"Well, you folks are on time. Bob's waiting for us."

Elliot's office is in the back building, behind the machine shop. We're introduced all around and listen to Bob's experiences.

"Well, I came to Alaska in 1969. I was in the military, and I got out of the service up in Anchorage and decided I'd stick around and see if I liked it. I haven't decided yet," he says grinning, "but I'm still here. It's an awful nice place to live. I got into the equipment business as a sales representative for Ingersoll-Rand. I moved to Ketchikan in 1974 selling IR equipment to the logging community. I started Coastal Machinery in 1978, and we haven't done too badly. We have this store here in Ketchikan and also one in Juneau.

"Primarily our equipment business is logging and construction-related. Logging provides the basis for the economy and because of that there's construction -- highways, city improvements like sewers. Logging is the hub of it, and everything else is a support or follow-along activity. Mining is just beginning to be a force of its own now, and we carry three major lines of underground mining equipment.

"One of our main product lines is rock drills and compressors. I don't know if you've noticed, but there's very little dirt in the Tongass, the glaciers carved this land. So when you build a house or build a road or dig a ditch, you generally have to drill it, load the holes with powder, and shoot it to blast the rock.

"We did about a million dollars in business the first year with three employees. Last year we did $8.5 million with twenty-five employees. During the timber slump of the early 1980s we struggled along, didn't grow much, but things are coming back strong, and we're anticipating growth for the next couple of years.

"I'm very concerned about the constant push by environmental groups for more Wilderness in the Tongass. I'd like to see less Wilderness area -- we should roll back some of those boundaries and release the timber. We should be more realistic about where we can log and under what restrictions. I think the pendulum has swung so far toward environmentalist extremism that it has to come back the other way. We have to have a livelihood, all of the people of the Tongass have to pay their bills to eat and enjoy life.

"Everybody can't live off the government, so there has to be something produced. Somebody has to harvest natural resources, whether it be logging or mining or farming or what have you, and there has to be some input to the funnel before useful products can come out the other end. I think that the conscientious people of this world would all agree with that. We have to have some type of economy, and it has to begin with a natural resource. There is no other way."

Three major dealers in the Tongass supply equipment to the timber industry: Coastal Machinery, Howard Cooper Corporation and NC Machinery.

Wind In The Treetops

The final leg of our day's journey will backtrack us by floatplane to Coffman Cove where the Alaska Women In Timber will be holding its annual meeting. We'll get there just in time for the picnic this evening and if the break in the clouds stays open you may just see a Tongass sunset.

Forty minutes later, here we are. Coffman Cove is a logging community with a population of about 200, tucked into a sheltered bay on the northeast rim of Prince of Wales Island. It's a land camp, not a float camp, and you can reach it by road from Thorne Bay.

The Cove has a few little shops of its own: a clothing store called Heart's Desire run by a couple of camp women; the Riggin' Shack, which is a general store run by Alaska Women In Timber director Judy Willis and her daughter Sandy; and you'll find camp folks wrapping themselves around a French dip sandwich or maybe a breakfast of hot cakes at Cove Market and Deli, run by Doug Quinlin and Terry Ellis. You'll find businesses called Gas Plus, High Hook Charters, the Calico Cupboard, Misty Isles Oysters -- we'll have some of their product at the picnic -- Coffman Bunkhouse, Island Taxidermy, Puffin Video and Aurora Satellite. Let's get up to the ball field next to the school. There's Pat Rowland outside her home. Hi, Pat! She's been one of AWIT's more tireless workers, and a past president. She's going to walk with us.

And here's Mike Valentine and his wife Leta.

Coffman Cove logging camp, looking northeast

Ron Arnold photo

Hi, Mike! Hi, Leta!

"Hello, you folks."

Mike's father pioneered Coffman Cove. Mike's been in logging all his life and was once president of Alaska Loggers Association. You two know how this community got here. Tell us about Coffman Cove in the beginning.

"Well," Mike says, "the community at Coffman Cove isn't all that old, you know, a little over twenty years. I think my dad and I came up from Washington State to look at the timber first in 1966 after getting a letter from Art Brooks of Ketchikan Pulp about a show R. H. Valentine Logging Company might be interested in. [Logger lingo: a "show" is a timber operation.]

"Don Finney was head engineer at that time and he took us out to Coffman Cove to examine the timber. We spent three days there in the darndest storm I'd ever seen. I wasn't sure if I wanted to log in a place that rough.

"We went back south. And a year later KPC decided they were going to put a contractor in there. We were it.

Leta says, "You know, Coffman Cove here is a nice little spot, it's a small protected bay on Clarence Strait. A good spot for a camp. Open to the sun. The weather there is actually better than in Ketchikan, it only rains about 150 inches a year.

Mike says, "When we first moved in it wasn't like just hitting the beach because KPC had built about ten miles of logging road in the area. An old guy named Pat LeMay lived here, he'd cat logged around Coffman for thirteen years. [Logger lingo: "Cat logging" consists of dragging the fell and bucked timber to the landings with a tracked dozer instead of hauling them by an overhead cable system. Not suitable for rugged terrain.]

"They already had a little logging camp here for a truck logging contractor, so there was something here. They even had a log dump. [Logger lingo: A log dump isn't a disposal site, it's a shore facility for lowering logs from the truck into the water where they are formed into rafts by boom boat operators for tugboat hauling to the mill.]

"That really saved us a lot of time. I remember our equipment barge got here some time in late March 1967 and we put our first logs down the log dump in late May. So in that time we set up our trailer house camp, made it livable, put in our pipe system and water system, and built a shop and put logs in the water. Ol' Art Brooks told that was as quick as he'd ever seen anybody do it.

"We started out with about 200 people as I remember. KPC wanted to harvest about 50 million feet a year and we were moving about 18 million. So KPC brought Cow Creek Logging Company to Coffman to get the 50 million -- they were a pretty big outfit with four sides [completely equipped crews]. But it wasn't more than about eight months and they went broke.

"Dad and I went to Art Brooks at the mill and said we think we can get you 35 million by adding just one more side to our operation. They revised their estimates of what they wanted and that was the size we remained. Art liked to put on this act that he was the emperor of the Tongass, but when it came to the nitty-gritty, he was a soft-hearted guy that would give you anything he could.

"We started out with a state operated school, right up here where we're walking. We provided the building and the state provided the teachers. It was apparent that the kids needed some kind of a covered playground, a decent place to play when the wind's blowing and it's raining. I told the community I would build a steel building and put in a concrete floor for some kind of a court, basketball and volleyball and that kind of stuff. The state came up with some money and I put up the rest and we built it, this building right here.

Ron Arnold photo

Author Jackie DuRette greets oyster supplier at AWIT picnic

"After a few years our enrollment went from about twelve to sixty-five. This was a big school for a while. The state put in these three main buildings and sent us some very good teachers. I have two boys and both of those kids went their full school career here at Coffman Cove Tech. Later the community named this school after my dad, they called it the Howard Valentine School."

We walk down the path from the school to the playground.

We're just in time. The picnic is drifting together now. You can see the outline of four or five men under the big shelter leaning over the charcoal pits ready to cook some fresh caught salmon and halibut. A couple of women have come in with big bowls full of salads and other goodies. An informal baseball game is in progress with nobody keeping score. If you foul out too far beyond first base the ball is likely to float away in the tide: the playfield drops straight to the rocky beach.

Women Of The Tongass

We can see walking from the school the reason we've come here: Helen Finney. She's just finished setting up her materials for tomorrow's Alaska Women In Timber meeting, no doubt.

Helen, come on under the shed and sit at the picnic tables with us.

"Hello, K.A., hello, Jackie. And all you people. Good to see you again. Been keeping busy on your book?"

Working on it now. Let's watch the sun set and wait for the salmon to bake. Hey, look at this mob of AWIT people coming to listen: Judy Willis, Donna Lewis, Judy Auger, Thyes Shaub. Well, Helen, you got an audience. Start at the beginning. The very beginning.

"Like Dickens, eh? 'I am born.' Well, I was born in Sitka in 1928, so I'm a native and a pioneer like you, K.A.

"And the reason I'm involved in forest issues is the movies. Stars of a different era, Fred MacMurray, Paulette Goddard and Susan Hayward, have a lot to do with it. I saw a movie when I was 12 years old called 'Forest Ranger,' and it made such an impression on me I decided I wanted to marry a forester and live in the woods and do all that romantic stuff like packing your water from a stream, with a barrel for a shower, fires in the fireplace, all that. It just seemed so romantic I wanted to marry a forester. Well, I finally found one and married him -- that's Don. But that wasn't for a while.

"I finished high school in Sitka. My dad worked in Sitka, he was in charge of Sheldon Jackson School, the Presbyterian mission school. I went to the public high school and then to college in Iowa for two years -- my parents had come from there. I transferred to Washington State University in Pullman, and got a degree in communications. This young man named Don Finney was going to the School of Forestry at the University of Idaho just nine miles away in Moscow. That's how we happened to cross paths.''

"Don had lived in Alaska one summer and wanted to come back. And the five

Helen Finney   Ron Arnold photo

years I was in college, all I really wanted to do was come home. After I graduated in 1951, I came back to Sitka and took a job while Don was Down South smokejumping and paying off college debts. He arrived in the fall and we were married in Sitka in December 1951.

"Don first went to work for the U.S. Bureau of Public Roads while we waited for Ketchikan Pulp Company to finish their pulp mill and start hiring. We figured we would move down to Ketchikan and move back to Sitka when they got the timber industry going up there. In 1953 we moved down and Don was immediately assigned as a cruiser in the woods out on Prince of Wales Island at Hollis at the mouth of Maybeso Creek. He went out that summer taking inventory so logging could start up, and I moved there that fall, and we lived in a Forest Service cabin on Cat Island near Hollis. We went out to the cabin with Debbie, who was born in Sitka in 1952 -- she was 9 months old when we moved.

"Don was transferred to working with the forest engineer, the cruisers moved on to another place, and we stayed in Hollis. We were there when the first loggers came to establish the first camp. That's how it happened that I was the first woman on the scene when they began the large scale logging for the pulp mill.

Here, have something to eat, Helen. The salmon's ready. Try to talk and eat at the same time. This is fascinating.

"I'll try. Well, we lived in Hollis for eight years, first in the Forest Service cabin on Cat Island, which was not what you would call a winter cabin. Then Don built a house for us on a homesite in Hollis. Kevin was born in 1954 -- I went back to Sitka to have him -- and Brad was born in 1955 in California.

"When the loggers built their camp, it became known as Hollis, but it was out on a little peninsula past Halfmile Creek and halfway around the bay from the original site of Hollis. We moved into Hollis camp and lived there for four years.

"In 1960 we moved to Thorne Bay. KPC was going to move the Hollis camp over there, and Don -- he was an engineer by then -- was going to lay things out and set things up. So we moved over there with the kids. Our friends Jan and Steve Seley and their three children moved there at the same time.

"When we went to Thorne Bay, it was still just a bay -- no town. It was just the two families while the engineers laid out and built the new camp around us. There was no school, so we taught the kids ourselves that year. Between Jan Seley and I, we had kindergarten, first, second, third,

Ron Arnold photo

Ketchikan Pulp Company foresters inspect a logging operation and fourth grade. Of course, we only had one kid in each class. She taught her kids, I taught my kids, and they all got together for recess.''

Look, Helen, we're going to see the sun go down.

We all watch, even the camp people who have come to the picnic and throng around the baked salmon.

The sun slides behind the Tongass with a glory that would make you believe in the mythological fire-chariot of Phoebus pulled by four long-maned suntreaders.

Nocturne of Clear Stars

Twilight. Go on, Helen.

''It's beautiful, isn't it? Well, the next year the loggers moved in from Hollis. They moved our house around and set us up in the main camp. We were there one year and then moved into Ketchikan. So actually my time in the logging camps was ten years, one month and three days.

''It seemed like a lot of fun at the time, but I remember when the kids were little it took eighteen-hour days just to keep them warm, clean, fed and dry. I did pack water a lot of the time, I scrubbed the diapers on a board -- I didn't have Pampers.

''When we settled into Ketchikan life, Don was gone four nights a week out to the various camps, so I stayed home with the kids. By then they were second, fourth and sixth grade and had a town school to go to. I started teaching Sunday School and PTA-ing and room mothering and going to Little League or Boy Scouts or Cub Scouts. We started ballet lessons, all those things you do when you live in town.

I found out what people's attitudes were about the forest industry. Even in Ketchikan, with a pulp mill seven miles north of downtown, they thought the logs just appeared miraculously by immaculate conception on Monday morning to keep the mill going that week. But what they knew of loggers is they came in on weekends and got drunk. Some of my friends in town -- I remember seeing the shades pull down on their eyes when you said you came from Thorne Bay. It meant you were a logger, that was trash in their eyes. They had no concept of who or what these people were. They didn't have a high opinion of them, they didn't know anything about them.

''I remember telling a group of women one time -- they were snorting about loggers -- and I said, 'You know, your husbands have never worked hard enough to sweat in their lives.' I feel very strongly that honest work should be honored, regardless. We ran into that prejudice in town for years. As time went by, though, it got better. A lot of people came from the camps to live in town like we did, and eventually people got to know loggers. Some of the most interesting, intriguing people you run into are loggers. There's nobody better when times are tough.

Scaler-grader tallying logs

Rollo Pool photo

"Eventually town people also saw the benefits that logging brought to them economically. Before logging came the Tongass was Poverty Gulch. There weren't many people and they weren't very well off. Logging changed that. It just took a while for people to see it. It took a tragedy to make even me realize it. While we were living in camp a good friend, Rex Strong, was killed in a plane crash. I was shattered. I remember the guys going to his funeral, but I didn't go because I couldn't face it. But I looked out my window down at the guys on the dock, on their way to the funeral service. The loggers were down there dressed in black suits. They had all gone to town to buy black suits. When they came to the Tongass they brought nothing but debts. Here they were now and they could afford the floatplane ticket to town and the price of a black suit. It just struck me. That's what the industry had done for them.

"They were able to pay their bills and get on their feet. You saw it in a lot of ways. Their kids' teeth were straightened. You saw it in our floors: We started out with bare shiplap lumber floors -- you were always warning the kids to watch for splinters -- then we went to plywood, then to vinyl tile over that, and eventually to carpets. Such a simple thing as carpets on the floor. That floor was like life all around you: it was

Log loader sorting logs in log yard   Rollo Pool photo

building, progressing, growing, in the same way. It was the timber dollars that were doing that.

"But once you have the nice carpet and you're comfortable, you go on to other things and the carpet doesn't seem so meaningful any more. I guess that depends on how long your memory is. So then came a day that my town activities took me totally away from the forest industry for years. I got into local politics.

"It started because we were living in the Carlanna area above Ketchikan and they didn't have a sewer system up there. Somehow we had to get the place cleaned up and annexed to the city, borrow the money and build the sewer system. So that's how I got my political start, working for a new sewer system.

"Then I went on the Ketchikan planning and zoning commission for four and a half years. I also kept busy on the local level and then state level of the League of Women Voters, and that involved some national conventions. I learned how to see both sides of an issue, get the facts straight, that there's more to it than meets the eye. It was a real revelation for me.

"I was elected to the Ketchikan city council in 1977, but had to resign when we moved outside the city limits in 1980. In 1972 I ran into the Tongass lands issues. That was the first that I became really aware of the greenie groups such as the Sierra Club and the Wilderness Society.

"In 1972 I was working on land use plans through the League of Women Voters. We were having public meetings, gathering information. I recall one particular meeting held in the old fish lab in Ketchikan where a fellow from the Tongass Conservation Society showed up in the same room as Jim Campbell, who was one of our major loggers. The preservationist was discussing the use of public lands and questioning whether logging should continue in the Tongass -- yes, even back in 1972 we had some who wanted to destroy the entire Tongass timber industry.

"The discussion became more and more exasperating because nobody was talking at the same level, they were talking through each other, and it wasn't working well. The situation was getting a little tense. The preservationist finally said, 'Well, I'm sure glad I made a tape recording of this meeting, because I can play it this winter when I want to be amused -- these loggers are so dumb I might as well talk to the wall.'

"Then Jim Campbell, who knew this man, had just about had enough and asked him 'What do you do for a living?' And the fellow said, 'I build houses.' Jim asked, 'What do you build them out of?' and the fellow said, 'Wood' without even realizing the contradiction between what he had said and what he did for a living. Jim suddenly realized the true depth of this preservationist's blindness and said, 'Maybe we should go outside and talk about this.' He was ready to get up and go fight it out, but then

Worker applying steel bands around log loads for water shipping   Rollo Pool photo

Log stacker places banded load on skids into water holding area   Rollo Pool photo

everybody kind of settled down. I will never forget that exchange.

"We had a whole lot of meetings with the preservationists about the use of the Tongass, but we had no idea the debate was going to grow into something so invasive and pervasive and devastating in the battle to come."

Everybody's been fed now. The coals glow where the salmon were. Many have gathered around us. Just to listen.

The Fireborn Are At Home In Fire

"By 1977 we were up to our ears in environmentalists. It was becoming obvious that if we did nothing we would be destroyed. A few of us who were connected to the timber industry heard that someone in California organized a group called Women In Timber -- WIT. K.A., you know this part of the story."

No, Helen. Somebody else should tell it, maybe you, Jackie.

How can I, K.A.? You were the one that was there. You were director of public information for Alaska Loggers Association when Don Bell invited Sandra Nutting up to Alaska. You were the one who made the arrangements for her to talk to the ALA annual meeting about the California Women In Timber. And you were really one of the founders of Alaska

Women In Timber. You tell about that.

Well, okay, Jackie. Don Bell was my boss at ALA when he heard about California Women In Timber. I had been involved with producing ALA's slide shows for the public -- and even a coloring book on logging. For some time Don had been getting the subtle message that ALA's womens programs were a little thin on substance. This new Women In Timber idea sounded like it might be what the Tongass women had been looking for, so Don extended the invitation to Sandra and I arranged the details.

Sandra gave a rousing speech, and the women then got together in the hospitality room of the Baranof Hotel in Juneau, and she addressed us separately -- people like Jewell Larrabee and Nancy Eliason and Linda Larson and Laverne Sullivan and Pam Chatham. We liked what we heard. Afterward we started a steering committee to decide what we should do. And finally we formed Alaska Women In Timber in 1978 and Thelma Cutler was the first president.

Helen said, "K.A., you spearheaded that whole early period."

Well, Helen, I was staff, you know. I worked for Alaska Loggers Association and attended the steering committee meetings and the early AWIT meetings, and kept all the books -- I was in effect AWIT's staff as well as ALA's. But this is your story, Helen. You go on.

Rollo Pool photo

Boom boat pushes banded log load into boom for haul

"When Thelma completed her term as president, I agreed to run, and I was elected AWIT's second president. I was elected president a couple of terms.

"Then, because I feel very strongly that you should keep moving, I didn't run again but stayed on as past president and then moved gradually into the background.

"Another thing: I feel very strongly about the necessity for the Federated Women In Timber in the different states. About a year after we started AWIT, we put the Federation together. Today there are eleven states in the Federated Women In Timber: California, Alaska, Oregon, Washington, Idaho, Montana, Wyoming, Colorado, Wisconsin, Minnesota, and Michigan. It's important that we all carry each other's story when we go to D.C.

"Our AWIT was kind of double purpose compared to the other WIT groups: The groups Down South are more involved with just the industry issues, but Alaska WIT also builds personal connections between the camps and the towns throughout the Tongass so the folks know they aren't alone out there.

"We emphasized the camps from the very start. I remember not long after we organized AWIT the schoolteachers in a camp asked permission to enlarge the playground so the kids wouldn't lose their baseballs in the

Rollo Pool photo

The aftermath of logging: a new forest rises above logging debris brush all the time. The Forest Service said no, they couldn't do that because if they did, the playground could be seen from the ferry channels, and they'd know there was a logging camp hidden there. The Forest Service made it very clear to the camp people that they were to be kept out of sight as if they were ashamed of them.

"We heard about that, and AWIT took the playground issue to the Forest Service as a group. With a little pressure, it was no problem: the teachers were allowed to enlarge the playground. That's also how we got satellite TV in the bush. Then just being able to get together and share common concerns, we felt AWIT was worth something.

"Meantime, we were also working on the legislative aspect of ANILCA, which was on the drawing board in 1979. AWIT went back to D.C. to testify. K.A. spearheaded that trip, organized our lobbying, acted as staff person in D.C. One woman wrote a letter on her child's school tablet, because that was the only paper she had. But she said she would wash dishes, weed gardens, scrub floors, anything, to get enough money to go to D.C. to testify about their lives in the woods, why they had a right to be there, and the good things they were doing. She said she'd even jump out of a cake if she had to. That's the kind of commitment to their lifestyle Women In Timber has: they are willing to put literally everything on the line.

"I believe in the people, I believe in the industry, I believe in the Women In Timber organization and the value of it. It's the last thing I think about at night and the first thing I think about in the morning. I feel these people are being done unto unfairly."

Everyone is hovering closer as the cool breeze wafts in off the sea next to the ball field. Up on the rise the town's lights scintillate. We feel the bond between us, all of us.

Against Fictions That Result From Feelings

"But today I'm bitter. Against my own government. We gave ANILCA our best shot back in the years from 1978 through 1980 -- we traded away 5.4 million acres into Wilderness in return for the Tongass Timber Fund to pay the Forest Service the extra money required to plan timber sales in more marginal areas. We put a lot of effort and money into that compromise. We operated in good faith, and we thought we had a deal. But we can't trust our own government. They're trying to change the deal. They're taking away our half of the compromise, but they're taking nothing from the environmentalists. In fact they're giving all of our timber harvest lands to the environmentalists. When you can't count on the government, the government is no good for the people, and that's what we're seeing now -- what hope is there?

"It's not fair to see timber people who work so hard and have their whole lives invested in the Tongass constantly threatened. And these people of the Tongass are not doing things wrong. I told Congress I've seen the trees grow back, I've seen the fish come back year after year, I've seen the timber people pay everybody's bills and get everybody on their feet. They've paved the streets and built the schools. Now people say, we've got this nice place, let's save it for the tourists and the fishermen. It's not fair. If we had done wrong it would be different.

"Since 1970 I've talked to thousands of visitors doing Alaska commentary on the cruise ships. Visitors understand what they see if you only explain it to them -- and they don't disapprove of logging. You're coming up the channel and you tell people that when you go around the bend, they're going to see an area that was logged. You tell them when it was logged, how tall the regrowth is now, and tell them what to look for so they can tell it from a muskeg.

"Probably the hardest thing for visitors to comprehend is that we're not connected by road. They get off on an island and cannot comprehend the extreme isolation from the rest of the world. They can't comprehend the vast distances. But they can comprehend logging. I think they'd like to have some operations right out in front where they can see them in work. They can appreciate logging as part of our culture, they understand honest work. The visitors today understand a lot more than the ones twenty years ago.

"Some people come looking for the devastation they've heard about from the press and the greenie groups, and they don't find it. They're awestruck when they come up here and see what it's really like. It's these people that reach other people, in my opinion.

"Of course, people entrenched in greenie groups Down South will not change their minds even when the evidence of their eyes demands it. Just as most of us have a preferred lifestyle, these people have a preferred mindstyle: If it's not in the environmentalist ideology, it can't be true. They're as far removed from reality as people who used to argue about how many angels can dance on the head of a pin.

"But the average visitor seems to be understanding that the timber industry is a valuable and respectable part of our economy and our heritage. I don't know if they'll be strong enough when they get back home to hold to it, to tell their neighbors that what they read in *Sports*

Illustrated wasn't true.

"To me, the loggers are the last of the mountain men. They have their place in the world, they do work that needs to be done, and they have a right to be proud of their work.

"Environmentalists have smeared the timber industry's reputation unfairly. It's not honest. It's slander. They ought to do better than come out here and pick on honest people who are doing honest work and fulfilling their role in the world. It's not fair."

No, Helen, it's not.

Not to the home-givers of the whole earth.

Forest Service photo

Island Princess cruises the Inside Passage, home of the home-givers

PULP MILLS

• •

If you're not a forester, you probably don't give it much thought, but forests have a finite life span.

Not just individual trees, which obviously live and die. But whole forests, which not so obviously go through numerous successional stages. Every forest goes through a pioneer stage of growing on bare ground cleared by some natural force -- floods, glaciers, volcanos, avalanches, fires in a pre-existing forest, insect or disease epidemics.

Usually the first invader in the Tongass is some hardy herbaceous species such as a moss or fireweed or a tough nitrogen-fixing tree like alder. Every forest goes through a stage of thrifty growth as numerous species vigorously shoot up to replace the pioneers that prepared their way -- and remember, there's a small "second growth" tree inside every old growth methuselah. Every forest goes through a stage of decadence and decline as the first individuals reach the end of their natural life span and begin to die off and rot, attracting insects and disease to the whole forest.

But not every forest can regenerate itself indefinitely. One or two species will inevitably prove most adaptable to the environment and become dominant, eventually wiping out the competing but less suited species -- and in the process becoming a different forest. The Douglas fir forest of the great Pacific Northwest, for example, is doomed to become a Western hemlock forest because Douglas fir cannot reproduce efficiently beneath its own stems: its seeds require mineral soil and plenty of sunlight, and anybody who's seen a mature Douglas fir forest floor know that it's made of impenetrable organic emerald gloom packed a foot deep over the mineral soil.

Hemlock seeds, on the other hand, can gain a foothold on practically anything from bare stone slabs to the bark of fallen trees to old stumps of anything that happens to have been cut down -- and hemlock is happy in dense shade. The Western hemlock and the Douglas fir may replace the pioneer species together, and they may form a long-lived *subclimax* forest together, but of the two only hemlock can reproduce under its own stems

213

forever as a *climax* forest. And so the Douglas fir counts on another strategy for survival: Periodic natural catastrophes to wipe the forest slate clean -- primarily gigantic fires that once devoured a million acres of Oregon and Washington at a gulp and burned for weeks.

If you're not a meteorologist, you probably don't give it much thought, but an extensive high pressure area settles off the coast of Oregon, Washington and southern British Columbia every year from about mid-May to mid-September.

That seasonal high pressure area diverts the prevailing westerly storm tracks northward toward the Gulf of Alaska. There the low pressure systems become semipermanent. Such cyclonic low pressure systems approaching from the sea are accompanied by precipitation. As a result, summer rain increases with latitude. Along the southeastern Alaska coast frequent light summer drizzle is the rule, with occasional fog along the outer coast. A trace or more of precipitation occurs about 20 days per month during June to September. And that's the dry season. So the Tongass is the most fireproof area in the West. Therefore, large scale forest fires are all but unknown. Therefore, there is no Douglas fir in Alaska. And therefore, there is a pulp mill in Ketchikan and a pulp mill in Sitka.

If the Tongass was less wet so that periodic forest fires could have permitted vast Douglas fir forests to thrive, nobody would have wondered what they could do with it as they once wondered what to do with the decadent Sitka spruce and Western hemlock forest that actually exists. Nobody would have wondered because Douglas fir yields some of the finest sawtimber in the world. Sawtimber goes to sawmills, not pulp mills. Sawmill construction costs are within the reach of many entrepreneurs and there would be a sawmill in every decent harbor in the Tongass. But the Tongass is very wet and there is no Douglas fir. Therefore there are pulp mills.

Pulp Talk

Back in 1911, first Chief of the Forest Service Gifford Pinchot knew there was no Douglas fir in the Tongass. He also knew that there was a great deal of Western hemlock, and a lesser amount of Sitka spruce in the Tongass, about fifty-five percent hemlock, thirty-five percent spruce, and about five percent each of red and yellow cedar, totaling an astronomical 78,000,000,000 board feet (which turned out to be low by 1950 estimates -- it's closer to 85 billion). In fact, Pinchot wrote an article about it in the *Saturday Evening Post* that year titled "Who Shall Own Alaska?" in which he stressed the need to develop and wisely use Alaska's resources. Pinchot also knew that both the hemlock and spruce components of the forest were beyond their prime, especially the shorter-lived hemlock. Even so, foresters calculated that a sustained yield harvest of a billion board feet per year could safely be logged in the Tongass.

There was a long-established spruce sawmilling industry taking advantage of the fine high-volume stands near tidewater when Pinchot wrote, mostly in small mills, but that did not answer two pressing questions in his mind: How can the Tongass be developed for settlement? and What can we do with all that timeworn hemlock?

Pinchot's foresters looked at the Tongass and swore that pulp mills offered the only way to use the elderly hemlock. Now, it's also true that we've stood and watched modern sawmill owners cutting high quality sawlogs out of our Tongass hemlock because sawn lumber sells for more than pulp logs. You *can* cut some Tongass hemlock as sawlogs. The quality is there if you're selective.

But back in 1913 with Pinchot's blessing, the Forest Service offered 300 million board feet on the Stikine River as a pulpwood sale, allowing the applicant a period of 20 years for removal and a reserve of an additional 300 million for future supplies. The applicant was unable to finance the deal. No pulp mill.

Forest Service photo

1918: Soldier guards spruce used for the war effort, Lituya Bay

So the Forest Service in 1914 hired an expert on pulp and paper to investigate pulp opportunities and potential mill sites in the Tongass. The investigation took four years.

In 1917, the Forest Service offered a billion board feet of timber in the Behm Canal area, but again the applicant couldn't get the financing together. No pulp mill.

In 1920, the Alaska Pulp and Paper Company applied for 100 million feet to supply a plant it actually built at Speel River, about 30 miles south of Juneau. Hurrah! A pulp mill at last. The mill produced about 15 tons of groundwood pulp per day and soon shipped 100 tons to Seattle. The low price of pulp and the high freight rates made the operation unprofitable. Like sensible people, APPC closed the plant in 1923 and the Forest Service cancelled the sale agreement in 1925. Boo! No pulp mill.

Historian Albert Wiener reports: "Two other failures of this period were West Admiralty Island, 3.35 MM cunits, and Cascade Creek, 3.34 MM cunits, for which bids were opened January 14, 1921, and May 1, 1923, respectively." (A cunit equals 100 cubic feet and MM is a symbol for a million.) Again the applicants zeroed out. No pulp mill.

By 1926 the Forest Service could release a confidently factual report noting that, "Western hemlock has a high value as a pulping wood...Sitka spruce compares very well in quality with eastern white spruce, the standard pulpwood of North America...The timber resources of the Tongass National Forest are managed by the United States Forest Service primarily for the development and maintenance of a permanent pulp and paper manufacturing industry commensurate with the available water power and timber resources."

That tells us two things: 1) Pulp was the answer to the Tongass question and 2) Pulp was what the Forest Service originally managed the Tongass for. Historically. Soundly. Without damage. Since the National Forest was created. That cannot be overemphasized with today's *Sports Illustrated* brand of amnesia so prevalent. Further evidence comes from another 1926 Forest Service document from the Tongass, "Statement of Priorities:"

> All policies and practices should be developed in such a manner as will contribute in the largest possible way to the welfare and prosperity of the individuals and communities which will eventually constitute a State of the Union, so far as this can be done without defeating the fundamental purposes for which National Forests are established....
> Encourage in every possible manner compatible with the

best interests of the Forest Service and the public in general, the development of a timber and paper manufacturing industry in Alaska which will utilize timber growth up to the full sustained yield basis in coordination with possible water powers naturally available.

Tough Times In The Tongass

That was the intent, but it wasn't working. Nobody could get the money together to make pulp mills work. Nothing daunted, the Forest Service kept trying, and in 1927 received bids from International Paper Company and I. & J.D. Zellerbach for 5 billion board feet on the Ketchikan pulpwood unit on Prince of Wales Island, the largest in the clusters of islands making up the Alexander Archipelago. The San Francisco *Chronicle* and the Los Angeles *Examiner* jointly bid on the Juneau unit, which, incidentally, included all of Admiralty Island and most of Chichagof and Yakobi Islands. The winning bidders, Zellerbach and the newspapers, were given conditional awards for the timber -- conditioned on obtaining power licenses from the Federal Power Commission. However, it took FPC bureaucratic bunglers of the day 42 months to approve the permits, which arrived in November of 1930. They were a little late: the Great Depression beat them by almost a year. The companies refused to sign the final contracts, which were cancelled in 1933 with the Forest Service retaining $5,000 damages each, which was about the only revenue from the Tongass that year.

The Great Depression of the 'thirties did nothing to help get a pulp industry going in the Tongass, nor did World War II. But the vision, energy and determination of one man finally made it happen.

His name was B. Frank Heintzleman. He came to Alaska with the Forest Service in 1918, advanced to regional forester and later served as Governor of the Territory of Alaska. He'd been hankering after a pulp industry for the Tongass all during the Depression and the War. It was 1937 when he succeeded to the position of regional forester in Alaska, where he served until 1953. When he came to that office he found his ambition to establish a pulp industry in the Tongass badly complicated by an issue he never expected: Native claims to possessory rights in the Tongass.

To be sure, this issue had been brewing for many years -- since the European explorers came to the Tongass. The Tlingit had frequently objected to encroachments on their traditional village sites and fishing waters, but they had few champions in the U.S. government. Theodore

B. Frank Heintzleman, 1947   Forest Service photo

Roosevelt was one of the first men of influence to consider the Alaska Natives seriously: He sent Lieutenant George Thornton Emmons to make a report. Emmons found the Indians of the Tongass a relatively advanced class of people, capable of self-support and mainly needing supervision, education and moral support to achieve economic success in the Western manner. They worked in mines, mills and lumber camps and were able to bridge the gap between tribal life and industrial civilization.

Roosevelt incorporated in his 1904 State of the Union message Emmons' recommendations that the Indians be provided technical education, hospitals and dispensaries, and legal status to acquire land and practice professions.

Congress acted upon these recommendations. Indians were entitled to take up land under the Forest Homestead Act of 1906. Under another act of that year Indian family heads were permitted to obtain allotments of 160 acres from the department of the interior. That meant two agencies, the Forest Service in the agriculture department and the General Land Office in the interior department would provide Tongass land to Indians. It took them until 1915 to work out arrangements that avoided conflicts between their two surveys of the land.

But conflicts over Indian claims were many. The possessory rights issue stopped its first timber sale in the Swan Lake watershed near Carroll Inlet on Revillagigedo Island and dragged on for years. One J. T. Jones of Tacoma, Washington, claimed all the Swan Lake watershed because of a deed he got from a Will B. Bell, who obtained it from the Indians, who asserted they had used it for hunting and fishing. In 1914 Jones planned to build a pulp plant, but he only installed a gauge in the stream that ran from Swan Lake to Carroll Inlet and made no waterpower application. The Forest Service was about to sell the timber in the area to Crown Zellerbach Corporation, so Jones asked a federal injunction to prevent construction of a dam on Swan Lake. Interior department agents could find no trace of Indian occupancy in the area and Jones lost. The case was formally closed in 1933.

By the time Heintzleman came to office as regional forester in 1937, the interior department had gained authority to set up Indian reservations in the Tongass but not to grant ownership in severalty. Any new reservation had to be endorsed in a special election by 30 percent of the Indian residents of the site. But the Tlingit did not want wardship, they wanted independence. The Haida-Tlingit Jurisdictional Act of 1935 entitled Indians to sue in court for any claims they might have against the United States. The Haida-Tlingit claim asking for hundreds of thousands of acres of land and tidewater filed under that act was not resolved in court until 1968.

The Curmudgeon Of The Potomac

But Franklin D. Roosevelt's interior secretary Harold Ickes came to their aid much sooner: He developed a new interpretation of Indian rights giving to the Indians lands or waters on which their ancestors had hunted or fished. That would include virtually all of Southeast Alaska.

If this interpretation were enforced, it would, of course, put an immediate end to any thought of a pulp industry in the Tongass. Heintzleman was alarmed. He still hadn't found any industrialist willing to buy into his pulp dream, and now Native possessory rights claims could frost any interest he might be able to arouse. He questioned Ickes' motives in an indiscreet letter to a Yale forestry professor friend named Harold Lutz:

> With the assistance of the Interior Department, and on the basis of some legal opinion given to the Secretary of the Interior by the Solicitor's office of that department, each village, as S.E. Alaska has never had a tribal organization, has made application for hundreds of thousands of acres of land and tidewater fishing areas that blanket all the fishing sites and large areas of trolling grounds. The thought is often expressed by private citizens that the move to set up vast Indian reservations in S.E. Alaska is based, in large part, on a desire to eliminate the National Forests in Alaska.

It was more than paranoia: Ickes was an aggressive bureaucrat who wielded power with a prickly personality and an eye to advancing the cause of the interior department. His close friendship with FDR made him a formidable competitor who gave more Forest Service officials than Heintzleman many sleepless nights.

Despite misgivings about Ickes, Heintzleman stuck to his vision. In June 1944, when the War was just about over, Heintzleman instructed C.W. Archbold, Supervisor of the Southern Division of the Tongass -- it was divided into two administrative parts then rather than the three current areas -- to set up timber cruising parties to prepare maps and reports to be used as the basis for reviving the old 1927 Ketchikan pulpwood unit timber sale. But Heintzleman knew he still needed somebody to sell it to.

During 1945 he contacted Fred Stevenot and Lawson Turcotte of Puget Sound Pulp & Timber Company of Bellingham, Washington and engaged them in long discussions. The company had a reputation for being aggressive, always in search of raw materials and ways to expand its operations. Stevenot and Turcotte sent their chief engineer along with a consulting forester and a consulting hydroelectric engineer to Ketchikan. The three experts conducted a study and submitted favorable reports on the feasibility of a dissolving pulp mill at Ward Cove, just north of Ketchikan. They emphasized the heavy financial requirements and the importance of an assured market for the plant's output.

Log pond at Coning Inlet sale, Long Island, 1945   Forest Service photo

The main problem was to find somebody to buy the mill's output: dissolving pulp cannot be used directly as a consumer product. It must be sold to another segment of the industry and changed by chemical processes into intermediate products such as viscose, nitrocellulose and microcrystalline cellulose which in turn are converted to finished products such as rayon, cellophane, explosives, lacquers, high grade pharmaceuticals and food additives.

Then Ickes came back into the picture. In a July 1945 ruling he declared that the public domain was both land and water and that submerged lands were available for Native possession. He asked that land to the extent of 176,000 acres be reserved for three villages. Decisions on an additional 2 million acres were postponed. Although Ickes departed upon Roosevelt's death, the possessory rights problem did not. Clearly something straightforward had to be done.

In order to permit timber sales without danger of the sales being terminated because of clouded title, a Tongass timber bill was introduced into Congress. The House committee on agriculture reported on the bill:

> A large-scale development of the timber resources in southeastern Alaska, involving the establishment of important business enterprises and the employment of many persons for extensive operations on a year-round basis, is essential to the maintenance of a prosperous and stable economy in the Territory...progress from the present dependence upon seasonal business operations...[provision of] valuable and sorely needed products...and...promoting the national defense through increasing the population and industrial capacity of Alaska as our 'Northern Rampart.'

The bill provided that the secretary of agriculture might make contracts for timber sales but that receipts from the sales be put in a special fund to remain untouched until the issue of Native claims was settled. Senator Warren Magnuson of Washington and Territorial Delegate E.L. Bartlett of Alaska played a major part in developing the bill. The draft bill was agreed on by the departments concerned -- Agriculture, Justice, Interior and the Bureau of Indian Affairs. The Tongass Timber Act was finally passed on July 27, 1947.

Pulp Mills At Last

Now, after almost three years of appraisal discussions and waiting for Congress, in 1947 the Forest Service could offer the old 1927 Ketchikan unit for sale once again. Nobody bid on it. The Forest Service extended the bid period 4 months. Still no bids.

Puget Sound Pulp & Timber had found nobody to buy the potential output of the potential Tongass pulp mill. Then in early 1948 the Puget Sound Pulp & Timber men finally talked American Viscose Corporation into sending a committee to investigate the Ward Cove pulp mill proposal. American Viscose was a pioneer American manufacturer of rayon and cellophane and quickly saw the possibilities. They immediately formed a joint venture with PSP&T, calling the new entity Ketchikan Pulp & Paper Company.

There were numerous obstacles to circumvent. The site of the mill was the former location of a real estate speculation called Wacker City, after its founder Eugene Wacker. When in need of money, Wacker had sold lots, sometimes selling and reselling the same lots numerous times and letting each purchaser think he had clear title. It took a while for local attorneys to sort out that can of worms, but the titles were finally cleared up and options on the land obtained.

The Ketchikan Pulp & Paper Company venturers requested the Forest Service to readvertise the sale for an August 1948 bid opening. Their bid was the only one submitted, it was opened and a conditional contract was immediately awarded, just as in 1927. And again, one delay after another forced the Forest Service to extend the pulpmill construction deadlines -- from 1948 to 1950 to 1954. During the interim, the Forest Service and the industrialists negotiated the first 50-year contract on the Tongass. The final award was made on July 26, 1951, and later that year the company shortened its name to Ketchikan Pulp Company.

The contract was technically called a timber purchase agreement, and it delivered to Ketchikan Pulp Company the exclusive cutting rights on approximately 786,000 acres of Tongass National Forest lands containing an estimated one-and-a-half billion cubic feet (eight-and-a-quarter billion board feet). The timber tract lay mainly on the north half of Prince of Wales Island and on the northwest portion of Revillagigedo Island. The contract price was 85 cents per cubic foot for wood cut for the manufacture of pulp prior to July 1, 1962, and was subject to review by the Forest Service every five years. The company also agreed to pay $3 per thousand board feet for spruce, $1.50 for cedar, and $2 for other species. The contract extends to the year 2004.

Ketchikan Pulp Company obligated itself to build a mill of not less than 300 tons daily capacity prior to July 1, 1954, with a proposed increase to not less than 525 tons by July 1, 1964.

Since this 50-year contract has generated so much heat among indus-
try-haters, it would be well to grasp the intent behind it. To reveal that
intent correctly, we'll show you something the environmentalists don't
want you to know about: We'll show you the contract. It's on the public
record.

The intent of the United States government is embodied in the preamble of the agreement:

> 1) The Forest Service, acting in behalf of the United States
> of America, is deeply interested in encouraging and bringing
> about the industrial development of Alaska;
> 2) The purchaser proposes to establish a new enterprise for
> the utilization of forest products, including a pulp mill, and the
> development of water supply with associated facilities within
> the boundaries of Pulptimber Allotments E, F and G, Tongass
> National Forest in Southeast Alaska;
> 3) Both parties recognize that this pioneering undertaking,
> involving a substantial long-term investment by the purchaser,
> will be accompanied by unusual risks due to many unknown
> conditions that may be encountered at the isolated site and
> during operations, great distances from markets, and present
> day costs of establishing the necessary facilities;
> 4) The Chief, Forest Service, having due regard for the
> interests of the United States and for the protection of the
> natural resources of Alaska, wishes to facilitate the establish-
> ment of such new industry by the purchaser and the operation
> of the industry on a commercially sound basis;
> 5) It is the policy and the intention of the Forest Service
> through sustained yield management of the Tongass National
> Forest, to afford an opportunity to purchase supplies of timber
> for permanent operations of such enterprise as is established in
> accordance with the terms of this agreement for the utilization
> of the timber embraced in this agreement.

Consequences

That's stunningly clear for government writing. The technical requirements, payment terms and operating details that followed in that
document were ironclad: No Congress today can impair the obligation of
that contract. Yes, Rep. Mrazek or Rep. Miller may convince their
colleagues to *breach* that contract, but Congress cannot escape *paying* just
compensation for doing so, plus damages for bad faith dealing.

And, just for amusement, consider the reaction in Mrazek and Miller's home districts if a congressman or a senator from Alaska were to stride imperiously into New York or California, tell the Nassau and Contra Costa yuppies that they don't have the proper respect for their environment, and spend months of effort to shut down their major industries. One imagines that the affront and injustice would cause a bit of indignation.

Anyway. To continue. Congress, as we said, cannot escape *paying* just compensation for breaching the long term contracts, if they breach them. The Constitution's Fifth Amendment "takings clause" has not been repealed.

What would it cost the taxpayer? Well, compare the situation with Redwood National Park: Congress took 58,000 acres of timberland away from three industry firms when the park was created in 1968 and then expanded in 1978. Congress originally authorized $92 million dollars to pay the just compensation. Industry officials figured the ultimate total at closer to $282 million. It went four times higher. Between court awards of more than a billion dollars directly to the timber firms, the cost of the Redwood Employees Protection Program (a worker dislocation program) and other economic mitigation measures, the costs went over $1.5 billion. That didn't include any damages for bad faith dealing, because there was no contract involved: In the redwoods, the government simply took private land for public use.

On Ketchikan Pulp's contract there are 786,000 acres involved, more than thirteen times the amount taken in Redwood National Park, but only the cutting rights, not the land, would be taken. It's not a directly *comparable* example, but it is a directly *relevant* situation in that Congress is the culprit in both cases and the issue is taking private rights for public use in both cases. The Tongass long term contracts created *valuable private property rights* in timber cutting that belong to the two pulp firms. Ask the Internal Revenue Service if you don't believe it. And if Congress insists that the contracts did not create valuable private property rights, think of the gigantic tax refund the government will owe the pulp companies for all their payments since the 1950s.

The Wilderness Society says there would be no compensation due if KPC's 50-year contract is broken, but the environmentalists stand alone in that opinion. As Sen. Frank Murkowski recently noted, such unilateral reneging on a deal and taking rights without compensation would be no different from Soviet President Mikhail Gorbachev deciding that Seward's purchase was a bad deal and he wanted Alaska back without having to return our seven and a half million dollars. Come on, smile. It's satire.

Depending on who you ask about cancelling KPC's contract, the amount runs from some $600 million to over $1 billion. If it were to unexpectedly escalate in court like the Redwood Park taking claims did -- well, do your own arithmetic. And we haven't started talking about Alaska Pulp Corporation's 50-year contract yet. Nor have we even thought about the existing short term contracts with all the 110 logging firms in the Tongass. And the federal government in the redwoods case ended up paying millions to the individual loggers in hardship payments and relocation claims so they could drive down the road and get another job. In the Tongass you can't drive down the road and get another job because there are no roads -- it would be airfare to another job and it would be clear out of Alaska. Because if the two pulp mills are shut down, that puts an end to *the largest year-around manufacturing plants in all of Alaska.* Bad faith can be very costly, in money and in human suffering.

Building On Ward Cove

But nobody was dealing in bad faith back in 1954. Ketchikan Pulp went ahead with construction on the site selected seven miles north of Ketchikan at Ward Cove, a small harbor the Russian traders used before Seward bought Alaska. It got its name from an officer of the U.S.S. Patterson, which surveyed the cove in the 1880s.

Ward Cove is just about ideal as a pulp mill site. A long bench above the shoreline perfectly contains the mill and its wharf. The Cove's waters are deep enough to accommodate barges and ocean-going vessels and the steep hills wrap around to provide quiet water adequate for log storage and handling. Ward Creek feeds into the cove from Connell Lake three miles upstream and 250 feet higher in elevation. A dam and aqueduct were built to supply water for pulp processing to run the mill, approximately 40 to 50 million gallons a day.

Water pollution was a major concern of the Forest Service, and intensive studies of the problem were made on potential sites for pulp mills at Ketchikan, Sitka and Wrangell. Heintzleman worked closely with the Alaska Water Pollution Board. Chemical engineers found that if the mill would adopt a magnesium-base process there would be no damage and that effluents could be safely piped out of the cove into the Tongass Narrows. Interestingly, Samuel Ordway of the Conservation Foundation raised the question of water pollution at the Tongass mill sites, and when Heintzleman told him of his studies and meetings with the state water pollution board, Ordway was apparently satisfied.

The construction of the mill had a tremendous impact on the city of Ketchikan. An established sawmill called Ketchikan Spruce Mills had

KPC MILL WARD COVE, ALASKA 11-27-53

Ketchikan Pulp Company mill construction, Ward Cove, 1953   KPC photo

been around since 1923 when the old Ketchikan Power Company reincorporated under the new name. It had flourished during World War II cutting spruce and hemlock for defense purposes. But the new pulp mill expanded timber employment enormously. The construction firms hired as many local workers and contractors as possible. Thousands of experts in dozens of areas were brought in, all requiring housing, utilities and community services. Meanwhile a logging camp was set up at Hollis on Prince of Wales Island -- remember Don and Helen Finney?

In May 1954 the first finished pulp rolled off the machines after years of frustration and false starts. A wood pulp industry was a reality at last! By then B. Frank Heintzleman was governor, and at the mill dedication he said:

> We now see the establishment of a major enterprise which will provide year round employment, based upon a renewable resource offering a supply of raw material in perpetuity under proper scientific management.

It was the fruition of a dream that went back to Bernhard Eduard Fernow, head of the Division of Forestry during the creation of the forest reserves, who had visited Alaska in 1899 on the celebrated expedition of railroad magnate E. F. Harriman. He was the first to suggest that the Tongass should support a pulp industry. It was a triumph for Heintzleman. It was a triumph for Ketchikan.

Petition After Victory

And now for Sitka. Their story begins in January of 1952 with a document from the government of Japan titled: "Plea to the U.S. Government to export softwood timber of the Alaskan (Tongass) National Forest." The Japanese government had written it in response to a petition it received in May 1951 from the Council for Integrated Counter-Measures for Forest Resources, an organization of twenty industrial and technical associations. The Council had asked for negotiations with the U.S. government for permission to import Alaska timber in log form.

World War II had reduced Japan's forest acreage 55 percent and its timber inventory 65 percent. It had also destroyed the Japanese Empire, stripping from it the nation of Manchuria and handing Sakhalin and the Kurile Islands to the Soviet Union. Japan's postwar annual harvest on remaining privately owned forests was three times the forest's growth -- a blueprint for certain disaster. These private lands contained 68 percent of Japan's accessible timber and provided 73 percent of its softwood timber supply.

The Supreme Commander of Allied Powers ordered American specialists to study Japan's over-cutting problem and make recommendations to the Japanese government. The Diet approved a new Forest Law in May 1951 "to enforce compulsory reforestation and to execute erosion and flood control, so that the maintenance and reproduction of forest resources be promoted and the crisis of national lands be averted.''

That solved one problem but created another. Japan's timber demand was increasing annually -- wood was a basic material essential for recovery from war damage: Pulp, mine props, shipbuilding timber, railroad crossties, telephone poles, rail rolling stock and on and on. The decrease of supply from cutting restrictions in the face of rising demand meant that Japan faced a long-term wood deficit. In 1951 the deficit was 38 percent of demand.

Japan had earlier turned to the Philippines as a source of round logs, but the Philippine government curbed export in order to develop its own industrial forestry. In 1951 the Council approached the Forest Service inquiring about timber sales being offered in Alaska. Their proposal suggested that Japan should furnish the labor and logging facilities. The Forest Service refused to sell them round logs for export on the grounds that they wanted to use Alaskan timber locally. That prompted the Council to make its petition to the supreme commander of the allied powers.

The Japanese government's plea explained: ''We choose the Alaskan forest because they are situated close to the seashore, the distance to Japan is comparatively short and their resources are abundant.'' The plea concluded with a request for information about what could be done within U.S. laws and regulations.

The plea was considered by the Defense, Interior, Agriculture, Labor, and State departments. They turned it down for a variety of reasons, mostly to avoid exporting potential domestic jobs along with the round logs. But that wasn't the end of it.

The American Embassy in Tokyo responded in June that ''it is feasible for Japan to procure forest products from Alaskan National Forests'' through ''incorporation in the United States of a United States or Japanese Company to produce lumber, pulp or other processes items.'' The American response also noted that the Forest Service ''has several pulp timber units for sale to an organization planning to establish a newsprint or pulpwood mill in Alaska....it is suggested that an application for a timber concession together with a specific development plan be submitted to the Department of State.'' It was clearly understood that any successful proposal would suggest the use of American labor only.

The Japanese government concluded that using American labor was better than getting no wood at all. They sent a mission of government and trade representatives to Washington, D.C. in October 1952 for two weeks of talks. They met with officials of the U.S. Department of State, Interior,

Agriculture, Labor, Justice, Commerce and Defense. Dr. Koichi Aki reported that overcutting was continuing in Japan despite the new Forest Law because of commitments to Korea, Okinawa and Japan, which could devour its entire domestic supply within twelve years.

The mission was assured they could create a U.S. corporation to establish plants in Alaska to produce products for Japan from federal timber under U.S. laws and regulations. The conditions were spelled out this time: The State Department wrote, "The United States Government will place no obstacle in the way of Japanese interests" and expressed the hope that the project "will prove a feasible step toward alleviating Japan's acute shortage of forest products." State affirmed, "A United States corporation owned and controlled by Japanese interests, could bid on an equal basis with other United States companies for timber...subject to the sale laws and regulations, including those requiring the utilization of available American manpower, and the processing of forest products within the Territory."

Friends Of The Pulp Mill

The Japanese announced they would send technical experts to Alaska to study the project. The team arrived in early 1953 and was well received in Southeast Alaska. They were given highly favorable publicity in the

Ship loading at Alaska Pulp Corporation dock, Sitka   Rollo Pool photo

press. The team found what it was looking for in Sitka: a good location at Sawmill Creek, a power site, and a climate and atmosphere attractive to the Japanese. They were astonished at the waste in American wood processing and asked if the waste could be baled and shipped instead of being discarded.

What seems to be ignored in today's debate over the Tongass is the original public sentiment in favor of the proposed Japanese-owned pulp mill in Sitka. The president of the Juneau Chamber of Commerce, O.F. Benecke, was one of its strongest supporters. The Alaska Development Board gave strong support to the Sitka project. Both houses of the Legislature of the Territory of Alaska petitioned the federal government in March 1953 to permit the sale of timber in the Tongass to any U.S. company under equal conditions. In fact, the only objection came from the Pacific Northwest timber industry through Rep. Walter Norblad of Oregon. Norblad felt the Sitka mill would hurt the Oregon economy, since Oregon mills needed the Japanese market. He was certain that some back-room deal had been made between the U.S. and Japanese governments years earlier. As the Seattle *Post Intelligencer* wrote:

> What the Pacific Coast pulp industry now fears, according
> to its spokesmen, is that after Japanese timber reserves were
> handed over to the Russians with the transfer of the Sakhalin
> and Kurile Islands in secret conference at Yalta, commitments
> were made to the Japanese that their timber deficiency would
> be made up by permitting them to draw on the American
> reserves in the Tongass National Forest.

A Forest Service official in Alaska said, "I am positive that no such agreement exists." He gave assurances that the Japanese could obtain timber only through competitive bidding. The State Department assured Oregonians that they would have equal opportunity to compete in the Japanese market, and added another important note to the discussion:

> Today, more than ever before, the Department of Defense
> looks upon the forest reserve as a resource which can strengthen
> that important link in our national defense, a stable civilian
> population in Alaska."

Nobody in Alaska had the slightest objection to hosting a Japanese-owned company. The Sitka newspaper editorialized, "It makes no difference whether foreign or domestic capital develops industry here, so long as the group in charge must form an American corporation, employ American labor and operate exactly like any other company.'' In a later edition, the paper noted, ''At the present time, the United States as a whole is receiving no benefit whatsoever from the timber resources of Alaska, which are being permitted to deteriorate for lack of intelligent harvesting.''

In June 1953 the Japanese company Toshitsugu Matsui formed the Alaska Pulp Development Company. On August 15 that year Alaska Pulp Co., Ltd. was formed with 750,000 shares of common stock owned by 81 stockholders, 76 of whom were Japanese companies with a direct interest in additional sources of wood. They held 97 percent of the stock, including 60 percent held by chemical fiber manufacturers, 21 percent by four trading companies, 13 percent by pulp and paper manufacturers and 3 percent by more than 40 lumber firms.

At the end of November the executive directors of APC visited the U.S. to form the wholly-owned subsidiary Alaska Lumber and Pulp Co., Inc. ALP was incorporated in Juneau on December 10 to serve as purchaser of Tongass timber, build a pulp mill in the timber sale area and produce pulp for export to Japan.

Funding for all this came from the capitalists and the Export-Import Bank of Japan, the Industrial Bank of Japan, the Long-Term Credit Bank of Japan and numerous Japanese commercial banks. The first three banks provided $38.9 million to APC, 13 commercial banks and four trust companies supplied nearly $5.8 million and APC contributed $2.4 million from capital stock, all loaned to ALP. U.S. lenders were facing the Suez crisis at the time, which made negotiations for U.S. capital difficult. The Japanese executives decided to raise $19 million through a bond issue of $12 million and long-term bank loans for the remainder in the U.S. In fact, $20 million in bonds were bought by The Prudential Insurance Company, the Equitable Assurance Society and the General Electric Pension Trust, and $7 million was raised from U.S. banks by issuance of Senior Notes to eight suppliers of machinery and equipment for the Sitka pulp mill including General Electric Company.

The U.S. government didn't put a penny in it.

At the end of December 1953 the regional forester wrote a six page letter detailing for APC the steps still required to qualify for award of a contract. APC had to identify stands of timber desired, present a logging plan, suggest the conditions under which the agency would advertise the timber, specify how the timber would be converted to lumber and pulp, and provide a detailed plan of operation.

Now began the long technical process of meeting the conditions for winning the contract. ALP leased a sawmill through Wrangell Mills Company in 1954. The Sitka city council arranged permits to obtain industrial water which facilitated construction of a hydroelectric development by the city. ALP funded water pollution studies in cooperation with various government agencies. Test drilling began on the mill site at Sawmill Creek.

On January 25, 1956 the regional forester announced that ALP had won a conditional award for timber harvest based upon its bid -- the only one received. Nearly 20 months would pass before the final award was made.

Finally, on October 15, 1957, nearly five years after the Japanese plea to the U.S. government, the contract was signed by Regional Forester P.D. Hanson and ALP President Tadao Sasayama, witnessed by Mike Stepovich, former mayor of Sitka, and B. Frank Heintzleman, former governor of Alaska Territory.

Like the Ketchikan Pulp Company contract, the Alaska Pulp Company contract contained an unusual preamble defining its intent. In fact, some of the language from the KPC contract was adopted as "boilerplate" for the APC document.

> In entering into this contract, the parties hereto are acting in recognition of conditions and intentions as follows:
>
> a. The purchaser proposes to establish a new industrial enterprise which will be an important and significant step in the industrial development of Alaska;
>
> b. The Forest Service desires to facilitate and encourage such industrial development of Alaska;
>
> c. Both parties recognize that this undertaking, involving a substantial long-term investment by the purchaser, will be accompanied by unusual risks;
>
> d. It is necessary that operations of this new enterprise be conducted on a competitive and commercially sound basis;
>
> e. It is the policy and intent of the Forest Service, through sustained yield management of the timber resources of the Tongass National Forest, to afford opportunities to purchase supplies of timber for permanent operation of the enterprise which may be established under the terms of this contract.

The meaning of "competitive and commercially sound" as used in this contract has been questioned: If the intent was to make the Tongass mills compete with other U.S. mills, why did they get 50 year exclusive cutting rights when mills in the Lower 48 had no such thing? It so happens that the issue came up in a 1978 lawsuit and the principal drafter of both long-term contracts, Ira J. Mason, former Director of Timber Management on the Tongass, answered the question in two parts: 1) The Forest Service had special concern to make its timber available to the pulp mills on such terms as would assist the industrial development of Alaska, which included equitable and competitive stumpage rates, to be redetermined every five years and based upon market prices; and 2) Shipping products to Japan directly from the Tongass is a shorter distance than from Puget Sound, a natural competitive advantage which, balanced against Puget Sound's developed economy and proximity to equipment, labor and services, yields equitable competitiveness.

The fifty year term was an agreed-upon recognition of the special risks involved in developing an industrial base in a new area in the midst of abundant timber but remote from markets and operating supplies, conditions which did not exist in Puget Sound. Even so, Congress in the Sustained Yield Act of 1944, authorized the Forest Service to enter into a 100 year contract with Simpson Timber Company in establishing the Shelton Cooperative Sustained Yield Unit that extended along the shores of Puget Sound. And if you stop to think of it, a long-term contract is the most effective instrument government has to make political lands behave economically like private lands -- short of actually selling the national forests to private owners.

The Sitka pulp plant was designed and built to produce 120,000 tons per year of high quality dissolving pulp (alpha cellulose for rayon production) or high grade bleached paper pulp. The total construction cost was $56 million. It uses the magnesium bi-sulfite recovery process providing for economical recovery of chemicals, heat recovery from the cooking liquor, and reduced stream and air pollution. Effluent, containing only minimal amounts of fibers and chemicals were discharged in the bay at Sitka to at least the 65-foot level. Continuous monitoring facilities are a part of the mill.

On December 7, 1959, continuous full scale production of pulp was begun and the first shipment of 2,060 tons of pulp left for Japan at the beginning of January, 1960. Now the pulp industry was firmly established in the Tongass, with strong economic growth for Sitka and all of Alaska as anticipated.

Wood, Brick, Steel and People

If you've never been in a pulp mill, prepare your mind for a new scale of physical scientific values. It's big.

We're going to tour Ketchikan Pulp Company's mill -- it's much like Alaska Pulp Corporation's Sitka plant, so we needn't visit both.

The approach to Ward Cove affords a panoramic view of the KPC mill with its heavily wooded backdrop and the foreground of deep tidewater. Here you can see the log rafts that supply the mill. Logs come here only by water, either by tugs towing rafts or self dumping log barges.

As we drive over Ward Creek and start up the hill to the mill, notice the five foot diameter wood-stave pipeline. It brings forty million gallons of water a day from KPC's 85 foot high reinforced concrete dam to the filter plant through that three mile long pipe. In the filter plant water is chemically treated and filtered prior to use for pulp processing and domestic service.

You drive around to the north side of the cove and up to the parking lot in front of KPC's mill office. Here we meet Martin Pihl, President and General Manager of Ketchikan Pulp Company. He puts this mill in context for us:

Martin Pihl   Ron Arnold photo

"Welcome to Ketchikan Pulp's mill. KPC is a wholly owned subsidiary of Louisiana Pacific Corporation based in Portland, Oregon. We are part of the pulp and paper industry, one of the ten largest sectors of the American economy. There are more than 700,000 pulp and paper workers and they cover all 50 states. The United States population uses about 650 pounds of pulp and paper products a year for every man, woman and child.

"This mill took two years to build and cost some $54 million. We began with a daily capacity of 300 tons, which our contract said must increase to 525 tons by July 1964. We surpassed that in 1959 with our current capacity approaching 650 tons of high quality dissolving pulp daily. Between 1977 and 1980 we spent $28 million installing air and water quality control systems. We also expanded our chemical recovery system to maintain a high recycle rate. The cost of mill construction now totals $120 million.

"Our product is dissolving pulp, which is used by other industries to manufacture dozens of finished products, the major one being rayon for fabrics and other fiber uses. Rayon cord is used to reinforce automobile tires and automotive fanbelts and other uses that seem unlikely at first. Dissolving pulp is also converted into cellophane, which you see today mostly in strapping tape.

"Dissolving pulp generates so many finished products you could hardly list them all. They include acetate fabrics, photographic film, pharmaceuticals, cigarette filters, rigid packaging, high quality plastics, cosmetics, detergents, food products, superabsorbents, additives for oil well drilling muds, explosives, lacquers, printing inks, rocket fuel, sponges and sausage casings.

"We employ about 520 workers at this mill and about 375 in the woods and at our saw mill on Annette Island. Our contractors employ about 465 workers. That's a total of more than 1,350 people at work. Our operations contribute about $5 million monthly to the economy of Ketchikan, Metlakatla and Prince of Wales Island. Let me hand you over to Steve Hagan, mill superintendent."

The pride we feel exuding from Martin Pihl is not the egotistic pride so often scornfully painted on industry executives, but the pride of contributing to the whole community of mankind, the pride of knowing that what you do helps everyone, even the ungrateful opponents who throw your products back in your face with hateful words printed on the paper your industry provided them.

Steve Hagan tells us, "I'll be walking you out to meet the production superintendent. We'll go down this main corridor. First you'll need these earplugs for hearing protection -- mills are noisy places. And you must carry this emergency respirator; it has a belt hook. You're not likely to need it, but if any unforeseen chemical gas leak should occur while we're in certain parts of the mill, you'll have to put it on quickly. Our workers carry this kind of protection at all times.

"Let me explain briefly what we do here. When you tour our mill, it looks very complicated. But it all boils down to four basic functions: First we cook wood to make dissolving pulp. Second, we recycle the pulping chemicals in a recovery boiler. Third, we manufacture the pulp into dry sheets which are baled for shipment. Fourth, we treat our wastes with state of the art equipment to protect the environment.

"The mill operates on a continuous round-the-clock schedule with a minimum of downtime for repairs. It's a non-stop operation.

"Here's Allyn Hayes, our production superintendent. He'll take you through the whole process."

Hayes marches us into a huge building and immediately hustles us onto a cargo elevator. We go

Allyn Hayes   Ron Arnold photo

down seven levels and follow him through a maze of pipes and tubing out a door facing Ward Cove.

Input

"Before we begin the milling process," he explains, "we have to get the logs out of the water. You can see these little one-man boom boats breaking up bundle rafts and pushing banded loads into position under our giant crane. These banded packages of logs are actually truck loads that were banded in the woods.

Huge crane claws lift logs from Ward Cove up to mill deck   Ron Arnold photo

"The crane lifts the loads to the log deck where the bundles are broken down and individual logs are sent to one of our two wood rooms for chipping. We chip about 3,500 logs each day.

Clay Hansen tends chip screen   Ron Arnold photo

"You'll also see a chip barge alongside the crane. Those are sawmill by-products shipped here from around the Tongass. These wood chips are blown by a blower system to storage silos.

There's Phil McElroy -- he's our wood preparation supervisor -- hey, Phil, tell us about your operation."

Phil says, "Our number one wood room handles large logs 38 inch diameter and up. A 108" diameter cut-off saw cuts the logs into 20 foot lengths. Logs are completely "barked" in 15 seconds by our 1,200-gallon-per-minute, 1,400 pound per square inch hydraulic barker.

"The number two wood room barks and chips logs up to 38 inch diameter in a continuous line, using a mechanical barker.

"All logs go to the chipper. George Beals there is the barker/chipper operator and Ken Chapin is his assistant. Quality pulp depends on a quality chip. Logs are cut into 3/4 inch chips in about ten seconds by a chipper disc containing eight sets of knives. The 140" chipper disc, driven by a

The beginning: a simple wood chip   Ron Arnold photo

2000 HP electric motor, revolves at 277 rpm. Uniformity of chip size is very important, and Clay Hansen, our chip screen tender, assures it. Fines and sawdust are conveyed to the boiler house to be burned as fuel to help power the plant. Our two power boilers also burn bark from the wood rooms and oil to drive two 10,000 KWH turbine generators and one 18,000 KWH turbine generator, enough power for a community twice the size of Ketchikan, which has an official population of 7,100 and several thousand more counting the surrounding area.''

Again, you can sense the pride and dedication of these people radiating everywhere they take us.

We leave McElroy and follow Hayes to the digester control room in the heart of the mill. Hayes introduces us to Jim Hinman, cook. He's not preparing filet mignon, but something more like a hemlock and spruce soufflé.

Jim tells us, ''Chips are conveyed to that bank of nine digesters on the deck outside the control room. Each is filled with 110 tons of chips and about 55,000 gallons of cooking liquor. Inside the digester, the cooking liquor breaks down the wood, separating the pure cellulose fiber from the lignin that binds wood together and from other wood chemicals. The temperature in a digester during the cooking process rises to about 300 degrees F under 120 pounds per square inch pressure. You can see the gauges there in front of John

Wood cook at work   Ron Arnold photo

Vandiver, my cook's first helper. Each cook takes nearly five hours. Three things come out: used cooking chemicals, lignin and pulp. We fill the digesters every forty-five minutes. The pulp goes from here to the washers.''

Now Hayes takes us to the acid plant. ''Keep your respirators handy. If any problem occurs, this is a likely place.'' We notice a sign on the wall saying there have been 696 accident-free days in this department.

Todd Sybesma is the Acid Maker. He explains: ''The acid plant is a

Acid maker checks a batch   Ron Arnold photo

chemical merry-go-round. Used chemicals and dissolved wood organics from the cooking and washing -- cooking liquor, it's called -- are recycled over and over again through an elaborate recovery process. It's a closed loop. We use the magnesium oxide recovery system here for environmental reasons -- it causes less pollution than other methods. The recycling process takes the cooking liquor and runs it to evaporators run by Rich Rold here. The evaporators distil it to a prescribed density, and then we burn it in four chemical recovery boilers operated by Glen Budge. We use the steam to drive electrical generators, and the used cooking liquor is restored through a complex chemical process that leaves ash and combustion gases recombined. Every new cycle, however, we have to add a little "make up" sulfur dioxide and magnesium oxide to compensate for the inevitable loss."

On our way to the wash plant we pass the maintenance shop, where most of the mechanical trades are represented. These workers have the skill, knowledge and tools to restore any part of the mill to production in case of a breakdown.

Now to the wash plant.

Bleacherman assistant Scott Diverty tells us: "Here cooked pulp is pumped to de-knotters which remove uncooked knots and chips. Then the pulp is washed on four stainless steel rotary washers. In the screen room -- no, it's not for movies -- pulp is directed over screens to remove particles of dirt that have been missed. Lindblad screens, which rotate and vibrate simultaneously, remove small pieces of bark and uncooked wood."

Bleacherman Larry Johnson runs the bleach plant where the continuous bleaching process takes five hours in six stages using varying quantities of chlorine, caustic and bleach liquor according to the type of pulp desired. Johnson continually monitors every stage of the bleach cycle,

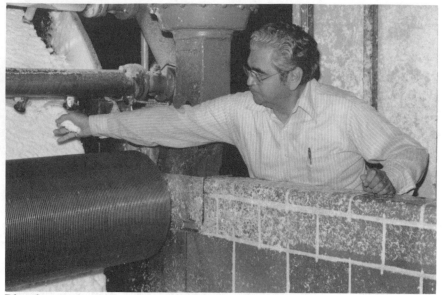

Bleacherman monitors pulp purity   Ron Arnold photo

insuring pure bleached pulp with no remaining defects.

Process engineer Steve Eilertson is doing special testing to determine better methods of bleach plant operation.

And now we troop along behind Hayes to the vast hall of the pulp machine. Primo Rodriguez is the pulp machine tender. He shows us the enormous contraption.

Primo Rodriguez and the enormous fourdrinier machine   Ron Arnold photo

Allyn Hayes and the dryer rolls   Ron Arnold photo

"The pulp slurry," says Primo, "has been diluted with ninety-eight and a half percent water and is piped into this steamy room. The slurry is fed into a head-box which evenly distributes the liquid pulp onto a moving endless mesh screen 192 inches wide called a Fourdrin-ier wire after its inventor. The wire, moving at speeds of up to 400 feet per minute, is designed to drain water out of the pulp. As water drains through the screen mesh, a layer of fibers forms, the first evidence of our product's final appearance. The farther down the screen the pulp travels, the more water is removed, first by gravity, then by suction, then by pressure and finally by the drying rollers. A wet felt belt helps carry the sheet through the press section. The pulp sheet is then 'weaved' through the block-long series of 147 steam heated drying rollers three stories high."

We walk the long distance to the "dry" end of the pulp machine. The dry pulp speeds out of the dryers looking like thick white paper, and is rolled onto "jumbo" rolls weighing from 17 to 20 tons each. As one rolls fills, another replaces it in a precision team maneuver. Backtender of the pulp machine is Rex Pope, who works with third hand Steve Cooper and grader John Cowan. The jumbo rolls are stored while each is thoroughly tested for quality.

The rolls are much too big for customers to handle. At the rewinder, cutter and layboy machines, cuttermen Jim Hendricks and Dave Wesley cut the rolls into sheets on an enormous and ingeniously designed machine that stacks the cut sheet pulp and sends it to the baler.

Stacker/baler operator Mike Fontana arranges the cutting machine's

Jumbo rolls of dry pulp ready for the cutter

short stacks into large shipping-size stacks.

Fontana tells us, "After the bales of pulp have been weighed, they are placed in a hydraulic press where pressure up to 1,000 tons is applied to increase pulp density and reduce shipping volume. The bales are then tied with wire and sent to the pulp storage area directly below."

Allyn Hayes walks us into a huge storage area. "Each pulp bale is identified by a unique number," he says, "and stored until shipped. If shipped by railcar on barges to Seattle, the

Cut sheets of pulp stacked into bales   Ron Arnold photo

Fork lift operator loads bales of pulp into rail car

Rollo Pool photo

Rail cars loaded onto barge for sea haul

Rollo Pool photo

pulp is loaded into boxcars inside the storage building. There's Wes Mollenhauer doing some loading now -- he's one of our truckers. Storage on a dock is provided for pulp to be loaded aboard ships.''

We follow Hayes out along the parallel rails.

"Rail cars are loaded off and on car barges over the ferry slip,'' Hayes says. "A biweekly barge service from Seattle brings chemicals, oil, general supplies and boxcars. The boxcars are filled with pulp for delivery to the various rayon and cellophane mills in the Eastern United States and Mexico.''

Hayes takes us back up the service elevator and out to the parking lot once more. Here we overlook the mill's wastewater treatment system.

"In the primary system about 14 million gallons of dirty water from barking, pulp washing and floor drains has the settleable solids removed in our 190 foot diameter clarifier. The water takes five hours to pass through this machine. The solids are raked to the center, pumped to the ''hog house'', filtered, then pressed and burned as hog fuel. Hog fuel is mill talk for low value raw materials which are burnt to recover their energy.

"The secondary treatment system consists of a 9.5 million gallon aeration basin, a clarifier and cooling tower. Here high strength waste streams are biologically treated to reduce discharge levels to limits required by the Environmental Protection Agency.

Pulp ship in Sitka Sound prepares for voyage to Japan's markets   Rollo Pool photo

''And that's it. You've now seen how a pulp mill works.''

Thanks, Allyn. It's a little overwhelming.

But what lingers is the feeling of humanity in a place that has been pictured as inhuman. This giant pulp mill is like a living organism whose life-blood is the people that flow in and around and out of it every day, a great creature tended and cared for by human beings producing basic human needs: meaningful work, useful products, an expression of the endless pride and the eager outstretching toward happiness of humanity, a wonder no less than the trees and the stars.

It's not just a pulp mill.

SAWMILLS

• •

W e're going back to downtown Ketchikan before we fly up to Wrangell to visit the sawmill there. We're going to talk to Cliff Taro, President of Southeast Stevedoring Corporation. That's another job sector environmentalists don't think of when they get the itch to put loggers out of business.

Cliff Taro's office is in a refurbished aircraft hangar on the waterfront. Cliff tells us what he does.

"We contract to load and unload ships, which means we employ longshoremen, furnishing supervision and all the gear and equipment, such as fork lifts, boom boats, cranes, and any other gear needed for proper loading and stowing of round logs, pulp, cants, lumber, and some fish products. We have about fifty people on our payroll every day -- and when ships are loading in every port we may have three or four hundred.

"But we're really here because of the timber industry. I just bought some stock in Louisiana Pacific, which I've waited many years to do because it was so high, but I wanted to be part of it, because if it wasn't for them I wouldn't be here -- and neither would my family. My son-in-law Bob Berto and my son Jim are vice presidents in our corporation.

"We've had the good fortune to ride on the progress of the timber industry because of the ports it developed. We stevedored the first shipment of pulp from Ketchikan Pulp Company in 1954 and shortly thereafter, the first shipload of sawn timber exported to Japan from Alaska at Wrangell Lumber Company. These jobs were followed by several 'first shipments:' of lumber from Haines and Ketchikan Spruce Mill; of pulp at Alaska Lumber & Pulp Company (as Alaska Pulp Corporation was known then); and subsequently of lumber from Juneau (the old Columbia Lumber Company during the Korean War). We also made first shipments of lumber from Metlakatla and Klawock, and first cargoes of round logs from Klawock, Kake, Hydaburg, Hoonah, Yakutat and Afognak Islands.

"As the Chairman of Cruise Lines Agencies of Alaska I wear another hat. We're steamship agents for some twenty large cruise ships, making

247

Cliff Taro   Ron Arnold photo

over a thousand port calls into the Tongass during the three or four summer months. We provide many services for these vessels including tugboats, pilot boats, pilots, line handlers, U.S. customs, Immigration -- if somebody's sick and needs medical aid, everything.

"If it wasn't for the timber industry's rock steady business in the Tongass, we'd have to charge much higher prices for services provided the cruise ships because of their short season, some years barely three months long. Thus the tourists would be paying a higher cost of passage to see our beautiful Tongass.

"So the truth is that the timber industry is heavily subsidizing the tourist industry. This vaunted boom in tourism many see on the horizon would go bust in a hurry if the timber industry were eliminated and trip prices went up thirty to fifty percent. There is no free lunch.

"Anybody who says that the timber industry is not compatible with tourism is ignorant at best. The timber industry is a good part of the reason there is a tourism industry at all -- it keeps the prices within reason."

Oh, foolish environmentalists who prate endlessly of the wonderful webs and chains and interconnections of ecology, will you never see that the same principles apply to the human economy? Will you never consider your own species part of the whole? You quote to us the poetry of Robinson Jeffers who said of nature, ''Love that, not man apart from that.'' Have you never wondered why Jeffers and your other heroes considered that man could be apart from nature in the first place? Loggers never consider man apart. Because loggers live and work in nature every day and it would never occur to them that there could be a separation. You write your diatribes against loggers in your crowded cities sitting in offices looking out over an alley or a traffic-clogged street and never realize that you're simply projecting your own alienation from nature onto us who are not alienated. We belong in this world. We're effective in this world. We achieve in this world. We're the home givers of this world.

You're the lawyers and the lobbyists of this world. Small wonder that someone has to preach to you about man apart.

The Care and Feeding of Sawmills

Alaska Airlines has a 737 scheduled for the Wrangell flight at just the right time. By jet it's hardly 20 minutes away.

The town of Wrangell has had a checkered sawmilling history. During World War II the Army Corps of Engineers put out a call for more lumber to be produced from its mill in Wrangell, and an outfit called Wagner Lumber Company answered the call, buying the existing sawmill, which had seen better days. The Army engineers were persuaded to put money into the Wrangell sawmill, which needed repairs and new machinery. In return for its investment the engineers would receive lumber at a fixed price.

However, things didn't work out and the mill ran for only a short time. Wagner left the country and the Army Corps of Engineers reacquired the property through default. It sold the mill to an American of Japanese descent named C.T. Takahashi. He operated it for a time and then sold it to the Japanese group that was building the pulp mill in Sitka. The Japanese formed a corporation, the Wrangell Lumber Company, as a subsidiary of the Alaska Lumber and Pulp Company.

Meanwhile, Oregon interests built another sawmill in Wrangell. Lumberman C.D. Johnson had formed the Pacific Northern Timber Company in order to create another 50 year contract with the Forest Service on the Tongass. The Forest Service offered for bid 3 billion feet of timber in the area with a provision that a 100-ton pulp mill be built in connection with the sawmill within three years. Nothing happened. Then an Oregon attorney, C. Girard ''Jebby'' Davidson (formerly an assistant secretary of the interior mentioned prominently in Don Hummel's *Stealing the National Parks*), reorganized the company, set up a sawmill, and got the operation going. It did not thrive and in 1968 the owners sold it to Wrangell Lumber Company. The Wrangell pulp mill was never built because Pacific Northern could not raise the capital, and the timber sale reverted from a fifty-year tenure involving 3 billion board feet to a fifteen-year sale of 790 million feet. Wrangell Lumber Company in the late 1970s drew a bad profit picture and Alaska Pulp had second thoughts about it.

Today things are different. Wrangell Lumber Company is now Wrangell Forest Products, which is a division of Seley Corporation and Seley Corporation is a success story of Steve Seley, a second generation Alaska logger. Steve was a Tongass logging camp kid, graduated from high school in 1971 at Thorne Bay and married his wife Lin in the fall. Steve happens to be in Wrangell today, although his headquarters is in Ketchikan. Let's ask him a few questions. How'd you get your start, Steve?

"We started a small repair business working on Louisiana Pacific equipment and later advanced to A-frame logging a few small sales around Thorne Bay. A-frame logging starts from the beach with a big log A-frame, opens up an entry road and then logs the timber behind a visual screen of trees. The environmentalists came in and stopped A-frame logging, you couldn't log where you could see the operation from a ferry passing down the passages. Which is a mistake. People on the ferries and cruise ships want to see our operations -- properly done logging is part of our cultural heritage they're being deprived of.

"So we were driven out of A-frame logging and we moved into marine construction, moved away from logging for a while."

But you moved back.

"Oh, yes. We run twelve to fourteen sides today feeding this mill." [Logger lingo: a "side" is one complete logging operation, including crew and the equipment.]

You've enjoyed success here with Wrangell Forest Products. This mill was a problem for Alaska Pulp Corporation when they owned it. You bought it and have had better luck.

"I don't pat myself on the back for that. I don't want to be one of those people they say is 'a legend in his own mind.' Our company is run by a group of people, and everybody shares the credit. Here, let's go talk in Win Smith's office, he's vice president and mill manager."

Hi, Win.

"And this is Richard Klinke, our mill superintendent. Get Roy Martin

Regrowing the Tongass for Tomorrow's Wood Needs

The three-photo sequence on this and the following two pages graphically illustrates the tremendous fertility of the Tongass for the purpose of tree growing. Virgil Byford of Wrangell posed in 1964 beside a recently logged area, little expecting to make a vital environmental point. Then on a 1975 visit, Byford posed as close to the same spot as he could locate, revealing vigorous regrowth in only eleven years. In 1988 Wrangell *Sentinel* publisher Alvin Bunch decided to continue the sequence and went with Byford to the same camera point and took the third photo. The forest regrowth of twenty-four years had become so thick and tall that they had to back away from the original spot in order to show anything but tree trunks.

courtesy Virgil Byford

Virgil Byford beside fresh clearcut in 1964

in here, too, will you? He's our industrial relations manager. He'll take you through the mill.''

Hi, fellows. Steve was just telling us the secret of the mill's success. Go on, Steve.

"I believe the difference is on-the-spot management. For one thing, Alaska Pulp Corporation had a labor contract that we judged was about five dollars an hour over market. Productivity was down. In a little outfit like mine even the managers will work any position required. When we first took over, any of us worked on the green chain or worked the night shift if we had to. [Sawmill lingo: the green chain is a conveyor chain where "green" or undried lumber comes out of the mill, and must be pulled from the chain into proper sort bins for later processing, the most physically demanding job in mill work.]

"I spent four years up here working like that, and that's the way we run the plant today. We've all done it. We've increased productivity tremendously. When we took over, this mill got about 1.6 thousand board

Virgil Byford and new forest 11 years later, 1975
courtesy Virgil Byford

feet per man hour. The mill had a reputation: alligator mouth and hummingbird fanny. Our goal is 3 thousand board feet per man hour and today we're about 2.7 - 2.8 thousand.

Was the turnaround rapid?

Steve laughs an ironic laugh.

"When we took over the mill in 1984 we thought the market was at the bottom. We thought we saw an opportunity to get in and make money cutting commodity items, cants and squares. And then we found out there was a basement under the bottom of the market. Our profits fell -- no, our losses increased -- for another two years with no end in sight. One day we realized that here we were with a facility that wouldn't cut to meet the market demand for finished products, which was rising at that time. Not only did we have to fund an operating loss, we had to borrow money to upgrade the facility so it could cut finished products for today's market -- about 7 million dollars. Go take a look at what we spent the money on."

Roy Martin hands us some familiar brown objects: "Better put on

1988: The forest has returned, vigorous and healthy   Wrangell Sentinel

these Tongass tennis shoes. It's been raining pretty good. And don't forget your ear plugs.''

We've walked past the sawmill to the docks where barges are taking on chips bound for Alaska Pulp Corporation's mill in Sitka to be turned into dissolving pulp. Since we want to start where the logs begin their complex trip through the mill, we're out here where they come in by water.

Roy tells us what we're looking at. ''The logs are lifted by crane from rafts in the water, unbanded, and fed into the mill on two tracks, one for large logs, one for small.

''Ron Rice runs our log yard, he's got two lift cranes over the water and three log stackers and four large front-end loaders to move logs with.

''Let's walk up the log path. Our logs come up the conveyor chain onto the cutoff deck where they'll be cut to proper lengths for the milling process further along. They first go through a 60-inch diameter ring barker run by ''Hoop'' Wellons and then through the cutoff saw run by Mack Pahang. Since we took over the mill, we've installed a new whole-log chipper so we can segregate cull logs that are only good for pulp chips from the lumber-quality logs we can use in our mill. Logs are diverted and the chipper is controlled by Mike Clark.

''Inside the mill we've changed machinery throughout. This is all new, state of the art log-break-down equipment. Let's stop by and see Ed Rilatos, the mill supervisor. He's directly responsible for this operation.''

We meet Rilatos, who takes us to the front end of the mill.

''First, we'll look at the head-rig bandsaw,'' he tells us.

He opens the headrig sawyer's glass-walled control room door and ushers us in.

Ed says, ''The large logs 23 inches diameter and bigger come up this side and feed our nine foot band saw operated by Randy Rasler. The sawyer is the most important person in the mill's chain of important people. Tell 'em what you do, Randy.''

Cull logs go to chipper   Ron Arnold photo

Headrig bandsaw's thin kerf gets the most from each log   Ron Arnold photo

Rasler says, "I do the initial breakdown of the larger logs into sizes and grades that can be cut into smaller dimensions by equipment farther down the line. Each log must be manufactured to its best economic return, so I have to judge many things on each log: Exactly where should the log be set for its first pass through the bandsaw -- the 'best opening face' -- because if I make a mistake on the opening cut, I could end up causing the people farther along to waste a third or even half of that log.

"My job is made easier because our logs are presorted out on the deck for diameter and grade, and I know the cutting patterns and the product we're trying to produce.

"We're intent on getting the most out of the forest, to waste nothing. We have thin kerf saws that make thinner cuts -- less sawdust, more lumber.

"I also have to look carefully for outside indications of inside defects, and judge where the high-quality clear wood is. Every time I pass the log through the bandsaw I'm narrowing my options for the remaining passes. I have to visualize the finished products coming out of every log as I cut it. I do my best to maximize high quality clear lumber recovery while leaving a minimum of factory or standard cuts."

Rilatos takes us to the other side of the mill's front end: a huge

machine with four bandsaws
mounted together called a quad-
band saw.

"Here on the other side
we feed the small logs to an
end-dogging quad-band saw on
a conveyor line of its own.
We feed it predominantly 16
inch diameter and smaller logs,
but we'll go 17 to 22 inch
from time to time. Penny Sims
is our quad-band sawyer. She'll
tell us about her job."

We enter her glass-walled
cubicle.

Penny says, "The small
logs require more finely-tuned
breakdown than larger logs, and

Penny Sims cuts for quality   Ron Arnold photo

that's why we use the quad-
band saw: Its four blades can be spaced by my control panel here so I can
get the best cuts possible from each log. The judgment problem is much
the same as on the headrig bandsaw, but there's usually less defect to cope
with on the smaller logs."

"I find that if I have a more consistent log, like a second growth type
-- which is what we've got going through the small log side -- then we
continually beat these environmentalists who tell us that second growth's
not any good, that you can't get good lumber from it. The more consistent
the logs I get the faster I can go."

She's a good sawyer.

Rilatos takes us further into the mill. After the initial log breakdown,
the wood goes to machines called edgers that do just what their name says:
They cut square edges onto rounded corners.

Rilatos says, "This mill has three edgers that together handle the
output of the headrig band saw and the quad-band saw. After being edged,
the wood goes to the trimmers which cut each piece to the best length,
removing defects where possible.

"As the lumber flows from one machine to another and becomes more
and more a finished product, we find that a larger low quality piece can be
resawn to produce a higher quality smaller piece, which will sell for a
higher price. So we have a resaw station that does nothing but improve the

Graders assign quality levels to each piece of lumber   Ron Arnold photo

grade of our product.

"When the green lumber has been cut, edged and trimmed to its highest value, we have to sort it, which we do over here at the end of the building in a J-bar sorter. We sort by lengths, by widths and thickness, by grade, and put the lumber in bundles. The J-bar sorter has 36 slots for 36 different sorts.

"On top of that we do numerous hand sorts in this mill. We continually pull in excess of 100 length and size sorts. That's the key to successful operation. We produce exactly what the customer wants. And that's the sawmilling operation."

Roy Martin takes us to the planer building.

"When we first took over the mill, this area was just a big sawdust pile. The planers take rough lumber from the mill and precision end trim and surface each piece to an exact thickness, right down to a millimeter. Then the finished lumber is loaded and shipped to market. Let's rejoin Steve Seley and he's explain our marketing strategy."

Back in the office Seley says over a cup of coffee: "We supply a group of wholesalers in Japan. We've identified the product mix that sells best in their market areas. Our mill workers each understand the mix, they know how we need to break our logs down into specific items that our customers

Loader sorts finished lumber for shipping to world markets   Ron Arnold photo

want. They know that different parts of a log will go to different wholesalers, so we can move each piece of lumber for the highest price in Japan. We have contact with the market every day by Fax machine and telephone.

"I think part of the success in our operation is that we not only own the mill, but we also have our own logging operations. We have the ability to fall the timber properly for the least breakage in the woods, we yard the logs efficiently, we're pretty good road builders to get to the timber, we have a couple of old tugboats to get the product to the mill, and once we get it here, we have the people that know how to cut for the highest and best use.

People. People of the Tongass.

The home-givers of the whole earth.

THE PEOPLE ASPIRING

Part Four

PROVING GROUND FOR LAWYERS

• •

Q: What's the difference between finding a dead lawyer and a dead skunk in the middle of the highway?

A: There are skid marks in front of the skunk.

A lawyer told us that joke, so don't assume that we have anything against lawyers. Yet, truth to say, most of our Tongass timber industry friends smile when they hear it. They have cause.

Think about this: The number of major national forest laws enacted in the last thirty years is about twice the number enacted during the previous sixty years. For the last thirty years every major federal law affecting the national forests has restricted the forest products industry. For the last thirty years every major federal law affecting the national forests has increased the costs borne by the forest products industry.

Arguably, only three obscure federal laws since 1960 have in any way helped the forest products industry, and that indirectly by supplying funds for roads or reforestation: The National Forest Roads and Trails Act of 1964, the Rural Development Act of 1972 and the Agriculture and Consumer Protection Act of 1973--Forestry Incentives. Even if you're a lawyer you probably never heard of these laws.

Big Laws, Little People

The timber industry in the Tongass has taken the full brunt of all this legalizing. Consider this compendium of ten major federal laws enacted since 1958:

● **The Alaska Statehood Act of 1958**. This law authorized the selection of up to 400,000 acres from the Tongass and Chugach National Forests for transfer out of the timber base and into state ownership. As of 1988, 172,606 acres have been or are in the process of being conveyed to the state, 142,700 of those acres in the Tongass, reducing the industrial timber base.

● **The Multiple Use - Sustained Yield Act of 1960**. It requires the Forest Service to administer the national forests "for outdoor recreation, range, timber, watershed, and wildlife and fish purposes." The law specifically rejects economic values as a guide for administration: multiple uses will be selected to "best meet the needs of the American people" and "not necessarily the combination of uses that will give the greatest dollar return or the greatest unit output." Since timber was historically the use that gave the greatest dollar return and the greatest unit output, this was a directive to de-emphasize the role of timber in the national forests. This de-emphasis has continued for nearly thirty years and is now virtually complete. Incidentally, this clause also vindicates the "below cost timber sale," since the law specifically orders administrators *not* to base their judgments on the greatest dollar return or the greatest unit output. But we notice that environmentalist lawyers who are so expert at finding flyspecks in the law to prove their points seem to develop instant Alzheimer's when it comes to boulders which prove them to be the fools they are.

● **The Wilderness Act of 1964**. It created a system of federal roadless areas of more than 5,000 acres each, "untrammeled by man" to be managed "without permanent improvements or human habitation," where there "shall be no commercial enterprise and...no temporary road, no use of motor vehicles, motorized equipment or motorboats, no landing of aircraft, no other form of mechanical transport, and no structure or installation within any such area." Not even primitive toilets. Congress designated 9.1 million acres of Wilderness in the act, with provisions to study all roadless areas for possible inclusion, and envisioned a Wilderness System of about 15 million acres in total. Today there are over 90 million acres designated Wilderness. Environmentalists have plans to double that. The act removes lands from multiple use classification and mandates a single use. It has pushed the timber industry out of 80 million acres that were previously available for timber harvest, 5.4 million in the Tongass.

● **The National Trails Systems Act of 1968**. Created a vast system of hiking trails excluding motorized vehicles and restricting adjacent lands "to avoid activities incompatible with the purposes for which such trails were established." Designation of national trails has caused the cancellation, relocation, redesign or delay of hundreds of timber sales in nearby lands otherwise completely suitable for harvest.

● **The National Environmental Policy Act of 1969**. Known as NEPA. Requires filing of Environmental Impact Statements for all major federal actions, including timber sales. Although an EIS is nothing more than a description of likely impacts, and is not a directive to adopt any specific on-the-ground improvement, hundreds of lawsuits over the adequacy of descriptions in EISs have raised the cost of planning a timber sale by millions of dollars in each national forest. These lawsuits involve nothing but word juggling and produce nothing but delays and thick documents. Many observers regard NEPA as "The Lawyer's Full Employment Act of 1969."

● **The Alaska Native Claims Settlement Act of 1971.** Provided cash settlements and authorized the transfer of nearly 44 million acres throughout the State of Alaska from federal management to private ownership by Native corporations. As of 1988, about 629,000 acres of the Tongass National Forest have been selected and have either been conveyed or are expected to be conveyed out of the timber base and into private ownership of Native corporations. Section 17(d)(2) of ANCSA provided for putting public lands into the "four systems," i.e. the Wilderness System, the National Wild and Scenic Rivers System, the National Wildlife Refuge System or the National Forest System. These "D2" lands included withdrawal not to exceed 80 million acres of Alaska lands into the Wilderness System.

● **The Forest and Rangeland Renewable Resources Planning Act of 1974.** Enacted a complex morass of planning requirements including the use of interdisciplinary teams; the specific requirement that all forest plans follow the NEPA process; limited the forester's ability to replant in desirable species (to prevent "monoculture"); forbade the selection of a harvesting system "primarily because it will give the greatest dollar return or the greatest unit output of timber;" required clearcuts to be "shaped and blended to the extent practicable with the natural terrain" regardless of the cost; that no stand of timber may be harvested until it reaches its full growth ("mean annual increment of growth") which pushed the harvest of second growth back many years from an economic (and biologically sound) harvest age; required the "non-declining, even-flow" harvest of timber, i.e., in an attempt to prevent over-cutting on any forest, required that the same low amount of timber be cut every year on all forests regardless whether the market demand was higher or lower.

● **The National Forest Management Act of 1976.** Amended and reinforced the Forest and Rangeland Renewable Resources Planning Act of 1974, again forbidding selection of harvesting systems primarily because of economic efficiency; limited the types of places where timber can be harvested by a long list of restricted areas; limited the size of clearcuts to a maximum size, generally 100 acres, regardless of biological conditions indicating larger harvest units.

● **The Federal Water Pollution Control Act** amendments in the late 1970s. Brought new constraints and required operating permits to be obtained from the Environmental Protection Agency. New standards caused both the Sitka and Ketchikan pulp mills to install primary and secondary treatment of mill discharges at a cost in excess of $60 million for each mill even though no biological harm to the waters of Ward's Cove or Silver Bay was ever shown.

● **The Alaska National Interest Lands Conservation Act of 1980.** Resulted in land transfers from the public domain that added 1.3 million acres to the Tongass National Forest, generally of low value for timber production; established 5.4 million acres of the Tongass National Forest as Wilderness, unavailable for timber production; created the Tongass Timber Supply Fund to pay $15 million a year to defray added costs of planning timber sales in marginal areas in addition to the normal $25 million annual Forest Service budget.

By 1980, Congress had reduced the 1950s billion-board-foot-per-year harvest on which the 50-year pulp mill contracts were based to 450 million board feet. The cost to log on the Tongass had been increased more than tenfold by Congressional demands. The public perception that government somehow favors the timber industry is grotesque.

Matrix of Destiny

And, sad to say, the public perception that the timber industry is a powerful lobby that always gets its way in Congress is worse than grotesque -- it's almost macabre. The fact is that for nearly two decades a powerful coalition of anti-timber environmental groups has completely overwhelmed the industry in Congress and the courts.

Dr. Rakestraw, help us out. Tell us, as a professional historian who has made a study of environmental groups, what really happened.

"What you've said so far is accurate, although it lacks somewhat in explanation. As I noted in my history of the Forest Service in Alaska, about 1977 there occurred important shifts in the alignment of political forces affecting the Tongass. One key shift involved the emergence of an Alaskan Coalition made up of groups such as the Sierra Club, Defenders of Wildlife, Environmental Defense Fund, Friends of the Earth, Western Federation of Outdoor Clubs, Wilderness Society, and National Parks and Conservation Association. These groups formed a strong and well funded lobby to push for the maximum acreage in single-use rather than multiple-use units. Those favoring multiple-use could not get a countervailing

force. Professional organizations such as the Society of American Foresters and the American Forestry Association, as well as industry groups
such as the National Forest Products Association and the Alaska Loggers
Association, came out for balanced bills on the current issues, but they
failed.

"A second key shift was the accession of Jimmy Carter to the Presidency. Rogers Morton, as previous secretary of the interior, had been a
suave and skillful politician, adept at reaching compromises; and Secretary of Agriculture Earl Butz had strongly defended his department's
multiple-use policy. Incoming Secretary of the Interior Cecil Andrus, on
the other hand, had a manner one Forest Service officer called a 'bulldozer
approach' not predisposed to bargaining. Incoming Secretary of Agriculture Bob Bergland seemed to lack the decisiveness of Butz, and Assistant
Secretary Rupert Cutler was quite unfriendly to the aims of the Forest
Service over which he presided and a ferocious enemy of the timber
industry: He later proved to be an environmentalist with allegiances sworn
in advance and was one of many who walked through the "swinging door
between government and environmental group employment" that Don
Hummel so eloquently described in his *Stealing the National Parks*.
Cutler now represents the National Audubon Society for a living."

Cutler's office during the Carter administration gave the environmentalists tremendous clout over the Forest Service and the timber industry.

"Indeed it did. But if we are to understand why Alaska became a
proving ground for lawyers, we must understand the fact that many
pressure groups evolved in Alaska during the 1960s and '70s. Several
things account for this phenomenon. One was the vast amount of legislation passed during this period. Some acts, such as the Multiple Use -
Sustained Yield Act you mentioned, were complex and, hence, controversial. The National Environmental Policy Act lent itself to litigation and
was as deadly and random in its operation as was the Allen Pepperbox in
the hands of the frontiersman. Old statutes came under attack, for example
the Izaak Walton League attack upon the Organic Act of 1897 in their
lawsuit against the Forest Service in 1973, which temporarily outlawed all
clearcutting. Had we possessed the understanding in 1973 of the origin
and legislative intent behind the 1891 forest reserves that you have
revealed in this book, that case would likely have had a different outcome.
Then too, the Alaska Native Claims Settlement Act of 1971 lent itself to
land-grabbing and pressure group action by its D2 Wilderness provision."

All this is so complicated you can never explain it in a debate. Or in a
rebuttal of an anti-industry magazine article.

"Ah, and then you write a book. Which you are doing. A second factor was changes in the composition of the courts. Courts have played an important part in shaping federal conservation policy, and their decisions have gone in cycles. The courts in the 1970s became as important in the development of environmental law as was the Taft-Wilson court in interpreting Pinchot-Roosevelt wise-use policies.

Standing To Sue

"Environmentalists would never have gotten into court had it not been for a 1965 case known as Scenic Hudson Preservation Conference v. Federal Power Commission. Traditionally, courts had recognized "standing" to sue as primarily economic standing; in other words, individuals had to show direct personal injury before being allowed to sue. "Scenic Hudson" was a complex case in which a group of wealthy New York estate owners fought construction of power facilities within their Hudson River view. The Second Circuit Court held that factors other than economic interest could be the basis for being an 'aggrieved' person, which, with other rulings gave environmental groups legal standing to sue in defense of scenic, historical and recreational values which might be affected by development. As a result, present courts give standing to noneconomic groups and individuals, and hence broaden the base of those who can litigate."

We've read somewhere that more than 500 lawsuits have been brought by environmentalists since 1965.

"There are more than 500 listed in one 1979 environmental law textbook. The actual number today is probably four times greater. A second change is that courts have taken the bare meaning of words, rather than congressional intent or administrative discretion, in interpreting statutes. This, of course, favors anyone who challenges an administrative agency's actions, and has worked heavily against the Forest Service and the timber industry.

"Third, the court has leaned in favor of participatory democracy rather than expert opinion. Thus virtually anyone can effectively thwart government action with a well-prepared lawsuit. Government action can also be frustrated for lack of sufficient public participation in the agency decision-making process, and 'sufficient' has proven to be a highly subjective standard. This too favors those who challenge the Forest Service and the timber industry. The cry against expert opinion has been raised that 'These lands are too important to leave to the experts,' and the courts have listened, giving great power to those who have nothing to lose and seriously handicapping those with economic interests in the federal lands. Now, expertise is enough to disqualify participation in certain federal environmental functions such as particular advisory board positions reserved for 'members of the public.'. It is amusing to think how these same participatory democracy advocates would react if they had a brain tumor and amateur neurosurgery enthusiasts raised the cry, 'Brain surgery is too important to leave to the experts.'''

So the courts have become more hostile to the Forest Service and industry.

"I think the record shows it. Now a third key shift that came to the Tongass and contributed to legal disputes and controversies is a basic change in the nature and tactics of pressure groups. Today's environmental movement evolved out of groups that began with substantially different views and approaches. You can find it in virtually every major environmental group today, but the Sierra Club is a typical example.

A Cancer of Advocates

"The Sierra Club began as a California organization. It began its expansion about 1940 when it took over the Western Association of Outdoor Clubs and made that organization a sounding board for its own policies. By 1960 it had begun a program of national expansion. It alone, of all major outdoor organizations, opposed the Multiple Use - Sustained yield Act of 1960, showing its early preference for single use designations and its strongly anti-industry orientation. Aided by grants from the Ford Foundation amounting to millions of dollars, the club began a series of litigations against the Forest Service beginning in California and by 1968 moving to Alaska. I once wrote of them, 'Noisy, unscrupulous, and adept in using the big lie and the glittering generality as publicity gimmicks, the Sierra Club epitomized the idea that the end justifies the means.'''

That sounds pretty judgmental for a professional historian.

"The task of the historian is to find out what really happened. I went back to many original sources and found the same comments in many different places. My statement about the Sierra Club is more a compendium of valid descriptions than a subjective opinion. Typical was that of one attorney who wrote: 'The abusive conduct of the Sierra Club includes a distasteful lack of respect for facts, and for opinions other than those of the Sierra Club. I have never seen such flagrantly misleading and deficient affidavits as those submitted by the Sierra Club. The Club has all too often embraced the principle that the end justifies the means.' Almost every attorney who has gone up against the club says the same thing of their tactics."

Our friend John Schnabel lived through one the Sierra Club's anti-social offenses back in the 1970s when he operated Schnabel Lumber Company in Haines. John, tell us your story.

"I found myself embroiled in a Sierra Club court action on some timber sales we had bought on Alaska state lands in the Haines Valley. One of the club's front groups, the Southeast Alaska Conservation Council, joined them in filing lawsuits against us to prevent us from cutting the trees we had purchased. They charged us with all kinds of violations, every one of them totally fabricated -- flat lies. One the court was willing to address was the question of sustained yield and the annual allowable cut: Would our sale volume exceed what was allowed by the State Forest Practices Act? So they challenged the volume, which had been set at 10.3 million board feet. The Sierra Club brought a good many witnesses here who perhaps were authorities somewhere but had little knowledge of Alaskan forests.

"We spent a couple of years in the lower court, which disrupted our operations because we were held in limbo until the court could rule. We had little income from the small amount of harvesting we'd been able to do on the sale and we had tremendous outgo to lawyer's fees. We eventually won the case after spending a few hundred thousand dollars, primarily because the Sierra Club lawyer had bragged around that he was going to stop our timber sale by using the courts as a delaying tactic. The lawyer *boasted* that his accusations against us were trumped up. Witnesses overheard this bit of arrogance and Judge Compton, a circuit judge on the supreme court, was not impressed. The judge ruled that the environmentalists had filed a frivolous lawsuit utterly without merit. The judge also said some very harsh things about the Sierra Club lawyer and awarded us $25,000 in damages. We were still the holder of the timber sale at the logging volumes set in the contract.

"But we lost anyway. Not only were we out the hundreds of thousands it cost to defend ourselves from a frivolous lawsuit, but the Sierra Club also appealed the damages decision to the State Supreme Court, which ruled that in class action suits, the loser is entitled to compensation for speaking 'in behalf of the public.' They overturned the damages award and forced us to pay $10,000 to the Sierra Club even though we won the lawsuit and there was no foundation for the complaint they had brought against us. That's justice in today's courts. If you're industry, you lose even when you win; if you're an environmentalist, you win even when you lose."

John, something has to be done about these people who are abusing their power and position in the community.

"I agree. But it got worse: The Sierra Club went to the national level and got senators from other states to put a rider on the ANILCA bill that would set aside the entire Haines Valley -- 170,000 acres -- as an eagle preserve. It took three years of study before the government decided maybe 50,000 acres would be more than adequate to take care of the eagles. During that study they denied us road access to our timber. Harvesting was totally wiped out and we ended up in default on lumber shipments to the Chinese because I couldn't get the logs out of the eagle preserve study area. In 1983 I finally gave up and shut the mill down."

The Imperial Environmentalists

And all of this is on the public record for anyone to see. But investigative journalists will not investigate it. There won't be a sensational *Reader's Digest* article "Time to Stop the Environmentalists From Destroying Alaskan Industry" or a *Sports Illustrated* exposé of the "Sierra Club Follies." Public opinion is so distorted today that nobody will let themselves believe anything good about industry or bad about environmental groups. It's like a collective national psychosis. The truth can't get through the false perceptions. We can't get a fair hearing.

That must change. Too many people all across America are being hurt by this kind of ferocious advocacy.

But, Dr. Rakestraw, you were in the middle of explaining the rise of the environmentalists' Alaskan legal machine.

"Yes. Sierra Club activity in Alaska had not been noticeable until the late 1960s. The Sierra Club then established an Alaskan chapter which spawned a large number of other organizations. It's the old story familiar in the Lower 48: The dozen local environmental groups consist of the same dozen people. Some of these cluster groups apparently were affiliated closely with the Sierra Club and followed its lines fervently. Some remained more independent. At least nine organizations formed chapters of the Alaska Conservation Society, claiming as its objectives wise use of renewable resources, preservation of the scenic, scientific, recreational, wildlife and wilderness values of Alaska. The Sitka branch, established in 1968 and apparently the one with closest ties to the Sierra Club, succeeded in obtaining a five year moratorium on logging in the West Chichagof - Yakobi Island areas. A coalition of clubs in the Tongass kept up a constant barrage of criticism of Forest Service policies.

"The first big Sierra Club lawsuit in the Tongass was brought in

February 1970 against the Forest Service. It is known as *Sierra Club v. Hardin*, and it complained that a long-term contract timber sale to U.S. Plywood - Champion Papers, Inc. was illegal. The sale of 8.75 billion feet of timber had been advertised in September 1965 by the Forest Service, with provisions that a pulp mill be constructed by July 1971. Numerous bids were received, and St. Regis Paper Company won with a bid of $5.60 per thousand with plans to cut 175 million feet per year. St. Regis spent 1966 examining the area and layout of tentative locations. It selected a mill site near Sitka, where the Japanese-owned Alaska Pulp Company mill was already in operation.

"The St. Regis sale fell through because of high construction costs for the plant and other economic factors. St. Regis forfeited its bond and gave

The Tongass Forest Speaks Sermons on Wise Use

Environmentalists denounced the "worst clearcut" in the Tongass, an experimental harvest of an entire creek drainage near the Hollis camp of Ketchikan Pulp Company in 1958. Thirty years later the drainage is a model of perfect forest regrowth.

Experimental block cut, 1958, in Maybeso Creek Drainage   Forest Service photo

up the sale. In 1968 the sale was offered to the second bidder, U.S. Plywood - Champion Papers, Inc., and was accepted on the same terms. The company hired an advisory commission of eminent scientists to give it advice on avoiding environmental damage, the first such industry effort. The company picked a mill site at Katlian Bay near Sitka, but the site was rejected on ecological grounds. An acceptable site was found at Echo Cove, north of Juneau.

''The Sierra Club complained that the sale violated administrative procedures and the National Environmental Policy Act of 1969. The Sierra Club was joined in the suit by local preservationist groups and the Forest Service was joined by U.S. Plywood - Champion and the state of Alaska, which wanted to foster the economic development of the Tongass.

''The case was tried in federal district court in Alaska in November 1970, and the Forest Service won. The Sierra Club was granted ''standing'' to sue, but lost on the merits: the court felt that the Forest Service had shown compliance with the Multiple Use - Sustained Yield Act. A major factor in the Sierra Club loss was the doctrine of ''laches'' -- unreasonable delay in bringing suit.

''But again, the environmentalist won even when they lost. Through a

Maybeso Creek, 1988, the ''worst case'' is now the best case. ^{courtesy Helen Finney}

long series of appeals, the Sierra Club waged a war of attrition, using all of the law's delays to postpone action, with the aim of putting the company to continued expense and killing the project by making it uneconomic. An appeal was brought in federal circuit court in California, where new evidence was presented. A. Starker Leopold and Richard Barrett had performed a study of the effect of clearcutting on wildlife, arguing that large clearcuts destroy the habitat of the Sitka deer and that cutting would endanger bald eagles. No replication of the study was permitted by other scientists to check its accuracy: the study was accepted by the court at face value -- a legal, not a scientific procedure.

"The case was remanded to the district court. The reduced clearcut areas proposed for the new trial would lessen the timber base to the point of diminishing returns. No consideration was given to mitigation measures such as thinning to protect habitat, and no consideration was given to the fact that the extent of habitat damage caused by logging even at its worst would affect only a small fraction of the total habitat. The mere suggestion of *any* damage had the same legal effect as proving *total* destruction. The Forest Service and Champion Plywood agreed to a bilateral cancellation of the sale in 1976. The Sierra Club had destroyed over a thousand lifetime jobs and incalculable economic benefits for the people of the Tongass, using grant money from large Eastern corporate foundations. Here again we see sectionalism as a contributing force in the continuing colonialization of Alaska."

Something must be done about their abuse of power, Dr. Rakestraw. We have to find a way to defend ourselves.

A Tyranny of Images

"Things got considerably worse. The Sierra Club was determined to shut down the Alaska timber industry, and in 1973 almost succeeded. It came through an attack on clearcutting, the only economic way to harvest timber in most West Coast forests. The Sierra Club mounted a resolute propaganda campaign based on a study of clearcutting practices by foresters at the University of Montana that purported to show irreversible damage to local hillsides due to carving bulldozer-wide benches on the hillsides to encourage reproduction in ponderosa pine forests. Soil erosion was the big issue, and a few photographs of the study's lead forester standing next to the scraped hillsides and beside a tiny scum-laden pond evoked furious emotional responses. As an embarrassing footnote, today the ugly benches carved by those bulldozers are among the most beautiful and best stocked stands of timber now thriving in Montana.

"But the matter came to a head in a lawsuit brought by the Izaak Walton League over clearcutting in the Monongahela National Forest in West Virginia. In the case of *Izaak Walton League v. Butz*, a loophole was invented in the Organic Act of 1897, the law that was added as a rider to the Sundry Civil Appropriations Bill of June 4 that year. As you recall from Chapter 3, it was the law that finally gave the government administrative power over the forest reserves created by Holman's rider in 1891.

"The 1973 court interpreted a few words of that law, in which the secretary of the interior, as administrator of the forest reserves, was empowered thus: "...under such rules and regulations as he shall prescribe, may cause to be designated and appraised so much of the dead, matured, or large growth of trees found upon such forest reservations as may be compatible with the utilization of the forests thereon, and may sell the same..." and rather than taking the meaning and practice used by foresters, held clearcutting illegal on the Monongahela, and by implication everywhere on Forest Service lands, including the Tongass.

"Obviously nothing in that clause literally forbids clearcutting, nor does any other part of the act, so the court's interpretation is not even literal. One can clearcut dead, mature or large growth as easily as one can selectively cut it. The court's ruling is invention *de novo*. It simply demonstrates a particular stage in the cycles of judicial practice in which one theory of legal interpretation supplants another -- reliance upon original intent, reliance upon the rule of reason and legislative history, reliance upon the literal text of the statute, reliance upon the novel arguments of a popular new movement with prejudice against an unpopular industry.

"Ironically, that very same 1897 law two paragraphs earlier stated that "No public forest reservation shall be established, except to improve and protect the forest within the reservation, or for the purpose of securing favorable conditions of water flows, and to furnish a continuous supply of timber for the use and necessities of citizens of the United States..." which the slightest historical understanding shows to have meant any harvest method then in practice, which in 1897 certainly included clearcutting.

"The 1973 court ruling also ignored the regulations of the Forest Service dating back to its creation in 1905. The handbook of regulations titled *The Use of the National Forest Reserves*, better known simply as *The Use Book* states in its first paragraph:

> The timber, water, pasture, mineral, and other resources of
> the forest reserves are for the use of the people. They may be

obtained under reasonable conditions, without delay. Legitimate improvements and business enterprises will be encouraged.

"The next page begins:

Forest reserves are for the purpose of preserving a perpetual supply of timber for home industries, preventing destruction of the forest cover which regulates the flow of streams,
and protecting local residents from unfair competition in the
use of forest and range. They are patrolled and protected, at
Government expense, for the benefit of the community and the
home builder.

"That has been the policy of the national forests from before they
were national forests. But modern courts have been at pains to disregard
these original Forest Service policies and regulations, that is, administrative law, because they are not statute law passed by Congress. However,
the discovery revealed in this book that Holman's legislative intent in
attaching the Section 24 rider is virtually identical to Pinchot's administrative policy makes the final connection and should have significant impact
on future lawsuits."

Perhaps there is hope. We may have at least a chance to show the
world that the forest industry, for all its faults, has been primarily in the
right. We may have at least a chance to convey our sense that we are not
evil, that we are decent people worthy of respect, the home-givers of the
whole earth.

The Rule of Unreason

"But the 1973's court's rejection of the rule of reason brought
instant alarm to the timber industry. The Sierra Club immediately added
Izaak Walton League v. Butz to Sierra Club v. Hardin. Meanwhile, the
Sitka branch of the Alaska Conservation Society and some residents of
Point Baker brought the suit Zieske v. Butz. The court ruled in Zieske that
only mature trees on Prince of Wales Island could be cut under a contract
by Ketchikan Pulp Company, and that clearcutting was forbidden only on
POW, holding that the actual legality of clearcutting was a matter for
Congress to decide. The court rejected charges by Point Baker residents
that KPC violated four other federal laws including NEPA.

"In 1976 Congress legalized clearcutting in the National Forest Management Act, but hedged it around with five stringent limitations: it must
be the optimum method to meet the objectives of the land management

plan; the interdisciplinary team must review each clearcut; clearcuts must be shaped to blend with the natural terrain; maximum size limits must be observed, generally 100 acres; and clearcuts must be carried out in a manner that will protect soil, watershed, fish, wildlife, recreation and esthetic resources.''

Dr. Rakestraw, again you've made the complex easy to understand.

The NFMA of 1976 also did something that brought the Tongass to the forefront: It required highly detailed Forest Plans to be prepared. As we know, the Tongass was the first national forest to complete its plan. And that planning process was soon to become entangled with another legal issue.

The next year, 1977, a long-smouldering question ignited: What to do with the 80 million acres of D2 lands from the Alaska Native Claims Settlement Act of 1971? Hearings on the alternatives were held. Rep. Morris Udall (D-Arizona), chairman of the House Interior and Insular Affairs Committee, had succeeded in introducing to the House HR 39, a bill strongly weighted in favor of the preservationist alternative that had been brewing since ANCSA was passed in 1971. Alaska Rep. Don Young and Senator Ted Stevens preferred an alternative weighted toward the multiple use of lands. Field hearings were held by the Subcommittee on General Oversight and Alaska Lands (How many colonies -- er, states have their own overseers in Congress?)

The hearings in Fairbanks, Sitka, Juneau, Anchorage, Fort Yukon, Bethel, Dillingham and Kotzebue revealed how many different kinds of Alaskans there are and how deeply divided we can be. We quarreled about the status of Admiralty Island, where the local Native corporation wanted to keep it untouched in order to preserve traditional ways. We quarreled about subsistence hunting and fishing; about transportation corridors; about using snowmobiles, airplanes and powerboats in wilderness; about ''rape of the land'' versus ''locking up resources;'' how much timber we needed from the Tongass to keep the industry viable; about who should administer what, the National Park Service or the National Forest Service; about nearly everything to do with using the land.

Predictably, the Alaska coalition of environmentalists united behind HR 39 which gave vast power to the National Park Service and the Fish and Wildlife Service. When it came to a vote in the House in 1978 it passed by a large margin. In the Senate, Senators Ted Stevens and Mike Gravel couldn't agree on tactics and strategy, but Gravel threatened a filibuster and the session ended with no Alaska Act.

By then, recall, President Carter was in office and his "termite infestation" of environmental activist appointees was firmly entrenched in the bureaucracy. Because there was no Alaska Act, environmentalists brought pressure to force presidential action. One hundred and forty six members of the House urged it; Secretary of Agriculture Bergland and Assistant Secretary Cutler urged it.

What could the president do that Congress could not? He could use an obscure law that Teddy Roosevelt cooked up. On December 1, 1978, President Carter used his authority under the Antiquities Act of 1906 to create 17 national monuments covering 55.9 million acres of Alaska. He also designated 38.9 million acres as national wildlife refuges in our state. The Alaska Coalition won a staggering victory without a single vote being cast.

The public is totally unaware of the stupendous power of the environmental movement. They are not the little tree-hugging David up against the Goliath of industry, no matter how they strive to foster that image. They are the most powerful single lobby in America in terms of goals accomplished, number of laws passed and court cases brought and won. They have destroyed hundreds of thousands of jobs and lives. They are radicalizing whole segments of America against environmentalism. Their imperial exercise of power will lead to their ultimate demise as more humane organizations come on the scene and co-opt their position through reason and balance.

Colonies Have No Rights

Two of the 17 Carter national monument proclamations affected the Tongass: Admiralty Island and Misty Fiords. Both were given to the Forest Service, which was a total break with tradition. Since the Transfer Act of 1933 was passed, the National Park Service has held sole jurisdiction over national monuments. Incidentally, the Forest Service was also given jurisdiction over Mount Saint Helens National Volcanic Monument after it blew its top in 1982, so the Forest Service now has three national monuments.

The State of Alaska was furious. It filed a lawsuit against the federal government complaining of the following points:

1. Creation of national monuments by proclamation violates the separation of powers doctrine.

2. The proclaimed national monuments conflicted with state land selections under the Statehood Act.

3. Withdrawal should not stop the state from filing on its land selec-

tions and getting state patent.

4. Failure of government to act on state selections violated the State-hood Act.

5. Failure to promptly convey native lands impedes the state's rights to select land.

6. Rejecting state land selections exceeded governmental authority.

7. The National Environmental Policy Act requires environmental impact statements and disclosures of the effects of the action, which was not done.

Now we're going to call on Jim Clark, general counsel for Alaska Pulp Corporation and the Alaska Loggers Association. He lived a great deal of the legislative history of the past decade lobbying for the timber industry. He can give us some behind the scenes insight into the Tongass and the law.

"Much of the period you're talking about, the mid-1970s, ties in with what is going on today in the Tongass. During that time I was one of the timber industry persons actively involved in the legislative efforts surrounding HR 39, which ultimately resulted in the Alaska National Interest Lands Conservation Act (ANILCA) of 1980.

Compromise With Disaster

"Today we are seeing the same arguments against Section 705 of ANILCA, which created the Tongass Timber Supply Fund, that were made during the four years of hearings that preceded passage of ANILCA. Congress weighed the arguments of all sides and fashioned the Section 705 compromise to resolve the matter. The current effort to repeal Section 705, to throw out the baby with the bathwater, is because the environmental community did not like the 1980 compromise to begin with and would like to get rid of the job protection measures that accompanied the massive wilderness designations made in Section 703 of the bill.

"Because Section 17(d)(2) of the Alaska Native Claims Settlement Act provided for putting public lands into the four systems', congressional action in the Tongass was not contemplated -- because the region was already part of one of the four systems -- the National Forest System. HR 39 was then introduced by Congressman Udall and involved the Tongass in the ANILCA process by proposing 5.2 million acres of wilderness.

"At that time representatives of the U.S. Forest Service and the timber industry argued that no wilderness should be designated in the Tongass until the Tongass Land Management Plan (TLMP) had been completed in late 1978. Nevertheless, Congressman Udall and Congressman John Seiberling (D-Ohio), both of the House Interior and Insular Affairs Committee, insisted that Tongass wilderness would have to be included in HR 39 and pressed the Carter Administration for wilderness recommendations.

"As I understand it, part of what caused the Forest Service to come forward with a recommendation in early February 1978 was the threat to transfer management of Admiralty Island to the Interior Department."

We remember the coercion and rough play the Carter environmentalists brought to Washington only too well.

"The recommendation, called the Regional Forester's Proposal, was embodied in the final TLMP EIS released on August 15, 1978: It tried to reconcile the congressional demand for massive wilderness with maintaining employment in the Tongass region at its then existing level, which was a harvest of 520 million board feet per year. It called for the use of intensive management funds to pre-road areas and use silvicultural practices that get higher timber yields from areas that were not economic to harvest under existing market conditions. This recommendation became the basis for the Tongass compromise: wilderness for a timber supply fund.

The recommendation had some unusual features: A number of major areas with high timber volume were divided into part "special management area" and part wilderness. Timber harvest on special management areas was prohibited without a further act of Congress, although the timber volume was to be included in the calculation of the forest's annual potential yield. For example, the east half of Admiralty Island was designated wilderness, while the west half was designated a special management area.

"This recommendation was part of HR 39 when it failed to pass at the end of session in 1978. HR 39 was reintroduced in the next Congress, and resulted in ANILCA as we know it today. But when the Senate version of the bill moved to the floor, Senator Paul Tsongas of Massachusetts sought to amend it. When a motion to table Sen. Tsongas' amendment failed, Senator Stevens began a long series of amendments to Senator Tsongas' motion. The Senate leadership pulled the bill off the floor and requested that the various parties attempt to work out a compromise bill which could pass without filibuster.

"This discussion led to the second compromise made by the timber industry. All of the special management areas were converted to wilderness. This was a particularly high priority of the Sierra Club and the

Alaska Coalition, which wanted all of Admiralty Island in Wilderness. The 520 million board feet per year harvest level was reduced to 4.5 billion feet per decade. For giving up the special management areas and reducing the timber harvest, the Committee agreed that the legislation would not be subject to the annual appropriations process. Rather, there would be an internal budget review by the administration leading to automatic funding of the intensive management program -- the Tongass Timber Supply Fund.

"The compromise passed the Senate immediately and the House passed it in a lame duck session after President Reagan was elected in November 1980.

"In short, there were two compromises by our industry. The first was to limit the timber base to 520 million feet a year, no more than would support the industry at its then current size, forgoing all hope of growth. Then that compromise was compromised by reducing the harvest to 4.5 billion feet per decade and giving up the special management areas in return for the Tongass Timber Supply Fund.

"Had we not compromised, there would have been no ANILCA. Even though Admiralty Island was a national monument, the Reagan administration planned to change that. Under TLMP the northwest portion of Admiralty Island would have been available for timber harvest in 1985. The environmentalists agreed to Section 705 because they needed Section 705."

And now that the environmentalists have their Admiralty Island wilderness safe and sound, they're coming back to get Section 705 because they don't need it any more. To the Sierra Club and the Defenders of Wildlife and the Environmental Defense Fund and the Friends of the Earth and the Western Federation of Outdoor Clubs and the Wilderness Society and the National Parks and Conservation Association, a deal is not a deal. It's merely a dispensable stepping stone to total victory.

Something has to be done to stop the environmentalists' abuse of power.

VOICES

• •

The Tongass mist swirls in our souls. So many things roil in our innards, so many lives have been lived in us that we want you to share. Out of the forest fogs come muted murmurs, sleepy sounds, almost dreamlike. The solid trees fade into infinite whiteness like a forest full of angels, inviting us to follow and find the spiritual in the ordinary.

Forest whispers ask us to let go of the branches we cling to, to take flight in clouds of story meditations, silent sounds poured out onto pages, outer forms by which the inner meaning of our lives may be known.

Come live with us a time. Be one with us. Listen now. The people speak.

Bunkhouse Window

I remember Sam Marsh and Don Hensley: the odd couple in the bunkhouse. These two veteran loggers were roommates for twenty years, yet it remains a mystery to all who know them how such men ever bunked together so long.

The only thing they had in common was that they were both early to bed and early to rise people. During their waking hours they were a study in contrasts. Sam was noisy and Don was quiet. Don would sit on his bed and read after dinner and Sam would make noise trying to be quiet. Sam said Don could even hear you chewing snoose. Yet they never came to blows about it in all those twenty years.

Don ate whatever he liked, but Sam was a health nut. Sam slept beneath a pyramid and spent Sunday recataloging his vitamins and dietary supplements. Sam claimed he was getting younger every day and actually believed that he was. If Don thought it was weird he never jumped on Sam about it.

One time Sam secretly tried to darken his hair, no doubt part of his rejuvenation regimen. He may have been knowledgeable about health foods, but he was no expert at hair coloring, and when the resulting orange tint exposed his covert activity, he assured everyone he had just taken too much vitamin C.

Don retired in 1984 due to a market-forced shutdown. He went home to his wife and younger children waiting for him in the Carolinas' Great Smoky Mountains. Sam retired to California on a pension shortly after Don left. He divided his life savings equally between paying off gambling debts, supporting Christian charities and contributing to right wing political causes.

The two inseparable bunkhouse buddies who always stuck together now reside on opposite sides of the country, surrounded by the families they seldom saw during their Tongass days. I hope they get along without us better than we manage without them.

-- K. A. Soderberg, personal friend

The Getaway

One of the reasons I work here and put up with this lousy weather is that I love to fish. The other evening after work I caught a beautiful king salmon. I docked the skiff, laid my fish on the planks of the airplane float and went up to the cook house to gather my tools and drink my congratulatory cup of coffee.

While vividly describing my wonderful catch to the crew, someone called to my attention that my salmon was no longer where I'd left it. I ran down to the airplane float and to my dismay found a hungry otter stealing away with my catch.

-- Jim Williams, camp cook

Talon

Life in the Tongass can be cruel. I remember one day being forced to explain the pitiless warp of nature to my small children as a bald eagle sat perched in a tree in front of our house devouring their beloved cat piece by piece. We live daily with nature and accept it, good or bad.

-- Ron Lindberg, boat captain

War Chest

Why doesn't the timber industry ever initiate legislation? The timber industry has not really attempted to get legislation because Alaska is a cheap environmental vote. We couldn't win. Members of Congress are able to make decisions with respect to Alaska in the abstract. They are able to look at their wants. There is nothing they have to trade off for it. So they write a laundry list of what they would like to have come out of

Alaska. And in so doing they pay no penalty whatsoever.

When you're a congressman from a swing state or swing district, you might trade off your vote to an environmentalist to prevent something bad from happening in your district. Alaska doesn't have a situation like that, like, say, the huge California delegation. They can act together, band in groups, protect one another, because there's enough critical mass there. We have one congressman and two senators. We have a little more critical mass in the Senate than in the House. There are only 100 senators and Alaska has one fiftieth of the Senate vote. There are 435 congressmen and we have one four-hundred-thirty-fifth of the House vote. We've always been more successful in terms of defending ourselves in the Senate.

Congress is a funny place. They're constantly cutting our baby in half. The environmentalists have nothing to lose in that process, but we're always subdividing and subdividing and subdividing what we have. You can't compromise for half the pie too many times before you run out of pie.

So far we've hung in there rather well given the fact that the Alaska Logging Association has $150,000 to spend on the timber supply fund issue and the Wilderness Society alone is spending over a million dollars on their Tongass campaigns. That means that just one environmental group's Tongass budget is ten times ours. They've got a sympathetic audience of liberal Easterners for whom the politics of going after Alaskans are just fine. The environmental groups have nothing else to do while everybody in the timber industry has a living to make, a work force to employ, loans to pay off, products to create, and the world to supply.

-- Jim Clark, attorney at law

In The Element of Antagonisms

It's hard for the individual contractor -- where do you find time for politics when you're busy ten hours a day just running your small business? If you want to take the time, you do it at night, you try to write letters to congressmen or try to make phone calls to alert your friends. Sometimes you're just too dog-tired and it gets neglected.

The stress alone is phenomenal. With our employees and us both, our financial survival is at stake. It's coping with the environment too, not just your job and the politics. There's harsh conditions here, the weather's a big thing. And our way of life -- if we don't save the lifestyle of our industry, if it isn't here, what opportunities will our kids or grandkids have? No matter who you are or what you're doing, the stress is there, and it's bad.

My own crew, I tell 'em what's going on, and they've been real good about making phone calls and letter writing. We have eighteen employees right now with a payroll over a million dollars a year. But on a long term basis it's hard to get them to keep putting out. They know they need to do it, but it takes all their time. Jackie and I, it's more critical to us. It's a fight for survival. We know what's going to happen. We know the environmental organizations have the power and the money. And they're beating us. We don't have the people or the resources to do what the environmentalists are doing. So we have to fight all the time.

But actually taking time off work to spend a week at committee hearings in Washington, D.C., that's real tough. In my position, I've got a small business to run, and if I'm not here seven days a week it goes down hill. I've got to stay on top of it. Other operators are the same: if they aren't on top of their business, production is lost.

Fortunately for us, Women In Timber is getting stronger. These little individual organizations can go back to D.C. and get their word across. The women are the citizen voice for this industry. I'm not saying the men are lazy, we just don't have the time, and that's not saying the women have all the time -- they're as busy keeping their companies alive as the men -- but they seem to get the thing done and have a lot more initiative in speaking out on industry's part.

So we help financially. I think it benefits our industry. The environmentalists can never take the power away from the women who believe in this industry.

The environmentalists will quit attacking us only when they've taken the whole Tongass. They're going to go on until they lock us out once and for all. I saw a program on the Discovery Channel the other night, that *National Geographic* program on the Tongass. They call Alaska a "pristine" state as if nobody ever lived here. What does that tell you? It tells you they want nothing touched. They want us out. They want this as a tourist colony and nature museum for the affluent of the Lower 48.

So my outlook is that you try to help our support organizations battle the environmentalists as much as you can. We're 'way behind as far as our message. We haven't conveyed a very good message yet. I hope this book helps. It's a start anyway.

But if the environmentalists win, Thorne Bay will be gone. Petersburg and Wrangell will roll up the few sidewalks they have. Ketchikan will dwindle to a village. Sixty percent of Sitka will vanish. I was in Sitka when both pulp mills shut down for six months once. Six hundred families moved out. They couldn't stay there for six months waiting for that mill to reopen. Sitka was a ghost town, the only thing that really survived was the fishing industry, and they have a good fishing industry where Ketchikan doesn't. If the environmentalists win, what's left of the Tongass will make Appalachia look like Beverly Hills.

-- Butch DuRette, road building contractor

Learning Logger Appreciation

When I graduated from college with a major in biology in 1973 I was a rabid environmentalist. I came to the Tongass with all my allegiances sworn in advance. But fate stepped in to change all that. My husband Rusty sold tires to logging contractors. After I got to know these loggers and their families and had a chance to see what they were really doing in the forest I was appalled by my own intolerance and bigotry toward them. It was almost like race prejudice. A blind feeling that I was better than them because of who I was or what I knew or what I felt about nature.

I reformed! That's the only way I can say it. I reformed. I found that one can be a conservationist and at the same time advocate industrial development with no contradiction. Conservation is the wise use of resources. Environmentalism is a blind bigotry toward all who want to use nature for commodity production. Conservation is what loggers strive for. Isn't that what we're all striving for?

I became active in the formative stages of Alaska Women In Timber. I served as AWIT president from 1983 to 1985 and was Government Affairs Consultant for Ketchikan Pulp Company in 1984 and 1985. Then I took a position with the Alaska Department of Commerce and Economic Development as a special assistant to the Commissioner for minerals and forest products.

Today I'm Director of Governmental Affairs for Alaska Loggers Association based in Juneau. My major responsibility is monitoring events and participating in timber-related affairs of government. I'm working on the Tongass Land Management Plan revision and on the Alaska Forest Practices Act revision initiated by the governor's office.

Even a rabid environmentalist can reform to become a wise use conservationist. Environmentalists must reform if America's industrial economy is to survive.

-- Thyes Shaub, Wise Use advocate

Quenching the Fire in the Belly

I originally came from Down South many years ago. Alaska's been very good to us. The pulp mill treated us very fairly. I have no regrets. It was tough, and we were prudent operators, or we wouldn't have survived.

Doing the work is a pleasure. Putting up with the politics wears a person out. It makes you want to get out of the business. It seems there's someone taking a shot at you every day from a different direction. You set up plans and do an excellent job and some uninformed guy flies over in an airplane and doesn't think what you're

Jerry Larrabee

doing is pretty and pretty soon you have a court injunction driving you out, like in the Kadashan project. It gets tougher and tougher in that respect.

We're not actively looking for logging jobs now. And to tell you the truth I'm not sure I'm ever going to again.

-- Jerry Larrabee, Alaska logger

Nationwide

Coffman Cove has been seen by folks across the country since the national TV show *20/20* filmed a segment a few years ago at our family logging operation on Prince of Wales Island.

My husband Mike didn't mind the intrusion of the media crews on his company's work. I thought my part of the operation was exaggerated but otherwise the program was well done.

Most Coffman Cove residents felt the same as Mike, but some were not anxious to become TV stars. The camera-shy guys were unusually quiet in the mornings as they prepared to go to work. Some even rode the crummy from the cookhouse across the camp to the shop just to avoid being filmed.

One guy left for work at 4 a.m. and didn't return until 11 p.m. -- and also went to the trouble of changing rigs [logger lingo: Rig: pickup truck or whatever you happen to be driving] so he wouldn't be recognized. He really didn't want to be filmed.

Despite a few camera-shy loggers, the production crew from New York spent as close to an ideal time at our logging operation as you could ask for. They were able to capture on film in a very short time the wide range of loggers' experiences and give the rest of the United States a glimpse of a unique lifestyle that we're proud to maintain.

-- Leta Valentine, Alaska Women In Timber

The Bear Sans Faulkner

My husband Butch's big-game hunting experience came during the early spring of 1981. We were at Freshwater Bay and bear hunting season had just opened. I remember the day only too well.

I had just unloaded a freight plane and made my way back to the office. I faced a pile of work and realized that I'd really have to hustle to find the top of my desk before the close of business that day. I picked up the phone and was ordering some parts from town for our mechanic when I heard some commotion outside the camp office.

I went and looked out the office window. Much to my surprise, there stood Butch next to his pickup proudly displaying a big brown grizzly bear to the crowd that had gathered around for an up-close inspection. I could see him grin from ear to ear as I heard him tell of the hunt and the bear he'd bagged. I was proud of him and he was proud of himself.

After devoting ample time for yarn-spinning, Butch drove the bear over to the shop where he hoisted it out of the pickup and left it there to hang until he could skin and flesh it out. But first he had to get back to the crew on the job site.

On his way out he came into the office and said to me, "Jackie, that bear is hanging in the shop and needs to be washed and taken care of now."

He had said "Jackie," but I was hoping that he meant somebody else. I looked around the office. I was the only one there. Without another word Butch left and went back to work. Evidently he hadn't meant anybody else.

Okay, I can handle this. Just another part of my job description, right? Wife, friend, partner, freight unloader, accountant, parts chaser, bear cleaner. *Bear cleaner?* Did I *really* want the camp knowing me as the bear cleaner?

Okay, I would do it, but discreetly. After all, no sense in making it a public event. I proceeded to the shop where my task awaited. There the bloody monster hung high on the hoist, almost nine feet long. Its rear claws dangled five feet above the floor. Now, I'm only five feet three inches tall, so my first task was obviously to find a ladder. I scrounged around and found one, then prepared a bucket of Ivory Snow detergent and climbed the ladder to face this hulking brute.

Little wisps of vapor from the dissipating body heat wafted off the bear. Blood and secretions dripped to a puddle on the shop floor. I knew the beast would have to be quickly and thoroughly cleaned or the hide would not hold up to the skinning and fleshing.

Well, have at it. With my scrub brush in hand I proceeded to give that bear the best darn bubble bath that any Tongass animal before or since ever got. I was careful to keep an eagle eye on the back door at all times. I couldn't *bear* the thought that someone would come in and find me doing such a thing. Bear cleaner! Hmph!

I scrubbed that bear until the pelt absolutely glistened, then rinsed it thoroughly with gallon after gallon of water. Can you imagine the soap commercial you could make from this situation? Just think of it: "Ladies, for all your chores around the machine shop, use Ivory Snow bear cleaner. Bubble, bubble, bubble, sparkle and furry snuggle! Makes your bear shine like new. Good for otters and martens, too! La-da!"

It was done! I eyed the back door. I hadn't been caught in the act!

As I climbed down the ladder, Ivory Snow bucket in hand, a round of applause and hysterical laughter erupted behind me. Several of my neighbors had come in the front door -- behind me!

-- Jackie DuRette, bear cleaner

Timber Wings

About 1976 the environmental movement started pressuring in the Tongass to do things that didn't matter at as far protecting the environment. Road standards, for one thing: A spur road was temporary before then -- we wouldn't ditch its edges because that spur would only be there a month or two and when we were through we'd water-bar it -- push up dirt piles across the road at intervals to divert water from turning it into a stream bed, sort of like speed bumps for water -- and we'd pull out and be gone.

Then the Forest Service started making us dig full ditches the full length of the road. And then we had to install metal culverts instead of the 3-log culverts made of cull logs, a low-cost system we'd been using successfully for years. That increased costs while actually making more of an impact on the environment: the old way left a natural gravel bottom on the watercourse and the new one left a corrugated metal bottom. And road building cost skyrocketed to $50,000 a mile -- each mile -- *in excess* of what they needed to spend to get the wood out.

Then the Forest Service became expert at coming back in May, two

months after you had negotiated the annual contract price, and adding
something like metal culverts for which you couldn't recover the cost until
the next year. So you were carrying their capital costs for them and paying
interest on the loans you had to get to carry them.

As time went on they reduced the clearcut sizes down to 160 acres,
then to 100 acres, and each time they did something like that it increased
the cost to log a unit by many thousands of dollars. When we started
logging in the Tongass, we were logging big units, 3 and 4 million board
feet per mile. Now our volume drops down to less than 1.5 million per
mile, and that's prohibitively costly. It's that kind of thing that made the
Tongass Timber Supply Fund necessary -- made it necessary to have road
augmentation money.

And the smaller clearcuts make multiple entries into the valleys
necessary. Instead of taking 300 acres once and leaving the valley alone
for a hundred years, you now take 100 acres three times, five or ten years
apart. You set up your logging camp and rebuild your roads and your
rafting ground and your log storage three times, so you've tripled your
initial entry cost. And you move out three times. The multiple entry idea
is very poor forestry strategy, and there's no way you can do it economically. You disturb the land more frequently and you don't gain a single

Author K. A. Soderberg interviews Mike Valentine   Ron Arnold photo

biological thing.

Utilization standards have been another sore point. When we first came to the Tongass we took nothing smaller than a 50 board foot log out of the woods -- smaller logs were left on the forest floor to recycle their nutrients. Then the Forest Service all of a sudden decided they wanted us to take 10 board foot logs -- that's 6 inches in diameter and 12 feet long. If you bring in a thousand of those logs you would have 10,000 board feet, and there's no way you could even buy the diesel for your cookhouse if you didn't have more than that. It's not a merchantable log, there's no way it could pay its way. but we have to bring it in anyway.

At the same time our logging costs were escalating so fast we could hardly keep up with them, the Forest Service brought in landscape architects, hydrologists, fish and wildlife biologists, everything imaginable in these interdisciplinary teams, all people that hadn't even studied logging in textbooks. Then every bridge crossing became a real challenge, trying to satisfy all of these people at once. They were out there watching everything we did -- with no understanding of what they were looking at. They sent out landscape architects that were absolutely inexperienced and designed clearcut edges to look pretty with no regard to prevailing winds, just asking for blowdown in the adjacent uncut areas. The ecology would have been better off if they'd paid them to stay home. You have to be cognizant of the winds blowing up and down these canyons. It was the loggers that finally wised them up a little bit, showed them how to lay out a successful cutline. But they only started listening after they came back enough times to see for themselves the pretty disasters they'd cooked up.

Log dumps, the log transfer facility sites were another big thorn in our sides. The environmentalists wanted these big fancy log transfer facilities built at a cost of eight or nine hundred thousand dollars each. You often have to put a bulkhead in for forty thousand dollars and put a large A-frame loader up for another forty thousand. You could do an environmentally sound job on a log transfer facility for less than $100,000. With the load lifters we have now, you can even put a log dump in for $25,000. We have also built just a very simple, gravity type dump that is non-violent, no big splashes that knock off bark, and it works perfectly without hardly any costs. But the environmentalists want to run us out of business.

One thing I can say about environmentalists is that they don't understand the environment. They have lofty emotions about it, but they have no feel for it. They grow up in cities, we grow up in the forest. I think loggers are the environmentalists. We can feel the forest in our bones. There's as much sawdust as blood in our veins. We wouldn't harm the forest for anything. It's our home! The Tongass is our home!

We can tell how good a logging job we did by watching the seedlings turn to saplings and fill up the cutover with thrifty trees. Those city environmentalists don't know what we know. They're actually preservationists. When their movement first started there were a lot of well-meaning people in it. But the leadership is completely out of hand now. Radicals have taken over and the rank and file doesn't know it. And from reading some of their publications, there's no truth to much of what they say. And even when they're proven wrong they don't change their minds.

-- Michael L. Valentine, logging contractor

November Thoughts

I am a senior at Juneau-Douglas High School in Juneau, Alaska. I have spent the last few days filling out reams of application forms to the college I plan on attending next fall. I hope to be accepted in the engineering department of Montana Tech University.

It occurred to me as I was filling in the paperwork how fortunate I was to have been able to save some money along the way to help with my education. All of those years that my brother Roby and I ran a trapline at Freshwater Bay really are beginning to pay off.

My Dad got us interested in trapping when we were small boys. I was only ten years old and Rob was seven. Now, trapping is a unique lifestyle that has a long history in Alaska. Not so long ago trapping was done by many people who lived in the bush. However, today it is done by only a few.

Trapping is hard work for the most part. The trapline has to be checked daily. Our line covered approximately twenty miles. We would cover it on snowmobiles as far as we could, and then walk.

The work really begins when the marten and mink and otter have to be skinned out and fleshed and hung on a drying board to properly dry. Many evenings we would spend several hours taking care of our pelts. Without proper care the fur buyer would not pay top dollar and when you are working this hard top dollar is something you strive for.

My Dad would help us some. He would check to see that we were doing the job right, and would teach us as to how to get the job done correctly.

We used to give our mother nightmares. She would often go into our rooms to find the overload of pelts that could not be put in the drying room hanging over the drapes in our rooms, or just about any place where they might dry. Mom was a pretty good sport about it. I know it drove her crazy at times, but after all, her sons were learning to be responsible and mothers will put up with a lot for that.

Dad and Mom can certainly see the benefits now. My trapping dollars are going to go a long way in the coming college years. And Rob will be using his soon too. I guess the most important thing, though, is that we have learned a unique business, we still have our traps. Someday I hope to be able to show my own son or daughter how it is done.

I only hope there is a place for me here in the Tongass to be able to live that lifestyle, or any other that I choose.

-- Corey DuRette, student

How Yesterday Looked

Don Brown's Mud Bay Logging Company was one of the bigger logging contractors in the Tongass. It would not have been uncommon to have over a hundred men in camp at one time. Don had seen everything and done everything and was more interested in giving "advice" than receiving it. He ruled his camp with an iron hand and his actions were reminiscent of a benevolent dictator more than anything else.

He was respected by men and feared by those who mistakenly thought they were. One rare summer the usually tepid hot spell became so intense that work in the woods was first restricted to morning-hours-only [the "hootowl shift" because you go to work at 4:00 a.m. with the owls] and then logging was completely shut down.

Too much good weather and idle time one morning produced a very drunk and unruly bunkhouse crew. Don fired forty-six men that day. He had to get down on his hands and knees to "better communicate" with the last three.

Some say that once it started raining again and work resumed, it took Don almost two days to round up and rehire the naughty men.

-- Virgil Soderberg, personal friend

A Long Memory

I served as General Manager of Alaska Loggers Association for more years than I'm willing to admit. ALA was chartered on August 25, 1957. Seventeen loggers attended the first meeting. Wes Davidson, owner of Davidson Logging Company, was elected the first president and served as a director until he retired in 1972. ALA didn't let the two pulp mills in as members until 1960. In 1966 ALA affiliated with the Pacific Logging

Congress, but in order to do so had to establish an Alaska Logging Conference, which was formally organized March 19, 1966, with Lloyd Jones named president and me as secretary. I told you I've been around a while.

I've seen a lot of water go under the bridge, and in the Tongass, that's a *lot* of water. And snow. Back in 1972 we had the longest winter on record. Normally, Southeast camps open in early March, but in '72 we still had five feet of snow on May first. I recall that Jim Campbell, Roger Gildersleeve, Lloyd Jones, Bill Menish and Alex Reid were unable to start operations until after mid-May.

It wasn't just the snow that got us, Forest Service regulations doubled logging costs in the three years between 1972 and 1975. How many people realize that all this "below cost" fuss resulted from unrealistic government regulations?

I served as General Manager under a lot of good presidents over the years. One year, 1976, we had a cat logger, Doug Ross, as president. He ran RBK Trucking up in Yakutat, the farthest northern reach of the Tongass National Forest. Yakutat is pretty much a flat land logging show, and Doug was one of the few cat loggers in the State. Most places in the Tongass the terrain's just too rugged to operate a cat, you have to go to tower logging. But Doug stacked up his logs in a row as he logged until a barge came and loaded out for the tow across the Gulf of Alaska to the mill at Sitka. Doug was quite a guy. He constructed, owned and operated the Glacier Bear Lodge at Yakutat. He was a guide for some of the best big game hunting in Alaska. He knew all the right spots and the right times to catch steelhead, sockeye, king, humpy and coho salmon. In addition to the fun things, Doug developed a sand and gravel business.

Probably the worst memory I have is hearing the news of the jet crash in Anchorage on December 4, 1978. It took the lives of some of our industry's best friends. Clarence Kramer, a founder of ALA, who served six years as president, was one of the victims. He'd spent over 50 years in the industry and was president of Alaska Lumber & Pulp Company when he was killed. Dick Sykes, an ALA member from 1965 to 1967, was the owner and pilot of the plane. Ann Stevens, wife of Senator Ted Stevens, died in the crash, and Ted himself narrowly escaped death. Tony Motley, Executive Vice President of CMAL, Citizens for the Management of Alaska Lands, was also spared.

The business side of ALA led us to establish a reciprocal insurance company, Alaska Timber Insurance Exchange in 1980. I served as its first president. The Exchange insures members of ALA domiciled in Alaska

Don Bell

for workmen's compensation insurance. It was the Association's second involvement in the insurance business. In 1967 the group organized Alaska Pacific Insurance Company, a stock insurance company, which was purchased by Insurance Company of North America in 1971 and we were dealing with a large insurance company again. The members weren't happy with the way costs kept going up, so we formed the Exchange to keep control within the logging community.

In 1984 the State of Alaska formed the Office of Forest Products in the Alaska Department of Commerce and Economic Development. It was an effort to make sure the timber industry has as much representation as the fisheries industry in government, which had always had powerful voices speaking for it in the Alaska Department of Fish and Game. It started out with two people and no budget, but it was a good idea anyway.

Even though I'm retired now I worry about the timber industry in the Tongass. I've seen it go through so much. Seen loggers and their families come and go. Seen the human side of the industry year after year. I wonder if we're going to survive the environmentalists. We have to. I don't know how, but we have to.

-- Don Bell, Alaska Loggers Association, retired

Is There Any Easy Road To Freedom?

Living in a logging camp in Southeast Alaska prepares a person for any travel difficulty you can imagine. I have learned to look forward to some small adventure every time I pack my suitcase for a trip to town.

"Town" in my case is Ketchikan. Often for the price of a ticket to town you get fascinating sidetrips thrown in at no extra cost. A trip to town takes about 45 minutes without interruptions, but can take as long as three hours depending on where circumstance dispatches the plane. So when I climb aboard a float plane I look forward to my flight with a sense of adventure.

Will we pick up anyone from a floathouse or will we land at a tugboat to take on a passenger? Will someone be on the way to the veterinarian with a pet rabbit that has been mauled by a marauding mink? Will we land at Point Baker, Edna Bay, Cape Pole, Craig, Klawock or Coffman Cove? Will we sit at Thorne Bay and wait for the fog to lift?

After seven years of flying out of Port Alice on Heceta Island with several different air taxi companies, I've learned to expect anything. So for the first leg of my 1985 trip to Washington D.C. I left Port Alice a day early to do some chores and to be sure I would get to town on time for the 8:20 am jet to Seattle.

On the day I was to leave camp I went to the office to talk to Rose Menish at 7:00 a.m. She said a plane was on its way and I could catch a ride on it. I went back home and, as things happen, the plane came in but I didn't hear it. Rose ran up, knocked on the door and we ran toward the floatplane dock. We weren't a quarter of the way there when the plane took off.

So Rose stopped at the office to radio the Alaska Loggers Association headquarters in Ketchikan and talked to public information officer Kirsten Held who then telephoned the airline in town. The airline said they would radio the plane and it would turn back and pick me up in about ten minutes.

We waited the ten minutes and no plane. We went back to the office and radioed Kirsten again. She called the airline again. They hadn't been able to contact the plane, so Kirsten contacted another airline that said they would be in Port Alice later in the day on a freight run.

Rose had another idea and radioed the Ketchikan Pulp Company helicopter which happened to be working in the area. Allen the chopper pilot said he'd be in after a while and I was soon en route to Ketchikan by way of Thorne Bay. Allen had to pick up someone at Thorne Bay and said he'd drop me off so I could catch a flight there. A plane was at the dock when we landed. What timing!

The pilot asked "Are you in a hurry?" I said, "No, I left a day early," and we were off for Meyers Chuck across Clarence Strait on Cleveland Peninsula to pick up a passenger he had dropped there earlier. We sat at Meyers Chuck enjoying the scenery for forty-five minutes while waiting for my traveling companion. Once he arrived in leisurely fashion we flew to town. With that part of my journey complete I was sure that the rest of my trip would be a breeze.

The next morning Kirsten and I caught the 7:15 ferry to the airport. From Ketchikan to Seattle we traveled with fellow Alaska Women In Timber activist Susan Oliver who had started from Haines at 4:30 a.m. In Seattle, Susan and Kirsten left me to catch a connecting flight to D.C. via St. Louis.

As I sat on my plane waiting to take off I thought how nice it is to cross the country on a beautiful day and how scared I had been on my first AWIT trip to D.C. five years earlier. In the midst of my pleasant reverie it dawned on me that we should be taking off. A voice came over the loudspeaker saying that we were waiting for a pilot but we should be taking off in less than forty-five minutes.

An hour later the voice came back telling us we could get off the plane but to stay in the boarding area of the airport. In the boarding area word went around that our pilot had broken his leg and we were awaiting his replacement.

Another hour later we Washington D.C. passengers were sent to another gate. I asked the attendant if our luggage was going with us and she said, "Happy Mother's Day! Check in with lost and found when you get to your destination."

I boarded the alternate plane, looked over my revised ticket and discovered I was going to Los Angeles and connecting with a plane there at 10:55 p.m. to Dulles instead of National Airport as originally scheduled. It was a long day.

After an uneventful flight to D.C. I reported my missing luggage and got on a bus to downtown. Forty minutes and $15 later I transferred to a cab to the Capitol Hill Hotel. More than twenty-four hours after we left Ketchikan, I was finally reunited with Kirsten and Susan.

We did our citizen lobbying and prepared to return home.

By then my airline was on strike, so I got to stay an extra day in our nation's capitol. Once I got back to the Tongass, it only took forty-five minutes from Ketchikan to Port Alice.

Ah, yes, travel in Alaska prepares you for anything.

-- Pat Rowland, Alaska Women In Timber

People Who Must

The Forest Service got the original idea of our Small Business set-asides. The whole thing came about in 1972 at a time when small logging operations had declined in number. The Forest Service and the Small Business Administration agreed to an annual set-aside program of about 80 million board feet for small firms in addition to the volume in the long-term sales for the pulp mill contracts. The volume is now pegged at 85 million feet per year.

Ketchikan Pulp went to Washington to oppose the small business set-asides, worried that the small business timber would be taken out of their allowable contract harvest. When it became clear that their contract would remain intact they dropped their opposition.

In all fairness to the two pulp mills, in truth we small loggers were protected from the large companies by those small business set-asides. The Forest Service did a great thing when they put them up. There are sawmills in Southeast that wouldn't be here otherwise if

John Schnabel

it weren't for the 85 million board feet per year that's outside the long-term contracts.''

But that's not the same thing as opposing the pulp mills' fifty-year contracts. Most of us are smart enough to realize that without those pulp mills there would be no place to sell half the logs we cut on the Tongass -- the unmerchantable pulpwood. We couldn't just leave it in the woods and we couldn't afford to pay stumpage for it and haul it out with no place to sell it.

-- John Schnabel, former sawmill owner

Balloons

Everybody wants to know about my balloon logging days. Balloon logging never paid and it ended up a short-term, impractical experiment. I did a conscientious job of logging for a whole career with every other system you can think of, and balloons is what people think of when they think of Pat Soderberg.

How it happened was that ALP had a sale for 264 million board feet of timber on Kupreanof island, and the north end of it was in the City of Kake watershed. They kept delaying the operation because no regulations had been written for logging in the watershed. The Forest Service finally decided to fully suspend the logs, and the only way they figured this could be done was by balloon logging.

So they asked us if we wouldn't go to balloon logging. There were about 7 million board feet in that watershed, so we negotiated how we were going to pay for this huge rig -- the balloon, the transport vehicle and all the other things we had to have. We worked out an agreement, bought the balloon gear and logged the Kake watershed.

Pat Soderberg's famous logging balloon

Forest Service photo

Technically it worked very well except for one thing: the balloon can lift logs completely off the ground for long distances, but it's very susceptible to high winds. This balloon is bigger than the hot air recreational ones you see Down South, so it can really catch the wind. We had to learn when to put it in the bedding grounds away from the high winds. After a couple of years we got pretty good.

We lost the helium out of it a couple of times by not knowing when to get it out of the high winds. We finally devised a way of getting through the winter: We deflated the balloon and pumped the helium back into tanks, and put the balloon on a big sled about 120 feet long. As we deflated the balloon, we laid it on this sled, and then we put plastic construction sheets on top of it and let the snow cover it. Then in the spring when the snow was gone we'd come back and inflate the balloon and go back to work.

-- Pat Soderberg, Alaska logger, retired

Balloon Shenanigans

Pat won't tell you how he packed his balloon for repairs one day. Pat's crew was working away, pulling the balloon with a dozer and the wind comes up. The balloon blew away into the woods and came down in a bunch of snags that punched holes all through it, and Pat had to send it back to the manufacturer for repairs.

Well, how do you ship something that big? Pat still had the box the balloon had come in, so he decided to return it the same way. This balloon is pretty big. They were using one of the log loaders to pick one edge of the balloon up in its grapple and fold it over again and again so it would fit in the box. They picked it up with the loader and put it in the box and when they had about two-thirds of the balloon stuffed in, the box was full.

So they just pushed the boom of the loader down and kept compressing the

Pat Soderberg

balloon into the box. And then the box started coming apart at the seams, so they went to the log dump and got their log banding equipment and banded the box with metal log-bundling straps. They forced the balloon in there with all the equipment they had, put the top on and banded it shut. I remember Pat telling me he'd like to be there when the manufacturer cut the banding and let that thing out. It must have been some Jack-in-the-Box. But nobody got hurt because Pat got the balloon back all repaired with no complaints.

-- Don Finney, executive director, Alaska Loggers Association.

Debris Of Life And Mind

I usually take the problems in stride. A businessman has to do that. The environmentalists have taken almost all of the Tongass now. We started with the abil-ity to log the whole forest and over the years they've whittled our logging area down to only a tenth of the forest, 1.7 million acres. They've put the rest into wilderness areas and national monuments. The base now is so small they're forcing the wood in-dustry into marginal areas where the log-ging is so low the government has to aug-ment the road costs.

J. R. Gildersleeve

But now the environmentalists are trying to do away with that *and* the fifty-year contracts with the pulp mills. I don't think there's going to be a wood industry in Alaska if this trend continues. Industry can't do impos-sible things.

But if any problem has troubled me, it's our internal industry dis-putes. That hurts our ability to present a united front when these political attacks hit us. And it presents a bad public image.

-- J.R. Gildersleeve, Alaska logger

Anything Is Ugly If You Say It Is

The worst black eye that internal dissension has given us recently was the Reid brothers' case. The civil suit they brought against the two pulp mills for conspiracy to drive independent loggers out of business has given the environmentalists a bludgeon they've used mercilessly. Rupert Cutler of the Audubon Society has really clobbered us with it.

Rupert Cutler was the Carter administration's Assistant Secretary of Agriculture and boss over the Forest Service yet a ferocious enemy of the timber industry.

He was giving a speech at the University of Washington in 1983 at a symposium on privatization:

> It is impossible for me to accept the Reagan privatizers' notion that individual maximizing decisions of independent economic agents will lead to both public and social optima. Atomistic choices often lead to antisocial outcomes. Another way of saying it is that private greed has often led to socially unacceptable results. Unfortunately, the history of forestry and range management in America is replete with examples of the phenomenon.
>
> One example is as recent as March 1, 1983, when the U.S. Court of Appeals for the Ninth Circuit sustained a June 1, 1981 finding by a U.S. district court to the effect that a Louisiana-Pacific subsidiary, Ketchikan Pulp Company, and the Alaska Lumber and Pulp Company had conspired to dominate all segments of the Alaska timber industry by refusing to compete with each other and excluding and destroying independent mills and contract loggers.

I was logging manager of the Ketchikan Pulp Company mill when the Reid brothers filed their suit in 1976. You have to understand that it was not a criminal prosecution in a criminal court. It was a civil suit in a civil court, which Rupe Cutler, true to form, does not mention. What environmentalists refuse to acknowledge is that Department of Justice investigations dating from the 1960s to this year have shown no anti-trust activity.

Why we lost in court has a great deal to do with the fact that the original judge died during the trial. The federal court then appointed Judge Barbara Rothstein to our case. Her whole history was as a consumer advocate on the consumer's side. From the day she first sat on the bench in our case it was clear that she believed in the Deep Pockets theory and that whatever big business did, it was wrong. Of course, you always think a judge who rules against you is biased, but consider the facts.

Judge Rothstein allowed arguments of the most absurd kind into court: That the Ketchikan mill and the Sitka mill never bid against each other, which constituted 'refusing to compete with each other.' But each mill has had exclusive cutting rights on its own area since the 1950s. The fifty-year contracts were deliberately arranged so that none of the five planned pulp mills would have to compete against the other. The point was to develop an industrial base for Alaska, using the Puget Sound region as the proper competitive comparison. The whole notion of the two Tongass pulp mills bidding on each others' contract timber is ridiculous. But Judge Rothstein wouldn't accept that argument.

When Judge Rothstein ruled against us, even with triple damages, the plaintiffs were awarded barely enough to cover their attorneys fees because they couldn't prove they had suffered economic harm. Not a very strong showing.

And as far as criminal charges of anti-trust violations, there have never been any despite almost continual investigations of the Alaska pulp industry since the 1960s. As recently as November of 1987, the Justice Department testified before Congress and told them there were no grounds

Don Finney

for prosecution.

The Department of Justice sent Deputy Assistant Attorney General Helmut F. Furth of the Anti-trust Division to testify and he said, 'In the past 15 years the Anti-trust Division has conducted several inquiries and investigations into alleged anti-competitive practices in the Southeastern Alaska timber industry.' He said they devoted substantial resources to the assignment and worked closely with the Forest Service for many years. Then he listed five separate inquires or investigations that were conducted prior to 1981. He mentioned one in 1968; then a 1970 investigation of collusive bidding; a 1971 investigation of Alaska Lumber & Pulp's market position; a grand jury investigation of ALP and KPC that extended from 1974 to 1976; and a review conducted in 1979 and 1980.

Yet the Justice Department has never taken an adversary position against the companies. They've come in and looked and looked. Now this part of Furth's testimony is significant:

He said, 'In the spring of 1981 a new investigation was initiated by us. The immediate cause of that investigation was the decision by Judge Barbara Rothstein of the United States District Court sitting without a jury in the Reid Brothers case. Our investigation continued from 1981 to the end of 1982. We reviewed the record of the Reid Brothers suit...'

Furth summarizes the Justice Department's opinion letter: 'There was no realistic prospect of attaining meaningful and effective injunctive relief against the two timber companies. We found that the economic power of the two firms in Southeast derives principally from their operation of only two pulp mills in that part of the country and their fifty-year contracts with the Forest Service.'

So in the final analysis, the internal dissension has given us a big black eye for very little substantive reason.

-- Don Finney

Moly In The Mountains

In 1974 U.S. Borax made some molybdenum discoveries at Quartz Hill in the Misty Fjords area, forty-five air miles from Ketchikan and near the Canadian border. A number of claims were established, and some were transferred to their affiliate Pacific Coast Molybdenum Company. An enormous deposit of molybdenum disulfide (molybdenite) was later verified near the surface, 1.5 billion tons, a unique and remarkable geologic feature of North America. It represents about ten percent of the world's known molybdenum reserves and the largest mineral discovery in the free world in the last twenty years.

At that time Misty Fjords was open to mineral entry, including mining activities. In 1976 the companies asked for a 'special use permit' to build an access road eleven miles in length to take out ore for analysis. The process is called bulk sampling and would allow enough ore to be removed to confirm the quality and uniformity of the deposit, as well as to evaluate appropriate milling technology.

The forest supervisor in Ketchikan sent a team of specialists to examine the proposed road site. They were aided by a state task force, appointed by Governor Jay Hammond. The completed EIS was submitted to the Council on Environmental Quality on July 18, 1977, and the permit was issued November 4, 1977 by the forest supervisor.

A group headed by the Sierra Club and including the National Audubon Society, Wilderness Society, Alaska Conservation Society, Tongass Conservation Council, and representatives from several fishermen's societies and the Ketchikan Native corporation made an administrative appeal. Regional Forester John Sandor held public hearings on the matter in Ketchikan on February 1, 1978. On March 31, 1978, he supported the supervisor's decision and issued a road permit.

The Sierra Club and its supporters appealed to Chief John McGuire in written and oral statements, but on October 4, 1978, he supported the regional forester's decision. However, inveterate industry foe Assistant Secretary of Agriculture Rupert Cutler reversed the road permit decision, holding that helicopters could be used for getting ore out for bulk sampling. Cutler denied the permit on December 1, 1978, the same day President Carter proclaimed nearly 100 million acres of Alaska as national monuments. Quartz Hill was withdrawn from mineral entry and proposed as a Wilderness area, casting the future of the project in doubt.

U.S. Borax and Pacific Coast Molybdenum brought suit against Agriculture Secretary Bob Bergland and Assistant Secretary Rupert Cutler, alleging that helicopter access was not feasible.

On December 2, 1980, Congress passed ANILCA, the Alaska lands act, confirming the establishment of the 3.2 million acre Misty Fjords National Monument and designated all of it except the Quartz hill area as Wilderness.

But Congress recognized the vital economic and national defense interest in developing this strategic mineral. Congress specifically authorized U.S. Borax and Chemical Corporation by name to develop the Quartz Hill mine and devoted more than two full pages to spelling out the procedures. Road access was guaranteed by Congress, overturning Rupert Cutler's overturning. What's more, the law says, 'It is the intent of

Congress that any judicial review of any administrative action pursuant to this section, including compliance with the National Environmental Policy Act of 1969, shall be expedited to the maximum extent possible.' If the EIS were to be challenged, Congress wrote that it should be expedited by every court. Every effort was made to thwart the destructive delaying tactics of the environmentalists.

ANILCA also required the Forest Service to publish two documents, a Draft Mining Development Concepts Analysis Document (CAD) to be followed three months later by a final CAD. It was not a decision document but intended to aid in understanding the engineering, economic, social and environmental implications of the total Quartz Hill project. The Draft EIS was issued on December 3, 1981 and a supplement in April 1982.

Over a period of thirteen years, U.S. Borax has spent over $100 million exploring and developing Quartz Hill. About $20 million has been spent on environmental protection studies -- just the studies. Without question, a greater amount of background environmental studies have been performed on the Quartz Hill area than on any equivalent area in Alaska. The presently planned construction phase will require an additional $800 million, and $200 in addition to that for subsequent developments.

The mine itself will eventually result in an excavation two miles long, a mile and a third wide and from 800 to 2,300 feet deep. The pit will become a lake after the fifty-five-year predicted life-span of the ore body, and the fringes revegetated as close as possible to natural conditions. Ore crushing facilities will be located at the mine site and primary processing will be at tidewater, the crushed ore conveyed there through a four and a half mile long tunnel.

The biggest environmental impact will be the mine tailings, which instead of just being left in heaps around the mining site, will be conveyed through a long tunnel for disposal at the bottom of the very deep Wilson Arm, one of the Misty Fjords. The tailings will be deposited in a biotic zone only sparsely populated by bottom life, and deposited gradually so that even what creatures there are -- pelagic and demersal fishes and benthic organisms -- will have time to adapt with minimal mortality. The tailings will spread by natural currents for about 11.3 miles to a natural sill in Smeaton Bay. Even after fifty-five years of mine tailings are deposited there, the top of the tailings will still be 580 feet below the water surface.

The economics of the project are significant. The payroll during construction is estimated at $162 million a year, with later standard operations payroll at $72 million. The tax contribution to the Borough and City of Ketchikan and the State of Alaska have not been calculated, but will obviously be tremendous.

In a letter to the *Ketchikan Daily News* on May 2, 1986, Governor Bill Sheffield stated:

> Over its 55-year life, Quartz Hill will employ thousands of Alaskans and provide tax revenue to both Ketchikan and the state. With proper safeguards for the protection of the environment, particularly water and air quality and the fisheries, as well as balanced consideration for economics, I support the careful consideration of projects like Quartz Hill.

The entire Alaskan congressional delegation wrote:

> We encourage the State of Alaska to do everything reasonably possible to assure the Quartz Hill Project is a competitive source of molybdenum and a stable long-term source of jobs and revenue.

The Forest Service in late October 1988 issued the Record of Decision from the final Environmental Impact Statement for the project and decided that the mine will go ahead. Even so, U.S. Borax will have to wait for better molybdenum prices in order to go ahead.

The environmentalists have indicated that they will continue to oppose the mine even though they have not yet read the new Environmental Impact Statement. Something has to be done about their abuse of power.

-- Don Finney

Mob Government

Our family of four relocated from Oregon to Alaska in 1985. It was a move dictated by special interest groups, environmentalists, that shut down the timber industry where we were. We saw numerous jobs lost and mills shut down because these "interest" groups were deciding how the forests should be managed.

Here in Alaska I enjoy watching eagles flying, fish jumping, deer walking on the roads, seals and otters playing in the bay, mink running on our floats and most of all, people working!

The "American Dream" of being a productive citizen of these United States is becoming a nightmare of unemployment. City people who have desk jobs and don't know what really living with nature is all about are telling me to move on because they don't think we treat our forests properly.

"Interest groups" will eventually be the fall of the hard-working man -- the man who feeds his family with his wages, not by welfare; the man who clothes his family and educates his children by himself, not by the handouts of a socialistic society.

Hardworking, honest Americans should be allowed to pursue their lifestyles, not told to roll over and die.

-- Mary Ann Lamb, homemaker

Not A Creature Was Stirring

The year when I was a third or fourth grader we were holding our Christmas program in the Rec hall in camp. One of my Dad's veteran employees, Johnny Banks, was to be Santa Claus. He had to go over to the Mallones' house to get his costume. We kids sang "Here comes Santa Claus, here comes Santa Claus" over and over but no Santa Claus appeared.

Again we sang -- over and over and still no Santa. We kept on singing because Santa Claus just had to come. Upon investigation they found the Mallones' dog had our Santa Claus cornered on the sofa and wouldn't let him off.

-- Virgil Soderberg, contractor

Reverie from a Sea-Gypsy Journal, 1982

I live in a float camp made up of log rafts lashed together with cable, each raft called a float. On the many floats we have trailer houses and small buildings such as work shops, a school, bunkhouses, our cookhouse, a small store and even a playground, everything needed to support a complete logging operation. Our camp is a quarter-mile long and is a registered marine vessel.

My husband Mick Cole and I are part of Don and Jan Harbour's logging company. We do high-lead A frame logging -- logging from the forest straight down to the water. We don't have to build roads or use log trucks so our operation is less expensive than other logging. We are the only A-frame logging show left in Southeast Alaska.

Float camps remain anchored in one place for the duration of the logging operation. Then we move to the next site. Getting there is always an adventure. Come with us on a typical move. We've just finished logging a timber sale at Naukati on the west coast of Prince of Wales Island in Tuxekan Channel. We'll be moving some sixty miles south to High Point on Dall Island. Here's our journal:

DAY ONE: *Exodus*

6:00 a.m. It's a beautiful morning with the sun coming up from behind Twin Mountain into a bright blue sky. You can feel the excitement in the air. The men have been outside for some time scurrying about getting things ready to depart -- a job that will take all day. They've already shifted all the "junk floats" to the front of the camp. These are the secondary floats carrying small equipment and working shacks.

6:30 a.m. Each end of the camp has been moored here at Naukati with a huge anchor to keep us from drifting. The A-frame crew just pulled up the big anchor in front of camp. The engines are roaring and the men are yelling and giving hand signals. The women and kids are taking pictures and watching all the action.

8:00 a.m. Because we will be towing, everyone must make sure they have enough water stored up for the next five days. I've filled up everything available -- garbage cans, big cooking pots, the bathtub, washing machine, sink and buckets. We'll be using sea water to flush the toilets.

9:45 a.m. Catastrophe at the Hicks home. Chris, a Harbour Logging employee, came in from helping with the sea-preparations to fill their bathtub for the tow -- and then left the house without turning the water off. His wife Laura found three inches of water in the hall, bathroom and bedroom! I ran and got the hand pump from our boat and took it to the Hicks flood. While one of us pumped the water into buckets, the other used a dustpan to push the water out of the carpet.

10:55 a.m. The Hicks home is dry now -- well, a little soggy, actually. But both anchors are up and the small tug, the Skookum, is towing us out of the Naukati Bay tide flats and into open water to wait for the big tug, the Mary Catherine, which will tow us to our destination.

12:30 p.m. All boats and skiffs have now been tucked inside the camp. Boomsticks [very substantial long logs] are lashed together outlining the camp, secured with cable to keep us in one piece during the tow.

2:30 p.m. The school floatplane just flew out to camp to bring my daughter Shawndell's correspondence course work. We didn't have enough kids for our own camp school this year.

7:00 p.m. The last detail has been taken care of. Everything has been locked down for the passage to Dall Island. We're all ready. The men have been fed and we're expecting the Mary Catherine any minute.

7:30 p.m. The Mary Catherine arrives and now begins the tedious process of connecting the tow cables that will pull a small sea-going town through sixty miles of treacherous Tongass waters.

9:50 p.m. It's dark out and we can't see much, but we're finally under way. Goodbye, Naukati! We'll remember you! There's something special, almost majestic, about this little camp of ours moving slowly through the Tongass waters in the dark between the mountains in the sea. The running lights of the Mary Catherine and the Skookum cheer the evening shadows. Shawndell, Laura Hicks and I decide to take a walk to the other end of camp. We walk across one section of the boardwalk that caves in just as we step off. We decide the kids better not be running around outside during the tow unless there is an adult with them.

11:30 p.m. The guys are out fixing things that have come apart, a routine job right after departure. One of the boomsticks in front of our trailer has separated and the men are repairing it.

DAY TWO: *Sea Beams*

6:00 a.m. We pass Chief Tonowek's grave and all throw food and Copenhagen in the water for him for good luck and smooth water. The Tlingit and Haida who worked these woods long before we got here felt the same sense of the spirit we get from working the forest of the Tongass.

6:30 a.m. My husband Mick, who is serving as our boat captain, drops anchor while we wait for the tides to change in Tonowek Narrows. A long wait.

2:00 p.m. We thread our way through the Narrows into Tonowek Bay.

3:00 p.m. A pod of killer whales goes by.

4:30 p.m. We are now passing Heceta Island and the peak of Bald Mountain. Ahead lies the Gulf of Esquibel, protected from the open ocean only by the scattered Maurelle Islands.

9:30 p.m. We've turned east into San Christoval Channel. Long swells are coming from the Pacific directly behind us. Things are beginning to rock pretty bad. I'm tying up the cupboards.

11:40 p.m. Even though we're passing behind San Fernando Island, the logs are groaning and creaking and every now and then there's a pretty good jolt that really shakes the trailer. It's difficult to write. My coffee cup just slid off the table.

11:50 p.m. Pilot Pete Amundsen of the Mary Catherine just called from the tug on the CB to say we lost something that he could see on the radar about a quarter mile behind camp.

Midnight. Mick and Chris leave in the skiff with spotlights to go and retrieve whatever we lost. The TV just went out. We were all hooked up with co-ax to Don's recorder -- it came tight and broke.

2:30 a.m. Mick and Chris are back. We lost three small floats and some logs. They called the Skookum and rounded them up. We decided to take turns sleeping in case something else goes wrong.

DAY THREE: *Tempest Tarry*

6:00 a.m. We are now passing through San Alberto Bay. We can see the village of Craig just beyond Fish Egg Island. There are gale warnings out and the wind is really blowing up Ursua Channel into the Bay.

7:30 a.m. Our tow is slipping past Balandra Island and behind San Juan Bautista Island where it is more protected.

8:00 a.m. They dropped the anchor and we are going to wait out the storm.

Noon. We're going to be here a long time.

8:30 p.m. Don Harbour just called on the CB. He stepped on a nail and wants some Epsom salts. We're still waiting for the weather to get better.

DAY FOUR: *Seaborne Once More*

6:30 a.m. The winds have died down. They just pulled up the anchor and we're on our way again.

10:00 a.m. We're approaching Cape Flores which leads into the protected Ulloa Channel behind Suemez Island.

5:30 p.m. The little community of Waterfall is coming up on our left. Mick, Chris, Shawndell and I jump in the skiff and take off for a visit to Waterfall Resort. It has a good store, so we buy some groceries.

9:20 p.m. Getting some more big swells.

DAY FIVE: *Last Leg*

9:00 a.m. Just as we pass Shelikof Island I fell on the walkway and scraped my arm and bruised my hip and leg.

Noon. I'll be all right, except for the aches. We're passing down the lee side of Dall Island now, making good time southbound in Tlevak Strait between Farralon Bay and Breezy Bay.

4:30 p.m. A bunch of people at View Cove are taking pictures as our tow goes by.

6:00 p.m. There's our destination dead ahead, High Point, a bluff on Dall Island facing across the strait to Sukkwan Island.

7:00 p.m. We're here. Our new home. An inlet behind High Point. We'll be logging here for several months. The camp is tied and anchored now and the kids are eager to explore the new beaches!

-- Kathy Cole, Alaska Women In Timber

The voices murmur on into the night, into the blanket of the Tongass night. They fade into the Northern Lights playing over the archipelago. A baby is being born somewhere on a lonely island. Another voice. Another one of us. Pick a lucky star for this baby. Pick a lucky star for the people of the Tongass. Sleep, you wonderful aspiring people. Be good to yourselves. Rest and listen. The voices will live in your dreams. And give you strength for the war ahead.

AGENDA FOR RENEWAL

• •

The time has come to change things. The people of the Tongass are not the ignorant rape-scrape-and-ruin savages environmentalists make us out to be. We are not faceless monsters running out-of-control engines of destruction. We are people. We are decent people deeply concerned about the environment, about our families, about our communities, about our forest, about our economies, about the world. We do a good job in the woods for mankind and for nature.

The people of the Tongass are tired of being victimized by the environmental lobby. For years there was no Wise Use counterbalance to the preservationist thrust of the environmental movement. Now such a countervailing Wise Use Movement is beginning to grow in America. The hundreds of thousands of ordinary people who have been victimized, pushed out of jobs, seen their towns die, seen their industries choked to death inch by inch, have been radicalized by their experience. They are beginning to band together to wrest the environmental movement from its arrogant and one-sided masters. The people of the Tongass are part of that new movement.

The Wise Use Movement is in its infancy. Its clout today is micro-scopic compared to the environmentalists. Its potential tomorrow is astronomical.

During 1988 two significant gatherings began to coalesce the Wise Use Movement. The underlying social force has been developing here and there for ten years or more in such groups as the Women In Timber organizations. In June 1988, the Wilderness Impact Research Foundation held the first National Wilderness Conference in Las Vegas, Nevada, to find ways to end the destructive spread of Wilderness designation into farms and ranches and forests and towns where it was never intended to be.

In August 1988 the Center for the Defense of Free Enterprise held the first Multiple Use Strategy Conference in Reno, Nevada, to plan the restructuring of all environmental law away from its present ideological ri-gidity into the rule of reason.

The growth of the Wise Use Movement is a challenge to anti-industry extremism and an invitation to people of good will everywhere to come and stand beside us under a new banner: People for Nature - Nature for People -- Sustainable Development Forever.

The National Wilderness Conference brought numerous old-line trade groups and citizen organizations together for the first time: The American Farm Bureau Federation, the National Rifle Association (hunters find themselves increasingly excluded from Wilderness), the National Cattlemens Association and many others that have realized they must work together if any are to survive.

The Multiple Use Strategy Conference brought more than 200 grass-roots Wise Use groups together from all over the United States and from all industrial and private sectors, mining, farms, livestock, agricultural chemicals, private property rights advocates, inholders groups, consumer advocates, civil rights groups. They voted to send the incoming presidential administration their Wise Use Agenda for the Environment. In that agenda they addressed every department of the federal government that deals with environmental issues. They addressed every environmental issue from global warming to safe pesticide application to timber issues affecting the Tongass.

The diverse elements of the Wise Use Movement have agreed to support one another in time of need. Now they stand in solidarity with the people of the Tongass. Their statements of support and belief in our cause bring a new reality to the public arena. Here are their endorsements of the people of the Tongass.

Statements of the Wise Use Movement

The Hannibal Hamlin Institute For Economic Policy Studies
Hallowell, Maine

The federal Administration should adopt a policy of environmental federalism which recognizes the appropriate federal and state government responsibilities governing allocation of public lands. No federal Wilderness area should be designated by Congress or approved by the President without prior approval of the state wherein such designation is contemplated.

The federal Administration should honor the obligation of its contracts with private industry for the extraction and conversion of natural resources from federal lands. Specifically, the federal timber harvest contracts with private firms in the Tongass National Forest of Alaska should be honored to their full terms without impairment of the obligation of contracts.

The federal Administration should affirm the right of the people of the Tongass to own property, to engage in profitable enterprises and to keep the fruits of individual labor.

Matthew J. Glavin
President

West Coast Alliance for Resources and Environment
(WE CARE)
Eureka, California

The West Coast Alliance for Resources and Environment is a community-based, grassroots group that promotes wise management and multiple use for our land and the protection of industry. We are concerned with resource-related issues which affect our lifestyle, both economic and historic. It is this rural lifestyle that we want to enhance and protect.

The United States Forest Service has the responsibility to the nation to professionally manage the forest for timber production, along with other commodities and amenities.

The Forest Service has the responsibility to each dependent community to offer an acceptable harvest level based on the biological capability of the forest. Statutory regulation should be sought to reach these goals. Special interest groups should not be allowed to subvert this responsibility.

WE CARE supports the people of the Tongass.

Liz Tomascheski-Adams
Executive Coordinator

American Freedom Coalition
Washington, D.C.

The American Freedom Coalition's Task Force on the Environment is committed to protecting Earth's environment and wise use of our natural resources to promote economic growth and human progress while assuring protection from pollution, overuse, and depletion. We therefore support legislation that will guarantee the sanctity of contracts between the

Forest Service, United States Department of Agriculture, and private firms operating the timberlands of the Tongass National Forest in Alaska, under multiple use and sustained yield principles.

Michael F. Beard
National Field Director

Taxpayers for the Environment And its Management
(T.E.A.M.)
Scotia, California

The decision-making process on our public lands, including national forests, needs to be revised.

All policy development should be based upon factually reliable studies. Only scientific reports that have been properly replicated to assure reliability should form the basis for each federal policy. No study which has originated from a special interest lobby should be allowed to stand by itself, but should be considered only if opposing interests have had an opportunity to submit comparable data.

Priority must be given to local legislation and management of natural resources to ensure economic stability and credibility. Federal policy must follow local policy, not lead it.

Only local judicial units should be permitted to review appeals on resource management disputes. Judges' schools should be instituted on community stability issues.

Government agencies should be required to provide a minimum of one year for regional study and local public input before allocating or approving any tax funds for wilderness designation or private land acquisition.

We support the people of the Tongass.

Gary Gundlach
Janet C. Baird
T.E.A.M. Organizers

North West Timber Association
Eugene, Oregon

In many parts of the west the continued economic and social stability of communities is dependent upon a reasonable and stable timber supply from dominant Forest Service and Bureau of Land Management lands. Over the past two decades legislative actions (Wilderness, National Park expansions, Wild and Scenic Rivers, etc.) have steadily reduced the timber landbase and thus the sustainable timber supply, causing reduced economic activity and higher consumer prices for wood products. Congressionally directed planning (NFMA, FLPMA) and legal hurdles (NEPA) have further increased the instability of our communities as wildlife, water, non-road recreation and visual management have been emphasized while community stability has been relegated to a residual position to be considered only after all other values are accommodated.

The portion of the public land base available for commodity production must be stabilized and protected much as areas have been reserved for non-timber use such as Wilderness.

A minimum level of timber and other commodity outputs necessary to stabilize and maintain the public timber dependent communities should be identified for each unit of the national forests. Minimum output requirements must be established by law.

These proposals should apply to the Tongass National Forest. We support the people of the Tongass.

Dennis Hayward
Executive Vice President

National Inholders Association
Washington, D.C. and Sonoma, California

An inholder is an owner of private property interests within government lands, which may include owners of real estate, cabin permits, grazing permits, timber contracts and other valuable private property rights. The National Inholders Association represents inholders to Congress and other forums to protect their rights.

The people of the Tongass are themselves a valuable resource that should not be dismissed lightly. Their life on the land, their natural wisdom and their productivity all give depth and shape to the meaning of America. Far from being a threat to the forest as extremists portray them, these diligent and dedicated people are good stewards who increase the natural gift of productivity on our timberlands through wise use and sound silvicultural practice.

Socially, the people of the Tongass are a priceless asset teaching our affluent society the forgotten value of basic economic commodity production, industriousness, foresight and endurance in the face of overwhelming obstacles, both natural and manmade.

Charles S. Cushman
Executive Director

Wilderness Impact Research Foundation
Elko, Nevada

The central theme of the Wilderness Impact Research Foundation is that no further Wilderness should be designated until the impact of the existing 90 million acres has been thoroughly assessed. Excessive Wilderness designation has wrought havoc in the fabric of American industry, economy, popular recreation and our society's vision. No further Wilderness designations should be made by Congress without the specific approval of the legislature of the state in which such designation is being considered. The Foundation specifically supports the people of the Tongass in their efforts to assess and redirect harmful Wilderness encroachment upon their livelihoods and way of life.

Grant Gerber
Director

Multiple Use Association
Gorham, New Hampshire

The Multiple Use Association is a grassroots membership group concerned about the needs of all forest users, the health of the forest now and in the future and the promotion of good forest management practices. The Forest Service has determined that less than five percent of the people who use national forests use Wilderness areas. One half of those Wilderness users would get as good or better experience in a multiple use area accord to the USFS.

Contrary to environmentalists' contentions that old growth forests possess values that second growth forests do not, a properly managed forest is healthier and more attractive. Younger trees are less susceptible to disease and insects. The forests of New Hampshire and Maine are attractive and healthy *because* they were harvested properly. To foster understanding in the general public we have distributed bumper stickers

which read: Promote healthy forests - Support multiple use.
We support the people of the Tongass.

Leon Favreau
President

Public Land Users Society (P.L.U.S.)
Tacoma, Washington

Forest Service policy should protect both the Wilderness and the public's right to enjoy the Wilderness by ensuring that use is dispersed in an environmentally sound manner More trails should be developed throughout the system which are open to hikers, horses and the handicapped. In addition, there should be *no* further inclusion of Wilderness on national forest lands other than the acres presently classified by Acts of Congress. P.L.U.S. fully supports the people of the Tongass.

John Hosford
Co-Chairman

California Women In Timber

Trees are one of America's renewable natural resources. Our national forests should be managed for multiple-use, balancing recreation and timber production. It is important that we maximize timber growth and increase timberland productivity in order to supply the people of our nation with the wood products they need.

The following criteria should be considered in the management of our national forests:

● Our national forests must be managed for sustained yield timber production.

● Timber harvest levels should be based on what the land base can biologically produce given mandated forest constraints.

● Forest plans must be developed and implemented in a timely manner in accordance with the law.

● Timber output should at least equal Resource Planning Act (RPA) goals set for each region.

● Community stability and the economic well-being of local communities must be considered when developing forest plans.

● The Forest Service should use their expertise to educate the general public on the differences in meaning between national forests, national parks, and wilderness. The meanings of these terms causes much confusion in the minds of the average American citizen. People *must* be educated about the restrictions associated with wilderness designation; and the benefits and rewards that can be derived from wise multiple-use of our national forests.

Acreage contained in our national parks and in wilderness areas is more than adequate. Existing parklands should be developed and maintained with no more new acreage set aside.

We support the people of the Tongass.

-- The Membership

The Blue Ribbon Coalition
Pocatello, Idaho

Trail enthusiasts using motorized vehicles pay millions in federal gasoline taxes annually which are used to construct highways, not aid motorized recreation programs. These monies should instead be returned to a National Recreational Trails Fund. The fund would provide matching grants to state and federal land management agencies, and local governments, coordinated through appropriate state agencies with the primary goal of encouraging multiple-use trail development. A provision should also be made for adding additional revenues to the fund in the future, revenues derived from trail activities which do not generate fuel taxes.

We feel that nationwide support for motorized trail use will help the people of the Tongass by promoting a wider spectrum of multiple uses.

Clark Collins
President and Executive Director

Mountain States Legal Foundation
Denver, Colorado

The public land management agencies, the Department of the Interior and the Department of Agriculture, must recognize that economic use of the public lands is a legitimate and essential part of the status quo of those lands. Timber production, livestock grazing, mineral development, and mining on the public lands means jobs, economic security, and increased state, Federal and local revenues. Time and time again environmentalists, bureaucrats, and the media use pictures of a logging cut or a mine as examples of environmental degradation and pollution. Such illustrations constitute gross misinformation. These actions are no more detrimental to the environment than the process that results in a field of corn stubble. They are simply evidence of land in production for the benefit of the Nation.

Economic utilization of the public lands is a right of the Western States. In the early years of the republic, Congress sold lands in those states seeking statehood. Although those sales ended prior to settlement of the West, the legislative histories of most of the statutes governing those western federal lands illustrate that Congress still wanted those lands to be developed for the economic benefit of the West. This right to the economic use of the federal lands is essential to the Western economies. It is their right under the law. This applies to the Tongass National Forest.

Eric Twelker
Attorney at Law

Timber Association of California
Sacramento, California

The United States is a net importer of wood products. Last year, we imported 12.2 billion board feet more softwood lumber than we exported. In wholesale lumber terms, that volume represents between $2 billion and $2.5 billion -- dollars that are contributing to an unfavorable trade balance. It is also nearly one-fourth of our total softwood consumption.

The harvesting of federally-owned timber (Forest Service, BLM, and others) generates more than one billion dollars annually in taxes of all kinds, and the private timber harvest adds another two billion. The imported lumber represents foregone taxes in an amount nearly equivalent to that generated by federal timber harvest.

The forest lands of this nation have the productive capacity to turn us from net importers to net exporters of solid wood products. The Tongass National Forest is a leader in export of solid wood products. We support the people of the Tongass in all their efforts.

William Denison
President

Wind River Multiple Use Advocates
Riverton, Wyoming

Over the past twenty years, federal land management agencies have been increasingly experimenting with a philosophy which holds that "nature" is best off where and when human involvement is the least. Many current policies reflect this philosophy, calling for human activities to be held to a minimum. The disastrous spread of Wilderness designations has seriously affected the economies of our Western states.

It is time to admit that the nature-without-man experiment has serious flaws, and that we now must turn our attention to finding management solutions in which humans are cast in a more active role. We support the people of the Tongass as a living example of mankind for nature, nature for mankind.

George Reynolds
President

Consumer Alert
Modesto, California

Consumer Alert is a nationwide consumer advocacy group with members in all fifty states. CA is funded by voluntary dues contributed by its members, by foundation grants and by sale of publications.

The environmental movement, although initially begun to make Americans more aware of the need to solve various ecological problems resulting from years of inattention to environmental affairs, today has taken on a life of its own involved only with maintaining its status as a going concern.

Movement leaders, more and more often referred to as anti-growth advocates, coercive utopians, and even fear mongers, show telltale signs of fanaticism. There is no rational basis to their negative pronouncements on mining of precious minerals, well managed forestry or prudent petroleum development.

American consumers are harmed when restrictions are placed on the wise development of natural resources. Consumers benefit from the efficient and ecologically sound development of all resources found in nature.

Housing costs rise when our national timber industry is saddled with unreasonable restrictions and is precluded from harvesting timber at a cost lower than imported supply. Likewise, higher costs of all timber-related products such as paper and packaging result when domestic harvesting is rendered uncompetitive by unreasonable federal regulations.

On behalf of American consumers, we urge that the federal government reconsider present restrictive forest policy and preservationist's artificial scarcity and move toward wise use and development of our nation's natural resources. We urge that a careful and reasonable balance be struck between consumer needs and demands and available supply of our nation's natural resources.

In particular, Consumer Alert stands in solidarity with the people of the Tongass in their struggle to supply the world's consumers with products and the American economy with jobs.

Barbara Keating
Executive Director

Waking Up To The Problem

There are more, many more contributions to the Wise Use Agenda that add their support for the people of the Tongass. There is no need to go on. The point should be clear. The people of the Tongass are gaining friends. But all too few, and perhaps too late. We need more. Many more.

As America's service economy grows steadily in relation to our total goods sector, Americans are coming to realize, slowly, painfully slowly, just how precious our basic resource extraction industries are. More than seventy percent of us work in service jobs today. Less than one-third of us produce all the physical needs of the whole nation. The number of people it takes to feed, clothe, shelter and protect us all is shrinking all the time.

But we have been slow in realizing the political consequences of that basic economic change: No longer can goods producing industry call upon a loyal workforce to defend it in the polling place because its majority no longer exists. It hasn't existed since 1952, the year that the total goods-producing sector was first surpassed by the service sector.

Today it's 70-30 in the other direction. The fisherman and the farmer and the logger and the miner and the steel worker and the automobile worker and the carpenter and the construction worker are outnumbered by the professor and the clerical worker and the doctor and the waitress and the store clerk and the accountant and the schoolteacher and the lawyer and the environmentalist.

The 70 percent in the service sector are seldom aware of the plight of the 30 percent in the total goods sector: They have enough problems of their own, e.g., their wages are barely half that of the total goods sector. Service workers need two incomes to thrive. That puts the nurturing extended family of yesteryear totally out of the question. It creates pressures on today's nuclear family which result in stress or violence on the one hand and on the other reinforces the trend toward tomorrow's subatomic family, the DINKs: Double Income, No Kids. And in the socioeconomic confusion, total goods has become The Forgotten Sector.

Post-Gratification Forgetting and Devaluation

When you're waiting table and your feet hurt and you have a note in your pocket from the high school teacher that your kid is doing drugs, it's hard to remember that somebody had to mine the metal to build the tools to build the equipment to mine the silica to make the glass you just spilled on your best customer. Mining: Forgotten Sector.

When you're late for the power lunch that could catapult you into the boss's suite of your computer software firm and you could lose it all because some clod has backed a front end loader into your lane of traffic during street repairs, it's hard to remember that someone had to explore the ground to find the oil to bring to the wellhead to pipe to the refinery to crack into asphalt to truck to the street so your tax dollars could work for you fixing the chugholes you've worn there in a thousand trips to the office. Petroleum: Forgotten Sector.

When you're a store clerk in a suburban mall trying to get over the chewing-out your boss just gave you for being late because the car wouldn't start again because you couldn't afford the extra money to join AAA last year so you couldn't use their car-starting road service and you're wondering where you're going to find the spare cash to buy a new battery, it's hard to remember that a team of tool and production planners had to call upon the capacity of eighty-five sectors of the economy to put the parts into the hands of the factory managers so the workers could assemble the car you roundly cuss. Manufacturing: Forgotten Sector.

When you're so well off that you don't have to worry about getting *enough* food so you can become concerned about *healthy* food and *moral* food and read all these books about how bad beef and lamb and pork are for your primate guts and how unethical it is to eat your fellow creatures so you can become a vegetarian and have to make sure each meal has the right combination of amino acids to make a complete protein, it's hard to remember that your distaste for eating dead cow carcasses which led you to oppose grazing on public lands which led to an anti-grazing law which put the rancher out of business is about to make you barefoot, because they still make shoe leather out of cowhide, unless you want to wear synthetic shoes made out of oil. Livestock: Forgotten Sector.

When you're a movie director jogging down the sidewalks of your exclusive residential neighborhood in your $1,500 exercise clothes trying to think of a way to make the scene work in which your $5 million female star narrowly escapes the clutches of the evil businessman so you can reinforce the negative public image of all those sharks that wouldn't back your first picture which flopped at the box office but now you're going to make them regret it with a real blockbuster, it's hard to remember that the Forest Service had to write a plan so the road contractor could get into the woods so the logging contractor could harvest the timber so the pulp mill could convert it to dissolving pulp so Eastman's wizards in Rochester could produce the motion picture film so you could make all your unrecognized benefactors in business look like greedy monsters so you could get rich and famous at their expense. Timber: Forgotten Sector.

When you're an environmentalist, it's hard to remember that the human race has to get its living somewhere. Total Goods: Forgotten Economy.

But now, after twenty years of dominance by the environmentalists' paradigms and assumptions, little by little the story is seeping out: American industry is on the Endangered Species list, and we put it there ourselves by uncritical acceptance of anti-industry misrepresentation, like Jack Skow's hatchet job on the timber industry in *Sports Illustrated*.

Restitution Is Not Enough

Is it so hard to realize that trying to destroy the forest products industry in the Tongass is anti-social? We don't think so. Is it so hard to understand that trying to put the people of the Tongass out of business is unethical? We don't think so. Is it so hard to grasp that unethical and anti-social behaviors are not to be tolerated? We don't think so.

But in order to think about environmentalists as unethical, one must not only know the devious and harmful things they have done, one must also have some kind of mental framework by which to understand that the environment can be protected without destroying industry. The National Environmental Policy Act of 1969 gave us a powerful clue in that direction: it declared "a national policy which will encourage productive and enjoyable harmony between man and his environment." Today's established environmental movement has emphasized the "enjoyable harmony" of that policy to the exclusion of "productive harmony." Productive harmony is the key concept by which we can understand that the environment can be protected without destroying industry. Productive Harmony.

The Tlingit and Haida and Tsimshian can log their lands without any federal environmental laws and still win environmental awards. Productive harmony. The timber industry in the Tongass can certainly do as sensitive a job working under the far more stringent rule of federal environmental law. Productive harmony.

A new life-philosophy based upon productive harmony is emerging with the new Wise Use movement. It indicates that a post-environmental society is somewhere on the horizon, a time when the pendulum of anti-industrial sentiment progresses, not back to some "industry-can-do-no-wrong" attitude, but to a new middle ground of "industry-can-do-things-right," an admission that the Sierra Club or the Wilderness Society would never embrace. Productive harmony is the key. Protecting our industry is implicit in the concept of productive harmony. Thwarting the enemies of industry is implicit in protecting our industry.

As a nation we must take measures now to protect our industrial base, which includes protecting our productive land base. This is not an easy task. A large and well financed lobby in Washington, D.C. is prepared to say anything in order to discredit industry. A necessary step to protecting America's industrial base, and one that is most distasteful, is that the environmental lobby itself must be discredited. To the people of the Tongass who are accustomed to working for a living and minding their own business, this is doubly distasteful: It demands that we enter the public arena, where we are not comfortable; and it demands that we neglect our true love, logging, road building, milling, shipping -- working as the home-givers of the whole earth.

To discredit the most local and most vocal opponents of our industrial base in the Tongass is, thankfully, not terribly difficult. Southeast Alaska Conservation Council, SEACC, a group noted for its efforts to deter development of natural resources in Southeast Alaska, is so extreme that its true intent to destroy the Tongass timber industry is perfectly clear. Their pronouncements are less skillfully contrived than those of many environmental groups.

In particular, SEACC has agitated for the elimination of key portions of ANILCA that protect the industry's timber supply. They tout a list of sixteen communities in Southeast Alaska that have allegedly passed resolutions denouncing forestry on the Tongass National Forest. What they don't say is that these sixteen communities represent at total population of 2,638 people.

The population of Southeast is 58,464. Two of the communities SEACC lists, Edna Bay and Port Protection, are classified as having no permanent population -- it varies with the fishing season. The two largest communities on the SEACC list are Hoonah, population 906, where Louie White and many other loggers live, and Yakutat, population 462. Both villages are surrounded by extensive logging lands of their own. The resolutions SEACC uses to buttress its efforts to destroy the timber industry certainly do not represent the views of most people in either Hoonah or Yakutat. The timber industry provides income to most of the sixteen communities on SEACC's list.

Notably absent from SEACC's list are Sitka, Ketchikan, Haines, Wrangell, Kake, Craig, Metlakatla, Hydaburg, Klawock and Petersburg, all of which depend heavily on the timber industry. SEACC is clearly manufacturing synthetic support for its views where in fact there is little or none. Such manipulation of people and the facts is completely unethical and without social conscience.

All the opponents of our industrial base, the Sierra Club, Defenders of Wildlife, Environmental Defense Fund, Friends of the Earth, Western Federation of Outdoor Clubs, Wilderness Society, and National Parks and Conservation Association must be reformed from their present unethical intent and antisocial goals, by congressional action if necessary. To the extent they act to destroy the forest products industry, which is a responsible renewable resource industry, they are no friends of you or me or the earth we live on. If they will not be reconciled to a healthy thriving forest products industry they must be reconstituted along more humane lines or cut out of society altogether. To the extent that they exclude productive harmony and emphasize only enjoyable harmony, they are unethical and anti-social.

In a word, the anti-industry aspect of environmentalism must be eliminated in favor of productive harmony. But how?

Respect For The Truth

What can we do to stop anti-industry activism? First, keep in mind the truth about the big lies:

1) A Forestry Truth: The Tongass National Forest is not being harmed by timber harvest. Even the most-logged area of the Tongass, Prince of Wales Island, is naturally regenerating its forest cover at prodigious rates. The second growth forests are producing more than one-and-a-half times as much wood as old growth and in many places twice the volume. The second growth forests are producing vastly more oxygen to cleanse the

atmosphere and absorbing carbon dioxide faster than stagnant and decadent old growth forests. The young forests, in all age classes, are healthy
and thriving.

2) A Wildlife Truth: The Tongass is richer in wildlife than almost any
other national forest, even after decades of logging. Brown and black bear
populations are high and healthy, the brown bear population more dense in
the Tongass than anywhere else. The bald eagle population is higher in the
Tongass than anywhere else. The Sitka blacktail deer presently enjoys
higher population levels than at any time measured in the past. The
salmon harvest in Tongass streams and open waters stands at record levels.
If logging had any adverse impact on wildlife, none of this would be true.
Environmentalist claims of logging damage to Tongass wildlife are flat
lies designed to discredit the timber industry for political reasons.

3) A Geographic Truth: Only ten percent of the Tongass National
Forest is scheduled for harvest during the 100-year rotation period. Thirty
percent of the Tongass National Forest is designated as Wilderness.
Claims that anyone is turning the Tongass into a "tree factory" are 90
percent wrong and 100 percent deliberate lies.

4) A Legal Truth: The Alaska National Interest Lands Conservation
Act represents two compromises by the timber industry that lowered its
annual allowable harvest to minimal no-growth rates but assured survival
in return for agreeing to a massive 5.4 million acre Wilderness designation
in the Tongass. Now that the Wilderness is safely under stable administration, the environmental community wants to revoke its agreement to
survivable timber harvest levels for the industry and is coming back to
Congress to repeal all harvest protections. The environmentalists are
reneging on a deal, revealing their unethical and anti-social nature.

5) A Budgetary Truth: The Tongass Timber Supply Fund of $40
million dollars a year is not a timber subsidy, it is a Wilderness subsidy. It
consists of $25 million dollars for the normal Forest Service budget on the
Tongass National Forest, while only $15 million is allocated to build roads
into submarginal areas, do some logging technology research for coping
with submarginal areas, and perform thinning to promote more rapid
timber growth.

6) A Political Truth: The environmental movement intends to eliminate the timber industry in the Tongass, a completely unethical and anti-
social goal. If they deny this, let them prove their benevolence by coming
forward with proposals that will *enhance* the survival of the timber
industry, for example by providing for expanded harvest to meet current
market demands at 600 million board feet per year instead of the compro-

mised 450 million.

But simply respecting the truth is only the beginning. An aggressive, practical, down-to-earth activist program is the basis of all change in this country. If we want to preserve the timber industry in the Tongass, then we have to fight for it. The opposition is powerful and intelligent, but they can be beaten.

This is what is needed:

Exposing Anti-industry Intent

All Forest Service policies should be analyzed for anti-industry intent and consequence. This analysis should be a required part of every Master Plan, Environmental Assessment, and Environmental Impact Statement. The true anti-industry intent of environmentalists is too often veiled over with blatant lies and seductive photography of appealing wildlife or awesome landscapes with no people in them. A "hard-look" doctrine needs to be brought to every step of the Forest Service planning process to explicitly state whether any given policy will help or harm the forest products industry. The findings must be stated in clear, plain English and not in Forest Service jargon, and must be stated on a separate, unbound one-page Memorandum of Anti-Industry Findings to avoid the old bureaucratic trick of burying the truth in volumes of facts that nobody will ever look at.

Release of Information on Anti-Industry Groups

A Right-To-Know Law concerning environmental groups should be adopted by Congress. It should require any group that lobbies or otherwise pressures agencies or legislatures to adopt anti-industry policies to disclose the names and addresses of its sources of income including private memberships, donations and grants, so that the general public can clearly identify those who support the destruction of American industry. The salaries of all officers should likewise be released. Our information, gathered from Form 990 Non-Profit Organization Internal Revenue Service Income Tax statements indicates that the leaders of top environmental organizations are paid more than $100,000 per year plus benefits.

Penalties for Obstructionism

Congress must enact legislation that provides for the environmental movement to indemnify American industry against harm when it uses the law to delay economic progress. The law must require that those who bring administrative appeals or court actions against timber harvest plans shall post bonds equivalent to the economic benefits to be derived from the challenged harvest plus cost overruns caused by delay. If the appellant or plaintiff loses, payment in full is to be made to the defendant in proportion to his losses and expenses.

Community Stability
Congress should enact statutory protection for timber-dependent communities by requiring the Forest Service to offer an adequate amount of timber from each Ranger District in the United States to meet market demands up to the biological capacity of the district and sell such timber only to local logging firms and milling firms.

National Timber Harvest System
A Timber Harvest Act is needed to create within our national forests a National Timber Harvest System reserved for the single purpose of timber harvest to counterbalance the incursive effects of the National Wilderness System, the National Trails System, the National Wild and Scenic Rivers System, the National Park System and the National Wildlife Refuge System. Timber is the only major use of the "multiple use" forest that has no system to protect the integrity of its boundaries.

The Tongass Timber Harvest Area should be the first dedicated single-use timber harvest area in America's National Timber Harvest System, to consist of the 3 million acres identified by the TLMP II planning process as suitable for growing commercial timber. Such areas should permit Multiple Use recreation where feasible. The timber industry should have its former logging lands restored to logging status for the 100 year rotation so that at least 20 percent of the Tongass is scheduled for timber harvest. We want our land base back! We want it protected against environmentalist attack!

The Timber Lease Act
Should permit the U.S. Forest Service to lease specific areas for 99 years to a single firm, allowing harvest based upon market conditions only, and not non-declining even-flow. Repeals the Renewable Resource Planning Act of 1974.

Private Rights In Federal Lands Act
Congress should enact measures which recognize that private parties legitimately own possessory rights to timber contracts, mining claims, water rights, grazing permits and other claims that are recognized by the

several states and by Internal Revenue Service estate tax collection policy as valuable private property rights. Establishes the principle of the Private Domain in Federal Land.

National Industrial Policy Act

Congress should enact a policy measure that explicitly recognizes the shrinking relative size of the total goods sector of our society's economy and takes steps to insure raw material supplies for commodity industries from public lands on a permanent basis. Should require preparation of an Economic Impact Statement for all major federal projects that clearly identifies each economic interest affected and cumulative economic impacts, and provide mitigating measures to lessen adverse economic impacts.

Perfect the Wilderness Act

The Wilderness System must be reassessed and reclassified into more carefully targeted categories according to the actual appropriate use, including: *Human Exclosures*, areas where people are prohibited altogether, including wildlife scientists who frequently harass to death the very animals they are supposed to protect; *Wild Solitude Lands*, managed exactly as present Wilderness areas; *Backcountry Areas*, which allow widely spaced hostels, primitive toilets to prevent unsanitary conditions that prevail today along Wilderness trails, and higher trail standards to prevent the trail erosion that plagues current Wilderness areas; *Frontcountry*, to allow primitive and developed campsites, motorized trail travel and limited commercial development; *Commodity Use Areas*, which will allow all commodity industry uses on an as-needed basis in times of high demand. The present Wilderness System would be redesignated with approximately 1 million acres of scattered Human Exclosures, 20 million acres of Wilderness, 30 million acres of Backcountry; 30 million acres of Frontcountry; and 10 million acres of Commodity Use Areas.

Standing To Sue In Defense Of Industry

Just as environmentalists won standing to sue on behalf of scenic, recreational and historic values in the 1965 case Scenic Hudson Preservation Conference v. Federal Power Commission, so pro-industry advocates should win standing to sue on behalf of industries threatened or harmed by environmentalists. Today, a specific individual or firm that is harmed must join a lawsuit as a plaintiff and pro-industry advocacy groups such as the Center for the Defense of Free Enterprise cannot bring a lawsuit on their behalf. Because industries must continue to live with their regulators after lawsuits are settled they are hesitant to bring legal action in all but the most horrendous circumstances, which chills their access to justice. There is no symmetry today between the rights of environmentalists to sue and the rights of pro-industry advocates to sue. This is not fair and must be changed in the name of justice.

Personal Ethics

If you presently support an environmental group that acts to destroy the forest products industry in the Tongass, you have a responsibility to yourself and your whole society to demand change. You cannot support the destruction of a responsible industry and consider yourself ethical. You cannot support the destruction of the hopes and lives of thousands of people and consider yourself ethical. And you cannot escape making a decision on this issue. Evading a decision is an act of conscious volition, and therefore has moral meaning. You have to come down somewhere on the issue of the Tongass timber industry's survival, and where you come down defines what kind of person you are. We urge you to come and stand beside us, to help us in our time of need. You will be most welcome among us and we will be most grateful for your good will. How can you help?

If you're a member of an environmental group (and about five million of us are) and you didn't realize your organization was engaging in such anti-social behavior as we've revealed in this book, you can do several things:

1. Ask your organizational leaders in a letter what their policy is about the forest products industry -- both in the Tongass and in general. Ask them if they intend to eliminate the timber industry in the Tongass. Ask them if they intend to further restrict the timber supply of the timber industry in the Tongass. Get the answer in writing.

2. Insist that a Forests Are For People policy be adopted by your environmental group's local chapter and national officers. If they don't want to talk about it, make it an issue. It's your group. It's your personal ethics they are compromising with your membership dues. It's our whole society they're damaging through anti-social efforts to destroy industry and disseminate unethical misinformation.

3. Get your environmental organization to put together a periodic Forestry Appreciation Day. Take your local group members to a forestry

area and include a meeting with timber industry representatives. They'll be happy to tell you what their company does and show you around.

4. Pressure the Forest Service to allow timber harvest operations at appropriate places that are clearly visible to cruise ships, and to publish cruise ship brochures explaining what is actually happening, and where the many outstanding examples of forest regrowth are thriving.

5. Pressure the Forest Service to begin a vigorous publicity campaign on the virtues of timber harvest, of multiple use, and of the wise use of resources. They have remained silent on the issue for fear of reprisals from the environmentalist pressure groups. Bolster their courage by applying the same pressure for timber harvest that environmentalists apply against the forest industry.

A Call to Action

Each citizen can and should act to restore justice to the Tongass and all national forest areas.

● If you're not a member of an environmental group, but are active in a social or civic group, organize a meeting on the situation in the Tongass National Forest. Invite a speaker from the timber industry in your area, or have a discussion about this book, or arrange a debate between a local environmentalist and forest industry representative. Get the issues out in the open. Get people thinking about both sides.

● If you're as outraged as we are about the destruction of forestry and the timber industry in Alaska, join People of the Tongass, a nationwide citizen gathering that supports the people of the Tongass. Cement the bond of solidarity with these fellow Americans whose lives are dominated by federal overseers and outside pressure groups. Make your voice heard to bring justice to this vast region of Alaska! Start a People of the Tongass group in your area. You can get information by writing to Alaska Women In Timber, 111 Stedman, Ketchikan, Alaska (AK) 99901, and they will send you up-to-date information on the issues.

● Apply political pressure on behalf of the people of the Tongass. Write your Congressman when issues come to committee and to a floor vote.

● Spread information about the real meaning of Wilderness.

● Expose the anti-people agenda of the environmental establishment. Make them change their anti-social ways.

● Learn to see through environmentalist propaganda. Don't fall for glittering generalities and false righteousness. Every time an environmentalist proposes a plan to ''protect nature,'' ask what it will do to people.

● Most of all, be true to others -- it is easy enough to be true to yourself. Honor the sense of justice. Acknowledge your bond to the people of the Tongass. We are calling upon you -- upon America -- to come to our aid.

Sendoff

If you have read this book carefully and with an open mind; if you've checked a few of our source notes against the original sources to verify that we're correctly documenting everything we say; if you believe in fair play; then we expect you to believe us now, just as we predicted in the prologue.

Let us remind you of why you should believe us, of why you should believe *in* us:

These are the roots of the word Tongass: People of the island. People of the sea lion island. Either way, the very name *Tongass* resonates with the human presence. That's the lesson to be drawn from the original meaning of *Tongass*. It's a lesson that The Official Version refuses to transmit. The Tongass is People. People of the Island. People of the Sea Lion Island. There's something symbolic here, and more than symbolic. The Tongass is not uninhabited wilderness. It *should* not be uninhabited Wilderness. It has been the home of people, humans, men and women and children, since the last ice age, and probably long before. People. Islands. Wildlife. We all belong.

We learn this: Those who die in us live in us. Their memories build us an inner determination and an inner force. Then when the Jack Skows and the Steve Richardsons and the Robert Mrazeks of the world come to destroy us we don't hate them. We despise them for what they are, insects of the spirit, worms of the soul. Skows, Richardsons and Mrazeks, how dare you make us suffer more who have suffered so much! You could not endure the thousand dangers we live with nor the thousand horrors we die with. Your hearts could not bear that hideous strength which dwells within us.

Keep your shameful lying selves elsewhere. You will never defeat us. We'll never give up. With your millions and your power you may destroy us, but you'll never defeat us. And if you come again and again and ask for roaring war, we will bring it to your doorstep. We will not go gentle into that good night. We are the people of the Tongass.

That's our message to you. We are the people of the Tongass. Don't destroy us. Don't help our destroyers. We cry out for justice, we cry out for truth. You, your family, your community, every American, should be one of us, one with us. We are your fellow citizens, your neighbors, your friends, even though we're hidden from your daily life. We are the people hidden not only in the rainforest mists of nature, but also in the shameful lies of shameless men.

Do you take American money here?
How high above sea level are we this far north?
Where's all the devastation?

SOURCES

We ruled out footnotes for this book because we wanted to make it readable with as few distractions as possible. But we also realized that any presentation running upstream against socially accepted mythology must be thoroughly documented. Therefore we elected to use the device of source notes keyed to phrases from the text in order to defend our thesis in as scholarly a fashion as possible.

We know that open-minded people will find these source notes welcome. We realize that ideological environmentalists won't get this far and it wouldn't make any difference if they did. We have provided the information because it's needed for the fair-minded critic.

Our major headings within chapters have drawn comment from pre-publication reviewers and perhaps need explanation. They were derived from many sources and are intended as symbols as much as topic descriptions. We borrowed freely from such American poets as Carl Sandburg, Wallace Stevens and Walt Whitman, as well as from scholars such as Joseph Campbell and Carl Jung. You'll find some Ridley Scott and George Lucas among other filmmakers in there, too. We made up a few of them ourselves.

Sources which are well-identified in the text will not be repeated here. After the first citation in these notes, only author and abbreviated title are used.

1: Liars

Meaning of Alaska: *Webster's Third New International Dictionary*; *Dictionary of Alaska Place Names*, United States Geological Survey Professional Paper 567, Government Printing Office, Washington, D.C., 1967; *Interesting Facts About Alaska* (brochure), Alaska Department of Commerce and Economic Development, Tourism Information Department.

Sports Illustrated article: Edition of March 14, 1988, pp. 77-88 gave little background on author John Skow. Skow is not a staff writer for SI and has written as a stringer for several other national periodicals. Circulation figures were provided by SI circulation director Michael Loeb in a telephone interview September 1988.

Environmentalist dishonesty: The forest products industry has recently begun to speak out strongly against the constant distortions by environmentalists. See *The Environmental Community Should Stop Mischaracterizing the Terms of the National Forest Management Debate*, National Forest Products Association, Washington, D.C., 1988.

Tongass National Forest statistics: The most recent comprehensive data are in *Status of the Tongass National Forest, 1987 Report*, U.S. Department of Agriculture, Forest Service, Alaska Region MB35, March 1988.

Muskeg mistaken for logging: The error is so pervasive that a photograph showing a muskeg foreground against a logged area background illustrates the tourist guide *Interpreting the Tongass National Forest via the Alaska Marine Highway*, by D.R. (Bob) Hakala, USDA Forest Service, Alaska Region, (no date), p. 26.

Wanita Williamson Interview: In her Juneau office, July 1988. **Carl Holguin Interview:** In his Juneau office, July 1988. **Wildlife statistics and David Anderson interview:** Telephone interview with Anderson September 1988.

Numerous studies have been carried out on logging and Alaska wildlife. Among the more classic: Ellis, Robert J. 1970. *Report on a study of effects of log rafting and dumping on marine fauna in southeast Alaska, June 6-9, 1970.* U.S. Department of Commerce, National Marine Fisheries Service, Auke Bay, Alaska; Erickson, Albert W. 1965. *The black bear in Alaska, its ecology and management.* Alaska Department of Fish and Game, Federal Aid in Wildlife Restoration, Vol. 5, Proj. W-6-R-5. Harris, A.S. 1968. *Small mammals and natural reforestation in southeast Alaska.* USDA Forest Service Research Note PNW-75, Pacific Northwest Forest and Range Experiment Station, Portland, Oregon. King, James G., Fred C. Robards and Calvin J. Lensink. 1972. *Census of the bald eagle breeding population in southeast Alaska.* Journal of Wildlife Management 36(4):1292-1295. Meehan, W.R., W.A. Farr, D.M. Bishop, and J.H. Patric, 1969. *Some effects of clearcutting on salmon habitat of two southeast Alaska streams.* USDA Forest Service Research Paper PNW-82, Pacific Northwest Forest and Range Experiment Station, Portland, Oregon. Writer John Skow appears to have been unaware of these and other studies and the continuing lively debate between scientists on the actual effects of logging on wildlife.

Tongass employment statistics: *ANILCA -- A Workable Compromise*, USDA Forest Service, Alaska Region, Leaflet R10-MB-21 (no date). *Statement of James F. Clark for Alaska Loggers Association* before the House Committee on Agriculture, May 25, 1988. Hearing Record on H.R. 1516.

"Bargain-basement" long term timber contracts: A factual account is contained in Rakestraw, Lawrence W., *A History of the United States Forest Service in Alaska*, Alaska Historical Commission, Anchorage, Alaska, 1981, p. 127ff.

Native claims: A comprehensive study of the claims and legislation is contained in Arnold, Robert D., *Alaska Native Land Claims*, Alaska Native Foundation, Anchorage, 1976. The Joint Federal-State Land-Use-Planning Commission has published a handy edition of the law. We are indebted to Bob Loescher of Sealaska Corporation for deep background information.

Timber contract chart: *The Tongass National Forest -- Current Issues in Resource Management*, USDA Forest Service, Alaska Region, Leaflet R10-MB-20, (no date), p. 13.

ANILCA legislative history: Unfortunately, no comprehensive scholarly history of ANILCA has yet been produced. The bottomless pit of detail available from the period of its progress through Congress, 1976-1980, will have to wait for a brave and talented historian with surpassing integrative powers. We have relied upon hearing testimony, interviews with lobbyists and elected officials involved in the debate, and Forest Service records in recording its impact on the Tongass.

Gaylord Nelson on eliminating industry from the Tongass: Among those present at the Juneau meeting were senior officials and senior staff from public affairs and technical departments, some of whom came and went during the meeting. A sufficient number of witnesses overheard Nelson's statement and provided the information to us coherently enough to meet the tests of author law in reporting that he actually said it. Even though our quotation is probably a close paraphrase, the exact wordings reconstructed by separate witnesses was sufficiently similar to validate our quote's accuracy beyond a reasonable doubt. We have no reason to believe our report is in any way false.

"Below-cost" timber sales: Definition: *Journal of Forestry*, August 1987, p. 37. We are indebted to Gary Peterson, group leader, timber valuation group, Tongass National Forest regional headquarters, Juneau, for his many patient explanations of the arcana of the "below-cost" argument. One environmentalist, Randall O'Toole of Oregon, has made a career of trying to put industry out of business on the national forests by using "below cost" as a value-laden code word in "studies" that studiously avoid counting the public benefits of timber harvest.

Native logging practices: Some observers have been concerned by Native logging practices, particularly because Native corporations can export round logs, which encourages "high grading," or "cut the best, leave the rest" attitudes. However, no environmentalist has published accusations of serious environmental degradation on Indian lands. Environmental groups, which have tried to ally themselves with the traditional lifestyle element among the Natives, have been strangely silent on Indian logging, which allows a much wider latitude of operator judgment than Forest Service timber harvesting. This double standard of complaining loudly about non-Native industry on tightly regulated Forest Service lands while turning a blind eye on the looser standards regulating Indian lands illustrates the environmentalists' hypocrisy, political cynicism and blatant racism.

Nicolls defense of the Forest Service: Wayne Nicolls prepared several drafts of a letter to the editor for Secretary of Agriculture Richard Lyng. The final letter did not contain the list of Forest Service accomplishments we selected for publication. We are indebted to Mr. Nicolls for other background on the Lyng letter and its rejection by *Sports Illustrated*. Douglas MacCleery, Deputy Assistant Secretary for Natural Resources, Department of Agriculture, Washington, D.C., verified the rejection and provided other background.

Ken Roberts: We interviewed Ken Roberts on several occasions to find out what really happened. Roberts never made any statement even similar to announcing that the Lisianski sites would be offered as timber sales. In fact, Roberts specifically stated during the time-frame Skow refers to that the Forest Service *wouldn't even re-examine the possibility* of timber harvest on the Lisianski sites until the 1991-95 plan period, and would even then obtain public comment from the Pelicaners once again.

Sports Illustrated's **neglect to check facts:** We interviewed everyone that Skow interviewed in the Forest Service. Neither Skow nor SI fact checkers, if SI has fact checkers, ever called anyone in the Forest Service. Receptionist records show no calls from Skow or SI.

Skow freeloading on Forest Service airplanes: Ken Roberts retrieved Skow's travel vouchers from Forest Service dispatchers at our request. The physical evidence is ironclad.

Skow's connection to the Wilderness Society: The diaries of Forest Service personnel show conclusively that Steve Richardson of the Wilderness Society accompanied John Skow in Juneau and on Noyes Island. Tongass National Forest Public Affairs Director Jim Caplan specifically offered Skow the opportunity to see logging and regrowth on Prince of Wales Island. Two members of the Udall junket's congressional staff overheard Richardson say, "I don't think that would be a good idea" about such a visit. Richardson at one time served on a congressional staff himself -- side by side with one Robert Mrazek who went on to become congressman from New York. Richardson and Mrazek are old friends. In addition, congressional staffers told us that Richardson and Skow were college chums, although we have been unable to verify it independently. One source said Richardson and Skow had been college roommates. The Wilderness Society was in a perfect position to engineer the entire *Sports Illustrated* project without detection.

George Miller 'Dear Friend' Letter: On congressional letterhead dated March 30 1988 and signed by Miller. We obtained a copy by request through the Forest Service.

2: Homeland

Imaginary but plausible trip: Throughout this book, every interview is authentic and contains only direct quotes transcribed from tape. The sequence of interviews has in places been altered and situations reconstructed for the sake of story flow. For example, interviews from several field trips may be combined into a single sequence. No significant fact has been altered or fictionalized. Every scene, whether in sequence or reconstructed, represents authentic situations. Where significant for the future researcher, actual interview dates have been included in these notes.

Blue canoes: An interesting newspaper story on the Alaska Marine Highway System is: Cross, Sue, "'Blue canoes' serve Alaskans on Marine Highway," *Seattle Times*, Sunday, September 25, 1988, B9.

Spellings of Fjords: Preferred English usage and U.S. Geological Survey maps spell it with a "j," but the Forest Service has settled upon "i." Therefore we use "Fiords" only in the proper name "Misty Fiords National Monument," and employ the standard spelling in referring generically to Misty Fjords as a geographical location.

Emma Williams: We are deeply indebted to Walt Begalka for introducing us to Emma Williams, and to Mrs. Williams for granting us an interview, and to her daughter Fran Hamilton for supplying important background information. The reader should be aware that Emma Williams' late husband Frank was Chief of the Tantakwan tribe and Emma Williams is still looked upon as we would think of a queen, to be regarded with the highest respect. Their work *Tongass Texts* remains the classic in the field.

Annette Island interviews: Recorded separately on September 12 through 15, 1988.

Precommercial thinning in Tongass forests: Thinning is done to stimulate tree growth by reducing competition in a young timber stand to an optimum level. The standard study in the field remains: Farr, Wilbur A., and A.S. Harris. 1971. *Partial cutting of western hemlock and Sitka spruce in southeast Alaska.* USDA Forest Service Research Paper PNW-124, Pacific Northwest Forest and Range Experiment Station, Portland, Oregon.

Rain jokes: Most of these rain jokes appeared in *Ketchikan Visitor's Guide, 1988,* published by Ketchikan Daily News.

Lew Williams interview: June 9, 1988 in Ketchikan at the Daily News.

Ken Eichner interview: June 9, 1988 in Ketchikan at Temsco Helicopters headquarters.

International Order of Illiterate Pigs: More information on IOIP and all of Prince of Wales Island can be found in *Profiles of Progress: A Photographic Journal of Prince of Wales Island, Southeast Alaska,* David Ray Dillman, The Prince of Wales Publishing Company, Thorne Bay, Alaska, 1988.

Nick Gefre testimony: Interview in Thorne Bay June 10, 1988. See *Statement of Nick Gefre, expert witness,* before the Subcommittee on Energy and Environment, House Interior and Insular Affairs Committee, May 21, 1987. Hearing record on H.R. 1516.

Becky Gay interview: August 6, 1988, at a conference in Reno, Nevada.

Bob Loescher interview: July 22, 1988 in Haines, Alaska.

Bob and Margaret Andrews interview: July 23, 1988 at their home in Haines, Alaska.

3: Stepchild of America

Dr. Rakestraw's analysis of forest history: The analysis first appeared in "Forestry History in Alaska: Four Approaches to Two Forest Ecosystems," *Journal of Forest History,* Vol. 23, No. 2, April 1979, pp 60-71. Our thanks to Forest History Society Executive Director Dr. Harold K. "Pete" Steen for his kind permission to adapt the original material. This chapter also relies heavily upon Dr. Rakestraw's two books: Rakestraw, Lawrence W., *A History of Forest Conservation in the*

Pacific Northwest, 1891-1913, New York, 1979; and *A History of the United States Forest Service in Alaska*, Alaska Historical Commission, Anchorage, Alaska, 1981.

Gruening: Gruening, Ernest, *The State of Alaska*, Random House, New York, 1968.

Sectionalism as a factor in environmentalism: Modern historians are returning to the old theme of sectionalism as a driving force in American history. For a recent study of sectionalist roots of environmentalism, see Feller, Daniel, *The Public Lands in Jacksonian Politics*, University of Wisconsin Press, Madison, 1984. For a specific examination of modern environmentalism as an expression of sectionalist rivalries, see Bensel, Richard Franklin, *Sectionalism and American Political Development, 1880-1980*, University of Wisconsin Press, Madison, 1984.

Rex Beach to Anthony J. Dimond: April 23, 1936, Dimond Papers, University of Alaska Library.

Origins of the Public Lands: This story has been told often, but evidently not in public. Hardly anyone knows it. See, Hibbard, Benjamin Horace, *A History of the Public Land Policies*, Macmillan Company, New York, 1924; and *The Public Lands: Studies in the History of the Public Domain*, edited by Vernon Carstensen, The University of Wisconsin press, Madison, 1962, pp. 7-34.

Growth of American forestry: The literature on early forestry is voluminous. See Hough, Franklin B., ed., *Report upon Forestry*, Washington, D.C., Government Printing Office, 1880; Fernow, Bernhard E., *A Brief History of Forestry in Europe, the United States, and Other Countries*, University Press, Toronto, 1911; Pinchot, Gifford, *Breaking New Ground*, Harcourt, Brace and Company, New York, 1947; other good secondary sources are: Cameron, Jenks, *The Development of Governmental Forest Control in the United States*, Johns Hopkins Press, Baltimore, 1928; Clawson, Marion, and Burnell Held, *The Federal Lands: Their Use and Management*, Johns Hopkins Press, Baltimore, 1957.

Emmons' report and Roosevelt's note: *Bulletin of the U.S. Fish Commission, 1890*, Miscellaneous Document 131, 51st Cong.,2d sess., Washington, 1891, p. 14.

Fox Farm report: F.E. Olmsted, "Alexander Archipelago -- Grazing," Dr. 38, Record Group 95, National Archives.

Steen's book: Steen, Harold K., *The U.S. Forest Service: A History*, University of Washington Press, Seattle, 1976, pp. 24-25.

Land fraud: Ise, John, *The United States Forest Policy*, Yale University Press, New Haven, 1920. U.S. Department of the Interior, Annual

Report (1886), pp. 95, 200, 213; and (1888), p. 85.

The Creative Act of 1891: 26 Stat. 1095 (March 3, 1891).

Dr. Steen's comments: Telephone interview, September, 1988. For Dr. Steen's comment on documentation, see his *U.S. Forest Service*, p. 26.

The first forest reserve bill: It was introduced in 1876 by Representative Greenbury L. Fort of Illinois and died in committee. U.S. Congress, House, 'For the Preservation of Forests of the Public Domain Adjacent to Navigable Rivers....', 44th Cong., 1st sess. (1876), H.R. 2075.

Newspaper articles advocating forest reserves: *New York Times*, September 18, 1885, p. 4, col. 4.

Forests attracting rainfall: The idea finally died in the late 1880s. See *New York Times*, August 5, 1888, p. 4, col. 4., "the old idea that trees directly induce a larger rainfall is now pretty much given up."

The American Forestry Association's role: Rodgers, Andrew Denny III, *Bernhard Eduard Fernow: A Story of North American Forestry*, Princeton University Press, Princeton, 1951, p. 142-43.

Hayes: Hayes, Samuel P., *Conservation and the Gospel of Efficiency: The Progressive Conservation Movement 1890-1920*, Harvard University Press, Cambridge, 1959

Ise and the Noble story: Ise, John, *The United States Forest Policy*, Yale University Press, New Haven, 1920, p. 115.

Dissertation: Kirkland, Herbert D., "The American Forests, 1864-1898: A Trend Toward Conservation," unpublished Ph.D. dissertation, University of Florida, 1971. References that Kirkland cites will not be included here because of their sheer volume. The diligent investigator, however, will find the perusal of Kirkland more than rewarding.

Hague letters: All are in Record Group 57, Hague Papers, letter book 3B, National Archives. Hague to E.M. Dawson, March 16, 1891; Hague to Brown, March 16, 1891; Hague to Noble, March 25, 1891; Hague to Grinnell, April 4, 1891; Hague to Grinnell, April 6, 1981.

Grinnell as Wilderness idea inventor: See Reiger, John F., *American Sportsmen and the Origins of Conservation*, New York, 1975, p. 262, n. 23.

House debate on forest reserve act: Congressional Record, 51st Cong., 2d sess., 22:4 (March 2, 1891), 3611-16.

1888 lands bill: U.S. Congress, House, *H.R. 7901*, 50th Cong., 1st sess. (1888), introduced by Holman February 29, 1888.

Committee report on 1888 lands bill: U.S. Congress, House, 50th Cong., 1st sess. (1888), *Report No. 778*, signed February 25, 1888 by William S. Holman.

Bowers' plan: U.S. Congress, House, *Public Timber Lands*, 50th Cong., 1st sess. (1888), H. Ex. Doc. 242.

Holman's biography: Blake, Israel George, *The Holmans of Veraestau*, The Mississippi Valley Press, Oxford, Ohio, 1943.

Why would Holman support forest reserves and why didn't he get credit for them? Marybelle Burch, manuscripts librarian at the Indiana State Library at Indianapolis and Holman admirer, writes that, "Holman was a resolutely modest man and he would be content to let others take the credit."

She also writes that, "The Holman papers have no mention of forest reserves, nor do the papers of his brother-in-law Allen Hamilton or his nephew Holman Hamilton. Holman was deeply interested in flood control, since he lived along the Ohio River and had seen what deforestation could do...I think his primary aim in setting aside forest lands was the protection of watersheds.

"In 1881, Prof. C.L. Ingersoll of Purdue University gave a talk on forestry before the Indiana State Board of Agriculture in which he pointed out the devastation caused by massive deforestation. Most of the arguments he uses are from Europe, but the point is, they were public knowledge in Indiana when a surprising number of Indiana men were in a position to do something about the problem." Burch to Ron Arnold, September 1988.

Mrs. Burch also notes at least four Indiana contemporaries of Holman who were connected to forestry issues: George Julian, Holman's fellow Democrat and member of the House Committee on Public Lands, was a strong enemy of the forest reserve idea. Ovid Butler of Indiana was Executive Secretary of the American Forestry Association. Robert S. Taylor of Fort Wayne was a member of the Mississippi River Commission from 1881 to 1914. Richard Lieber, a German immigrant, wrote a book titled *America's Natural Wealth*, Harper & Brothers Publishers, New York, 1942. Lieber's only comment on the forest reserves is:

> In 1891, Congress passed an act giving the President authority to withdraw areas of the public domain as forest reserves. There were, of course, loudly voiced protests that the forest reserves were being locked away from the people. Unfortunately, the Act did not make any provisions for protecting or administering the reserves.

4: The Forest Service

Sandor interview: At his home in Douglas, Alaska, in September

1988. We are deeply indebted to Mr. Sandor for other background on the issues that arose during his administration of the Tongass. His influence pervades this whole book.

Lyon interview: At his office in Juneau in September 1988.

About TLMP: Lyon's team publishes a periodic newsletter for the Forest Plan revision called *Tongass Review*. It is available from Forest Plan Interdisciplinary Team, 8465 Old Dairy Road, Juneau, AK 99801.

Barton interview: In his office in Juneau in September, 1988.

Thompson interview: By telephone in October 1988.

Forest Management: For comprehensive discussion of the technical issues and an extensive bibliography, see Ruth, Robert H., and A.S. Harris, *Management of Western Hemlock-Sitka Spruce Forests for Timber Production*, USDA Forest Service, Gen. Tech. Rep. PNW-88, Pacific Northwest Forest and Range Experiment Station, Portland, Oregon, June 1979.

Gate System: *Forest Service Manual*, Amendment 141, October 1985, Title 2400 - Timber Management, Section 2431.

5: Loggers

Virgil Soderberg interview: At Haines, July 22, 1988, additional tape recorded aboard the Wavos Rancheros at Hawk Inlet, July 24, 1988.

All Whitestone Logging interviews: At Whitestone Logging in Hoonah and associated woods, July 20, 1988.

Walt Whitman reference: *Leaves of Grass*, "Song of the Broad-Axe," The Inner Sanctum Edition of The Poetry and Prose of Walt Whitman, edited by Louis Untermeyer, Simon and Schuster, New York, 1949, p. 213-221.

On logging: Numerous texts on logging engineering are available, along with hundreds of technical and professional journal articles. We recommend the systems approach which includes road building as reflected in: Conway, Steve, *Logging Practices: Principles of Timber Harvesting Systems*. Miller Freeman Publications, Inc, San Francisco, 1976.

Janice Harbour: Interview taken in Ketchikan in June 1988.

Arnold Johnson interview: On Chichagof Island and in his helicopter, July 20, 1988.

Kirsten Held: Kirsten arranged most of the interviews for this book and helped in many capacities. The hours she spent digging out facts and finding sources to interview are deeply appreciated.

Bob Elliot interview: In his office at Ward Cove, June 10, 1988.

Helen Finney interview: In Coffman Cove, June 11, 1988 and in

Haines, July 23, 1988.

Cruise ship visitors interested in logging: A number of logging sites are described in the tourist guide *Interpreting the Tongass National Forest via the Alaska Marine Highway*, by D.R. (Bob) Hakala, USDA Forest Service, Alaska Region, (no date).

6: Pulp Mills

On forest succession: Probably the most comprehensible discussion for the layman that remains technically uncompromised is Scott, David R.M., "About the Resource: Plants" in *Clear-cutting: Impacts, Options, Trade-offs*, University of Washington, College of Forest Resources, Seattle, 1971, proceedings of conference number one, Institute of Forest Products, held at the University of Washington December 16, 1971.

History of the mills: This chapter relies heavily upon Rakestraw, Lawrence W., *A History of the United States Forest Service in Alaska*, Alaska Historical Commission, Anchorage, Alaska, 1981.

All KPC interviews: At the KPC mill, September 1988. We are indebted to Martin Pihl not only for allowing us free rein in the KPC pulp mill, but also for making helicopter transportation available to our editor Ron Arnold to remote sites for photography and verification.

Pulp Technology: Clark, James d'A., *Pulp Technology and Treatment for Paper*, second edition, Miller Freeman Publications, 1985. Libby, C. Earl, editor, Vol 1., "Pulp," in *Pulp and Paper Science and Technology*, McGraw Hill Book Company, New York, 1962.

7: Sawmills

Taro interview: At his office in Ketchikan, June 1988.

Wrangell Forest Products interviews: At Steve Seley's office in Ketchikan June 1988, and at the mill in Wrangell September 1988.

Sawmill technology: An outstanding up-to-date text on sawmill technology is Williston, Ed M., *Lumber Manufacturing: The Design and Operation of Sawmills and Planer Mills*, Miller Freeman Publications, San Francisco, 2nd edition, 1988.

8: Proving Ground for Lawyers

Legal history of the Tongass: We are indebted to John Sandor, former regional forester, Alaska region, for many insights into the legislative battles of the 1970s in particular.

This chapter relies heavily upon Rakestraw, Lawrence W., *A History of the United States Forest Service in Alaska*, Alaska Historical Commission, Anchorage, Alaska, 1981.

Standing to sue: This is a complex issue that extends far beyond the scope of this book. For a competent legal discussion, see: Rodgers, William H., Jr., *Handbook on Environmental Law*, West Publishing Company, St. Paul, 1977, pp. 23-30.

Schnabel interview: At his home in Haines, July 23, 1988.

Clark interview: At Haines, July 22, 1988. Portions of this commentary are taken from testimony Clark gave before various House committees as lobbyist for the timber industry.

9: Voices

Personal anecdotes were recorded on tape during 1988 and diary entries were taken from editions of the newsletter of Alaska Women In Timber. Only formal interviews will be cited for this chapter; personal anecdotes and diary entries will not be individually cited.

Clark interview: At Haines, July 22, 1988.

Michael Valentine interview: Haines, July 22, 1988.

Pat Soderberg interview: Lake Chilkat, July 23, 1988.

Don Finney: Don provided much background information and helped in many ways. His interview was taken at Lake Chilkat with additional interview time at various other locations including Alaska Loggers Association headquarters in Ketchikan. Don's breadth of experience in timber and mining is unmatched in the Tongass.

J.R. Gildersleeve interview: Haines, July 22, 1988.

Don Bell interview: In Ketchikan, September 28, 1988.

Jerry Larrabee interview: Lake Chilkat, July 23, 1988.

Cutler's diatribe: *Selling the Federal Forests*, edited by Adrien Gamache, University of Washington, College of Forest Resources, Institute of Forest Resources Contribution No. 50. Proceedings of a Symposium held April 21-23, 1983 at the University of Washington. Seattle, Washington, 1984.

Quartz Hill information: Quartz Hill brochures, six editions. Available from United States Borax and Chemical Corporation, 3075 Wilshire Boulevard, Los Angeles, California 90010.

Mining lawsuit: *U.S. Borax and Chemical Corporation and Pacific Coast Molybdenum Company v. Bob Bergland and M. Rupert Cutler*, May 17, 1979.

10: Agenda for Renewal

Wise Use Movement statements: These statements of support were originally statements of policy recommendation to the federal government for the Free Enterprise Press publication, "Agenda for Wise Use of the Environment." They were converted to statements of support for the people of the Tongass through an action committee organized by editor Ron Arnold that contacted over 100 groups to obtain specific commitments from each group contacted. The nationwide web of support thus organized is a new political reality in the Tongass debate.

Ideas for renewal: The ideas for renewing wise industrial development in the Tongass came from many sources. We are indebted to Merrill Sikorski of the American Freedom Coalition, Alaska Chapter, for background on a Wise Use philosophy now being developed by many minds.

Some of the activist approaches to correcting environmentalist distortions were offered for our use by the dean of national park concessioners, Don Hummel, before he passed away August 18, 1988. Don will always stand high in our regard as an outspoken champion of free enterprise in partnership with government. He will be sorely missed.

Charles S. Cushman, executive director of the National Inholders Association, provided outstanding guidance in lobbying tactics and advice on citizen strategies in support of industry.

Ron Arnold has been our guiding spirit in this venture, encouraging us when things looked bleak, and offering ideas for positive action to restore faith in American industry. Some of the ideas in this chapter are his.

INDEX

A

A-frame logging, 188-190, 308
Admiralty Island, 10, 46, 72, 155, 162, 216-17, 275, 278-79
Admiralty Island National Monument, 276, 303
Afognak Forest and Fish Culture Reserve, 99
Afognak Island, 99, 168, 247
Air Force Academy, 8
Aki, Koichi, 229
Alaska, novel by James Michener, 76-77
Alaska
        Meaning of the word, 58
        Russian occupation, 93-94
        Territory, 5, 33, 98ff., 217, 230
        Statehood Act of 1958, 261
Alaska Airlines, 66, 249
Alaska cedar, 55-56, 61, 81, 214
Alaska Conservation Society, 269, 304
Alaska king crab, 71
Alaska Loggers Association, 32, 194, 197, 206ff., 265, 277, 286, 293, 296, 306
Alaska Lumber and Pulp Company, Inc, 231ff., 247ff.
Alaska Marine Highway System, 53ff, 172
Alaska National Interest Lands Conservation Act of 1980, 36, 269, 277

Alaska Native Claims Settlement Act of 1971, 41, 80-81, 99, 263ff
Alaska Native Language Center, 58
Alaska Pulp Corporation, 26, 32ff
Alaska Pulp Development Company, 231
Alaska Pulp and Paper Comany, 216
Alaska Timber Insurance Exchange, 295
Alaska Women In Timber, 15ff., 19, 155, 196ff, 284-85, 287, 295ff., 333
Alexander archipelago, 23, 72, 93-94, 100, 217
Alexander Archipelago Forest Reserve, 100, 102
American Farm Bureau Federation, 314
American Forestry Association, 111ff., 122-23, 135, 265

American Freedom Coalition, 315-26
American Viscose Corporation, 33, 222
Anderson, David, 30, 71
Andrews, Bob and Margaret, 83ff., 185
Andrus, Cecil, 265
Annette Island, 59, 235
Annette Hemlock, 59
Antiquities Act of 1906, 276
Archbold, C.N., 220
Arnold, Andrea, 116ff.

Arnold, Ron, 108ff.
Atkinson, Harris, 59
Auger, Judy, 199
Aurora (ferry), 53ff.

B

Bacus, Oliver, 172-74
Baker, Richard, 112
balloon logging, 9, 298-300
Baranof Island, 71, 73
Bartlett, E.L., 5, 221
Barton, Michael, 27, 47, 140-41
Beach, Rex, 94
Beacher, The, 10, 160-61
Beals, George, 237
bear, black, 71
bear, brown, 71
beaver, 72
Beck, Tom, 69-70
Beecher, Perry, 166, 181
Begalka, Walt, 57
Bell, Don, 292-94
"below-cost" timber sales, 26, 38-
42, 149ff., 262, 293
Benecke, O.F., 230
Bergland, Bob, 265, 276
bird refuges, 20
Blue Ribbon Coalition, 320
Bobbe, Tom, 143ff.
Bowers, Edward A., 106, 111ff.
Brooks, Art, 197
Bruns, John, 60
Budge, Glen, 239
buffer zones, 144
Bureau of Indian Affairs, 60
Buschman, Dierdre, 135
Butz, Earl, 265

C

California Women In Timber, 319-20
Caplan, James, 27, 46
caribou, 71
Carter, Jimmy, 265, 276

Center for the Defense of Free Enter-
prise, 313-14
Chapin, Ken, 237
Chatham, Pam, 207
Chatham Strait, 14
Chichagof Island, 23, 100. 166, 217
Chickamin River, 68
Chilkat Dancers,56
Chilkat Indians, 55
Chilkoot Barracks, 6
Citizens for Management of Alaska
Lands (CMAL), 293
Clark, Jim, 277ff., 282-83
clearcutting, 22ff., 132ff., 270-71
Cleveland, Grover, 97
climax forest, 97
Chugach National Forest, 47, 141
Coastal Machinery, 194-95
Coffman Cove, 155, 196ff., 286-87,
295
Cole, Kathy, 307-311
Columbia (ferry), 53
Cooper, Steve, 241
Conde Nast's *Traveler*, 49
Conservation Foundation, 225
Consumer Alert, 322-23
Council on Environmental Quality,
304
Cowan, John, 241
Creative Act of 1891, 108ff.
Crown Zellerbach Corporation, 219
Cutler, Rupert, 265, 276, 301, 304
Cutler, Thelma, 207

D

"D2" lands, 263, 265, 275
Davidson, C. Jirard "Jebby", 249-50
"Death Star," 25, 140
deer, Sitka blaktail, 25, 71
Defenders of Wildlife, 264, 279
devils club, 15, 56
Dimond, Anthony J., 94
dissolving pulp, 39, 221

Diverty, Scott, 239
Division of Forestry, 98, 101. 105, 111, 113,
Douglas Island, 130, 133
Duncan, William, 59
DuRette, Butch, 13, 69, 83ff., 184ff., 284-85, 287
DuRette Construction Company, 17, 69, 156, 194
DuRette, Jackie, 12ff., 83ff., 155ff.

E

eagles, bald, 5, 31, 73, 282
Egleston, Nathaniel, 98, 111
Eichner, Ken, 61, 65-68
Eilertson, Steve, 240
Eliason, Nancy, 207
elk, 71
Elliot, Bob, 194-95
Emmons, Lt. George, 99-100, 218
environmental assessments, 143, 329
Environmental Defense Fund, 264, 279
environmental impact statements, 26, 40-41, 139-40, 143, 262, 277,306, 329
Equitable Assurance Society, 231
erosion, 165, 171, 174
Export-Import Bank of Japan, 231

F

Federal Power Commission, 271
Federal Water Pollution Control Act, 264
Federated Women In Timber, 208
Fernow, Bernhard E., 111ff., 227
fifty-year contracts, 33 ff., 70, 78, 82, 130, 141, 193, 222ff., 232ff., 264, 297, 300, 302, 314-25
Finney, Don, 197, 199, 227, 300, 302ff.
Finney, Helen, 19, 20, 199ff., 227
fire, 55-56, 214

fishing, 25, 31, 53, 56, 60ff.,
Fontana, Mike, 242
Forest History Society, 110
Forest Homestead Act of 1906, 218
forest industry, 9ff., 22ff., 104ff., 213ff., 247ff.
forest inventory, 137ff.
forest management, 133ff., 155ff.
Forest and Range Renewable Resources Planning Act of 1974, 41, 263, 330
Forest Reserve Act of 1891, 97, 99, 108ff., 129
Forest Reserve Administration Act of 1897, 97, 129, 265, 273
forest reserves, 97, 99, 129
Forest Service, 21ff., 98ff., 129ff., 161ff., 214ff., 249, 262, 264ff., 283, 288ff., 315ff.
Forest and Stream (magazine), 115, 128
FORPLAN, 138
Fort William S. Seward, 6
fox farms, 99, 102
Freshwater Bay, 14, 83, 184, 287, 291
Friends of the Earth, 264, 279
Friends of the Tongass, 135
Furth, Helmut F., 303

G

Garfield, James A., 124, 127
Gate System, 142ff.
Gay, Becky, 77-79
Gazzaway, Ken, 59-61
Gefre, Nick, 69-71
General Electric Pension Trust, 231
General Land Office, 98ff.
Geographic Information System, 136
Gildersleeve, Colleen, 63

Gildersleeve, Roger, 293
Gildersleeve, J.R., , 300
Glacier Bay National Park and

Preserve, 83
Gorbachev, Mikhail, 224
Gravel, Mike, 275
Greens Creek Mining Company, 10, 155ff.
Gregg, Alan, 8
Gregg, Mimi, 5
Gregg, Ted, 6
Gregg, Tresham, 8
Griffin, Richard M., 20
Grinnell, George Bird, 115ff.
Gruening, Ernest, 94

H

Hagan, Steven, 235-36
Hague, Arnold, 115ff.
Haida Indians, 93, 55, 79
Haida-Tlingit Jurisdictional Act, 219
Haines, 4ff., 71, 83, 268, 296
Halstead, Leona B., 112
Hammond, Jay, 304
Hannibal Hamlin Institute, 314-15
Hansen, Clay, 238
Hanson, P.D., 232
Harbour, Janice, 188ff.
Harriman, E.F., 227

Harriman expedition, 227
Harrison, Benjamin, 97, 111ff.
Harvard Graduate School of Business Administration, 8, 159
Hawk Inlet, 10. 155, 166
Hayes, Allyn, 236ff.
Hayes, Samuel, 111
Heintzleman, B. Frank, 33, 217ff.
Held, Kirsten, 194
Hendricks, Jim, 241
Hensley, Don, 281
Hinman, Jim, 238

Hitchcock, Ethan Allen, 100
Holguin, Carl, 27-28
Hollis, 200

Holman, William Steele, 116ff., 129, 273
Homestead Act of 1862, 98, 104-05
Hoonah, 44-45, 79, 100, 155, 166ff., 247
Hough, Franklin B., 98
House Interior and Insular Affairs Committee, 48, 70, 78, 275, 278
horizontal rain, 62, 67

Howard-Cooper Corporation, 195
Hudson's Bay Company, 94
Hummel, Don, 250, 265
hunting, 29-30, 56, 66, 172, 219, 275, 287
Hydaburg, 83, 247
hydroelectric development, 62, 220, 232

I

Ickes, Harold, 219-221
Inside Passage, 19, 53
interdisciplinary teams, 130ff.
International Order of Illiterate Pigs, 69
International Paper Company, 217
Ise, John, 105, 112-13, 128
Islands College, 20
ITT Rayonier, 60
Izaak Walton League v. Butz, 123, 265, 273

J

Japan, 34, 60, 73, 75, 82, 227, 247, 249, 257, 270
    forest law of 1951, 227
    mission to Alaska, 34ff., 228ff.
Jeffers, Robinson, 249
Jones, J.T., 218-19
Johnson, Arnold, 192-94
Johnson, Larry, 239
Johnston, Pete, 46

Juneau, 23, 27, 32, 38, 42, 45ff., 54, 62ff., 101, 166, 172, 186, 195, 207, 216ff., 247, 271, 275, 291, 285
Juneau Chamber of Commerce, 230

K

Kadashan timber sale, 16, 88
Kaelke, Michael, 75-77
Kake, 9, 247
Kennel Creek (logging camp), 14, 46, 83ff., 184ff., 287, 291
Ketchikan, 235
Ketchikan Daily News, 63-65, 306

Ketchikan Pulp Company, 26, 32ff., 57, 59, 66, 69, 130, 141, 172, 194, 197, 200, 213ff., 247, 264, 274, 285, 295, 297, 301ff.
Kirkland, Herbert D., 113ff.
Klawock, 247, 295

Klinke, Richard, 250ff.
Klukwan, (village), 70, 83
Klukwan Forest Prodcuts, 70
Korea, 220
Kosciusko Island, 168
Kuiu Island, 72, 100
Kupreanof Island, 9, 72, 100, 192
Kurile Islands, 227, 230

L

Labouchere Bay, 72
Lamb, Mary Ann, 306-07
landscape architects, 134-35, 143
Langille, William A., 101ff.
Larrabee, Jerry, 14, 84ff., 286
Larrabee, Jewell, 207
Larson, Linda, 207
Leer, Jeffry, 58
Lewis, Donna, 199

Life, 49
Lindberg, Ron, 282

Lisianski Inlet, 23ff.
Loeb, Michael, 22
Loescher, Bob, 23, 79-83
logging techniques,
      falling and bucking, 163, 175ff.
      yarding and loading, 180ff.
long-term contracts, *see* fifty-year contracts
Los Angeles Examiner, 217
Louisiana Pacific Corporation, 26, 59; *also see* Ketchikan Pulp Company and Annette Hemlock
Louisiana purchase, 96
lumber mills, 247ff.
Lutz, Harold, 219
Lyng, Richard, 42
Lyon, Don, 133ff.

M

McConnell, Chuck, 136
McElroy, Phil, 237-38
McMinnville, Oregon, 13
McRae, Thomas C., 118
Magnuson, Warren, 221
Malaspina (ferry), 53
Marsh, Sam, 281
Marshall, Bob, 43
marten, 72
Martin, Roy, 250ff.
Mason, Ira J., 233
Matanuska (ferry), 53
Maybeso Creek, 200, 270-71
Metlakatla, 59-61
Michel, Peter, 112
Michener, James, 76-77

Miller, Rep. George, 44, 48-49, 78, 193, 223
mining, 3, 10, 38, 155ff., 303ff.
mining claims, 303ff.
Missouri Historical Society, 112
Misty Fiords National Monument, 54,

168, 276, 303
Mitkof Island, 168
Mollenhauer, Wes, 244
molybdenum discoveries, 303-04
moose, 71
Moran, Bill, 62
Morton, Rogers, 265
Motley, Tony, 293
mountain goats, 71
Mountain States Legal Foundation, 320-21
Mrazek, Rep. Robert, 133, 187, 193, 223
Multiple Use Association, 318-19
Multiple Use Strategy Conference, 313ff.
Multiple Use - Sustained Yield Act of 1960, 262
Murkowski, Senator Frank, *ix*, 22, 224
muskeg, 26, 62, 66-67, 137, 170-73

N

National Audubon Society, 304
National Cattlemens Association, 314
National Environmental Policy Act of 1968, 41, 139, 262-63, 265, 271, 277, 305, 325
National Forest Management Act of 1976, 41, 131, 133, 263-64, 274
National Forest Products Association, 265
national forests, 21ff., 97, 99ff., 129ff. 161ff., 214ff., 249, 262, 264ff., 283, 288ff., 315ff.
National Geographic, 20, 22, 284
National Inholders Association, 317-18
National Park Service, 275
National Parks and Conservation Association, 264, 279
National Rifle Association, 314
National Wilderness Conference,

313-14
National Wilderness Preservation System, 43, 330
Native claims, 41, 80-81, 99, 263ff.
Native corporations, 41, 59, 70, 80ff., 168, 174, 188, 263, 275, 304
NC Machinery, 195
Nelson, Gaylord, 38
New Archangel, 93
New Republic, 49
Nicolls, Wayne, 42
Noble, John W., 111ff.
Norblad, Walter, 230
North West Timber Association, 316-17
Noyes Island, 47
Nutting, Sandra, 15, 206-07

O

Okinawa, 160-61, 229
Olmsted, Frederick Law, 105
Ordway, Samuel, 225
Organic Act of 1897, *see* Forest Reserve Administration Act of 1897
O'Sullivan, Louis, 103
Outdoor Writers Association of America, 47

P

Pacific Coast Molybdenum Company, 303ff.
Paulson, Thad, 75
Payson, Lewis E., 116ff.
Pelican (village), 25ff.
Peterson, Gary, 149-50
Pettigrew, Richard E., 116ff.
Phillips, W. Hallett, 115ff.
Pickler, John A.,116ff.
Pihl, Martin, 234-35
Pinchot, Gifford, 43, 98, 109, 123, 129, 214-15
Pioneers of Alaska, 7
Plumb, Preston B., 116ff.

Pope, Rex, 241
porcupine, 72
Powell, John Wesley, 111
Prince of Wales Island, 17, 46, 58-59, 65ff., 72, 100, 136, 155, 194, 196ff., 217, 222, 227, 235, 274, 286, 308
Prince Rupert (British Columbia), 53-54
Prudential Insurance Company, 231
Pruett, Darrell, 62
Public Broadcasting System, 20
Public Land Users Association, 319
Puget Sound Pulp and Timber Company, 34, 220ff.
pulp mills, 213ff.
pulp production, 234ff.

Q

Quartz Hill mine, 303ff.

R

raccoon, 72
Rakestraw, Lawrence, 56, 92ff., 264ff.
Rancho de las Palmas, 11, 160
Ranger Districts, xix, xx, 140,41
Rasler, Randy, 254-55
Readers Digest, 49, 107, 269
Redwood National Park, 224-25
Reid brothers lawsuit, 301ff.
reforestation, 60ff., 151ff., 270-71
regional forester, 27, 47, 101, 140
reservations, Indian, 59ff., 108
Resource Development Council of Alaska, 77-79
resource management,26ff., 129ff., 155ff.
Revillagigedo Channel, 54
Revillagigedo Island, 61, 71, 72, 139
Richardson, Steve, 46ff., 187
Rilatos, Ed, 254
road building, 155ff.
Roberts, Ken, 43ff.

Rodriguez, Primo, 240-42
Rold, Rich, 239
Roosevelt, Franklin D., 34, 219
Roosevelt, Theodore, 58, 99ff., 106, 218, 266, 276
Ross, Doug, 293
Rothstein, Barbara, (Judge), 301ff.
Rowland, Pat, 196
Ruckel, Johnny, 178-79
Russian-American Company, 93

S

Saint Lazaria Island National Wildlife Refuge, 20
Saint Regis Paper Company, 270-71
Sakhalin Island, 34, 227, 230
salmon, 31, 71
Sandor, John, 130ff., 304
San Francisco Chronicle, 217
Sanyakwan, 55
Sasayama, Tadao, 232
Saturday Evening Post, 214
sawmills, 247ff.
sawtimber, 148ff., 174ff. 247ff.
Scenic Hudson Preservation Conference v. Federal Power Commission (lawsuit), 266
Schnabel, John, 268-69, 297
Schnabel Lumber Company, 268
Schurz, Carl, 106, 123
Sealaska Corporation, 79ff.
Seattle Post Intelligencer, 230
Seattle Times, 75
Selcy, Steve, 15, 201, 250ff.
Seward, William Henry, 73
Shaub, Thyes, 199, 285
Sheldon Jackson College, 75ff.
Shelton Cooperative Sustained Yield Unit, 233
short term timber sales, 141ff.
Sierra Club, 18, 35, 66, 193, 205, 264, 267ff., 279, 304ff., 327
Sierra Club v. Hardin, 270-72

silviculture, 147ff.
Simpson Timber Company, 233
Sims, Penny, 256
Sitka, 20, 26, 35, 44ff., 73ff., 92, 130, 141, 171, 174, 199, 214, 225, 227ff., 249, 254, 264, 269ff., 284-85, 293, 302, 326
Sitka blacktail deer, 31, 71

Sitka spruce, 25, 44, 56, 93, 214
Skagway, 71
Skow, John, 21ff., 78, 167, 187, 297
skunks, 72
Small Business Administration, 36, 297
Smith, Grant, 63
Smith, Win, 250-51
Smithsonian Institution, 58
Society of American Foresters, 265
Soderberg, K.A., 3, 83, 155ff., 282
Soderberg Logging and Construction Company, 9, 156ff.

Soderberg, Hazel, 9
Soderberg, Pat, 9, 298ff.
Soderberg, Virgil, 9ff., 155ff., 292, 307
soil maps, 137ff.
Southeast Alaska Conservation Council, 268
Southeast Stevedoring, 60, 247-48
Spasski Creek, 78, 167, 174
Sports Illustrated, 21ff., 64, 107, 167, 210, 216, 269, 325
spruce, see Sitka spruce
Stalin, Joseph, 34
Standerwick, John, 147ff.
Steen, Harold K., 105, 110ff.
Stepovich, Mike, 232
Stevens, Senator Ted, vi, 22, 275, 293
Stevenot, Fred, 226
Stewart, Bud, 167ff.
Stikine Indians, 55
Stikine River, 71, 94, 215

Sullivan, Laverne, 207
Sustained Yield Act of 1944, 233
Sybesma, Todd, 238-39

T

Takahashi, C.T., 249
Taku (ferry), 53
Tantakwan, 55ff.
Taro, Cliff, 247-48
Taxpayers for the Environment And its Management, 316
Temsco Airlines, 65ff.
Ten Year Action Plan, 142ff.
Tenakee Springs, Alaska, 14
Thompson, Gordon, 60
Thompson, Joe, 141ff.
Thorne Bay, 17, 46, 60, 65ff., 194, 196, 201ff., 250, 284, 295

timber
        cutting, 22ff., 155ff.
        harvest, 22ff., 155ff.
        sales, 19ff., 129ff.
Timber Association of California, 321
Timber Culture Act of 1873, 105
Timber and Stone Act of 1878, 105
Time-Life, Inc., 21
Tlingit, 7, 54ff., 73, 79ff., 93, 166, 182, 217, 309, 326
Tongass, meaning of, 58
Tongass Conservation Council, 304
Tongass Island, 54-55
Tongass Land Management Plan, 133ff.

Tongass Narrows, 61
Tongass National Forest, 21ff., 100, 129ff.
Tongass Timber Act of 1947, 33
Tongass Timber Supply Fund, 37, 132, 172, 264, 277, 289, 328
Toshitsugu Matsui, 231
totem poles,56

tourism, 32, 62
Trade and Manufacturing Act of
1898, 101
Transfer Act of 1933, 276
transportation, 10, 53
        air travel, 45, 65ff., 166,
        192ff.
        boats, 10, 53, 244, 277ff.,
        307
        canoes, 55
        trucks, 158ff.
Truman, Harry, 49, 77
Tshimshian Indians, 59ff., 93, 108,
326
Tsongas, Paul, 278
Turcotte, Lawson, 226
Tyler, Wes, 166ff.

U

Udall, Morris, 43, 78, 275, 277
U.S. Borax and Chemical Corpora-
tion, 303ff.
United States Department of Agricul-
ture, 98, 101, 111, 218, 221, 228ff.
United States Department of the
Interior, 97, 99ff.
United States Fish and Wildlife
Service, 275
United States Geological Survey, 105,
111, 114
U.S. Plywood - Champion Papers,
270-71
University of Alaska, 20, 58
Unuk River, 68, 71, 73, 100

V

Valentine, Leta, 196
Valentine, Michael L., 196, 288ff.
Value Comparison Unit, 169
Vandiver, John, 238
Vaughan, Ken, 72-74
Von Logging Company, 13
von Wrangel, Baron Ferdinand, 93-94

W

Wacker City, 222
Wacker, Eugene, 222
Walker, Keith, 170ff.
Walthall, Edward C., 116ff.
Ward Cove, 66, 222ff.
water pollution, 225, 232, 239, 264
Wavos Rancheros, 11, 155
Waterman, Thomas J., 58
Wesley, Dave, 241
West Coast Alliance for Resources
and Environment, 315

Western Federation of Outdoor Clubs,
264, 279
Western hemlock, 56, 213
Western redcedar, 56, 214
Wiener, Albert, 216
White, Louie, 166, 182-84
White, Trish, 73-75
Whitestone Logging Company, 166ff.
Wilderness Act of 1964, 43, 262
Wilderness areas, 30, 130

Wilderness Impact Research Founda-
tion, 313ff.
Wilderness Society, 5, 18, 38, 43,
46ff., 70, 133, 193, 264, 279, 283,
304, 326-27
wildlife,
        conservation, 32, 58, 75,
        133ff., 191-92, 262, 275
        habitat, 29, 36, 48, 138
        management, 41, 71, 132,
        146
        refuges, 20, 36, 263
Williams, Emma, 57ff.
Williams, Frank, 58
Williams, Jim, 282
Williams, Lew, 63-65
Williams, Pete, 58
Williamson, Wanita, 27

Willis, Judy, 196, 199
Wind River Multiple Use Advocates,
322
Wise Use Movement,313ff.
wolf, 31, 70-71
wolverine, 72
woodworking crafts, 55
Wrangel, see von Wrangel
Wrangell, 71, 168, 249
Wrangell Lumber Company, 249
Wrangell Forest Products, 250ff.
Wrangell Island, 94
Wrangell Mills Company, 232

Y

Yakobi Island, 217, 269
Yakutat, 71, 83, 139, 247, 293
Yalta, 34, 230
Yellowstone Forest Reserve, 110,
112, 114, 117
Yellowstone National Park, 105, 110,
112, 114, 125, 128
Young, Don, *xi-xii*, 43, 275

Z

Zarembo Island, 100, 168
Zarembo, Lt. Dionysius, 94, 100
Zieske v. Butz, 274
Zellerbach, I. & J. D., 217